The CAREERS DIRECTORY 2018
- the one-stop guide to professional careers

edited by
Guy Nobes

COA

The CAREERS DIRECTORY 2018

This edition published in 2017 by Cambridge Occupational Analysts Ltd
www.coa.co.uk

Editorial and Publishing Team

Editor Guy Nobes
Cover Design PFD
Design and typesetting Simon Foster and Paul Rankin

© Cambridge Occupational Analysts 2017

British Library Cataloguing in Publication Data
A catalogue record for this book is available from the British Library.

ISBN 978-1-906711-29-0

Typeset by Cambridge Occupational Analysts Ltd
Printed and bound in the EU by Graphius, Ghent, Belgium

Contents

Foreword

Most people, when they look back on their lives, agree that there is a gap between what they once aspired to and what they eventually settled for. The bigger the gap, the more likely they are to feel dissatisfied.

Career planning, while not claiming to guarantee a lifetime of success and fulfilment, can help you to clarify your aspirations and can identify relevant routes for you to achieve your goals. At COA, we are convinced that *The Careers Directory* can make a major contribution to setting out the options available to you and can suggest suitable directions for the road ahead.

Making career decisions is never easy. Apart from reading this book, you will find that it helps to talk things through with friends, family, teachers, lecturers, training providers, employers and - last but certainly not least - a professional careers or personal adviser.

Conscious that careers information is constantly changing, we are committed to keeping *The Careers Directory* as up to date as possible. For this edition, completed in June 2017, we have checked every entry.

In addition, we have made every effort, in keeping with established practice in professional career guidance, to ensure that the information in *The Careers Directory* is accurate, objective and impartial.

Guy Nobes, Editor

Disclaimer

While we have made every effort to ensure that The Careers Directory is accurate and up to date, we recognise that careers information is always changing and that broad descriptions cannot always cover every detail of every person's individual circumstances. We cannot, therefore, accept any liability for errors, omissions or apparently misleading statements.

*We welcome comments and suggestions for improvement. Please email any observations to: **info@coa.co.uk***

Introduction

Welcome to *The Careers Directory 2018*.

The aim of this book is to help you plan positively for your future career. At the same time, we try to look realistically at the current state of the labour market and to comment on career prospects for the coming years. The good news is that the UK economy is now in a state of recovery after the long recession that started in 2008, creating new opportunities for ambitious school leavers and university graduates.

If we look, for example, at 'The Graduate Market in 2017' - a study of the latest graduate vacancies and starting salaries at 100 of the UK's best-known and most successful employers, conducted by High Fliers Research during December 2016 - we read that:

- the number of graduate vacancies available at the country's top employers rose by 1.6% in 2016, compared with recruitment in 2015

- employers have increased their graduate recruitment targets by a further 4.3% for 2017, the fifth consecutive year that graduate vacancies have increased

- this significant rise in graduate vacancies for 2017 takes recruitment beyond the pre-recession peak, in the graduate job market in 2007, to its highest-ever level

- graduate recruitment will rise in 6 out of 13 key employment areas this year, with the biggest increases in vacancies reported in retailing, the public sector, engineering and industrial companies, oil and energy companies, IT & telecoms and the law, which together intend to recruit more than 1,200 extra graduates in 2017

- the median starting salary for new graduates at the top 100 employers is expected to be £30,000 in 2017. The most generous salaries last year were those on offer from investment banks (median of £47,000), top law firms (median of £43,000), oil and energy companies (median of £38,000) banking and finance (median of £32,500)

- the highest published graduate starting salaries for 2017 include Newton Europe (£45,000), law firms Baker & McKenzie (£45,000), Herbert Smith Freehills (£44,000), Freshfields Bruckhaus Deringer, Linklaters and Slaughter and May(all £43,000) Aldi (£42,000) and the European Commission (£42,000)

- the 10 universities most often targeted by Britain's top graduate employers in 2016-2017 are Warwick, Manchester, Bristol, Nottingham, Cambridge, Leeds, Birmingham, Nottingham, Oxford, Durham and Bath

It is worth noting, by the way, that up to a third of last year's entry-level positions were filled by graduates who had already worked for their organisations - either through internships, industrial placements, work experience placements or vacation work. Indeed, some three-quarters of the graduate vacancies advertised by City investment banks and half the training contracts offered by the leading law firms were filled by graduates who had already completed work experience with the employer.

Over 90% of the UK's leading graduate employers now offer paid work experience programmes for students and recent graduates, with a record 13,917 places available this year. At least half of employers provide industrial placements for undergraduates (typically for 6 to 12 months) and three-quarters offer paid vacation internships lasting more than three weeks.

More than a third of recruiters taking part in the research warn that graduates who have no previous work experience at all are unlikely to be successful during the selection process and have little or no chance of receiving a job offer for their organisations' graduate programmes.

You can read more about the High Fliers *Graduate Market in 2017* research by visiting the website at: **www.highfliers.co.uk**

Fierce Competition For Top Jobs

Investment bank Goldman Sachs reports that it has attracted more than a quarter of a million applications from students and graduates for summer positions in 2017, according to figures provided to the Financial Times.

There were 223,849 undergraduate applications for summer jobs and for new analyst positions this year, while 30,542 still studying or completing their Master of Business Administration (MBA) applied for new associate positions.

Goldman Sachs has not revealed how many jobs are actually on offer but competition is clearly tough. Getting a job at JPMorgan is no easier: the rival investment bank has hired only 2% of graduate applicants to its investment banking division. Chances are marginally better at Citigroup, at 2.7%.

The news comes as a report from jobs website Glassdoor reveals that the tech industry has overtaken banking in a new ranking of the top paying companies in the UK.

"Tech salaries in particular," says Glassdoor Chief Economist Dr Andrew Chamberlain, "tend to be high because of a shortage in specialist skills such as software development and programming, with a bidding war for these workers now under way."

A separate piece of research from salary benchmarking website Emolument confirms that leading technology firms are outpacing the financial sector in terms of entry-level pay, adding that Amazon is ahead of rivals Google, Apple and Microsoft as the best paying tech firm for junior employees in the UK.

Skills shortages are most often cited by recruiters looking for programmers/software developers and web design/development professionals. An inadequate supply of candidates with the required Microsoft skills is the most common cause of these shortages (e.g. .NET, Dynamics, SharePoint, Visual Basic and C#) although difficulties sourcing applicants with PHP and VMW are also noted.

The technical skills most often called for by employers last year were:

SQL, C, C#, .NET and Java, and this was true for both permanent and contract positions on offer.

For more information, explore the Tech Partnership website at:
www.thetechpartnership.com

The Confederation of British Industry (CBI) maintains a positive message in the annual CBI/Pearson Education and Skills Survey. Last year's report revealed that demand for skills is rising fast. More than three-quarters of businesses (77%) expect to have more job openings for people with higher-level skills over the coming years while just 3% expect to have fewer. The proportion of businesses not confident there will be enough people available in the future with the skills to fill their high-skilled jobs has reached a new high (69%).

Read the full CBI/Pearson survey report on the website at: **www.cbi.org.uk**

According to the Department for Business, Innovation and Skills (BIS), future UK economic growth will be driven by innovation in four key sectors: Emerging & Enabling

Technologies, Health & Life Sciences, Infrastructure Systems, and Manufacturing and Materials. These four areas underpin the development of high-value products and services across many industrial sectors.

Part of the BIS, 'Innovate UK' is the UK's innovation agency. It has invested £1.8 billion since 2007, supporting innovation in 7,600 organisations and creating around 55,000 new jobs. Its delivery plan for 2016 to 2020 aims to accelerate UK economic growth and help keep the UK at the forefront of technological innovation.

New products and services might range from lightweight materials and nanotechnologies to biological products, sensor systems, power electronics, use of data and improved computing experiences.

For full details, visit the website at:
www.gov.uk/government/organisations/innovate-uk

Research by PricewaterhouseCoopers, suggests that robots increasingly pose a threat to some occupations. Around 30% of UK jobs could potentially be at high risk of automation by the early 2030s. The risks appear highest in sectors such as transportation and storage (56%), manufacturing (46%) and wholesale and retail (44%), but lower in sectors like health and social work (17%). On the other side of the coin, new automation technologies should both create some totally new jobs in the digital technology area and, through productivity gains, generate additional wealth and spending that will support additional jobs of existing kinds, primarily in service sectors that are less easy to automate. The net long term impact of automation on total UK employment could therefore be either positive or negative. For more information, visit the website at:
www.pwc.co.uk/services/economics-policy/insights/uk-economic-outlook.html

Across the Atlantic, US and Canadian careers specialists CareerCast identify the following as their Top Ten Careers for 2017:

1. Statistician
2. Medical Services Manager
3. Operations Research Analyst
4. Information Security Analyst
5. Data Scientist
6. University Professor
7. Mathematician
8. Software Engineer
9. Occupational Therapist
10. Speech Pathologist

We do not promote any one career suggestion over another - it is for you to identify the opportunities that best match your own ideas, abilities and aspirations - but we can draw some useful conclusions from our brief overview of highly-rated and apparently recession-resistant areas of employment.

Firstly, just about all require a high level of education, not to mention highly specialised training. (Interestingly, CareerCast also publish their 10 Worst Jobs of 2017, a list dominated by jobs seen as unskilled, poorly paid, insecure, stressful and dangerous.)

Secondly, almost all are based on well developed STEM skills, which - as we have seen above - are widely regarded as essential in creating sustainable economic growth.

To find out more about the national Higher Education STEM programme in the UK, visit the website at: **www.hestem.ac.uk**

You might also be interested in the Big Bang programme of events for young scientists and engineers at: **www.thebigbangfair.co.uk**

Explore the CareerCast best and worst career ratings at: **www.careercast.com**

The Importance of Staying Up-to-Date

Despite our very best efforts to keep abreast of new developments and to maintain our database of careers information, we are aware that the world of work is constantly changing and that some details of training, qualifications or remuneration will alter during the lifetime of this book.

The same message therefore applies to every entry in this book: always check for the latest information by exploring the web links we supply for each career covered.

Looking Ahead

We must also acknowledge the fact that most readers of this book will not be entering the labour market before 2019 at the very earliest. If you are about to undertake a period of sixth form or further education study, followed by three or four years in higher education, you won't be looking for a job until around 2023. It is impossible to predict with any degree of certainty what the labour market consequences will be of the UK referendum vote to leave the European Union (EU). We will, of course, keep a very close eye on negotiations as we try to gauge the impact on employment opportunities of the UK's new relationship with the remaining 27 EU member states and of its success in forging new trade deals with other countries.

GCSE Reforms

GCSEs in England are being reformed and will be graded on a new scale from 9 to 1, with 9 being the highest grade. At the same time, new GCSE content will be more challenging and fewer grade 9s will be awarded than A*s. English language, English literature and maths are the first to be graded from 9 to 1 in 2017. Another 20 subjects will have 9 to 1 grading in 2018, with most others following in 2019. During this transition, you will receive a potentially bewildering assortment of letter and number grades.

The new grades are being brought in to signal that GCSEs have been reformed and to offer better differentiation between some of the old grades. Grade 9, for example, equates to something more like A**, while grade 8 should be seen as equivalent to the old A*. The important cut-off point is grade 4, which broadly matches the old C. Where we refer in this Directory to GCSE passes, or their Scottish equivalent, for entry to certain careers, we now say 'a good spread of GCSE/S Grade passes 9-4/A*-C/1-3.'

Wales and Northern Ireland are not introducing the new 9 to 1 grading scale as part of the changes to GCSEs, although independent schools in these countries - as in England - remain free to choose whichever system they like.

The Workbrief Analysis

In this publication, we cover some 300 career ideas in 176 carefully chosen chapters, each analysed under our unique WORKBRIEF headings. We cover a further 278 careers in shorter brief outlines.

What is Involved?

What sort of work would I be doing? What kind of responsibilities would I have to deal with in a typical day or week?

Opportunities for Training

What sort of courses and qualifications are available? Do I need qualifications before I start? Can I work towards these on a part-time basis? Is there a choice of qualifications and/or routes?

Requirements for Entry

What exams would I have to pass in order to be considered for entry to this kind of course or work? Are there any other specific requirements?

Kind of Person

What personal qualities would help me succeed in this type of work? What skills are particularly important?

Broad Outlook

Is there likely to be a demand for this type of work in the future? What are the promotion prospects? Is there a chance of self-employment?

Related Occupations

Are there any similar careers for me to consider at this stage?

Impact on Lifestyle

How would this type of work affect my overall lifestyle? Would my work limit my free time, especially in the evening or at weekends? Is it likely to be hot/cold, dirty/clean, noisy, active, dangerous or whatever? What levels of stress would be involved?

Earnings Potential

How much would I be paid? Am I likely to be on salary/commission/bonus or whatever? Could this type of career give me an adequate or very good lifestyle? Are there any benefits apart from the salary?

Further Information

Where can I obtain more detailed information about this type of work? (Especially in terms of website addresses).

Why Workbrief?

Well, the chapters are brief and they're about work! Much more than that, Workbrief allows us to brief you about a type of work by answering questions about both the 'hard' facts (What will I be doing? What entry qualifications do I need?) and the equally important 'soft' aspects (Will doing this job affect my family or social life? What personal qualities might be important?). With each title analysed under identical headings in a double-page format, you get a clear briefing about a specific occupational area and you should find it easy and beneficial to compare and contrast a number of different career options.

The Workbrief Focus

The Careers Directory is aimed at young people who anticipate achieving or already have a range of GCSEs/S grades or equivalent at 9-4/A*-C/1-3, who hope to achieve AS/A level/Higher/Advanced Higher or equivalent qualifications and who are likely to progress to higher education. (See our comments below regarding equivalent qualifications). Much of the information is also relevant to undergraduate and postgraduate students.

Alternatives to Higher Education

University isn't for everyone and, if you feel this way, you might try exploring NotGoingToUni.co.uk. The award-winning jobs portal provides advice on many viable alternatives to the traditional university route.

For full details, visit the website at: **www.notgoingtouni.co.uk**

You may, in particular, be interested in considering opportunities on the Apprenticeships programme. An apprenticeship is a real job with training, which means that you can earn while you learn and work towards recognised qualifications as you go. With over 25,000 apprenticeship vacancies available online, you may well be able to find a route that matches your needs. If you live in England, are over 16 and not in full-time education, you can apply.

There are four levels of Apprenticeship available:

1 **Intermediate**
   You would work towards a nationally recognised vocational qualification at Level 2, which is broadly equivalent to five GCSE passes at 9-4/A*-C

2 **Advanced**
   You would work towards a nationally recognised vocational qualification at Level 3, which is broadly equivalent to two A levels

3 **Higher**
   You would work towards a qualification at Level 4 or above, where Levels 4 and 5 are equivalent to a foundation degree, Level 6 is equivalent to a bachelor degree and Level 7 is equivalent to a master's degree

4 **Degree**
   You would work towards a qualification at Level 6 or Level 7 as above

There is no set rate of pay for apprentices, although all employed apprentices must receive a wage of no less than £3.50 per hour, together with at least 20 days paid holiday per year, plus bank holidays. Pay is dependent on the sector, region and apprenticeship level; some higher apprenticeships can pay as much as £500 per week.

As your skills develop, your pay will increase accordingly. You may also get additional money for essential books, clothing or equipment, or to help with a disability. As an apprentice, you will receive the same benefits as other employees such as pension contributions, and subsidised canteen and leisure facilities.

To find out more, visit the website at: **www.getingofar.gov.uk**

Choosing the Right Subjects

Many of the careers covered in this book require a degree as a starting point. It is, therefore, important that you do not put yourself at a disadvantage by choosing a combination of subjects at A level or equivalent that will not equip you with the appropriate skills and knowledge for your university course or that may not demonstrate effectively your aptitude for a particular subject.

With this thought in mind, the Russell Group of universities has published a guide (revised for 2016/17) to post-16 subject choices. Produced in collaboration with the Career Development Institute, *Informed Choices* is aimed at all students considering A level and equivalent options. It includes advice on the best subject combinations for a wide range of university courses, together with guidance on subjects that will keep options open if you don't yet know what you want to study at university.

Broadly speaking, Russell Group institutions tend to favour a combination of mainly 'facilitating' subjects, which are identified as:

- Mathematics and Further Maths
- English
- Physics
- Biology
- Chemistry
- Geography
- History
- Languages (Classical and Modern)

If a particular subject is not listed as a facilitating subject, this is because it is not generally required for entry to degree courses. The classification does not imply any judgement about the importance of the subject per se; it merely reflects typical university entrance requirements.

There are some advanced level subjects which provide suitable preparation for entry to university generally, but which are not included within the facilitating subjects because there are relatively few degree programmes where an advanced level qualification in these subjects would be a requirement for entry. Examples of such subjects include Economics, Religious Studies and Welsh.

If you have talent in music and want to study it at university it is important that you take Music to advanced level (along with performance grades).

If you have a talent in art you may well be thinking about an art foundation course as a precursor to a degree programme. You might want to consider an advanced level qualification in either Art or Art and Design. Either of these will provide you with the basis for your portfolio, which you will need to gain entry to an art foundation course.

Some Medicine, Veterinary Science and certain Engineering courses may require three specific facilitating subjects. For most other courses, however, you won't necessarily need to have studied three facilitating subjects at A level. Some courses require one or two facilitating subjects, whilst for other courses there are no specific subject requirements. Some institutions publish a list of preferred A level subjects which are acceptable for general admission, as well as specific requirements for individual courses. If you don't know what you want to study then it's a really good rule of thumb that taking two facilitating subjects will keep a wide range of degree courses open to you.

Informed Choices is available on the Russell Group website at: **www.russellgroup.ac.uk/informed-choices**

The Russell Group universities are:

- Birmingham
- Bristol
- Cambridge
- Cardiff
- Durham
- Edinburgh
- Exeter
- Glasgow
- Imperial College London
- King's College London
- Leeds
- Liverpool
- London School of Economics
- Manchester
- Newcastle
- Nottingham
- Oxford
- Queen Mary London
- Queen's University Belfast
- Sheffield
- Southampton
- University College London
- Warwick
- York

Equivalent Qualifications

While we are aware that the majority of our readers will progress from GCSEs/S grades to AS/A level/Higher/Advanced Higher examinations, we acknowledge that there are many equivalent qualifications - notably the International Baccalaureate (IB), European Baccalaureate (EB), Irish Leaving Certificate (ILC), recognised vocational qualifications, Scottish Baccalaureate, Welsh Baccalaureate or England's new Technical Baccalaureate. For certain types of work, moreover, the Apprenticeship route might be more appropriate than traditional full-time study. You might also find that an Access course could help you return to higher education opportunities after taking a break from your studies.

If you are aiming high, you might try to achieve an A* at A level. This means that you must score at least 90% of the A2 marks available for a given subject.

Some schools and colleges have abandoned A levels in favour of the Cambridge Pre-U, a qualification devised by Cambridge University and seen as a return to traditional A level standards.

To be eligible for the two-year Diploma, students complete three Principal Subjects and a Global Perspectives and Research (GPR) component, a course focusing on global issues, which leads to an independent research report on a topic chosen by the student. The Diploma is flexible enough to accommodate students who wish to import existing A levels.

To find out more about Cambridge Pre-U, visit the website at: **www.cie.org.uk/programmes-and-qualifications/cambridge-advanced/cambridge-pre-u**

Another sixth form qualification is the AQA Bacc, a baccalaureate qualification designed to sit alongside a normal A level programme.

Unlike other baccalaureate qualifications, such as the IB or Welsh Bac, AQA Bacc retains A levels at its heart. You must also be careful not to confuse it with the English

Bacc, an initiative designed to promote a broad range of academic study in England up to the age of 16.

The successful completion of three A levels, in any combination, is key to success in the AQA Baccalaureate, with three additional elements required:

- An Enrichment Programme, recognising students' accomplishments away from the classroom, perhaps through the Duke of Edinburgh Award, work-related activities, community involvement or sporting achievement. The Bacc encourages students to go out into the world, to develop people skills in a non-academic context and to broaden the scope of their interests

- An Extended Project Qualification (EPQ), developing students' abilities to manage tasks using their own initiative and resources

- Broader Study, designed to develop critical thinking/citizenship skills through, for example, Level 3 Core Maths or an A or AS level examination that differs from the main programme of study

For full details, visit the website at: **www.aqa.org.uk/programmes/aqa-baccalaureate**

Rather than fill each page of this book with lengthy and repetitive listings of every possible alternative qualification, we mention the most commonly cited entrance requirements and add 'or equivalent'. Professional bodies and higher education institutions try to be fair and flexible when considering entry qualifications, so it is always worth making specific enquiries if you feel uncertain about matching the requirements for entry to a course or career.

In the requirements sections of each Workbrief chapter we refer to A levels. We do not normally mention Advanced Subsidiary (AS) level qualifications because these have in recent years provided the first half of the eventual A levels awarded. AS can now be taken as a stand-alone qualification in many subjects and can be counted as 40% of an A level.

You should be aware that the entry levels shown do not guarantee automatic acceptance by professional bodies or higher education institutions.

You can find out more about these qualifications and the most recent changes from:

Department for Education
www.gov.uk/government/organisations/department-for-education

Apprenticeships
www.getingofar.gov.uk

Access to Higher Education
www.accesstohe.ac.uk

Ofqual – Office of Qualifications and Examinations Regulation (England)
www.gov.uk/government/organisations/ofqual

Qualifications Wales
www.qualificationswales.org

Northern Ireland Council for the Curriculum, Examinations and Assessment
http://ccea.org.uk

Scottish Qualifications Authority
www.sqa.org.uk

UCAS and Higher Education

Many of the articles in this book highlight the need for a higher education qualification. You can access a complete database of UK higher education provision and full details of how to apply via the Universities and Colleges Admissions Service (UCAS) website at: **www.ucas.com**

The Open University is not part of UCAS but you can explore the courses it offers at: **www.open.ac.uk**

The UCAS Tariff

UCAS operates a points system known as the UCAS Tariff for entry to higher education. This allows you to use a range of different qualifications to help secure a place on an undergraduate course. The Tariff has recently been revised and we give examples here of the new version.

Not all higher education providers use the UCAS Tariff but many do to make comparisons between applicants with different qualifications. Tariff points are used in many entry requirements, although other factors are often taken into account. You will find that entry requirements on the UCAS database provide a fuller picture of what admissions tutors are seeking.

The Tariff helps universities and colleges when deciding on course entry requirements and making conditional offers, although conditional offers that use Tariff points will often require a minimum level of achievement in a specified subject (for example '120 points to include grade A (48 points) in A level chemistry', or '100 points including Scottish Higher grade B (27 points) in mathematics').

Use of the Tariff may also vary from department to department within any one university or college, and may in some cases be dependent on the programme being offered.

Key features:

- The new Tariff only contains qualifications at Level 3/SCQF Level 6 or equivalent. This means that, for example, it does not include Key Skills qualifications at Level 2 or 4. For European Union (EU) qualifications this is EQF Level 4 or equivalent, therefore the Irish Leaving Certificate at Higher Level is included, whilst the Ordinary Level is not. For qualifications outside the EU, evidence is reviewed to make a judgement about their equivalence to this level

- For composite qualifications the new Tariff allocates separate points to each separate constituent qualification rather than the overall qualification. For example, for the International Baccalaureate (IB) Diploma, the new Tariff allocates separate points to the Higher Level, Standard Level, Extended Essay and Theory of Knowledge qualifications. There is no overall allocation to the whole IB Diploma

To find out more about the Tariff and how it relates to your qualifications, visit the website at: **www.ucas.com/ucas/undergraduate/getting-started/entry-requirements/tariff/tariff-tables**

Engineering Qualifications

When covering engineering careers in this publication, we focus primarily on training and working as a professional engineer. There are many other valuable roles in engineering - at operative, craft and technician levels - but they are outside the immediate scope of this book. The professional level can be divided into two groups: chartered and incorporated.

As a *chartered engineer*, you would be involved with the processes of innovation, creativity and change that drive technological progress. You would develop and apply new technologies, promote advanced designs, improve production efficiency and pioneer new management methods. You could lead projects and work towards a senior management role in your organisation.

As an *incorporated engineer*, you would be more concerned with maintaining and managing applications of current technology, seeking to extract maximum efficiency from existing systems and processes. As with a chartered engineer, you could work towards a leading management role.

Aspects of the roles often overlap in practice and there is a corresponding closeness in the training routes available. The quickest route to either qualification is to obtain a degree accredited to Engineering Council standards by one of the professional engineering institutions. If you want to be a chartered engineer, you should select a four-year MEng course, for which you would need high grades at A level/Advanced Higher/Higher or equivalent. Maths is generally an essential requirement.

If you want to be an incorporated engineer, you should select a three-year BEng (or BSc or BTech) course. This would have a greater focus on practical applications than the more mathematical and theoretical syllabus of the MEng. Entry requirements for BEng courses are usually lower and more flexible.

You can convert your incorporated engineer qualification to chartered status by following an extra period of learning, known as a matching section, to bridge the gap between the BEng and MEng standard. You can do this over several years, while you are working, if you wish.

Whichever route you take, you could seek sponsorship for all or part of your course. You would gain industrial experience by working for your sponsor during the summer vacation and you would receive a salary to offset your student loan. You could also extend your course by a year in order to incorporate longer periods of industrial experience in a sandwich course.

When you have finished your degree, you would enter a period of initial professional development with an employer, during which you would apply your knowledge to solve real problems in a working environment. The final stage of this process is a professional review, in which you would have to show that you have the necessary competence and commitment. When this is successfully completed, you can call yourself a chartered or incorporated engineer and add the letters CEng or IEng after your name. Chartered status would also entitle you to register with the Fédération Européenne d'Associations Nationales d'Ingénieurs and claim the title European Engineer (EurIng).

Further Information

Young Engineers
www.youngeng.org.uk

Engineering Leadership Scheme
www.raeng.org.uk/grants-and-prizes/schemes-for-students

Royal Academy of Engineering
www.raeng.org.uk

Year in Industry
www.etrust.org.uk/the-year-in-industry

Smallpeice Trust
www.smallpeicetrust.org.uk

EngineeringUK
www.engineeringuk.com

Engineering Council UK
www.engc.org.uk

Institution of Engineering and Technology
www.theiet.org

Fédération Européenne d'Associations Nationales d'Ingénieurs
www.feani.org

Engineers Ireland
www.engineersireland.ie

About the Editor

Guy Nobes has spent his career in UK and international schools, and presently is Head of Guidance at Marlborough College, advising pupils on career and university matters. He serves on the schools' advisory board at UCAS, and has written books on planning and writing university personal statements.

Contributors

The entries in the Careers Directory are based on original articles supplied by:

Jennie Barnes

Annie Edgar

Sue Eynon

Graham Garrett

Jill Garrett

Bob Jackson

Joyce Lane

John Mainstone

Ken Reynolds

Joanna Roberts

Godfrey Thomas

The WORKBRIEF Career Descriptions

*W*hat is Involved?

What sort of work would I be doing? What kind of responsibilities would I have to deal with in a typical day or week?

*O*pportunities for Training

What sort of courses and qualifications are available? Do I need qualifications before I start? Can I work towards these on a part-time basis? Is there a choice of qualifications and/or routes?

*R*equirements for Entry

What exams would I have to pass in order to be considered for entry to this kind of course or work? Are there any other specific requirements?

*K*ind of Person

What personal qualities would help me succeed in this type of work? What skills are particularly important?

*B*road Outlook

Is there likely to be a demand for this type of work in the future? What are the promotion prospects? Is there a chance of self-employment?

*R*elated Occupations

Are there any similar careers for me to consider at this stage?

*I*mpact on Lifestyle

How would this type of work affect my overall lifestyle? Would my work limit my free time, especially in the evening or at weekends? Is it likely to be hot/cold, dirty/clean, noisy, active, dangerous or whatever? What levels of stress would be involved?

*E*arnings Potential

How much would I be paid? Am I likely to be on salary/commission/bonus or whatever? Could this type of career give me an adequate or very good lifestyle? Are there any benefits apart from the salary?

*F*urther Information

Where can I obtain more detailed information about this type of work? (Especially in terms of website addresses).

Accountant (Professional)

What is Involved?

As a professionally qualified accountant, you would be working with financial and management information, using your specialist knowledge to advise a range of clients, from individuals to large organisations. There are several different professional bodies in accountancy and your initial employment could be linked to the specialist activities of the body you choose. You would find, however, that there is considerable overlap between the various professional qualifications and you could move between sectors later in your career.

Major areas of work include private practice (also known as public practice, which is not terribly helpful), the public sector and industry/commerce. In the first of these, you would work in a specialist firm of accountants offering services ranging from basic bookkeeping to audit (independent assessment of your client's current financial position), taxation advice, management consultancy and corporate financial planning. Working in the public sector could see you handling very large budgets in local or central government, the National Health Service, colleges or universities. As an accountant in industry/commerce, you could be involved in keeping financial records for a company, overseeing credit control systems and possibly participating in strategic planning for the organisation's future development.

Opportunities for Training

To gain recognition as a qualified accountant, you would need to spend several years pursuing the professional training route of one of the six main bodies, all listed in the Further Information section.

With so many different bodies, there are many routes to professional qualification. Most take three to five years and usually involve work experience in an approved organisation, part-time study and lots of exams. You may also opt to start as an accounting technician and then work your way towards professional status.

Requirements for Entry

As with training routes, entry requirements vary from one body to another. You would need at least two A level/Advanced Higher, three Higher or equivalent qualifications, together with three GCSE/S Grade passes 9-4/A*-C/1-3, including English and maths, to enter a training contract with ICAEW, ACCA, CIMA or CIPFA.

ICAS, on the other hand, would require a degree, unless you come through the accounting technician route. In practice, the most common entry route to professional accountancy training is with a degree in any academic subject. If you choose an accountancy-related degree subject, you should gain exemption from some of the exams set by the professional bodies.

Kind of Person

You need to be very computer, figure and systems literate. You do not have to be brilliant at maths but you should enjoy working with figures and problem solving, as well as being diligent and accurate. Employers have indicated that they are looking for good academic results together with other skills such as leadership, communication, numeracy, interest in finance and business, self-motivation and commitment.

Broad Outlook

An accountancy qualification is a very useful tool and demand for accountants is currently growing in all sectors. As your career develops, you could choose to work for a very large organisation, you could become self-employed and work as a freelance consultant or you could take advantage of the worldwide recognition of UK accountancy qualifications and travel extensively.

Related Occupations

You might also wish to consider: accounting technician, investment analyst, banking executive, chartered/company secretary, economist, stockbroker, tax professional, insurance underwriter, actuary, management/business consultant or financial adviser.

Impact on Lifestyle

Normal working hours are Monday to Friday, nine to five, but your lifestyle as an accountant would depend very much on the sort of organisation you join and the area of specialisation you choose. Audits can take you all over the country and a large international partnership would expect you to travel. High salaries are possible but are usually associated with increased stress and longer working hours. You may have to move a few times to develop your career. One of the main lifestyle challenges for trainees is balancing part-time professional study commitments with the pressures of the day-to-day job.

Earnings Potential

Accountancy positions tend to pay well, which can mean anything from a reasonable to a considerable salary. Starting salaries for graduate trainees vary from around £20,000 to £30,000; salaries for school leaver trainees are rather lower. The ICAEW Salary Survey 2015 reports that the average global salary of a chartered accountant in business, six to nine years after qualifying, is £90,800 plus £20,600 bonus. Accountants working in banking and capital markets are the highest earners, with an average salary and bonus of £172,800. A newly qualified ICAEW chartered accountant with two years' experience can expect to earn, on average, £48,100 plus bonus.

Further Information

Institute of Chartered Accountants in England and Wales (ICAEW)
www.icaew.com

Institute of Chartered Accountants of Scotland (ICAS)
www.icas.com

Chartered Accountants Ireland
www.charteredaccountants.ie

Association of Chartered Certified Accountants (ACCA)
www.accaglobal.com

Chartered Institute of Management Accountants (CIMA)
www.cimaglobal.com

Chartered Institute of Public Finance and Accountancy (CIPFA)
www.cipfa.org

Institute of Certified Public Accountants in Ireland
www.cpaireland.ie

Accounting Technician

What is Involved?

As an accounting technician, you could be working alongside professionally qualified accountants in activities such as keeping financial records, auditing accounts, preparing tax returns or providing information for management reports. You could be running a payroll or credit control system. There are opportunities in virtually every sector of the labour market: you might be based in a specialist accountancy practice, in industry or commerce, in the public or voluntary sectors or you could work from your own home for a variety of clients. Unlike a professional accountant, you would not be legally qualified to conduct a full-scale audit but you could be responsible for much of the groundwork. As a broad rule, you would be more likely to be involved with the detailed, practical applications of day-to-day accounting issues than with the wider areas of financial management dealt with by professionally qualified accountants. As your career develops, you may choose to specialise in a particular area of work, such as taxation or insolvency.

Opportunities for Training

The Association of Accounting Technicians (AAT) and the Association of Chartered Certified Accountants (ACCA) both offer training and qualification routes for accounting technicians. Several major chartered accountancy bodies sponsor the AAT and the qualification would make you eligible for entry to their professional examinations. You would work your way through introductory and intermediate levels 2 and 3 (levels 5 and 6 in Scotland) to the advanced diploma at level 4 (level 8 in Scotland). While each level counts as a qualification in its own right, completing the final level leads to the full AAT accounting qualification. The training scheme is offered at many different centres, including local colleges, the workplace and training providers.

With ACCA, you would work towards the Certified Accounting Technician (CAT) qualification. To obtain this, you must pass a suite of examinations within the ACCA foundation level programme and have at least a year's relevant practical experience. You would be automatically transferred to the ACCA Qualification register when you successfully complete your CAT examinations. Passing the remaining ACCA Qualification examinations and gaining three years' relevant experience would lead to full ACCA membership. The experience you have already demonstrated to become a Certified Accounting Technician would count towards the work experience you would need for ACCA membership.

It is possible to train via the Apprenticeship programme, although you must check to see if a suitable scheme is available in your home area.

Requirements for Entry

There are no formal academic requirements for training with one of the organisations that award qualifications as an accounting technician, although you must be over 16 years old and should be reasonably numerate with a good command of English.

You may be able to gain exemption from part of the AAT qualification if you have relevant work experience or suitable A level/Advanced Higher, Higher or equivalent qualifications.

Kind of Person

As an accounting technician, you would need to feel completely at ease when working with numbers. You would also need to be accurate, with a sharp eye for detail, and you would need good communication skills in order to explain details of accountancy and finance to those less numerate than yourself. You would usually be working as part of a team. Good computer skills are essential. The work would often require you to keep to strict deadlines.

Broad Outlook

Opportunities for accounting technicians have grown in recent years, in line with the trend of shifting financial responsibility and decision making away from large central offices towards local, independent control. Qualifying as an accounting technician can be a step on the career ladder leading to full professional status, although many technicians enjoy their work as it is and do not wish to take further exams. With experience, you could move to a senior management position in a company or you could pursue the option of self-employment.

Related Occupations

You might wish to consider: accountant (professional), banking executive or financial adviser.

Impact on Lifestyle

Accounting technicians are office based, working traditional office hours five days a week. You may have to move across the private and public sectors - and possibly to different parts of the country - in order to gain experience and develop your career. There may be opportunities for working from home and for part-time work.

The work can often be intense and pressurised with a constant need to meet important deadlines.

Earnings Potential

The 2015 AAT salary survey shows an average of £17,865 at the introductory level, rising to £18,563 intermediate and £20,940 advanced. You can earn considerably more in a senior management post or if you are successful in running your own business. AAT and ACCA qualifications are recognised globally, meaning that you could work overseas if you wish.

Further Information

Association of Accounting Technicians
www.aat.org.uk

Association of Chartered Certified Accountants
www.accaglobal.com

Accounting Technicians Ireland
www.accountingtechniciansireland.ie

Accountancy Age
www.accountancyage.com

Accountancy Apprenticeships
https://3aaa.co.uk/apprentice/accountancy

Actor

What is Involved?

As an actor, you would be a creative interpreter of dramatic works, comedies or musicals, performing in the theatre, in films, on television, video and radio. You should be prepared not merely to act but also to sing, dance and maybe undertake fights and stunt work. Glamour, fame and self-fulfilment might spur you on but can seem far away when you are rehearsing lines or sitting around while scenery and lights are adjusted. The varied working life of an actor might also see you doing voice-overs for advertisements, recording talking books or narrating documentary films.

Opportunities for Training

It is possible to become an actor without any formal training but you would be well advised to consider a Drama UK accredited training course at a drama school. This would give you a much better chance of gaining employment and acquiring an Equity (the actors' union) Card.

Courses vary a good deal in style, so you should do plenty of research to determine which would be the best for you. Straight from school at the minimum age of 18, you would normally follow a three-year course. There are shorter courses available for graduates and mature candidates. The syllabus should include movement, voice projection, improvisation, singing, dancing, audition techniques, and make-up.

You must be careful not to confuse Drama UK accredited courses - often at degree level and run in association with a university - with the many drama or performing arts degrees offered by universities and colleges. The latter tend to be more academic, concentrating on the history of drama and the analysis of texts rather than vocational training.

Requirements for Entry

Entry to accredited courses is fiercely competitive and you may find that you are one of 20 or so applicants competing for a single place. Admission is usually by audition and interview, with experience of performing regularly in amateur productions or youth theatre a great advantage. For the audition, you will usually be expected to prepare two or three speeches and sometimes a song to present to the audition panel. Speeches should usually be between two and three minutes long, although you should check each school's audition guidelines for details, and you will often be asked to present contrasting classical and modern pieces. As part of your preparation, ask a teacher, friend or relation to time your speeches at your normal performance speed and try to make any cuts required before you learn them by heart.

You may not need any special academic qualifications, although some drama schools ask for five GCSE/S Grade passes 9-4/A*-C/1-3 or equivalent and even two A level/Advanced Higher or three Higher or equivalent qualifications.

Kind of Person

Apart from possessing outstanding acting talent - the intelligence, sensitivity and imagination to understand and interpret various roles and the ability to present them to a theatre full of people or to a camera - you must be dedicated, determined and disciplined.

You would need to be strong enough, both physically and mentally, to withstand the long hours of rehearsal, the emotional demands of public performance, the disappointment of rejection at audition and the pain of negative criticism. A good memory is clearly important, together with a mixture of self-confidence and willingness to work in an ensemble. A feeling for music and movement would also be of great benefit.

Broad Outlook

You can build a name for yourself by working hard and giving good performances. There is often a degree of luck involved in having the right talents and being available at the right time for a particular project. Many actors, it must be said, spend more time looking for work than they do performing. You need to bring yourself to the notice of casting directors and producers whenever possible and you might find it useful to have an agent to help you get work. Networking and personal contacts are also invaluable tools in the hunt for work. Many actors provide themselves with other qualifications as well, so that they can earn some money in other fields when the going gets tough.

Related Occupations

You might also consider: drama teacher, dramatherapist or speech and language therapist. If being in the theatre is your main motivation, you might look at: stage manager, musician, dancer, production assistant/runner or TV/film camera operator.

Impact on Lifestyle

As an actor, you would probably be seen as a member of a glamorous profession. There certainly are great rewards for some in terms of fame and personal fulfilment but you should be aware of the restrictions this could put on your private life. Most performances take place in the evening and at the weekend, and a long run in the theatre could take you out of social circulation for weeks on end. You may find that you would spend a considerable time away from home, staying in a variety of surroundings.

Earnings Potential

Be prepared for the fact that, on average, actors work professionally for only 11.3 weeks per year. When working, you should be entitled to the pay rates negotiated by Equity, with a current minimum wage of, for example, £603 per week for TV work with the BBC, or a £400 programme fee with ITV, plus £55.53 per day worked. There are no agreed rates for TV commercials but Equity recommends a basic studio fee for featured artists of between £300 and £500. There are separate weekly rates for theatre work, and a lodgings allowance could be available if you are on tour. In all cases, your agent may be able to negotiate a rate for you above the minimum level. If you are not a member of Equity, you may be expected to work for less than the minimum rate. Stardom would entitle you to demand whatever sum you or your agent can command!

Further Information

British Actors' Equity Association
www.equity.org.uk

Creative and Cultural Skills – theatre careers
http://ccskills.org.uk/careers/advice/any/theatre

Gaiety School of Acting – National Theatre School of Ireland
https://gaietyschool.com

Youth Theatre Ireland
www.youththeatre.ie

Arts Award on Voice
www.voicemag.uk/artsaward

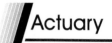

Actuary

What is Involved?

As an actuary, you would use your specialist statistical skills to make financial sense of the future. Using a database of previously accumulated information, statistics, probability theory and compound interest, you would design solutions to questions of financial risk, particularly in the fields of insurance, pensions, risk assessment and investment. For example, you might be asked to consider how much money a company would need to invest in order to pay its employees a reasonable pension when they retire.

You could work for the Government Actuary's Department (GAD), reporting to Parliament on such matters as projected population growth or forecasting funding needs for the National Health Service. Alternatively, you might advise an insurance company on the premiums required to make life insurance policies competitive while still offering a reasonable return for customers and shareholders.

Opportunities for Training

To become an Associate or Fellow of the Institute and Faculty of Actuaries, you must pass a series of examinations, or be granted exemption from them, and also attain a satisfactory level of work-based skills. This usually takes between three and six years.

The examinations cover topics such as statistical modelling, economics and financial actuarial maths. You study by distance learning, and many employers offer support for study, some offering paid study leave during your training.

Requirements for Entry

For entry to a degree course, you would need at least two or three A level/Advanced Higher or three or four Higher or equivalent qualifications, including a good pass in maths, together with five GCSE/S Grade passes at 9-4/A*-C/1-3 or equivalent, including maths and English.

For most actuarial employers, a 2:1 degree or better is essential. Any subject is acceptable, but employers prefer candidates with numerate degrees, such as actuarial science, mathematics, statistics, economics, engineering, chemistry or physics. You would be expected to gain relevant work experience during your university holidays. Many actuarial employers encourage internships and often use them as opportunities to evaluate suitable candidates for future positions.

You can also get a taste of what it's like to study as an actuary by taking the Certificate in Financial Mathematics (CT1) examination. This is open to non-members of the professional body and would demonstrate to employers that you are an enthusiastic candidate. Full details of how to apply can be found on the Actuarial Profession website.

Kind of Person

You would need to be the sort of person who finds solving difficult numerical problems very satisfying. Employers would expect you to be highly numerate and analytical, with sufficient people and communication skills to explain your work to non-mathematicians, work with other professionals and manage teams of colleagues. Accuracy and attention to detail would be very important, as would excellent time management, prioritising and IT skills. The training is long and difficult and you would need determination to see it through.

Broad Outlook

Employment prospects are excellent. Very few actuaries are unemployed and hardly anyone feels the need, once qualified, to leave actuarial work. As the UK qualification is highly valued throughout the world, it is possible to spend part or all of your career abroad.

Actuaries' skills are in great demand throughout the financial sector, particularly in investment, insurance and pensions. Actuaries are also increasingly employed in risk management for large companies. However, actuarial consultancies are probably the biggest employers of actuaries in the UK.

Consultancies offer advice on issues such as acquisitions, mergers and financing capital projects, and also on occupational pension schemes. Investment work involves research on the pricing and management of investments, particularly in mitigating the risk of investments, and using an understanding of insurance or pension liabilities to manage the corresponding assets. In insurance, you would provide a service to companies which need a huge range of numerical information investigated, analysed and explained; for example to create and price polices, or to ensure they have the money to cover claims. Pensions work includes designing and advising on company pension schemes, especially placing a value on accumulated pension commitments.

Although there are many opportunities available to actuaries, most trainees start working either for an insurance company or for a consultancy firm.

Related Occupations

You may wish to consider: accountant (professional), chartered/company secretary, insurance underwriter, investment analyst, stockbroker or financial adviser.

Impact on Lifestyle

You could expect your life as an actuarial student to be dominated by long hours and examinations, which could mean temporarily giving up any aspects of your social life that conflict with your professional studies. A good training package from your employer would be very important as you would need their support and study leave for exams. This is very responsible and demanding work, which can be stressful, especially when huge financial risks are involved.

Earnings Potential

The actuarial profession is very well paid. Average basic salary figures from current survey data show £39,520 for a student actuary, rising to £50,007 on qualification. A function head typically earns £122,472 a year and a chief actuary/senior partner £209,292 plus bonus.

Further Information

Institute and Faculty of Actuaries
www.actuaries.org.uk

Government Actuary's Department
www.gov.uk/government/organisations/government-actuarys-department

Association of Consulting Actuaries
www.aca.org.uk

Society of Actuaries in Ireland
https://web.actuaries.ie

Advertising Account Executive

What is Involved?

As an Account Executive or Account Handler in an advertising agency, you would liaise with one or more clients to assess the message they wish to promote and work out and cost a suitable campaign. You would be working with an account planner and media buyer in your agency to devise a campaign that meets the client's needs and budget, and with the agency's creative team to find the right words and images. You would then monitor the whole programme and ensure it is completed on time, within budget and to the client's satisfaction.

You would normally start by handling around three or four accounts at the same time, which is important in terms of gaining experience across a range of client needs. The outcome of a number of successful campaigns may see you entrusted with one major, high-profile account.

Opportunities for Training

You would usually start as a junior account executive and learn on the job, possibly as part of an agency's structured graduate training scheme, perhaps working at the same time towards qualifications offered by the Institute of Practitioners in Advertising (IPA). These are available mainly online and range from the entry-level Foundation Certificate to the IPA Excellence Diploma. An alternative is the Diploma in Marketing Communications offered by the Communication Advertising and Marketing (CAM) Education Foundation.

You might also consider the level 4 advertising and marketing communications higher apprenticeship, equivalent to a foundation degree or higher national diploma, details of which are available from Creative Skillset.

Requirements for Entry

There is no fixed entry route into advertising and there are no minimum academic requirements. Many new advertising account executives do, however, have a degree. While any degree subject is acceptable, some employers may prefer one related to the industry, such as advertising, marketing, communication and media studies or business/management.

Pre-entry work experience, perhaps through an internship, is a very highly valued way of developing a clear understanding of the industry, meeting key people and building up appropriate contacts.

You might find it useful to visit the Diagonal Thinking website and take the *Diagonal Thinking self-assessment test*, an online tool designed to aid recruitment. It tests the hypothesis that the most successful individuals in advertising are both Linear and Lateral thinkers - they think 'diagonally'.

Kind of Person

Handling successful campaigns calls for a passion for advertising linked with keen commercial awareness. You would need excellent written and spoken communication skills, a high level of numeracy and effective team working and organisational skills. It is also important to be IT-literate and aware of how the advertising industry is developing in the light of new communication technologies and the growth of social media.

Broad Outlook

The total UK advertising spend rose to £20.1 billion in 2015 . This confirms a return to levels last seen before the recession. Advertising is an extremely popular career choice, with many applicants competing for every vacancy. Once you are in employment, promotion tends to be based on experience and proven track record. Mobility and flexibility are important factors in career progression, and may require moving between agencies and working for several different clients.

Related Occupations

Other options in advertising include: advertising creative or copywriter. You might also consider: marketing executive, sales executive, public relations executive or market researcher.

Impact on Lifestyle

This job is mainly office based, although you would have to travel to meet clients. To bring in a campaign on time, you might have to work long, irregular hours. Advertising is a young person's world and the great majority of people employed in this field are under 40. A job in advertising tends to be seen as glamorous, but it is recognised as a demanding and difficult world to enter.

Earnings Potential

Earnings differ greatly from agency to agency. Those based in London tend to pay the most and as a graduate recruit you could expect to earn between £19,000 and £26,000. With experience you could earn about £45,000 to £90,000, while the most senior posts pay £150,000 plus.

Further Information

AdMission
www.theadmission.co.uk

Institute of Practitioners in Advertising
www.ipa.co.uk

Account Planning Group
www.apg.org.uk

Communication, Advertising and Marketing (CAM) Education Foundation
www.camfoundation.com

Advertising Association
www.adassoc.org.uk

Creative Skillset
www.creativeskillset.org

Diagonal Thinking
www.diagonalthinking.co.uk

Institute of Advertising Practitioners in Ireland
http://iapi.ie

Advertising Creative

What is Involved?

Creatives in the advertising industry usually come in pairs: a copywriter and an art director.

As an Advertising Copywriter, you would provide the verbal or written 'copy' for advertising campaigns, using suitable slogans, catchphrases, messages and straplines for printed material, text for web advertising, and scripts and jingles for radio, TV and online commercials; as an Art Director, you would work with a copywriter to plan the visual aspects of a campaign. The visual concept must flow from a briefing about the client, the product, the target audience and the key message to be communicated.

While the two roles may seem quite distinct, they tend to fuse into one in a successful creative partnership, with both copywriter and art director contributing to the visual and verbal content to produce the right end result for an advertising campaign. They often stay together, moving from agency to agency as a team. Once an idea is agreed, the partnership manages and commissions artworkers, photographers, illustrators, film-makers and designers to make the concept a reality.

Opportunities for Training

Training is often on the job, with agencies expecting you to develop your skills as you work. You may be able to study for the Institute of Practitioners in Advertising (IPA) Foundation Certificate, which will give you an overview of brand communications. This is aimed at new creatives who have been in the role for up to one year.

The Design and Art Directors Association (D&AD) also offers a series of workshops and short courses, which aim to develop skills and inspire creativity.

Requirements for Entry

Although it is not essential, most art directors have studied design to degree level, usually specialising in advertising design, graphic design, illustration or fine art. There are no specific requirements for copywriters, although many new entrants are graduates with skills in English, journalism, communication and media studies or public relations. More than formal qualifications, the work requires a combination of business acumen, creativity, versatility and writing ability.

The most important entry requirement for a creative is an outstanding 'book' or portfolio of work to showcase your talent. You may find it useful to form an art director/copywriter team, perhaps on an introductory course, and create a 'book' together as you approach agencies to secure work experience placements. A good starting point is the IPA *Ad School Creative Programme*, which is open to undergraduates and recent graduates, or the *Creative Pioneers Challenge* programme of internships and apprenticeships for school leavers.

You might find it useful to visit the Diagonal Thinking website and take the *Diagonal Thinking self-assessment test*, an online tool designed to aid recruitment. It tests the hypothesis that the most successful individuals in advertising are both Linear and Lateral thinkers - they think 'diagonally'.

Kind of Person

Creating successful campaigns calls for a passion for advertising linked with a keen Interest in brands, branding and the commercial world. You would need an original imagination, with a limitless supply of new ideas to apply to business problems. Excellent written and spoken communication skills, a high level of numeracy and effective team working and organisational skills are all important. It is also vital to be IT-literate and aware of how the advertising industry is developing in the light of new communication technologies and the growth of social media.

Broad Outlook

The total UK advertising spend rose to £20.1 billion in 2015. This confirms a return to levels last seen before the recession. Advertising is an extremely popular career choice, with many applicants competing for every vacancy. Once you are in employment, promotion tends to be based on experience and proven track record. Mobility and flexibility are important factors in career progression, and may require moving between agencies and working for several different clients.

Related Occupations

You might also consider: artist/illustrator, author/creative writer, journalist, marketing executive, public relations executive, publisher or technical author.

Impact on Lifestyle

This job is mainly office based, although you would have to travel to meet clients. To bring in a campaign on time, you might have to work long, irregular hours. Advertising is a young person's world and the great majority of people employed in this field are under 40. A job in advertising tends to be seen as glamorous, but it is recognised as a demanding and difficult world to enter.

Earnings Potential

Earnings differ greatly from agency to agency. Those based in London tend to pay the most and as a graduate recruit you could expect to earn between £20,000 and £26,000. With experience you could earn about £45,000 to £90,000, while the most senior posts pay £150,000 plus.

Further Information

AdMission
www.theadmission.co.uk

Institute of Practitioners in Advertising
www.ipa.co.uk

Creative Pioneers
www.creativepioneers2.co.uk

Communication, Advertising and Marketing Education Foundation (CAM)
www.camfoundation.com

Advertising Association
www.adassoc.org.uk

Design and Art Directors Association
www.dandad.org

Young Creative Network
www.ycn.org

Creative Skillset
www.creativeskillset.org

Diagonal Thinking
www.diagonalthinking.co.uk

Institute of Advertising Practitioners in Ireland
www.iapi.ie

Advocate

See also Barrister for England, Wales, Northern Ireland and Republic of Ireland

What is Involved?

As an advocate, you would work as a member of the Scottish Bar, representing clients in courts of law and giving specialist legal advice. You would work as an expert in a specific area of the law and would be consulted by solicitors or other professionals. You would not work directly for the general public. As well as appearing in court, you might be consulted on a particular point of law or you may appear at a tribunal or enquiry. Advocates can also find employment working for the government or as part of the in-house legal team in a large organisation.

Most advocates work as self-employed independent professionals, based in Parliament House in Edinburgh. A group of advocates who share a clerk are known as a 'stable'. This system offers some support to newly qualified advocates but you would need to build your own reputation in order to get work. It would help to establish a good relationship with the clerk of your stable, who would be, to some extent, responsible for allocating the work that comes in.

Opportunities for Training

The process of becoming an advocate is currently under review. At the moment, after completing a degree of the requisite standard in Scottish law and the one-year, full-time Diploma in Legal Practice at a Scottish university, you must undertake a period of full-time training (usually 21 months) in a solicitor's office approved by the Faculty of Advocates. After you have been formally admitted by the Faculty as an Intrant (trainee advocate) and passed certain examinations there comes a further eight/nine month period of unpaid practical training ('devilling') with an experienced advocate (a devilmaster) and finally a competency assessment, which covers written and oral advocacy skills. Current advice is that you should complete a two-year solicitor's traineeship so that you can qualify and practise for some years as a solicitor before going to the Bar.

Requirements for Entry

Degrees in Scottish law are popular and you would need to get good results in your Higher/Advanced Higher subjects in order to be accepted. It would also be helpful if you could show, through work experience, that you have a genuine interest in the law and its processes.

Kind of Person

You would need complete integrity of character and must be deemed to carry the 'seven lamps' of advocacy: honesty, courage, industry, wit, eloquence, judgment and fellowship. Self-confidence, the intellectual capacity to assimilate large volumes of information in a short time, and the ability to work long hours with tight deadlines and high levels of responsibility are all essential. In addition, you would need the motivation and determination to succeed in what can be a daunting profession, particularly in the early years.

Broad Outlook

In the early days as an advocate, you may have to work for a reduced fee or work in lower courts in order to get yourself known. It can be hard work for little reward for the first few years, after which it is usually clear whether you are going to be successful.

There are no guarantees of employment, meaning that your job security would depend entirely on your own ability and reputation. You would be part of a small profession, with only 460 advocates currently in practice at the Bar. This compares with around 8,000 solicitors in practice in Scotland. Alternatively, you could choose to work as a specialist legal adviser for a corporate company or in local or central government (known as the 'employed Bar').

With experience, you could become a sheriff or a depute in the Crown Office and Procurator Fiscal Service. After around ten years of practice, you could apply to 'take silk' and become a Queen's Counsel (senior advocate) or become a judge.

Related Occupations

You might consider: solicitor, civil service executive officer, civil service fast streamer, barrister or legal executive (England and Wales).

Impact on Lifestyle

The hours of work can be very long, especially when you are starting out, and can be unsocial as you have to prepare late into the evenings and travel to courts. However, you should be able to do quite a lot of work from home and, if you are successful, to be selective in the sort of work you prefer to do. Payment often comes in some time after the work has been done and this can be a particular problem in the early years.

Advocates who are employed would have the security of receiving a regular wage but may not have the potential for the very high earnings that are possible for advocates in legal practice.

Earnings Potential

Whilst you are working as an intrant in a solicitor's office, you would normally receive a recommended minimum salary. This should be £17,545 at present for the first year, rising to £21,012 in the second year, although some large commercial firms pay considerably more. You would not receive any money during your nine months of devilling. There are scholarships available but you are more likely to be funding yourself. As a practising advocate, you would be self-employed so your earnings would vary enormously, depending on the nature and extent of the instructions you receive and the reputation you develop. Salaries might range from £30,000 to £35,000 in the early years but can rise dramatically, to £300,000 a year or more, with relevant experience.

Further Information

Faculty of Advocates
www.advocates.org.uk

Crown Office and Procurator Fiscal Service
www.copfs.gov.uk

Aeronautical/Aerospace Engineer

What is Involved?

As an aeronautical or aerospace engineer, you would be concerned with all aspects of making things fly and keeping them flying. This could range from missiles or one-man microlites right up to the largest passenger planes. You could be involved at all stages of the planning, design and testing of the aircraft. In addition you might be concerned with developing new technology. You would need to consider factors such as aerodynamics, the most appropriate materials to use, electrical systems and the means of propulsion. You could find yourself involved with the design of any aspect of the aircraft, from the wings to the guidance system used. You might choose to become a specialist in one particular field, such as thermodynamics or onboard computer technology. You could find yourself developing ideas for either civil or military aircraft. This is an industry where you would be likely to be working with new, cutting-edge technology.

Opportunities for Training

There are more than 30 UK universities and colleges offering degree and related courses in aeronautical or aerospace engineering. Some focus more on production and some on electronics or research, so you should read the prospectuses carefully; there is also a variation in the degree of specialisation as some courses are designed to show the integrated nature of engineering degrees. You should certainly check that your course is accredited with the Royal Aeronautical Society.

In order to become a chartered engineer (CEng), you would need to complete at least four years of academic study on a course leading to an MEng. There are also three-year courses leading to a BEng degree, which could take you to incorporated engineer (IEng) status.

Requirements for Entry

In order to study for a degree course in aeronautical engineering or one that incorporates aeronautics options, you are likely to need at least five GCSE/S Grade passes at 9-4/A*-C/1-3 plus three A level/Advanced Higher, four Higher or equivalent qualifications, to include maths, physics, and/or another science or technology subject.

Kind of Person

You would need a keen interest in aviation, a very logical and practical approach to problem solving and an ability to understand and to keep up to date with modern technology. You would need to be able to check technical specifications accurately and to follow detailed designs. You might be involved with conducting lengthy equipment tests and would need to show attention to detail. You are likely to be involved with analysing data, so would need to be numerate and able to use computer technology in your work. In addition to your scientific and practical engineering skills, you are likely to be working as a member of a team so you would need to be able to get on well with others. You would be expected to communicate both with fellow professionals and with others who do not have your specialised knowledge.

Broad Outlook

Aeronautical engineers may work for manufacturing companies, airline operators, the armed forces and the Defence Science and Technology Laboratory (Dstl). There are also opportunities to work abroad. Many employers would be interested in sponsoring you for at least some of your time at university. The UK has the second largest aerospace industry in the world after the United States, with more than 3,000 companies employing some 230,000 people. Since 2011, the sector has grown by 14%, spurred on by the Aerospace Growth Partnership, a joint government and industry initiative that has made significant progress in boosting innovation, skills and enhancing technology development in the supply chain.

Related Occupations

You might wish to consider: Royal Air Force officer, airline pilot, automotive engineer, control and instrumentation engineer, mechanical engineer, electrical engineer, electronic/electronics engineer, naval architect, materials scientist/engineer or metallurgist.

Impact on Lifestyle

Whilst you may have set conditions of work, there are times when you may need to work long hours in order to meet a deadline or to solve a particular problem. You might be based in a laboratory but you could have to work outside or possibly on a wind tunnel project for example. You might be expected to travel to conferences or meetings, which could be in another part of the country or abroad.

Earnings Potential

As a recent graduate you could expect to start on around £22,000 to £30,000, rising after a few years to £35,000 to £55,000. Once you are experienced, your salary is likely to rise to £50,000 to £65,000. Average earnings for incorporated engineers in the aerospace industry are around £50,000.

Further Information

Careers in Aerospace
www.careersinaerospace.com

Royal Aeronautical Society
www.aerosociety.com

Advancing UK AeroSpace Defence, Security and Space Industries
www.adsgroup.org.uk

UK Space Agency
www.gov.uk/government/organisations/uk-space-agency

Aerospace Growth Partnership
www.theagp.aero/the-agp

Association of Aerospace Universities
www.aau.ac.uk

Defence Science and Technology Laboratory (Dstl)
www.gov.uk/government/organisations/defence-science-and-technology-laboratory

Institution of Mechanical Engineers
www.imeche.org/industry-sectors/aerospace-engineering

Engineers Ireland
www.engineersireland.ie

Federation of Aerospace Enterprises in Ireland
www.faei.ie

Agricultural/Land-based Engineer

What is Involved?

As an agricultural engineer (or land-based engineer), you would be working as a specialist in technology related to agriculture or one of the allied land-based industries, including forestry, food engineering and technology, renewable energy, horticulture and the environment. These are highly mechanised industries and you would be involved with the design, development and maintenance of the specialised equipment currently in use. You could expect to be involved with: tractors and tillage machines, harvesting equipment, crop processing, animal welfare (handling and transport), irrigation and drainage schemes, earth moving and other construction equipment, pioneer road and bridge construction, forestry machines, horticultural machines and fish farming equipment.

You could also work in areas such as field engineering, land reclamation, drainage and irrigation and the systems used for this or the management of the field-to-table supply chain. You could combine your technical engineering skills with management and economic knowledge and play a valuable role in many aspects of an industry that is undergoing rapid change at the moment.

Opportunities for Training

This is a specialised area and there are few universities or HE colleges that run courses in engineering for the land-based sector. It is possible to take a three-year course that leads to the BEng or a four-year course leading to the MEng degree. There are also sandwich courses available, which allow for time to be spent working in industry as part of the course, and you could combine agricultural engineering with another subject, such as management. In order to become a chartered engineer, you would need to take an accredited course and to complete at least four years of academic study; to become an incorporated engineer, you would need at least a three-year accredited course (see separate article on engineering qualifications).

A new chartered environmentalist (CEnv) award is now available from the Society for the Environment. It is available through a number of professional institutions, and is open to members of the Institution of Agricultural Engineers involved in environmental work.

Requirements for Entry

Some universities would require you to have maths at A level/Advanced Higher, Higher or equivalent qualification, but even those that do not actually insist on maths would prefer you to have it. Most universities would also prefer you to have physics at A level/Advanced Higher, Higher or equivalent as well.

Kind of Person

You would need to have a strong interest in and understanding of agriculture, horticulture or forestry and the ways that these industries work. You should have a very practical and logical approach to problem solving and a strong mechanical interest. You would need to be able to analyse problems clearly and then to produce workable solutions. In addition to your technical and engineering skills, you would need to be able to communicate your ideas to others. You may well find yourself working as part of a small team, in which case you would be required to tell others what you think and to listen to their points of view. You could find yourself explaining your proposals to others who do not have your expert knowledge, or having to 'sell' your ideas in other cases.

Broad Outlook

There are good opportunities for well-qualified and knowledgeable engineers who can help to bring solutions to the range of problems facing the land-based sector. The industry needs to change and adapt to different demands and conditions both in the UK and abroad. There is a constant need to find more efficient and sustainable ways of using natural resources and more profitable ways of farming, with implications for recycling and environmental concerns. There are opportunities to work abroad, particularly in developing countries. You may be able to use your skills to work in development and relief projects, such as those organised by People and Skills for Disaster Relief.

We are currently seeing the emergence of a new profession of biosystems engineer, combining knowledge of biological systems and processes with a strong engineering background. This allows practitioners to be involved with issues concerning human health and welfare, including biomedical engineering, regenerative medicine, innovative materials and biomaterials, bio-mechatronics, bio-fuels and alternative energy sources.

Related Occupations

You might be interested in working in another branch of engineering as, for example, a mechanical engineer, automotive engineer, manufacturing engineer, mining engineer or water engineer. Alternatively, you might consider soil scientist or farm manager, horticultural manager or estate manager/land agent.

Impact on Lifestyle

Whilst you might find yourself working normal office hours, you are also likely to be required to travel out to farms or factories, which could involve longer hours. You may need to be outside in all kinds of weather, which may involve you getting wet, cold and dirty, or hot and dusty in developing countries with primitive facilities. You may have to travel to get to your clients or to the areas where they need your advice. At times you might find yourself working with potentially dangerous equipment and be required to take the necessary safety precautions.

Earnings Potential

You are likely to be paid around £22,000 to £25,000 when you first graduate. This can rise as you gain experience to around £50,000 to £70,000 for a chartered engineer and £36,000 to £42,000 for an incorporated engineer.

Further Information

Institution of Agricultural Engineers
www.iagre.org

Agricultural Engineers' Association
www.aea.uk.com

Society for the Environment
www.socenv.org.uk

RedR UK (People and Skills for Disaster Relief)
www.redr.org.uk

International Commission of Agricultural and Biosystems Engineering
http://cigr.org

Farm Tractor and Machinery Trade Association, Ireland
https://ftmta.ie

Air Traffic Controller

What is Involved?

As an air traffic controller (ATCO), you would be part of a team ensuring the safety of all aircraft taking off, landing and overflying the United Kingdom. You could work at the main control centre at Swanwick, near Southampton, or at Prestwick, near Glasgow, monitoring flights en route to their destinations; alternatively, you may be based at a specific airport, dealing with arriving and departing flights. In all situations, you would be communicating with pilots by radio, providing them with a radar-based picture of all the air traffic in their vicinity and authorising their movements in relation to the flight plans they submit before take-off.

Most air traffic controllers work for National Air Traffic Services (NATS) and this article is concerned primarily with a typical NATS career structure.

Opportunities for Training

Under the NATS training scheme, you would begin your training with a three-month basic course at the NATS College of Air Traffic Control, based at the Corporate and Technical Centre in Whiteley, Fareham, followed by further specialist training. You would develop teamwork skills, undertake practical training in simulators, do some private flying and visit air traffic control units. In the process, you would work towards ratings for a specific type of work: aerodrome approach, approach control, approach radar control or area radar control. You can't do everything and your specialist rating would determine whether you work at a control centre or an airport.

On successful completion of the student phase, you would be posted to an operational unit as a trainee controller and would continue to develop your skills as you work towards your Certificate of Competency as an operational controller. The training and assessment process takes around three years and typically sees 20 people – from 3,000 applicants – qualify for a licence.

Requirements for Entry

You must be at least 18 when you apply and in good overall health, with particular reference to hearing, eyesight and colour vision. Glasses or contact lenses are acceptable within certain limits. You would need at least five GCSE/S Grade passes 9-4/A*-C/1-3, including English and maths. You must be eligible to work in the UK and you must be security vetted. Following a series of psychometric tests and personality assessments, you would proceed to a second stage of interviews and computer tests.

Kind of Person

Because of the intense nature of the work, much of it sitting at radar screens and computer displays, you would need a high level of concentration and the ability to stay alert for sustained periods. You would need to be able to work both quickly and accurately under pressure and stay calm and focused; to think logically and to react quickly if required. Although the international language of air traffic control is English, you would need to be tolerant when communicating with pilots whose English is not strong, particularly in emergency situations. You must have a clear speaking voice.

You should be a good team player but able to work on your own. You should also have an aptitude to work with complex radar systems and the ability to think in 3D and calculate distances and angles.

NATS have devised five games, each of which has been designed to help you decide if you have the kind of skills and competencies required. Give the games a try online at: www.nats.aero/careers/trainee-air-traffic-controllers/games

Broad Outlook

With the continuous increase in air travel, despite the recent economic downturn, the further development of air traffic control is assured. European air space is some of the busiest in the world and the current system of air traffic management is under constant review. Under the *Single European Sky* initiative, the design, management and regulation of airspace is in the process of being harmonised throughout the European Union.

Once qualified, some 80% of ATCOs remain operational throughout their career. However, opportunities do exist for those who are interested in moving on to other areas. You could, for example, become a watch manager, or even a unit manager. Air traffic controllers can also apply to become trainers of new controllers.

Reducing the impact of air traffic operations on the environment is a top priority for the future and NATS has pledged to reduce the total CO_2 emissions by aircraft it controls by an average of 10% per flight by 2020. NATS is the first company in its sector to create this kind of environmental aim.

Related Occupations

You might wish to consider: aeronautical/aerospace engineer, air traffic controller in the armed forces, airline pilot, helicopter pilot, Royal Air Force officer or air cabin crew.

Impact on Lifestyle

Although you would work a 40-hour week, you would be expected to complete this in eight-hour shifts, including nights, weekends and public holidays. The work is entirely indoors, mostly wearing headphones and speaking into a microphone. It is extremely tiring and you would normally expect a break of at least 30 minutes after two hours of sitting in front of a radar screen.

You must be prepared to work at any NATS operational unit, depending on vacancies and your specialist qualifications. NATS has over 40 manned sites across the UK, including radar and radio stations, control towers at airports, area control centres, corporate headquarters, and the College of Air Traffic Control.

Earnings Potential

On joining, you would receive a basic salary of £13,154, together with a benefits package including a contributory pension scheme and generous annual leave. You would also be paid a weekly accommodation allowance of £60 and a further £1,000 on completion of your college-based training to cover travel and other expenses. After the college training phase, your salary would rise to between £17,066 and £20,479, depending on where you're posted. Once you've fully completed your training, your salary would rise to £32,522 to £36,247, again depending on the unit.

When you become an ATCO, on your third joining anniversary, your salary rises to £46,461 to £51,781 plus shift pay of £5,543. After qualifying, you could potentially earn over £100,000 (inclusive of shift pay) at Swanwick and Heathrow.

Further Information

National Air Traffic Services Careers
www.nats.aero/careers

Guild of Air Traffic Control Officers
http://gatco.org

Irish Aviation Authority
www.iaa.ie

What is Involved?

As an airline pilot, you would fly aircraft on scheduled and chartered flights, transporting passengers and cargo. You would normally be one of two pilots on the flight deck, starting as first officer or co-pilot and working up to promotion as captain or commander. You would be in overall charge as captain, responsible for the safety of the aircraft and everyone on board. A typical flight would follow a logical sequence of tasks: before take-off, for example, you would decide on a flight plan, taking into account the weather conditions, the number of passengers and amount of cargo. You would supervise loading and fuelling operations, brief the cabin crew and carry out all the necessary pre-flight checks of operating systems. When ready for take-off, you would liaise with air traffic control for permission to proceed to the runway. During the flight, you would maintain a series of checks on the aircraft's position and technical performance, monitor weather conditions and other air traffic, communicate with air traffic controllers and advise passengers of flight details. Finally, you would land under instruction from air traffic control and would write a report on the flight.

Opportunities for Training

You would need to complete a lengthy and expensive training programme in order to obtain your Airline Transport Pilot's Licence (ATPL). Traditionally, this was sponsored by the airlines, leading to employment after graduation from a Flight Training School. However, there is currently little airline sponsorship available and most pilots are self-sponsored. Given that pilot training is very expensive, you should research all the options available and seek impartial advice.

There are two routes to achieving an ATPL: an 'integrated' course lasting about 18 months, where the training is condensed into a very intensive programme, or a 'modular' course, where you can complete the various phases of training in more manageable chunks.

A possible alternative training route is to qualify as a pilot in the armed forces and take a conversion course at the end of your military career.

Requirements for Entry

You must hold a special medical certificate to be able to fly passengers. It is advisable to obtain this before even starting training to ensure that you meet the medical criteria. You need to be physically fit, with normal colour vision and good hearing and eyesight. Glasses may be allowed and some airlines specify minimum height requirements.

Most flying schools look for a minimum of five GCSE/S Grade passes at 9-4/A*-C/1-3, including English, maths and a science. Airlines offering sponsorship usually ask for more than this and would normally expect two A level/Advanced Higher, three Higher or equivalent qualifications, preferably including maths and physics.

Kind of Person

Your spatial aptitude must be very high, including the ability to think clearly in three dimensions and to interpret maps quickly and accurately. You would also need a high level of numeracy for making mathematical calculations. Excellent communication skills would be essential for linking with air traffic control, briefing the cabin crew, liaising with passengers and producing written reports.

Qualities of leadership, initiative, adaptability and the ability to work well with other people would be required, together with high levels of concentration and attention to detail, the ability to stay calm under pressure and the authority to take charge in an emergency.

The Honourable Company of Air Pilots provides an aptitude test and assessment scheme for people with little or no flying experience. Although not a requirement for flight training, it could help you decide whether you are suited to this career before you make a financial commitment to training.

Broad Outlook

The airline industry is currently undergoing considerable change and has been severely affected by the recent economic downturn. Market conditions at present tend to favour new, low-cost companies rather than the traditional 'flag carriers'. A protracted decline in airline recruitment has resulted in a large pool of unemployed newly-qualified commercial pilots, far outnumbering the demand for pilots as the airlines themselves struggle to stay in business.

Related Occupations

You may consider: aeronautical/aerospace engineer, air traffic controller, helicopter pilot, pilot in the armed services or Royal Air Force officer.

Impact on Lifestyle

You could be away from home for extended periods of time, especially on long-haul flights. Your social and family life would have to be fitted around your job. Your hours of work would vary enormously but would usually include nights and weekends. While your time in the air would be restricted to 900 flying hours per year, your workload would not necessarily be spread evenly throughout the year; on charter airlines, for example, the summer months tend to be busier than the winter months. As a short- or long-haul pilot, you could expect to have 12 to 15 days off per month, but you would be lucky to have a regular day or night off each week. Long-haul pilots may suffer tiredness, particularly when flying regularly through different time zones.

Earnings Potential

It is a common misconception that all airline pilots earn very high salaries. Your salary would actually vary according to the type of aircraft you are flying, the airline you are working for and your experience. As a first officer, for example, you might start at between £22,000 and £24,000 a year, depending on the operator. The starting salary for a captain in a medium UK airline is from £57,000 to £78,000, rising to more than £100,000, or up to £150,000 with a major operator. Many airlines expect you either to pay for your own 'type training' to qualify you to fly a certain type of aircraft, or to pay the airline a bond of £20,000 to £35,000 to cover part of your training. Your bond would be repaid to you over a period of several years if you continue to fly with that airline.

Further Information

British Air Line Pilots' Association
www.balpa.org
Civil Aviation Authority
www.caa.co.uk
Honourable Company of Air Pilots incorporating Air Navigators
www.airpilots.org
Royal Aeronautical Society
http://aerosociety.com
Irish Airline Pilots' Association
https://ialpa.net

Ambulance Paramedic

What is Involved?

As an ambulance paramedic, you would respond to 999 and other urgent calls, travelling by ambulance, helicopter, car or motorbike to be at the scene of an emergency as soon as possible. You would be highly trained in all aspects of pre-hospital emergency care from crush injuries to cardiac arrest. Your aim would be to treat and stabilise patients before movement but not to delay hospital admission unnecessarily in order to achieve this. You would be working primarily in a vehicle designed to provide a clinical workplace with maximum mobility. It would be equipped with a wide range of emergency care equipment, including a heart defibrillator, spinal and traction splints, rescue equipment, intravenous drips, oxygen and a range of drugs for medical and traumatic emergencies. You would carry sophisticated patient monitoring equipment such as a pulse oximeter and cardiac and blood pressure monitors.

Opportunities for Training

Traditionally, staff joining the ambulance service could work their way up with experience and additional training from care assistant, through ambulance technician to paramedic. However, this route is no longer open to new entrants. Anyone wishing to work as a paramedic will now need either to secure a student paramedic position with an ambulance service trust, or to attend an approved full-time course in paramedic science at a university.

Courses tend to be modular, with flexible entry and exit points related to your academic qualifications and any relevant experience. They last from two to five years, depending on whether you study full- or part-time. The training comprises both theory and practical clinical experience, including several weeks in various hospital departments. Much of the training of paramedics is carried out under the supervision of senior doctors.

As a paramedic, you would have to register with the Health and Care Professions Council, sitting a one-day paramedic refresher every year, and a five-day paramedic refresher every three years.

Requirements for Entry

The range of paramedic science courses at university varies in terms of entry requirements and you must contact each university directly for information on their admissions policy.

In order to drive an ambulance, whether emergency or non-emergency, you will need a full, manual driving licence. Ambulance services use vehicles of different gross weights and you must hold a driving licence with the appropriate classifications to enable you to drive ambulances in your chosen service. In some ambulance services, a 'standard' driving licence may be acceptable, but if you passed your test after 1996, you will need an extra driving qualification to drive larger vehicles and carry passengers. Some services may provide support for staff who need to gain further licence classifications but this is not standard across the UK.

Kind of Person

You would have to be highly skilled, quick thinking and decisive, yet able to provide a calm and reassuring environment for the patient and relatives. You would also need to be a good team worker, with excellent communication skills. Physical fitness would be essential to deal with moving and lifting patients and equipment. At the same time, you would need the manual dexterity to carry out treatment in awkward conditions.

Broad Outlook

As the ambulance service is run on a local basis, the demand for staff varies across the country, with more vacancies occurring in London and other urban areas. You should contact your local ambulance service for more details. There are some opportunities with ambulance services run by private hospitals or with large industrial companies who run their own on-site ambulance service. There is also some scope to train and work within the armed forces. Promotion to senior management positions can come after successful experience.

With further experience, you might take on one of the developing roles in the community such as an emergency care practitioner. Here you could be based in one of a number of different settings, such as a GP surgery, minor injuries unit or hospital accident and emergency department. You would usually need extra training and qualifications for this.

Related Occupations

You might also wish to consider: fire fighter/fire officer, health visitor, nurse, or police officer.

Impact on Lifestyle

You would have to work on rotating shifts, going out in all weathers at night, over the weekend and during public holidays. Most of the population respect ambulance personnel for the vital work they do but you should be prepared for the occasional hostile reception, especially when dealing with people under the influence of drink or drugs. As you would be wearing uniform, you would be immediately identifiable. The work can be stressful in that you would rarely know in advance the severity of the emergency to which you were responding; you could be dealing with a train crash or motorway pile-up involving seriously injured casualties.

Earnings Potential

As a paramedic, you can earn £22,128 to £28,746 once you have completed your training, rising to around £26,565 to £35,577 as a service manager.

Further Information

College of Paramedics
www.collegeofparamedics.co.uk

NHS Ambulance Services (England)
**www.nhs.uk/NHSEngland/AboutNHSservices/Emergencyandurgentcareservices/
Pages/Ambulanceservices.aspx**

Scottish Ambulance Service
www.scottishambulance.com

Health and Care Professions Council
www.hcpc-uk.org

Welsh Ambulance Services
www.ambulance.wales.nhs.uk

Health Careers
www.healthcareers.nhs.uk

Paramedic Resource Centre
www.paramedic-resource-centre.com

Irish Ambulance Training Institute
www.ambulancetraining.ie

Archaeologist

What is Involved?

Archaeology is the study of the past through objects left behind by previous generations. Studying the remains of the past can involve anything from old coins to buried cities. As an archaeologist, you could choose to take up teaching, lecturing, museum work, research or fieldwork. You would need a broad academic understanding of your subject before specialising in an area such as conservation, heritage management, underwater, computing or environmental archaeology; other specialisms include coins, weapons, ancient languages, chemical analysis and dating of specimens, as well as geographical areas (e.g. Egyptology) or historical periods (eg the Iron Age).

To show evidence of your commitment and enthusiasm, it would be a very good idea to do as much voluntary work as possible during your university holidays. The Council for British Archaeology (CBA) can help you arrange this, providing information about excavations requiring volunteers.

Opportunities for Training

Nearly all archaeologists are graduates and most have a first degree in archaeology. For some areas of archaeology (eg museum work) a postgraduate qualification is normally required.

There is great variation in the course content but most single honours courses include a basic core of archaeological methods, a broad geographical and chronological view of the subject, science, history and the role of archaeology in today's society. There is a trend also towards the more scientific aspects of archaeology, with several institutions offering BSc courses in archaeological science. Most courses offer a varying amount of practical fieldwork experience, often on research projects in Britain and abroad.

The Chartered Institute for Archaeologists is currently working to establish an overarching qualification of Historic Environment Practitioner, with apprenticeships intended to cover levels 3 to 7 (equating to academic qualifications from A level to postgraduate standard).

You can develop your own Archaeology Skills Passport and explore potential career pathways via the British Archaeological Jobs and Resources (BAJR) website.

Requirements for Entry

The minimum requirement for a degree course in archaeology is normally three A level/Advanced Higher or four Higher or equivalent qualifications, together with five GCSE/S Grade passes 9-4/A*-C/1-3, including English and maths. Geography, history and a foreign language are all useful subjects. Some science-based degree courses ask for physics and chemistry. Archaeology has become a popular subject and high grades are, therefore, required.

Kind of Person

Archaeologists need a dual approach: digs require physical stamina and teamwork, whereas writing up your finds requires attention to detail and patience. You would need to have an academic interest in the past and it is important to realise that the finds made are not always glamorous. You would examine pieces of pottery, coins, human skeletons and bone fragments, which may reveal DNA evidence, together with organic matter which may need dating by processes such as isotopic analysis.

Broad Outlook

In the current economic climate, jobs are scarce, competition is fierce and projects are poorly funded. Advice from Current Archaeology includes "if archaeology is your passion, why not consider sitting out the current recession and study for a Masters, even a PhD? The job market will surely be better in the future."

The main areas of work for archaeologists are in commercial archaeology units, museums, local authorities or specialist consultants. Many also work for the national heritage agencies (English Heritage, Historic Scotland, Northern Ireland Environment Agency and Cadw) or conservation charities, among which the National Trust is probably the biggest employer.

Related Occupations

You may be interested in other careers in this field, such as heritage manager, historical researcher, museum keeper - art gallery curator, archaeological illustrator or archaeological surveyor.

Impact on Lifestyle

Your hours of work would vary according to the type of archaeological activity being undertaken. Museum work usually involves a 36-hour week and some weekends. If you work for a local authority or national agency, you could also expect to work normal office hours. Work on excavations, however, is likely to involve long and sometimes unsocial hours, not to mention a potentially muddy, wet and windswept or achingly hot and unshaded workplace.

Earnings Potential

At the bottom end of the career ladder, salaries are often quite low, with many positions on fixed-term contracts. Even at higher levels, salaries are frequently lower than in correspondingly similar positions in other fields of employment. You might expect to earn between £20,000 and £21,000 on graduating, rising to between £29,000 and £40,000 with experience. BAJR has implemented a grading system, creating a recommended minimum level of payment based on duties and experience. This currently starts at £18,960 for a G2 site assistant, with appropriate increases for, say, a G4/5 supervisor or a G7 senior manager.

Further Information

Council for British Archaeology
http://new.archaeologyuk.org

Archaeology Training Forum
http://archaeologytraining.org.uk

Young Archaeologists' Club
www.yac-uk.org

Chartered Institute for Archaeologists
www.archaeologists.net

Current Archaeology
www.archaeology.co.uk

British Archaeological Jobs and Resources
www.bajr.org

Institute of Archaeologists of Ireland
http://iai.ie

Architect

What is Involved?

As an architect, you would be involved with designing and constructing new buildings or restoring old ones. You would have the power and the responsibility to shape the environments in which people spend their daily lives. Your designs must be attractive, practical, soundly conceived and not too expensive to turn into reality. You would need to combine both the creativity of using shape, colour, materials and space to meet your client's design requirements and the practicality of understanding planning and building regulations while meeting the physical demands of the construction process.

Opportunities for Training

In order to practise as an architect you would need to complete a seven-year training programme, which involves three stages:

- Firstly, a five-year degree at a recognised school of architecture; this consists of a three year intermediate degree (Part 1) and a two year further degree (Part 2);

- Secondly, two years in professional practice in an architect's office. The first year usually follows Part 1 and the second year follows Part 2;

- Thirdly, the Professional Practice Examination (Part 3).

The title 'architect' is protected in the UK by law. It is only by following this route - or an equivalent route recognised by the Royal Institute of British Architects (RIBA) and the Architects Registration Board (ARB) - that you could be eligible to call yourself an architect.

Requirements for Entry

To be accepted for a degree course at a school of architecture, you would normally need three A level/Advanced Higher, four Higher or equivalent qualifications, plus five GCSE/S Grade passes at 9-4/A*-C/1-3 to include maths, English language and either chemistry or physics. Some courses may require maths or physics at A level/ Advanced Higher or Higher, or art at A level/Advanced Higher/Higher or equivalent.

You could expect an interview by the schools you have applied to and they may want to see your portfolio. Your portfolio may include a mixture of photos, sketches of buildings, short notes, collages, still life and life drawings. They would be looking for evidence of creative skills together with an awareness of architecture. Work experience in an architect's office would be especially valuable here.

Kind of Person

Three-dimensional awareness is important, together with the ability to explain complex structures in the form of drawings. A balance of creative flair and technical skill is essential and you would almost certainly be using computers quite extensively. You should enjoy problem solving and you must have a keen interest in how people react in different types of built environment. You would also need an awareness of and interest in current trends and fashions.

Architects must be able to work as part of a team. They need to be good communicators both with clients and with construction personnel on site. Good management skills are also important. You would need to be able to work to deadlines.

You would need to be physically fit for the site inspections, which would involve climbing around part-constructed buildings, and the ability to drive would be a considerable asset.

Broad Outlook

Like the construction industry generally, architecture has highs and lows reflecting the state of the national economy. After the recession of 2008, the building sector shrank considerably and with it opportunities for architects. However, the UK construction industry has turned around to become one of the fastest-growing sectors in the economy, offering new hope for architecture graduates in the years to come.

Training is very long with no guarantee of employment at the end. Most architects work in small private practices with usually fewer than ten staff. To start with, you might be on a short-term contract and then progress with experience to junior and then senior partnerships. Alternatively, you could start your own practice. The environmental field is a growing area of work, offering opportunities for professionals to become involved in the planning process for environmentally sensitive development schemes.

Related Occupations

You may consider: architectural technician/technologist, civil engineer, structural engineer, environmental consultant, town planner, interior designer, surveyor (general practice) or landscape architect.

Impact on Lifestyle

Architecture is a prestigious and highly regarded profession in any community. Training does, however, take a long time and you can expect to still be a student when your friends are working. Most architects work normal office hours unless there are deadlines to be met. As a self-employed freelance architect, you might experience periods of inactivity and other periods of high workload.

You could expect to work some of the time in a light, bright office and some of the time on a potentially hazardous construction site.

Earnings Potential

As a Part 1, first year out student, you should earn £18,000 to £22,000. This should rise to £24,000 to £31,000 for a Part 2 student and to £31,000 to £40,000 for a Part 3, newly qualified architect, varying according to location and size of your employer. The public sector tends to pay less. With experience you could expect to earn £50,000 to £90,000 and, at the top of the profession, considerably more. RIBA publishes an annual salary survey.

Further Information

Royal Institute of British Architects
www.architecture.com

Architects Registration Board
www.arb.org.uk

Architecture Students Network
http://theasn.org

Architecture Jobs
www.ribaappointments.com

Royal Incorporation of Architects in Scotland
www.rias.org.uk

Royal Institute of Architects of Ireland
www.riai.ie

Architectural Technician/Technologist

What is Involved?

As an architectural technologist, you would be a specialist in the application of building science and technology to architectural design and construction projects. You would be able, when fully chartered, to set up in practice and provide a full architectural design service to the public and other clients. As a technician, you would support architectural technologists, architects and other professionals in the construction industry. You might specialise in collating technical information during the development of a project design, preparing drawings and writing specifications for construction work.

The design process requires many activities to be undertaken by the architectural team: you would start by deciding exactly what is required, establishing with the client such factors as how the building might be used, how much it would cost, how it would be built and what sort of site might be available, before thinking about its outward appearance.

In addition to the design drawings, detailed specifications and documents would have to be prepared in conjunction with other consultants. You would have to negotiate with the planning and building authorities and you would work closely with other professionals such as architects and building surveyors. Finally, a 'package' would be prepared to enable the building project to be carried out, often including a management role for your team in supervising work on site.

Opportunities for Training

To graduate as an architectural technologist, the recommended route is to enrol on an honours degree in Architectural Technology. This programme can be studied over a period of three or four years, full- or part-time. The four-year degree will include a sandwich year (excluding Scotland), allowing you to gain industry experience before returning to complete the degree. There are currently 33 accredited degree programmes across the UK and Ireland. You can then work towards the title chartered architectural technologist and will be able to use the designation MCIAT.

To become a professionally qualified architectural technician it is recommended that you complete an Architectural Technology Associate degree, Higher Diploma (HND), Higher Certificate (HNC) or Foundation degree in Architectural Technology (or built environment equivalent). You may also be able to start with a company on an advanced apprenticeship in, for example, Built Environment and Design.

Requirements for Entry

Entry to an architectural technology programme is subject to individual university requirements but you should have a broad secondary education with particular focus on science and technology subjects. It is recommended that your GCSE/S Grade passes should include art, design and technology, English, information technology, mathematics and science. A/AS levels/Highers or equivalent should be in relevant subjects such as science, technology, building services engineering or construction.

Kind of Person

As a specialist in the science of architecture, building design and construction, you should be able to analyse and solve working problems, both at a computer terminal in the drawing office and on construction sites in all weathers. You would need to be flexible and able to work with others as part of a motivated and effective team.

You would need to be creative as well as technically minded, so you should have an ability to draw in addition to good IT skills. You would need to take an interest in your surroundings and to be able to visualise objects in three dimensions. You would need a good memory for facts and figures, including all those building regulations, and you would have to be fit enough to climb around building sites on a fairly regular basis.

Broad Outlook

Prospects in architectural technology are linked to the overall health of the construction industry. The recent economic climate has been far from encouraging but the UK construction industry has turned around to become one of the fastest-growing sectors in the economy, offering new hope for architectural technologists and technicians in the years to come.

Employment can be found in a variety of national and international organisations, from private architectural practices to local authorities and construction companies, and can include new build, conversion, adaptation, restoration or management and maintenance work on many types of commercial, industrial and residential property.

As an experienced and chartered architectural technologist you could eventually set up your own practice or work in partnership or as director with fellow architectural technologists, architects and other professionals within the construction industry.

Related Occupations

You might also consider: architect, landscape architect, environmental consultant, town planner, civil engineer, surveyor (general practice), building surveyor, construction manager, site engineer/construction estimator or structural engineer.

Impact on Lifestyle

Your working week might vary from one contract to another but you would be mostly office-based and could expect a fairly typical Monday to Friday, nine to five timetable. Particular schedules might demand unsocial hours from time to time to meet deadlines and you might be required to travel to site meetings.

Working conditions on building sites can be hazardous, wet, muddy and cold. You may have to climb ladders and scaffolding, and would need to comply with all health and safety requirements.

Earnings Potential

There are no set salary scales and how much you earn could depend on your employer and how good you are. As a guide, a junior architectural technologist could expect to earn around £17,000 to £25,000, rising to £24,000 to £40,000 with some three years' experience. In a more senior post, you could expect to earn from £45,000 to over £100,000. To attract the highest salary, you would need both considerable experience and the ability to run complex contracts.

Further Information

Chartered Institute of Architectural Technologists
www.ciat.org.uk

Building Design Online
www.bdonline.co.uk

Royal Institute of Architects of Ireland
www.riai.ie/architectural_technologists

Army Officer

What is Involved?

As a British army officer you would be part of the service that carries out tasks given to it by the democratically elected Government of the United Kingdom. Your primary task would be to help defend the interests of the UK, which may involve service at home or overseas.

The army is composed of divisions and brigades, each made up of smaller units bearing historically significant names. While you would be first and foremost an officer, rather than a particular specialist, you can express an interest in one of four different areas:

Combat - the army's fighting regiments, whose work can involve engaging the enemy on the battlefield, peacekeeping or delivering humanitarian aid. This area encompasses the Household Cavalry, Royal Armoured Corps, Infantry and Army Air Corps

Combat Support - made up of the Royal Artillery, Royal Engineers, Royal Corps of Signals and the Intelligence Corps, providing the Combat Arms with direct support on the battlefield, as well as indirect support such as intelligence

Combat Service Support - helping the Army to function effectively, from maintaining machinery and vehicles to ensuring the physical wellbeing of personnel. This area includes the Royal Army Chaplain's Department, Royal Logistics Corps, Army Medical Services, Royal Electrical and Mechanical Engineers and the Adjutant General's Corps

Professionally Qualified Officers - including doctors, pharmacists and physiotherapists; dentists; nurses; barristers and solicitors; vets; and Ministers of all faiths. These normally qualify professionally before joining the army

Your exact duties as an army officer would depend on the area you work in and what type of job you do. In the combat area, for example, you could be a battlefield helicopter pilot, or a platoon commander leading a team of 30 trained soldiers on operations.

Opportunities for Training

Most officers follow the commissioning course at the Royal Military Academy Sandhurst (RMAS), which lasts 44 weeks. The course includes training in leadership and management, tactics, weapons and fitness. After leaving RMAS, you would complete an additional course and receive a commission. You begin your career as a Second Lieutenant, following the Officer Career Development programme, which develops leadership and management skills and concentrates on the development of professional military knowledge both in barracks and on operations.

At the age of 16, you could apply to attend the Welbeck Defence Sixth Form College near Loughborough to study at A/AS level.

Requirements for Entry

The minimum entry requirements are seven GCSE/S Grade passes 9-4/A*-C/1-3 and two A level/Advanced Higher, three Higher or equivalent qualifications. Nearly all new entrants are graduates and you must be of degree calibre even if you choose not to go to university. For some specialist sections a degree in a relevant subject, e.g. in engineering, would be necessary, while some jobs require you to be professionally qualified before applying.

You must pass the Army Officer Selection Board, where you would be put through a series of selection tests and interviewed at length about your motivation and interests.

Kind of Person

Above all else, the qualities of leadership are important. A high standard of physical fitness is also vital and the programme at Sandhurst ensures that you would leave not only in top physical condition but also able to supervise the fitness training of the soldiers placed under your command. Expeditions involving climbing, sailing, caving, kayaking, diving, trekking and other activities are all encouraged at Sandhurst, with the success or failure of each expedition depending entirely upon your initiative, resourcefulness and courage.

As an officer you must be able to command the respect of those in your care, through your ability to lead in difficult and potentially dangerous situations. You must be able to exercise responsibility, be fit, prepared to work closely with others in combat and mix easily with all sorts of people in whatever context. You must be a team player but able to work alone if required, able to listen but also to make on-the-spot decisions.

Broad Outlook

In common with other branches of the UK's armed services, the army has faced severe cuts following the 2010 Strategic Defence and Security Review (SDSR). The SDSR target, known as Army 2020, is that the army will be reduced from 102,000 to 82,000 personnel by 2018. At the same time, the army reserve is set to double in size from 15,000 to 30,000. The army continues to recruit, although competition for places will inevitably become fiercer.

Related Occupations

Royal Air Force officer, Royal Navy/Royal Marines officer, or police officer.

Impact on Lifestyle

You would be paid to be available 24 hours a day, seven days a week, although when you are not on exercise or operations you are likely to work a normal five-day week.

You could expect to be posted, often at short notice, anywhere around the world, in combat or in humanitarian work like peacekeeping or famine relief. You would need to be highly adaptable and broad-minded for you may not always be welcomed by the local community.

Earnings Potential

How much you get paid as an officer in the Army is determined by your rank and how long you have served. Sixth form sponsorships and undergraduate sponsorship and bursaries are offered to suitable candidates and special rates of pay may be offered to undergraduates whilst studying. An officer cadet currently earns £25,727, and a Second Lieutenant £30,922, while a newly appointed Lieutenant starts on £32,008, and a Captain £39,628. At the top of the tree, a Brigadier is paid £101,147. Many allowances are provided in terms of accommodation and food.

Further Information

Visit an Army Careers Centre or call 0345 600 8080. You can create an account and apply online via the Army website below:
British Army
www.army.mod.uk
Welbeck Defence Sixth Form College
www.dsfc.ac.uk
Defence Forces of Ireland
www.military.ie

Artist/Illustrator

What is Involved?

As an artist, you would use a range of techniques, from painting and drawing to collage, installation, performance, photography, sculpture and printmaking, to create original works of art for exhibition and sale. You might receive commissions for some of your work from individuals, private companies or public authorities, or you might seek galleries or art dealers to exhibit your work. You may specialise in, say, landscape, portrait or abstract work.

As an illustrator, you would be employed to carry out a brief or project set by a client, producing drawings, paintings or diagrams to help make products more visually attractive. You might work on books, comics, magazines, newspapers, websites, advertisements, packaging, or on detailed technical diagrams in medicine, science and technology. As either an artist or illustrator, you would spend some time travelling or contacting potential clients to show them examples of the work in your portfolio.

Opportunities for Training

Some successful artists/illustrators are entirely self-taught but talent is seldom enough and a good starting point would normally be to take an art foundation course before going on to a further course of training at an art school or university. Most foundation courses allow you to explore several areas of artistic work before you choose a specialised degree or higher national diploma (HND) course.

Requirements for Entry

Entry to foundation courses can be from GCSE/S Grade or A level/Advanced Higher/ Higher or equivalent qualifications, with great importance placed on a current portfolio of your own artistic work. The courses last for one or two years full-time, and can be found at sixth form colleges, further and higher education colleges, art colleges and some universities.

Entry to an HND course would normally require a minimum of four GCSE/S Grade passes 9-4/A*-C/1-3 and one or two A level/Advanced Higher or two or three Higher or equivalent qualifications. The course would last for two or three years, with the possibility of conversion to a degree course. Entry to a degree course would normally require a minimum of five GCSE/S Grade and two or three A level/Advanced Higher or three or four Higher or equivalent qualifications. These requirements might be waived if you have foundation course experience and/or an impressive portfolio.

Kind of Person

You would clearly need a high degree of creative artistic talent but there is also a call for other skills. As an illustrator, in particular, you would need to be very well organised, able to stick to deadlines and to interpret the wishes of your clients. IT skills would almost certainly be helpful. As either an artist or an illustrator, you would need to be very determined but able to deal with disappointment if a client or dealer rejected your work. Communication skills, particularly powers of persuasion, would be very important, as you would have to deal with a wide variety of people. Some business sense and an understanding of budgets would also be a great asset.

Broad Outlook

The traditional image of the starving artist in a lonely garret still has some relevance. It is not easy to make a living purely as an artist but that should not stop you trying if you feel that you have the necessary talent and determination. The position is brighter for illustrators, although permanent contracts are still something of a luxury.

According to a survey conducted by Artists' Interaction and Representation (AIR the average artist earns only £10,00 a year, and only 16% of them pay into a private pension fund, raising questions about how professional artists might support themselves in retirement.

Related Occupations

You might wish to consider: advertising creative, fine art dealer, art gallery curator, art therapist, art restorer/conservator, art valuer, cartographer, ceramics designer, fashion designer, graphic designer, interior designer, photographer, textile designer, set designer or costume designer.

Impact on Lifestyle

Working as an artist or illustrator would put you in a very competitive field, with very little security. You would most likely work on a freelance basis, with extremely variable hours, and you might have to work during the evenings or at weekends if you had a deadline to meet. Also, your earnings might be far from regular and you would have to plan your budget and your domestic and social activities accordingly.

Earnings Potential

The price you could ask for your work is governed by many factors and could vary tremendously, possibly requiring you to supplement your income by undertaking some other work. As an illustrator, you would usually receive a fee for each piece of work, the amount being dependent upon the size and scope of the commission. Alternatively, you might charge a daily rate, ranging from, say, £200 to £300. You should also remember that any artists' agent you might employ would charge you a fee. The Association of Illustrators has extensive information about pricing for its members. The Artists Information Company can help members calculate how to price their work. It is suggested that artists might reasonably aim at a similar income to teachers.

Further Information

Association of Illustrators
www.theaoi.com

Creative and Cultural Skills
www.ccskills.org.uk

Creative Scotland
www.creativescotland.com

Artists Information Company
www.a-n.co.uk

Society of Artists Agents Illustration Hub
http://saahub.com

Artquest
www.artquest.org.uk

Illustrators Ireland
www.illustratorsireland.com

Visual Artists Ireland
http://visualartists.ie

Auctioneer/Valuer

What is Involved?

As an auctioneer, you would be expected to sell at auction such items as bankrupt stock, commodities, collectables, furniture, household goods, property, land, motor cars, farming equipment or whatever else owners wish to sell in this way. You might work for a firm of surveyors or estate agents who undertake general auctioneering, or for a specialist auction house in the worlds of fine art, furniture, sculpture, antiques, literature, philately, postcards, militaria and celebrity memorabilia, where you would need a very high level of expertise.

In addition to conducting the auction itself, you would assess the value of items for sale, advise clients on setting reserve prices, arrange items into lots, organise a catalogue, insure the goods against loss or damage, arrange the transport of sold and unsold lots and ensure adequate pre-sale publicity.

Opportunities for Training

There are many possible routes to a qualification such as those offered by the Royal Institution of Chartered Surveyors (RICS). You could, for example, complete a degree or diploma course accredited by the RICS or, if your degree is not accredited, a postgraduate conversion course. You would then undertake two years of practical, on-the-job training leading to the RICS Assessment of Professional Competence. The major international auction houses, Christie's and Sotheby's, run their own courses in the art business.

Developed in consultation with the National Association of Valuers and Auctioneers are the Real Property Auctioneering and Chattels Auctioneering qualifications offered by the National Federation of Property Professionals. These can be achieved using home study training manuals produced by Manchester Open Learning.

Requirements for Entry

Two to three A level/Advanced Higher, three to four Higher or equivalent qualifications, together with supporting GCSE/S Grade 9-4/A*-C/1-3, would normally be required to secure entry to most relevant degree or diploma courses. There are no specific requirements for open learning, although employers may determine their own minimum standards.

Kind of Person

You would need to be capable of inspiring confidence in your clients and of understanding the minds of collectors or purchasers. A sound grasp of the market and its trends and fashions would be essential, as well as a willingness to steep yourself in your specialist field. You would need to have good commercial and business flair. You should be a good public speaker, capable of controlling the auction room and able to explain the special features of items for sale. You should be extremely quick-witted and observant in spotting bids, with excellent hearing and eyesight.

It would be important to know the particular features involved in establishing authenticity, supply and demand, market price and provenance of important or valuable items for sale, especially in the fields of fine art and antique furniture. Writing skills would be needed to produce catalogues, numerical skills to assess bids quickly and IT skills to keep accounts, produce inventories and perhaps maintain a website.

Broad Outlook

There are openings from time to time for those with the necessary drive and enthusiasm in this relatively small field of employment. However, securing a position in one of the large international auction houses is extremely competitive. You may have to work in a range of practical activities before being accepted into a specialist department and it may take up to five or six years to acquire the necessary expert knowledge in a specialised field, such as in 18th century painting or furniture. Even then becoming an auctioneer would not be automatic.

General auctioneering within an estate agency would usually be less demanding. Late starts are feasible in the smaller undertakings but far less easy in the major international auction houses.

Related Occupations

You might also consider: antiquarian bookseller, antiques dealer, surveyor (general practice), estate manager/land agent, estate agent, museum keeper/art gallery curator or rural practice surveyor.

Impact on Lifestyle

Within a big organisation, travel is likely to be a major consideration. In all auction houses, much pressurised time would be devoted to preparatory activities in itemising and valuing the goods for sale, producing catalogues and displaying and storing the items to avoid awkward delays during sales. Conducting an auction can be very demanding on you mentally and physically.

Earnings Potential

There are huge variations in potential earnings, depending on the location, the level of business and the profit margins involved. As an auctioneer or valuer in a big company, you are likely to start on around £22,000 to £26,000, moving on to £28,000 to £36,000 with some experience and over £40,000 as a chartered valuer. Where you are running your own business or are an employed director of a firm of auctioneers, hard work and a successful track record would largely determine your financial rewards. The auctioneer normally takes a percentage of the value of each item sold and your own earnings could be directly related to the sale prices you achieve.

Further Information

Royal Institution of Chartered Surveyors Course Search
www.ricscourses.org

University College of Estate Management
www.ucem.ac.uk

National Association of Valuers and Auctioneers
www.nava.org.uk

Sotheby's Institute of Art
www.sothebysinstitute.com

Christie's Education
www.christies.edu

Propertymark
www.propertymark.co.uk

Society of Chartered Surveyors Ireland
www.scsi.ie

Audiologist

What is Involved?

As an audiologist, you would work directly with patients to identify and measure hearing loss, detect balance problems and neurological diseases and work closely with patients to develop rehabilitation programmes. You would be qualified to see people of all ages but most of your work would be with children and older people because hearing problems are most common in these groups. The rehabilitation of hearing-impaired adults would require both the prescription and evaluation of hearing aids, using objective and subjective methods and measures. You would have to be proficient in all procedures for testing hearing and balance, together with interpreting and reporting the results of these tests.

As you progress through the career grades, you would be expected to undertake more complex and non-routine tasks. These may include electrophysiological testing of the auditory pathways and the fitting of more complex hearing aids. Senior grade audiologists are also involved with the training and supervision of junior grades.

You could develop a special interest and expertise in one area of audiology, such as paediatrics, balance disorders or complex procedures like cochlear implants.

Opportunities for Training

Guidance on training has been complicated in recent years because of the implementation of the Department of Health Modernising Scientific Careers (MSC) programme. This has created three main routes into a career in audiology:

- With three GCSEs at grade C or above, or equivalent, and preferably a nursery nursing or childcare-related qualification, you can train as a newborn hearing screener

- With A levels or equivalent, the NHS Practitioner Training Programme (PTP), an accredited BSc Healthcare Science (Audiology)

- With a relevant science degree, the NHS Scientist Training Programme (STP), working towards MSc neurosensory sciences on a part-time basis

In a related but separate field, several universities offer a Foundation degree in hearing aid audiology.

Requirements for Entry

The minimum entry requirement for the PTP is typically a good range of 9-4/A*-C grade GCSEs plus two A levels or equivalent, including a science subject. However, this is just a guide and you must check with each university you are considering to confirm the exact requirements. For STP training places, a 2:1 in a relevant science degree is the minimum required. Each NHS organisation advertising STP vacancies is free to determine what constitutes a relevant degree.

Kind of Person

You would need the ability to listen carefully to problems and, when necessary, to break bad news in a caring and sensitive way. You must be deaf aware, comfortable looking directly at your patient and speaking at a normal level but slightly slower. You should be easy to lip-read. In the assessment of children, you would need a wide range of skills and strategies to test babies, toddlers and older infants.

In all types of audiology work, a scientific, evidence-based approach would be essential, together with a keen interest in working with people in a clinical environment.

You should have the enthusiasm to keep up with modern trends and technological developments.

Broad Outlook

The profession of audiology is currently undergoing a period of considerable change and it is difficult to predict how career prospects will develop over the coming years. You should regularly check the British Academy of Audiology and Health Careers websites to keep abreast of the very latest implementation of the MSC programme, and contact your local audiology departments to see if they have vacancies. Given that a national study of hearing shows some 16% of the UK population suffering significant hearing loss, work in audiology will continue to be a significant area of the NHS.

Audiologists can also work outside the NHS, in the private sector or in a university where you could undertake teaching and research.

Related Occupations

You might also consider: speech and language therapist, medical physicist, physiotherapist, teacher of the deaf or doctor specialising in ear, nose and throat surgery.

Impact on Lifestyle

Most audiologists work office hours from Monday to Friday in a hospital outpatient department. Some audiology work is also carried out on hospital wards, during surgery or in a community setting. In order to progress to higher grades, you would often be expected to attend courses and meetings at weekends or study outside working hours.

Earnings Potential

Working as a registered audiologist in the NHS, you would normally be paid on the healthcare scientist practitioner scale in Band 5, which runs from £22,128 to £28,746, or the healthcare scientist specialist scale in Band 6, which runs from £26,565 to £35,577. With further training and experience, you could move up the career structure to Band 7, earning from £31,696 to £41,787. Additional allowances are paid for appointments in and around London, ranging from 20% of basic salary for Inner London, to 15% for Outer London and 5% for the London Fringe.

Further Information

British Academy of Audiology
www.baaudiology.org

Health Careers
www.healthcareers.nhs.uk

British Society of Hearing Aid Audiologists
www.bshaa.com

Irish Society of Hearing Aid Audiologists
www.ishaa.ie

Automotive Engineer

What is Involved?

Working as an automotive engineer, you would be involved in a specialised area of mechanical engineering that deals with all facets of the production of motor vehicles and their components. Your job would be to apply mechanical principles to issues related to the design, development or maintenance of all aspects of motor vehicles. You could be involved with designing new cars or with developing a specific part of a vehicle, such as the transmission system. You would be likely to be working as part of a small team on a particular project, seeing it through from the beginning to the production phase.

Opportunities for Training

There are a number of universities offering degrees in automotive engineering, sometimes combined with mechanical engineering. In order to become a chartered engineer, primarily concerned with research, design and development, you would need to complete at least four years of academic study and would usually achieve this via an MEng degree. If you want to be more involved with the day-to-day management of production processes as an incorporated engineer, you could take a three-year BEng degree.

You don't always have to choose your specific training route from the start, so you should read prospectuses carefully. See also our separate article on engineering qualifications. There are sandwich courses available for both types of degree; these add an extra year but give the opportunity for a period of work experience, which can be very valuable when you are looking for a job. After graduating, you would need to complete a period of industrial training and responsible work experience before you achieve chartered or incorporated engineer status.

Requirements for Entry

For degree entry, you are likely to need A level/Advanced Higher/Higher or equivalent qualifications, including maths and/or physics plus one or two other subjects. If maths and physics are not required, they are certainly preferred by universities. In addition, you would need at least five GCSE/S Grade passes at 9-4/A*-C/1-3. You would normally need higher grades for MEng than for BEng admission.

Kind of Person

Your job would involve understanding and solving complex engineering problems. For this you would need a practical and logical mind that might need to show creative approaches to problems. You are likely to find yourself using maths and statistics in your work and you would make extensive use of computers, including specialised and sophisticated software packages.

You would usually work as part of a multi-disciplinary team, which means that you would need to be able to communicate with a variety of people. These could be fellow engineers, who would share your technical expertise and understanding, or non-technical specialists in other fields, who would expect you to explain your ideas clearly to them. You could also find yourself managing a team of people working on a project. In addition, you may need to take into account the costs and budget of a project, so you would need some business skills.

Broad Outlook

The UK excels in the design and development of motor vehicles, as evidenced by the number of Formula One racing teams based in 'Motorsport Valley', a business cluster centred in Oxford. Most global manufacturers carry out research, design and development activities in the UK and there are also specialist consultants, such as Lotus, who employ around 1,000 engineers. The motor industry was severely affected by the economic downturn between 2008 and 2012 but has since seen its fortunes transformed. The UK is the third-largest automotive producer in Europe and the 13th-largest globally.

You may choose to develop skills in emerging fields in order to stay ahead of the game or take advantage of skills gaps. Environmentally friendly, ultra-low carbon vehicles, for example, are currently the subject of intense interest within the automotive sector.

Related Occupations

You might also consider: manufacturing engineer, mechanical engineer, aeronautical engineer, electrical engineer or electronic/electronics engineer. Alternatively, you might want to consider working as an industrial or product designer, perhaps specialising in motor vehicle design.

Impact on Lifestyle

Whilst you may have set hours of work, you could expect to be under pressure sometimes to meet commercial deadlines and may have to work overtime. You could be based in an office but you are also likely to be working in a more practical, hands-on environment for a large part of your working week. You may occasionally be expected to wear protective clothing of some sort.

Earnings Potential

Average salaries on graduation are currently in the range of £25,000 to £35,000, rising to £35,000 to £45,000 after four or five years. Managerial positions usually offer £50,000 to £65,000. A top engineer in a Formula One racing team, with 10-15 years experience, can earn over £100,000 a year.

Further Information

International Federation of Automotive Engineering Societies
www.fisita.com

Motorsport Industry Association
www.the-mia.com

Institution of Mechanical Engineers
www.imeche.org

Engineering Council UK
www.engc.org.uk

Lotus Engineering
www.lotuscars.com/engineering

Institute of the Motor Industry
www.theimi.org.uk

Engineers Ireland
www.engineersireland.ie

Banking Executive

What is Involved?

The banking industry has undergone radical change in recent years, with many mergers and acquisitions taking place and increased competition from supermarkets, building societies, insurance companies and large retailers to provide financial services to individuals and organisations.

As a banking executive, you might choose to build your career in an area such as:

- Clearing, retail and private banking - providing advice and financial services such as authorising loans and overdraft facilities or setting up saving accounts and bonds on behalf of private customers, sole traders and partnerships

- Corporate and commercial banking - dealing with business clients ranging from small start-up companies to major international corporations

- Wholesale banking - involving corporate finance, investment management and dealing in capital markets, usually on a global basis

Opportunities for Training

There is such diversity in the banking sector that there are many possible training routes. All banks/financial institutions recruit school leavers and graduates in varying numbers from year to year. However, each institution has its own specific recruitment and training preferences and you should contact individual banks for current details and an application pack. You can access the websites of all major organisations through the British Bankers Association. You may find it useful to study part-time for qualifications from the Institute of Financial Services (ifs) School of Finance.

Most management training schemes require a degree as a starting point. The exact subject is not critically important but study in such fields as economics, finance, business or marketing could prove useful. Once in post, you could work towards the Chartered Banker Certificate and Diploma qualifications.

It is sometimes possible to join a management training scheme through internal promotion after gaining experience as a cashier or customer services adviser.

Requirements for Entry

For entry to a degree course you would need two to three A level/Advanced Higher, three to four Higher or equivalent qualifications, together with a minimum of five GCSE/S Grade passes 9-4/A*-C/1-3. The degree would usually last three years, although you might like to consider a sandwich course, which would last four years, including a period of paid work experience.

Kind of Person

Since much of your work would be concerned with dealing with a wide variety of people, both colleagues and customers, you would need excellent communication skills, as well as a good head for figures and an understanding of the economic climate. Accuracy and organisational skills would be very important.

As a manager you should be able to inspire confidence and loyalty in your team, and also be capable of selling the bank's services effectively. A high degree of computer literacy would be of benefit, as would proficiency in a foreign language. You would generally be expected to maintain a neat, formal appearance at all times.

Broad Outlook

Technology has dramatically changed the face of banking over the past few years and has resulted in such initiatives as telephone and e-banking. If you enter the banking industry, you would almost certainly face the prospect of continuing change.

Banking was at the heart of the financial meltdown that severely affected the world economy in 2008 and the Chartered Banker Institute is now trying to rebuild public confidence in the banking sector. Explore its website to learn more about how the Institute is working to help bankers and banks embed a culture of ethical and professional standards.

Related Occupations

You might also consider: accountant (professional), actuary, economist, financial adviser, insurance broker, insurance underwriter, investment analyst, investment fund manager or stockbroker.

Impact on Lifestyle

In retail banking, you might work normal office hours from Monday to Friday, although increasing competition may mean evening and weekend work. Promotion in this sector of the industry often entails moving to another part of the country.

In wholesale banking, you would need to be available when colleagues and clients are at work in other parts of the world, which could involve evening and night-time attendance at the office. You may be required to travel extensively.

Earnings Potential

Pay scales would vary widely according to your experience, level of responsibility and the type of banking in which you specialise. Starting salaries for new entrants to graduate management trainee programmes in retail banking range from £20,000 to £28,000. You may also qualify for a London allowance, funding for study for professional qualifications, and relocation expenses. Typical salaries at senior level range from £50,000 to £80,000 plus, depending on your level of responsibility. Salaries in corporate and wholesale banking have traditionally been considerably higher - starting at around £35,000 to £40,000, and rising with significant experience to around £150,000 plus performance related bonus of up to four times the base salary - although they are currently under close political and media scrutiny.

Further Information

British Bankers Association
www.bba.org.uk

Financial Skills Partnership
www.financialskillspartnership.org.uk

Bank of England
www.bankofengland.co.uk

Association for Financial Markets in Europe
www.afme.eu

Chartered Banker Institute
www.charteredbanker.com

The London Institute of Banking & Finance
www.libf.ac.uk

Institute of Bankers in Ireland
www.iob.ie

England, Wales, Northern Ireland and Republic of Ireland. See also Advocate for Scotland

What is Involved?

As a barrister, you would work as an expert in a specific area of law and would be consulted by solicitors or other professionals. As well as appearing in court, you might be consulted on particular points of law or you may appear at a tribunal or enquiry. Your job as a barrister in a higher court would be to present the facts of the case to the judge and jury, using evidence collected by a solicitor. You would cross-examine witnesses and seek to persuade the court to find in favour of your client.

Opportunities for Training

The academic stage of training requires an approved first degree in law or a degree in another subject, which you then 'convert' by taking a postgraduate qualification known as the Graduate Diploma in Law (GDL) or Common Professional Examination (CPE).

Traditionally for the professional stage of training, you must pass the Bar Course Aptitude Test and join one of the four Inns of Court (Gray's Inn, Inner Temple, Lincoln's Inn, Middle Temple). You would then take the Bar Professional Training Course (BPTC), a one-year full-time or two-year part-time course of study, which includes practical training in mock trials, drawing up evidence and interviewing clients. It also covers litigation, sentencing and specialist options. Once you have successfully completed the BPTC, you will be 'Called to the Bar' by your Inn. Before Call can take place you will also have to undertake 12 qualifying sessions (previously known as 'dining') with your Inn. In April 2017 the Bar Standards Board announced that it will in future offer a number of alternative routes to qualification which will be more flexible, accessible and affordable. See the Bar Standards Board website for the latest information.

Having completed the BPTC you must, if you intend to practise, complete two pupillages of six months each, working under supervision while you gain experience in all aspects of the job. During the 'first six' you would simply observe your supervisor and other barristers in chambers, whereas you would be able in the 'second six' to supply legal services and exercise rights of audience as a barrister, representing your own clients in court. This is when you start to build up your reputation as a barrister.

At the end of the 'second six', provided certain training conditions are met, you would be granted a full qualification certificate. After this you must find a tenancy in a set of chambers, from where you must work for at least three years while you follow a compulsory system of professional development. Most chambers select their junior tenants through the process of pupillage.

A similar system applies in the Republic of Ireland. For details, visit the Irish websites listed under further information.

Requirements for Entry

You would need a minimum of a 2:2 Honours degree but in fact most chambers are looking for at least a 2:1. Competition for places to read Law is exceptionally strong and university admissions tutors expect high grades at A level/Advanced Higher, Higher or equivalent. No particular subjects are specified. You will have to take the National Admissions Test for Law (LNAT) to secure a place on a Law degree at several of the most prestigious UK universities.

Kind of Person

Bar Council research shows that the following abilities make an important contribution to success as a barrister: intellectual ability and the ability to cope with large volumes of information to be assimilated in a short time; the ability to withstand the stress of working long hours with tight deadlines and high levels of responsibility; the ability to deal with a wide range of people, to listen to them and then to put across a point of view convincingly. In addition, barristers need the motivation and determination to succeed in what can be a daunting profession, particularly in the early years. You need to be confident both in your work and socially.

Broad Outlook

Most barristers work as self-employed independent professionals, often based in chambers, which means they share the offices and costs of support staff. However, you have to build your own reputation and may have to work very hard for little reward in your early days. It is usually clear after a few years whether you will make a successful barrister. For many barristers, the eventual aim is to become a Queen's Counsel (QC), which involves leading in very serious cases, or entering the judiciary as an assistant recorder prior to becoming a judge.

The recent Legal Education and Training Review (LETR) has recommended a number of changes to the training and professional practice of barristers. There is currently considerable concern in legal circles about the greatly increased number of law schools, law graduates and people qualifying as barristers, solicitors and legal executives, at a time when the number of law jobs available is diminishing. See the Bar Standards Board website for the latest information.

Related Occupations

You might be interested in other legal professions such as solicitor, barristers'/ advocates' clerk or legal executive.

Impact on Lifestyle

The hours of work can be very long, especially when you are starting out, and can be unsocial, as you have to prepare late into the evening and travel to courts. Your life may very well start to revolve around your chambers. However, if you are successful, you can later be selective in the work you choose to do. Payment for work often comes in some time after the work has been completed, which can present problems in the early years.

Earnings Potential

All pupils must be paid no less than £1,000 per month plus reasonable travel expenses. As practising barristers are self-employed, your later earnings can vary enormously. Typical earnings/receipts for self-employed barristers, before deduction of tax and chambers' charges, range from £40,000 to £200,000 gross within five years of call. Typical earnings/receipts at senior levels range from £65,000 to £1,000,000 gross after ten or more years of call. A top QC can earn well in excess of £1,000,000 per year. Barristers who are employed have the security of receiving a regular wage but may not have the potential for the very high earnings that are possible for the self-employed.

Further Information

Bar Standards Board
www.barstandardsboard.org.uk
Law Careers
www.lawcareers.net
National Admissions Test for Law
www.lnat.ac.uk
Bar of Ireland
www.lawlibrary.ie

Barristers'/Advocates' Clerk

What is Involved?

As a barristers' clerk (advocates' clerk in Scotland) you would work for a set of barristers practising in chambers; the equivalent in Scotland is to work for a stable of advocates based in the Advocates' Library in Edinburgh. Your job would be to operate as a member of a small team keeping the chamber or stable running efficiently as a business. Each barrister/advocate is self-employed and the senior clerk acts as an agent for them. As such, you would be expected to make and maintain contacts with solicitors to ensure that briefs come to your set or stable. Negotiation of fees and keeping diaries for the barristers would also be your responsibility.

There are 12 stables of advocates in Edinburgh, each with a clerk and at least one deputy. Their remit includes organising members' diaries, scheduling court commitments, arranging consultations, liaising with instructing solicitors, distributing work and negotiating fees.

Opportunities for Training

There is no quick route to becoming a successful clerk to chambers. Training is 'on the job', learning through observation and helping the more senior clerks. When you become a practising Junior Clerk working in London, chambers may offer training associated with the Institute of Barristers' Clerks (IBC). This leads to a BTEC Advanced Award at level 3 in chambers administration. Much of the work for this is undertaken in chambers under the guidance of a mentor.

On becoming an associate member of the IBC and completing five years service in chambers, you could apply for qualified membership. To enable clerks to keep abreast of current legal issues, market changes and administration needs, the Institute organises regular seminars.

In Scotland, there is no formal training or resulting qualification, although there are short courses run by the Faculty of Advocates and junior clerks are encouraged to attend.

Requirements for Entry

While there are no official entry requirements specified in England, the majority of new barristers' clerk entrants start after completing their GCSE, A level or equivalent qualifications. The IBC recommends to chambers a minimum qualification of four GCSE grades 9-4/A*-C in academic subjects, including maths and English.

In Scotland, advocates' clerks need Higher English and must be computer literate and numerate.

Kind of Person

This is still a very small and in some ways old-fashioned profession and in many respects this aspect of the legal profession is still very hierarchical. You would need to be prepared to tackle menial jobs and to respect the established pecking order that exists within the system. Good manners and a smart appearance are important attributes. You would be expected to be loyal to the members of your set or stable.

You must have the confidence to deal with enquiries and problems that arise without having to bother the barristers/advocates. You would have to be tactful, discreet, honest and reliable. At times, you would be expected to think on your feet to solve a problem. To be involved in negotiating the fees, you would have to be reasonably competent at maths. As there is a lot of administration and paperwork, you need to be well organised.

Broad Outlook

There are limited opportunities for work as this is a small and close-knit profession but the Institute does run a scheme whereby, for a small fee, you can receive notification of vacancies. Most jobs for barristers' clerks are in London, although there are some openings in chambers in towns on the court circuits. *In Scotland, there are very few advocates' clerks and deputies and turnover is low.*

The role of barristers' clerk has changed significantly with the advent of legislation allowing barristers to advertise their services rather than wait for work to come to them. Clerks can now be much more proactive in seeking work for chambers and in promoting the expertise of both the chambers and individual barristers.

There is no scope for progressing to professional qualification as a barrister/advocate.

Related Occupations

You might be interested in other law-related work such as a legal executive or paralegal; alternatively, you might consider administrative work in local government or the civil service.

Impact on Lifestyle

The hours worked can be long and can include evenings and weekends. *In Scotland, deputy clerks are paid overtime but this is unlikely to be the case for junior clerks in England and Wales.*

Earnings Potential

Starting salaries are around £15,000 to £18,000 in London for a school leaver or university graduate. These can rise with experience to £50,000 to £100,000. Some senior clerks are paid a salary or a percentage of the fee due to each barrister; alternatively, they may combine a small salary with a percentage of the earnings. This gives senior clerks the potential for very high earnings if they are in a large and successful set of chambers.

Advocates' clerks, all employed by the company responsible for the administration of the advocates' library, earn from £22,000 to £24,000 as a deputy, rising to £28,000 to £40,000 as a senior clerk.

Further Information

England and Wales: Institute of Barristers' Clerks
www.ibc.org.uk

Chambers People
http://chamberspeople.co.uk

Scotland: Faculty of Advocates
www.advocates.org.uk

Biochemist

What is Involved?

Working as a biochemist, you would be a scientist applying the principles of chemistry to the structure and functioning of living things. This is a science at the heart of all areas of biological or life sciences. You might be concerned with organisms from viruses and bacteria to plants and humans; you might find employment in the food, brewing or pharmaceutical industries, where you could help to develop new products or monitor the quality of existing ones; you might work in the agricultural industry, developing high-yielding, disease-free crops; you could be involved in monitoring the environment and advising on pollution or water quality. There are also opportunities for biochemists to work in hospitals. (See Clinical Biochemist)

Opportunities for Training

Although it may still be possible to start a career as a biochemist straight from school, a degree in a subject such as biochemistry, biology, chemistry or a related scientific area is now becoming the more normal requirement. Many employers will also want you to have a postgraduate qualification (such as an MSc in clinical chemistry or clinical biochemistry, an MPhil or PhD) and relevant work experience, which could be part of a four-year sandwich degree course.

There are degree courses in biochemistry at most universities and it is possible to study for joint honours degrees with a range of other subjects. It is important to read the prospectuses carefully, as the content and emphasis of the degrees can differ enormously.

It is also possible to start work as a technician without a degree, taking part-time study leading to a Higher National Diploma or Foundation degree.

Requirements for Entry

Universities differ widely in their entrance requirements for biochemistry. Most would be looking for an A level/Advanced Higher/Higher or equivalent qualification in chemistry and some would want at least another science at A level or equivalent. Some universities or colleges will accept an AS or Higher in chemistry together with another science or maths and some will specify GCSE/S Grade passes in maths or the sciences at particular levels of achievement. It is best to check directly with the universities to find out what they expect. At some universities, it is possible for candidates without science A level/Advanced Higher, Higher or equivalent qualifications to take a year-long conversion course before they start a degree course. You would need GCSE/S Grade passes at 9-4/A*-C/1-3 in science if you wish to do this. In order to work towards a Higher National Diploma, you are likely to need at least four GCSE/S Grade passes at 9-4/A*-C/1-3, together with one or two A level/Advanced Higher, two or three Higher or equivalent qualifications in appropriate subjects. Some colleges specify that the GCSE/S Grade passes must include maths, English and a science.

Kind of Person

You would need to have a strong interest in science and in laboratory techniques. If you do not enjoy your practical science sessions at school, this may not be the right choice for you. You will be expected to show a logical and analytical approach to problem solving. At times you may need to show persistence in order to solve particular problems. Some problems may need to be approached with creative thinking and imagination. In addition to your scientific skills, you should be able to communicate well with others. You are likely to be working as part of a team and may have to explain your findings to others, some of whom may not have your scientific background.

Broad Outlook

If you are set on a career as an academic researcher, you will need to apply for a PhD or Master's degree. For other careers, a postgraduate course may also be advisable or even essential. To enter some careers, you may have to consider a period of short-term or voluntary work. More general graduate recruitment programmes require early application during your final year, whereas for science-related work you normally apply only as jobs are advertised.

You will find job opportunities in healthcare, education and research. You could also work in the pharmaceutical and chemical industries, in agriculture, food and drink production, and biotechnology. Progressing in your career will often include moving into a team leader or management post. With experience, you could move into research, sales and marketing or scientific journalism.

Related Occupations

You might be interested in other careers in a scientific field such as clinical biochemist, pharmacist, microbiologist, or forensic scientist.

There are close links with other specialist life sciences, such as cell biology, genetics, microbiology, molecular biology, physiology and pharmacology. In fact, in many cases the distinctions between these disciplines are becoming increasingly blurred.

Impact on Lifestyle

You are likely to be working regular hours without working at weekends or late into the evenings, although there may be occasions when you are required to work late and under pressure in order to meet deadlines. In the laboratory, you may need to wear protective clothing and to take scrupulous care over hygiene; at times you may need to work in sterile conditions. You may need to move around the country in order to find the right job for you.

Earnings Potential

Graduate trainees should earn in the range of £25,000 to £28,000 a year, rising with experience to £36,000 to £44,000. Higher earners can make £60,000 to £90,000 a year, depending on their employer, role and responsibilities.

In the National Health Service, qualified biochemists are generally in Band 7 of the pay scale, earning from £31,696 to £41,787 a year.

Further Information

Biochemical Society
www.biochemistry.org

Health Careers
www.healthcareers.nhs.uk

Biomedical/Clinical Engineer

What is Involved?

Working as a biomedical or clinical engineer, you would be using your engineering knowledge and skills to help with the treatment and rehabilitation of patients with serious diseases or disabilities. You would work with medical consultants to develop the instruments necessary for diagnosing or monitoring patients. You could be concerned with designing new equipment, such as that used in keyhole surgery, aids for the handicapped, such as replacement joints and limbs, or implants like pacemakers. Your work might be said to harness the techniques of electrical, electronic and mechanical engineering to supplement the mechanics of the human body.

Opportunities for Training

Guidance on training has been complicated in recent years by the gradual implementation of the Department of Health Modernising Scientific Careers Programme, which offers two entry points into clinical engineering: the Practitioner Training Programme (PTP) or the Scientist Training Programme (STP). You can check on the latest developments via the Health Careers and Institute of Physics and Engineering in Medicine (IPEM) websites.

For the STP, you could start with an IPEM-accredited degree (MEng if you plan to qualify later as a chartered engineer) in a relevant engineering discipline, aiming for at least a 2:1. You could then apply for a place on the NHS Scientist Training Programme for Medical Physicists and Clinical Engineers. This would lead to an MSc in your chosen area of clinical engineering, combined with vocational training in a hospital department. Finally, you would apply to the Health and Care Professions Council for state registration.

The alternative under the new programme is to enter at undergraduate level through the NHS PTP route. This would involve an accredited BSc Healthcare Science degree specialising either in clinical engineering or medical physics. These are three-year programmes which combine academic study with practical experience gained in the NHS.

The IPEM Clinical Technologists Training Scheme, developed with the Association of Renal Technologists on behalf of the Register of Clinical Technologists, is a degree programme supporting the regulation of clinical technologists by the Health and Care Professions Council.

Requirements for Entry

In order to be accepted on a suitable engineering degree course, you would need at least three A level/Advanced Higher, four Higher or equivalent qualifications, normally including maths and physics, together with five GCSE/S Grade passes at 9-4/A*-C/1-3. These should include maths, another science subject and English. You should check with individual universities the entry requirements for the new Healthcare Science degrees.

Kind of Person

You would need to be interested in discovering practical solutions to the problems experienced by patients. You would therefore need a logical but creative approach to problem solving. In addition to your technical and engineering skills and knowledge, you would have to be able to work as part of a medical health team providing care for your patients. You could find yourself dealing with fellow professionals, patients and their carers as well as with technical and administrative staff. You would need to keep abreast of developments in your field and to share your own specialist knowledge with other professionals at meetings, courses and seminars.

Broad Outlook

The medical engineering industry is currently valued at approximately £50 billion worldwide and it is growing. This sector offers a great opportunity for graduates with entrepreneurial ideas to carve out lucrative careers. Students with enthusiasm and a sound engineering background can use medical engineering to make a difference to healthcare and can have a direct influence on the health of people around the world.

There is a need for engineers in companies that research and manufacture medical products, such as artificial heart valves, replacement joints and monitoring equipment. Some private sector manufacturers operate internationally and may offer scope to work in mainland Europe and beyond.

Related Occupations

You might be interested in one of the related engineering professions, such as electronic/electronics engineer, electrical engineer, mechanical engineer or telecommunications engineer. Alternatively, you might like to consider another of the professions allied to medicine, such as biotechnologist or medical physicist.

Impact on Lifestyle

You are likely to be able to work regular hours but may need to work overtime if there are tight deadlines to meet. As this is a field that depends extensively on research and new technology, you may find that you have to travel to conferences and meetings in order to exchange ideas with other experts or clients.

Earnings Potential

Starting salaries for healthcare scientist practitioners in NHS Band 5 are currently £22,128 to £28,746. A medical engineering team manager in Band 7 would earn £31,696 to £41,787. Senior manager or consultant posts can offer salaries ranging from £56,665 to £100,431. Additional payments are made for employment in and around London. Work in the industrial sector is, in general, better paid than research and development positions in university and government medical research departments.

Further Information

Institute of Physics and Engineering in Medicine
www.ipem.ac.uk

Academy for Healthcare Science
www.ahcs.ac.uk

National School of Healthcare Science
www.nshcs.hee.nhs.ukNHS Education for Scotland

www.nes.scot.nhs.uk

Institute of Biomedical Science
www.ibms.org

Health Careers
www.healthcareers.nhs.uk

Biomedical Engineering Society
www.bmes.org

National Centre for Biomedical Engineering Science, Ireland
http://ncbes.nuigalway.ie

Biomedical Scientist

What is Involved?

As a biomedical scientist, you would carry out tests on samples of tissue and body fluids to support healthcare professionals in diagnosing disease and monitoring the treatment of patients. You would usually specialise in one of three specific areas: *infection sciences, blood sciences* or *cellular sciences*.

Rapid diagnosis is particularly important in *infection science* in order to prevent the spread of infectious diseases and ensure the most appropriate use of antibiotics. You might specialise in:

- medical microbiology - detecting diseases such as meningitis, food poisoning and legionnaires disease
- virology - testing for infections such as rubella, herpes, hepatitis and HIV, or screening selected populations at risk from virus disease.

Blood sciences could include:

- clinical chemistry - analysing blood and other biological materials to assist the diagnosis of, for example, diabetes. You would carry out, thyroid, kidney and liver function tests and help monitor therapies
- transfusion science - supporting hospital blood banks and the blood transfusion service and ensuring that the blood groups of both donors and patients are compatible
- haematology - identifying abnormalities within blood cells to diagnose different types of anaemia and leukaemia You would also carry out tests to diagnose other life-threatening conditions including thrombosis and malaria
- immunology - dealing with the conditions of the body's immune system and its role in infectious diseases, allergies, tumour growth, tissue grafts and organ transplants

Specific areas of *cellular sciences* include:

- histopathology - processing tissue samples from surgical operations and autopsies, using specialist techniques to detect cancer
- cytology - analysing tissue and fluid samples including cervical smears but also providing a non-gynaecological service
- reproductive science - analysing samples to detect infertility

Opportunities for Training

Entry is usually via an accredited integrated BSc degree in Healthcare Science (life sciences), or at postgraduate level if you already have an honours degree in biomedical science accredited by the Institute of Biomedical Science (IBMS) and approved by the Health and Care Professions Council.

It is also possible, with A levels or equivalent in life sciences to start work as a trainee biomedical scientist, provided your employer is willing to offer financial support and the time off to study for a degree on a part-time basis.

Requirements for Entry

University entry qualifications usually include A level/Advanced Higher/Higher biology and chemistry and GCSE/S Grade passes at 9-4/A*-C/1-3 in mathematics and English. Consult the IBMS for full details.

Kind of Person

Your work must be accurate and efficient because patients' lives could often depend on your skills. You would be using sophisticated automated equipment, microscopes and other hi-tech laboratory equipment, but you would need to control and understand the technology in order to recognise false signals. You would have to be prepared to update your skills as laboratory techniques develop and as research paves the way for new applications of science and medicine. You would normally work with other professionals as part of a healthcare team.

Broad Outlook

In the NHS, there has been a structured career path for qualified biomedical scientists. To progress after registration you would usually need a higher degree such as an MSc. This could then qualify you for Fellowship of the IBMS. Many biomedical scientists take charge of a section within the laboratory or manage a department. You might also become involved in advanced scientific work, research or training. However, career pathways may change as a result of the current *Modernising Scientific Careers* programme. Consult the NHS Careers and IBMS websites for the most up-to-date information.

Biomedical scientists are also employed in a variety of roles including the veterinary service, the Health and Safety Executive, university and forensic laboratories, pharmaceutical and product manufacturers, the Armed Services and various government departments. There could be opportunities to use your training and skills in healthcare posts and projects around the world, and you might consider undertaking a period of voluntary work in a developing country.

Related Occupations

You might also consider: medical physicist, pharmacist, pharmacologist, clinical biochemist, forensic scientist, food scientist or technologist, research biologist/ bioscientist or research chemist.

Impact on Lifestyle

You would normally work a 37.5-hour week, with some shift working on a rota basis to provide 24-hour cover to support clinical services. Working conditions try to ensure that, while biomedical scientists may sometimes work unsocial hours, they are not working excessive hours.

Earnings Potential

Qualified biomedical scientists in the NHS currently start in Band 5, on a scale currently ranging from £21,909 to £28,462. Earnings can rise to £35,225 for a specialist biomedical scientist at the top of the scale and to £41,373 at the top of the advanced scale. Additional allowances are paid for appointments in and around London, ranging from 20% of basic salary for Inner London, to 15% for Outer London and 5% for the London Fringe. Earnings in the private sector are generally likely to be higher, depending on where you live and the hours you are prepared to work.

As a new entrant to the profession, you will find that a professional portfolio will assume major significance. You will need it to provide evidence of specialist and higher specialist training to support any claims for promotion to a higher pay band.

Further Information

Institute of Biomedical Science
www.ibms.org

Health Careers
www.healthcareers.nhs.uk

Academy of Clinical Science and Laboratory Medicine, Ireland
www.acslm.ie

Biotechnologist

What is Involved?

Working as a biotechnologist, you would be involved with using tiny living organisms such as bacteria or yeasts in industrial, environmental or medical processes. You might find yourself, for example, producing enzymes for use in manufacturing and preserving food and drink; developing fertilizers or animal foodstuffs; or studying human genetics, proteins, antibodies and viruses to research and treat disease. There are also opportunities to work with pollution control, renewable energy sources or biodegradable plastics.

You might become involved with the production of complex molecules, such as hormones or enzymes, which could be particularly useful in the medical field. One area of biotechnology that is expanding at the moment is that of harnessing genetic engineering.

Opportunities for Training

There are several courses in Biotechnology at undergraduate level, but degrees in biological sciences, molecular biology, genetics or biochemistry could also provide a good foundation for postgraduate work in this area. The main recruitment for work in the biotechnological field is from scientists with two to three years' postgraduate experience. To obtain this you would need a first class or upper second class degree, followed by specialist research in the area.

Pure research in biotechnology is concerned with subjects such as: proteomics - the structure and function of proteins, including the way they work and interact with each other inside cells, body fluids and tissues; functional genomics - the function of individual genes and interactions amongst groups of genes; structural genomics - the three-dimensional structure of proteins.

Requirements for Entry

To gain admission to a degree course, you would need three good A level/Advanced Higher, four Higher or equivalent qualifications, including biology and usually chemistry, together with five GCSE/S Grade passes at 9-4/A*-C/1-3 including English and maths.

Kind of Person

You would need a keen interest in biology and chemistry and in the application of specialised techniques. Attention to detail and a logical approach to problem solving would be essential. If you were involved in research, you would need to be persistent in the face of setbacks because it can take a long time to make headway in solving scientific problems. In return, you could be breaking new ground in an ever-changing world of discovery.

Some of the work would be routine testing and you should enjoy your current laboratory practical work. You would need a facility with statistics as well as good communication skills, as you would be called on to explain your experiments, results and conclusions to others, some of who may not have your technical knowledge. You are also likely to be working as part of a team of scientists and, as you become more senior, would need to direct the work of other members of the team.

Broad Outlook

Once qualified, there would be a range of career options available to you. Not only is there choice in the area in which you could work but also in the type of job that you could do. You could, for example, continue with research or move into technical sales and marketing in your particular field. It is often possible to move between industries and so apply your knowledge and expertise in different fields as your career and interests develop. There is normally a shortage of qualified specialised scientists of this nature, although you may need to move to find the job that you really want.

Funded by Government, and with an annual budget of around £500M, the Biotechnology and Biological Sciences Research Council (BBSRC) supports research and training in universities and strategically funded institutes. Major challenges include food security, green energy and helping people lead healthier, longer lives. BBSRC research underpins important UK economic sectors, such as farming, food, industrial biotechnology and pharmaceuticals.

Related Occupations

You might be interested in working in another area of scientific research by becoming a biochemist, microbiologist, research biologist/bioscientist, pharmacist or pharmacologist. You could consider the broad areas of biomedical/clinical sciences.

Impact on Lifestyle

You are likely to be based in a laboratory, although you may also be working in an office attached to a factory, university or hospital. You may need to travel to other laboratories or to meet other scientists or attend conferences or lectures. At times you may have to work late when you have an important deadline to meet or when you are coming close to a breakthrough with a particular experiment.

Earnings Potential

Your salary when you first start working as a graduate biotechnologist is likely to be around £22,000 to £26,000. Having a postgraduate qualification would boost your starting salary. Earnings should rise with experience to £35,000 to £60,000 and could exceed £65,000 if you were working in industry and had a particular specialism that is in short supply.

Further Information

Biotechnology and Biological Sciences Research Council
www.bbsrc.ac.uk

Royal Society of Biology
www.rsb.org.uk

Biotechnology Young Entrepreneurs Scheme
www.biotechnologyyes.co.uk

Bioindustry Association
www.bioindustry.org

Vitae - realising the potential of researchers
www.vitae.ac.uk

Institute of Food Research
www.ifr.ac.uk

European Biotechnology Network
www.european-biotechnology.net

National Institute for Bioprocessing Research and Training, Ireland
www.nibrt.ie

Broadcasting/Media Researcher

What is Involved?

As a researcher working in the broadcast media, you would generate new and original ideas for programmes, source information, contacts and contributors and turn ideas into actual broadcasts. As the person responsible for making first contact with potential contributors to programmes, you would have to ensure that they are good speakers and that the stories they provide are accurate and fair. All your sources must be thoroughly corroborated.

On the day of the programme, you would meet the guests you have booked and brief them about what to expect. You may be researching something topical and currently in the news or something more human interest led, and you could spend some time delving into archives, combing newspapers or surfing the internet for background information.

You would have to keep meticulous records of the work you do, notes of interviews with people, copyright details, where permissions to use material have to be obtained and so on. You would also have to work strictly within the constraints of time and budget.

Opportunities for Training

There is no single way to train to become a researcher. It is likely but in no way essential that you would have a degree or bring to the industry transferable skills from another area such as print journalism. Much more important than qualifications would be to prove you have the talent, commitment and knowledge of the industry to make a positive contribution to production research.

Creative Skillset, the Sector Skills Council for the audio visual industries, is the central information point for relevant training courses.

Requirements for Entry

You would need two or three A level/Advanced Higher, three or four Higher or equivalent qualifications for degree course entry. The subject of your degree is not important, although you could consider a course in journalism or media studies. Three or four years at university would be an opportunity to build experience in student journalism or broadcasting. You should take every opportunity to gain relevant work experience because that is often more highly valued than academic qualifications.

Kind of Person

You must be a team worker, with constant energy, a passion for programming and the ability to generate a variety of ideas for a range of programmes. You must be able to get on with people, particularly contributors, and able to make them feel at ease. You would need a high level of literacy and numeracy skills, together with intellectual rigour. You should be able to work independently and under pressure, to extract relevant details and write detailed notes or reports.

Wide general knowledge would be useful, together with good organisation and accuracy, and a high degree of computer literacy. As important as anything would be excellent intellectual and analytical skills. You would have to be very organised and have good communication skills, as you would be dealing with a wide variety of people. You would need mental and physical toughness, to cope with frustration as well as success, and probable long hours. Knowledge of and an ability to analyse different types of programmes would be essential.

Broad Outlook

Competition for contracts is intense. Most researchers work on freelance contracts, either directly for broadcasters or for independent production companies. Factual programmes regularly employ researchers, and sometimes drama and light entertainment programmes will too (particularly specialist researchers in, say, music or stills research).

Much of the work is in London and the south east, although there has been a marked shift in recent years to MediaCityUK at Salford Quays near Manchester.

Related Occupations

You might also consider: producer (film/television/video), film/tv director, floor manager (TV/film), presenter (radio/TV), journalist, broadcast journalist, author/creative writer, production assistant/runner, advertising account executive or scriptwriter/screenwriter.

Impact on Lifestyle

You should be prepared for short-term contracts, unpredictable hours and tight deadlines. You may have to supplement your income with other work between contracts, especially in the early days as you build up your network of contacts. Your work would probably involve you in a good deal of travel, so a driving licence would be a virtual necessity.

Earnings Potential

It is very difficult to define annual earnings for a freelance researcher. Rates vary considerably, from nothing initially to around £400 per week for a junior researcher, rising to £650 per week with experience. The BECTU website gives details of current agreed rates.

You would normally be paid expenses for travel, accommodation and subsistence when you spend time away from home.

Further Information

BBC Careers
www.bbc.co.uk/careers/home

TRC Media
http://trcmedia.org

Producers Alliance for Cinema and Television (PACT)
www.pact.co.uk

Creative Skillset
www.creativeskillset.org

Broadcasting Entertainment Cinematographic and Theatre Union (BECTU)
www.bectu.org.uk

Broadcast Journalism Training Council (BJTC)
www.bjtc.org.uk

MediaCityUK
www.mediacityuk.co.uk

Radio School, Dublin
www.radioschool.ie

Building Services Engineer

What is Involved?

As a building services engineer, you could be involved with the design of energy efficient buildings, renewable energy, green architecture, ventilation, lighting, acoustics, electricity and control, many or all of which are necessary in modern buildings. You might also use your skills to meet demands for building energy management systems, fire/smoke control, indoor air quality standards and environmental pollution control. You could design the sophisticated systems that are required and draw up the necessary plans on paper or computer. You would also be expected to supervise the installation of all of these services and ensure they meet the correct specifications and safety regulations. You would often work alongside architects, allowing you to input your creative expertise at the concept stage in the design process.

Opportunities for Training

To qualify as a chartered engineer, responsible for research, development and senior management, the simplest route would be to complete a four-year accredited MEng degree, followed by about four years of structured training with an employer. To qualify as an incorporated engineer, responsible more for the day-to-day management of projects, you could take a three-year accredited BEng degree, followed by a similar period of structured training.

If you are more interested in working at a practical level, you could join a building services apprenticeship programme. This takes up to 24 months to complete and requires the achievement of a level 2 vocational qualification, a technical certificate level 2 and the appropriate key skills. You would also have the opportunity to progress to or join directly a level 3 Advanced Apprenticeship, which can take up to four years and may provide a more direct route to technical, supervisory or junior management roles. You would be in full-time employment and would receive an appropriate wage.

Requirements for Entry

Entry requirements vary for different degrees and at different universities. Generally speaking, you would need three A level/Advanced Higher, four Higher or equivalent qualifications for the MEng route, including maths and physics, and two A level/ Advanced Higher, three Higher or equivalent qualifications for the BEng route.

For an apprenticeship, a broad platform of GCSE passes at 9-4/A*-C or equivalent would be useful.

Kind of Person

You would need to be able to display initiative and enterprise in planning and executing a programme for the development of an engineering project and able to work effectively both as an individual and as a member of a team. You should have excellent numeracy and problem-solving skills and the ability to communicate ideas verbally, in written reports and by means of presentations to groups.

You would also need good awareness of management methods and of the financial environment in which you would be working. This is a rapidly changing work environment, so you would need to keep up to date with new developments and technology. Computer skills would be essential in your design work - using computer-aided design (CAD) software packages. You would find yourself analysing and solving practical problems and taking responsibility for your decisions and possibly for large projects. You would need to make site visits during the construction phases, which would require agility and physical fitness.

Broad Outlook

Employment statistics show that the UK construction industry is now recovering from the 2008 recession to become one of the fastest-growing sectors in the economy, offering new hope for building services engineers in the years to come. Potential employers include large building contractors, architectural or design practices and equipment manufacturers. Large companies with a buildings portfolio also need building services engineers and there are jobs in companies responsible for the maintenance and servicing of buildings.

The skills and knowledge of building services engineers are becoming increasingly valued as the UK strives for zero carbon. Heating, ventilation, water and lighting all have an impact on the earth's resources and professionals able to minimise their use, through the installation of low carbon footprint systems like solar water heating, photovoltaics and micro wind turbines, will be highly sought after.

Related Occupations

You might also consider: construction manager, quantity surveyor, building surveyor, civil engineer, electrical engineer or mechanical engineer, architect or town planner.

Impact on Lifestyle

If you were office based, you would expect to work regular hours, probably a 36-hour week Monday to Friday. However, you might need to work longer hours when there were important deadlines to meet. If you were working on site, you could expect to work longer and less regular hours than this, including evenings and weekends.

You might need to travel a long distance to reach the site or even to stay away from home whilst you were working. You would also be expected to work all around the site, which could involve climbing ladders or scaffolding. You would need to be prepared to get wet, cold and dirty and probably to wear protective clothing.

Earnings Potential

You could expect to start earning around £25,000 to £28,000 when you first graduate and should be able to increase your earnings fairly rapidly, to around £40,000 to £55,000 within a few years, rising to £65,000 to £85,000 plus for an experienced manager.

Further Information

Chartered Institution of Building Services Engineers
www.cibse.org
BESA Training
www.thebesa.com/training
Summit Skills
www.summitskills.org.uk
Modern Building Services Online
www.modbs.co.uk
Chartered Institution of Building Services Engineers, Ireland
www.cibseireland.org

Building Surveyor

What is Involved?

As a building surveyor, you would provide detailed advice on the design, construction, maintenance, management or repair of proposed or existing buildings. You would be looking for defects in, or ways to improve, all types of existing buildings. You would also advise on the feasibility and possible costs of repair to the building, of conversion and the suitability of the building for particular purposes.

Your clients would include prospective purchasers, vendors, building societies and property owners. You might find yourself drawing up detailed plans, advising on government or health and safety regulations and on whether a grant might be available for the work. You could also be involved with instructing an architect to prepare detailed plans and with obtaining estimates for carrying out the work.

Opportunities for Training

In order to become a member of the Royal Institution of Chartered Surveyors (RICS) or the Chartered Institute of Building (CIOB), you would need an accredited degree (or equivalent), together with a minimum of two years training whilst you are employed. This on-the-job training must normally be approved before you start. There are full-time degree courses in a range of property and construction related subjects, which take three years to complete. There are also sandwich courses, which include a year of practical work experience that can count towards the required two years' training. During this time, you will need to demonstrate effective interpersonal and business skills, core competencies specific to building surveying and optional competencies. You will need to provide written evidence of your experience, together with critical analysis and a report.

If you want to 'earn whilst you learn' there are part-time degree courses available, which you take whilst you are employed. In addition, there are some accredited distance-learning degree or diploma correspondence courses, which can be taken whilst you work, and relevant postgraduate courses.

Requirements for Entry

Degree courses in surveying normally ask for a minimum of two A level/Advanced Higher, three Higher or equivalent qualifications, together with at least four or five GCSE/S Grade passes at 9-4/A*-C/1-3, often specifying English and maths.

Kind of Person

You would need a practical approach to problem solving. There is likely to be quite a lot of paperwork involved. You would be drawing up and interpreting plans and for this you need to be accurate. You might be involved with reading and evaluating both tender documents and documents relating to the law. You could be involved with making decisions relating to deadlines and budgets for work for which you will need to have a good grasp of maths.

Above all, you would need to bring common sense and logic to your decision making. In addition to this, you are likely to be working with a large number of different people. These can include your employers, who you may need to persuade to your point of view, and the site workers, who you may need to instruct and lead. At times you would be imparting complex technical information to people without your specialist knowledge. You are also likely to be working as part of a team of building professionals, with whom you may need to negotiate the best solution to a problem.

Broad Outlook

The entire construction industry was severely affected by the economic downturn that started in 2008, but demand for building surveying expertise is now recovering well. The largest employer is the private sector, which ranges from very small practices to large companies with overseas operations. Your qualification would be recognised in many countries if you wanted to work abroad. Local authorities also employ a number of building surveyors, as do well-known companies with a large amount of property, such as major retailers or hotel chains. There are also opportunities to work with large historical buildings for the trusts or charities that manage them and are concerned with their maintenance.

Related Occupations

You might consider: building control officer/surveyor, town planner, architect, estate manager/land agent, estate agent, civil engineer, rural practice surveyor, structural engineer, surveyor (general practice), auctioneer/valuer.

Impact on Lifestyle

You are likely to be involved in inspecting buildings very thoroughly; this can involve going into dirty, damp and dark areas such as attics and cellars. You would need to be reasonably fit and agile in order to carry out your surveys effectively. At times you may need to climb ladders or scramble around on scaffolding. Your work could involve you being outside in all kinds of weather and you could need to walk for quite long distances.

A driving licence is likely to be essential to get you to the sites and you may be expected to travel quite long distances within the UK and in some cases to spend time abroad.

Earnings Potential

Graduate starting salaries are generally around £20,000 to £26,000, slightly higher in the London area. The average salary for chartered surveyors is around £45,000, and for a partner around £70,000. Top-end salaries can be over £100,000. Most surveyors receive additional benefits as part of their salary package. These may include a performance-related bonus and a company car.

Further Information

Royal Institution of Chartered Surveyors
www.rics.org

Chartered Institute of Building
www.ciob.org

Chartered Association of Building Engineers
www.cbuilde.com

Chartered Institution of Civil Engineering Surveyors
www.cices.org

Society of Chartered Surveyors Ireland
www.scsi.ie

Business Manager/Executive

What is Involved?

As a business manager, you might be working for a large multinational organisation with a turnover bigger than the economy of a small country or you might be part of a small, family-run concern with no more than a handful of staff. Whatever the size or type of the organisation, you would soon play a key role in helping it achieve its goals, through managing resources - such as people, money, materials - and work activities.

Your precise responsibilities would vary according to the type of organisation and your position within it. At the first level of management, for example, you may have responsibility for only a small team and are likely to have limited influence on the organisation's policies. As a more senior person, on the other hand, you may be responsible for a specific function - such as finance, human resources, IT/ management services, marketing/sales or production - and could have a high degree of responsibility for, and influence on, the organisation's policies and future development. Frequently, you would be seen by clients as the 'face' of the company for their purposes.

Opportunities for Training

Most business managers undertake training on the job. This can be supported by a wide range of management qualifications at business schools and colleges, including level 4 in management and leadership or the Executive Diploma in Strategic Management and Leadership. Details of accredited courses are available from the Chartered Management Institute (CMI) and the Institute of Leadership and Management (ILM). The ILM offers a range of management apprenticeships, levels two to five, which could give you the chance to study part-time for a recognised qualification while working.

An alternative route is to progress to higher education and continue your studies with a degree, foundation degree or HNC/HND. Useful subjects would include business studies, management science, business information systems, accountancy, economics, law and modern foreign languages, but most good degree subjects would be acceptable for new entrants. You might even undertake a postgraduate Master in Business Administration (MBA), usually after several years of business experience.

Requirements for Entry

There are no set academic entry requirements for business managers. Most people do not go directly into a key executive role, as it is important to start by building considerable experience of relevant work. If you do want an executive role as early as possible in your career, you might consider a trainee post as offered by some of the larger organisations, particularly in the retail industry. Entry requirements vary, but for school leavers are usually a minimum of five GCSEs/S Grade passes (9-4/A*-C/1-3) including English and maths, plus either two A levels/three Higher grades or equivalent. Employers may also ask for specific skills, such as communication, problem-solving or teamworking.

Kind of Person

It goes without saying that you will be motivated by achieving set goals or targets. You should also be decisive, willing to take responsibility, and able to work well in a team under pressure, to delegate when appropriate and to motivate and encourage others. Excellent communication and number skills should make you effective at planning, monitoring and reviewing, and able to analyse and interpret information. You should also possess effective presentation and public speaking skills.

You must be persuasive in order to influence people, able to command respect and trust and be good at problem solving. It would help if you can speak at least one major foreign language.

Broad Outlook

Depending on the size of your organisation, there may be opportunities for internal promotion to a more senior management level, or it may be necessary to move elsewhere. With the right experience and a proven track record of success, you may be promoted to company director level. With even more experience, you may progress to the role of chief executive and subsequently chair of an organisation. There may also be opportunities to become a non-executive director, usually on a part-time basis, for one or more organisations. Another option could be to set up your own business for which your training would provide invaluable experience.

Related Occupations

You might consider: chartered/company secretary, marketing executive, human resources manager, sales executive, health service manager, retail manager, civil service executive officer, civil service fast streamer or accountant (professional).

Impact on Lifestyle

You may nominally work office hours, which are usually 9am to 5.30pm, Monday to Friday. However, many managers work additional hours in order to meet the demands of the job. You would be largely office based, but may be required to travel to visit clients or attend meetings at other sites within the organisation. This may be within the UK or overseas.

Earnings Potential

Salaries for managers vary considerably according to the size of the organisation, the nature of the business, its location and function. You might start on, say, £18,000 to £25,000, rising with experience to £45,000 to £65,000. As a director, you might earn anything from £80,000 a year to over £2,000,000. In addition, you may receive bonus payments and share options.

Further Information

Chartered Association of Business Schools
http://charteredabs.org

Chartered Management Institute
www.managers.org.uk

Institute of Directors
www.iod.com

Institute of Leadership and Management
www.i-l-m.com

Chartered Quality Institute
www.quality.org

Irish Management Institute
www.imi.ie

Buying Executive

Also called Buyer or Purchasing Officer

What is Involved?

As a buying executive, you would be responsible for obtaining the products and services needed by your organisation to support its key activities. This could include, for example, purchasing the raw materials or components for a manufacturing process, sourcing spare parts for machinery maintenance, ordering the merchandise for a retail outlet or updating the IT facilities in an office environment. You would be expected to negotiate competitive prices at the same time as building relationships with suppliers who understand your needs, can meet your quality specifications and can deliver the right quantity of materials on a reliable basis.

You would have to maintain adequate reserve stock levels to cope with fluctuations in demand and ensure that supplies reach their intended destination on time. You would probably set up automated systems to cope with some of these functions but you would need to discuss contracts with suppliers, monitor deliveries and stock levels, challenge price changes, check sources of new materials and keep pace with technological and design improvements. You could work in almost any sort of manufacturing or service organisation, although you would need special skills to act as a buyer in, say, the retail fashion business or a technical background before you could purchase engineering components.

Opportunities for Training

Some employers would expect you to work towards the Chartered Institute of Purchasing and Supply (CIPS) portfolio of five qualifications in procurement and supply. These are available on a full- or part-time basis or by distance learning. You could also take an accredited undergraduate or postgraduate degree. The CIPS qualifications would be supported in many companies by an internal training scheme. With appropriate qualifications and experience, you could become a member and then a fellow of CIPS.

There is now a wide variety of UK universities offering purchasing and supply related degree courses. General business degrees also often include some core elements of purchasing and supply disciplines in their syllabus.

Requirements for Entry

While there are no specific entry requirements, most employers look for a degree, HND or equivalent qualification. This could be in any subject, although supply chain management, business studies, management science, computing or logistics could be useful. In the engineering/manufacturing industries, a technological qualification would be an advantage, as would chemistry in the chemical industry or computing in IT. For degree entry, you would normally be expected to have at least two A level/ Advanced Higher, three Higher or equivalent qualifications, together with four or five GCSE/S Grade passes at 9-4/A*-C/1-3, including English and maths.

Kind of Person

As an essential link in the supply chain, you would be in a very demanding and responsible position. You would need to understand the overall requirements of your own organisation and to be able to assess the relative merits of suppliers' goods or services. A logical and analytical mind would be essential, together with good powers of judgement and the ability to negotiate contracts. You should have strong numerical skills and a grasp of finance and accounting, since you would often be handling large sums of money. In addition to these technical qualities, you would need excellent written and verbal communication skills, a liking for others and a sense of fairness and integrity.

Broad Outlook

You might achieve promotion - to senior management or even to board level - within your existing organisation. Alternatively, you could develop your career by moving elsewhere. All kinds of organisations throughout the country need buying executives, so many opportunities to move should be possible. There may be scope to specialise in a particular field calling for special expertise, such as buying art at auction, next season's designs for a fashion store or lorries and vans for a freight company.

CIPS publishes, in association with business data specialist Markit, a regular Purchasing Managers' Index. This covers transport and communication, financial intermediation, business services, personal services, computing and IT and hotels and restaurants. The February 2017 survey reports a solid rate of expansion, with the current period of growth lasting over three years despite import cost increases due to the pound's weakness since the Brexit referendum.

Related Occupations

You might also consider: logistics/supply chain manager, sales executive, retail manager, freight forwarder, or shipbroker.

Impact on Lifestyle

You would work normal office hours but would occasionally need to take work home at night or over weekends, so that you could formulate your strategic plans and analyse your departmental performance, check levels of stock or write a monthly report for directors. You may need to travel fairly extensively, including making trips overseas, in order to check suppliers' procedures, transport systems and quality controls.

Earnings Potential

You could expect to start at around £21,000 to £26,000 as a graduate trainee, with your income rising after five years to £35,000 to £45,000. Once you reach middle or senior management levels, say after ten years in the business, you could expect a salary of £55,000 to £70,000. If you can demonstrate that your buying skills lead to savings in costs and improvements in efficiency, you could earn significant performance-related bonuses.

The most recent Purchasing and Supply Rewards research from CIPS and Croner Reward claims that procurement and supply professionals are better paid than colleagues in equivalent posts working in marketing, sales, finance, IT and human resources.

Further Information

Chartered Institute of Procurement and Supply
www.cips.org

Chartered Institute of Logistics and Transport
www.ciltuk.org.uk

Skills for Logistics
www.skillsforlogistics.co.uk

Supply Management Jobs
http://jobs.supplymanagement.com

Irish Institute of Purchasing and Materials Management
www.iipmm.ie

Careers Adviser/Guidance Counsellor

What is Involved?

As a careers adviser or guidance counsellor, you would provide information, advice and guidance (IAG) to help people make decisions about their future. You might work in a careers centre, in schools and colleges, a university or an adult guidance centre, and your clients might need guidance on, for example, their long-term career goals or help with decisions related to their education and training. You would usually work with people individually, although you may occasionally lead groups, using your counselling skills and your knowledge of education, training and employment to help them decide on next steps. You may use psychometric and other interest and ability tests to support the guidance process. After your interview or group work session, you would provide a written report summarising the outcomes of the guidance interview and the implications in terms of career plans. In an educational establishment, your work may involve preparing education programmes related to careers and personal development, taking classes and leading group discussions. You would also be expected to have close, regular contact with employers and other opportunity providers.

In England at present, guidance provision is in a state of flux. Since September 2012, schools have been responsible for arranging impartial guidance for pupils, while adults can use the new National Careers Service.

Provision is much more settled in Scotland, Wales and Northern Ireland.

Opportunities for Training

Many entrants hold the Qualification in Careers Guidance (QCG), which is available full- or part-time at four institutions in England, or the Qualification in Careers Guidance and Development (QCGD), which is offered by two universities in Scotland.

Alternatively, you could start work as a trainee or administrator in a careers organisation and study part-time for a qualification such as the:

- Level 6 Diploma in Career Guidance and Development.

Training preferences vary from one employer to another, so you should research information carefully. Advisers working in higher education have their own qualification organised by the Association of Graduate Careers Advisory Services.

Requirements for Entry

There are no specific entry requirements for the QCG/QCGD, although you would have to demonstrate your ability to cope with the academic aspects of the training. Many new entrants are graduates, with a degree in any subject, but employers also value a broad range of life and work experiences. Career co-ordinators and career teachers are usually qualified and experienced teachers who choose to specialise in careers work.

Kind of Person

You would need enthusiasm, flexibility and a real interest in helping people to make the most of the opportunities available. Depending on the client group that you were working with, you would also need a wide range of counselling and guidance skills, an understanding of educational systems and knowledge of local, national and international labour markets.

You would need to be able to plan and organise your own time and to be able to work as part of a team. Computer systems are widely used for record keeping, maintaining occupational databases and administering tests, so you would need good IT skills. If your clients are facing difficulties in obtaining employment, you may need advocacy skills as well as the ability to network with relevant agencies.

Broad Outlook

With considerable change in guidance provision in England, not to mention severe public spending cuts, many posts have been offered in recent times on a temporary or fixed-term contract basis. This is far from encouraging for potential new entrants to the profession and the immediate future appears equally unpromising.

Outside England, the main national employing organisations are Skills Development Scotland, Careers Wales and the Northern Ireland Careers Service. Other employers include higher education institutions, voluntary organisations and private careers consultancies, providing services on a fee-paying basis.

Several professional bodies have worked together in recent years to create a single professional body known as the Career Development Institute (CDI). As well as providing a qualifications framework, the CDI has created a Register of Career Development Professionals.

Related Occupations

You might also consider: recruitment consultant, human resources manager, teacher (secondary), teacher (primary), community development worker, social worker, probation officer or youth worker.

Impact on Lifestyle

The work has traditionally been based on normal Monday to Friday hours, with occasional evening and weekend events and some time spent away from home on training courses.

Earnings Potential

You would probably start as a trainee on around £19,000 to £22,000, rising to £23,000 to £27,000 on full qualification. With experience and increased responsibility, your earnings should increase to £35,000 to £50,000. Some senior posts offer £55,000 plus.

Further Information

Career Development Institute
www.thecdi.net

Association of Graduate Careers Advisory Services
www.agcas.org.uk

National Careers Service England
https://nationalcareersservice.direct.gov.uk

Skills Development Scotland
www.skillsdevelopmentscotland.co.uk

Careers Wales
www.careerswales.com

Careers Service Northern Ireland
www.nidirect.gov.uk/campaigns/careers

Institute of Guidance Counsellors, Republic of Ireland
www.igc.ie

Cartographer

What is Involved?

As a cartographer you would be dealing with the making of maps. You must be careful not to confuse the work of the cartographer with that of the surveyor, nor expect employment to involve strenuous outdoor activity and travel to remote places. With very few exceptions, you would normally be found seated at a desk or graphics workstation, processing original survey data collected and recorded by specialists in the field. The work falls into two areas: the editorial side, where the contents of the map are chosen and its appearance is designed, or the drafting side, where the map is actually produced.

Cartography has been revolutionised by information technology and traditional methods of map-making continue to change. For example, information is now obtained by photography from satellites. Unlike earlier mapmakers, whose challenge was to obtain the relevant information, today there is so much information available that the problem has become how to select what is required. What we are able to map has also changed and will continue to do so. We can now map the seabed with great accuracy and our increasing exploration of space will bring with it new demands for maps and charts.

Opportunities for Training

See the 'Go Geo' website for a list of undergraduate and postgraduate courses with content of direct relevance to working in cartography. These usually include such terms as Surveying and Mapping Sciences or Geographical Information Systems (GIS) in their titles.

Some courses focus on how computer systems and software are used to analyse satellite images, aerial photographs and digital surveying data. Students undertake high levels of practical and field work; other courses focus more on the science, technology and maths behind geographic data collection and analysis. It is important to read prospectuses carefully.

At postgraduate level, one course with a substantial element of cartography (map design and visualisation) is the MSc in Geoinformation Technology and Cartography at Glasgow University. There are also postgraduate distance learning courses offered by Unigis UK.

Requirements for Entry

Degree entry would require a minimum of two A level/Advanced Higher, three Higher or equivalent qualifications, ideally including geography, together with five GCSE/S Grade passes 9-4/A*-C/1-3, including English and maths.

Kind of Person

You should have a genuine feeling for maps, combined with the patience and powers of concentration necessary to undertake work which may be both mentally and physically demanding, as the preparation of a single sheet may take several weeks or even months. Artistic flair and a sense of design are valuable assets, as is an ability to work with precision and sometimes against the clock. This is very precise work using complex equipment and techniques.

Cartographers have to be experts in communication: in real life roads are not red, nor motorways blue, and there are no dotted lines marking the borders between countries, but we see these things on a map and immediately know what they mean.

In short, you need to love maps, be interested in design, like geography and enjoy designing on a computer screen.

Broad Outlook

The IT revolution has meant that far fewer cartographers are needed than before and there is enormous competition for the comparatively few employment openings which occur. Potential employers include government departments and national organisations like the Ordnance Survey, Met Office, and Civil Aviation Authority; local, district and regional authorities; and the private sector such as publishers of road atlases. There are also opportunities to work abroad, for example for oil companies and private consultancies.

Employers with vacancies tend to approach the universities that offer cartography- or surveying-related degrees. Membership of the two main professional groups, the Society of Cartographers and the British Cartographic Society, is useful for making contacts and keeping up with developments.

Related Occupations

You might wish to consider: land/geomatics surveyor, hydrographic surveyor, meteorologist, surveyor (general practice), town planner, graphic designer or artist/illustrator.

Impact on Lifestyle

This is an office-based job and you could expect to work regular office hours. Many cartographers work freelance on a contract basis and enjoy the freedom of being their own boss. If you have the right qualifications, you can progress from being a map drafter to a map editor and gradually assume responsibility for whole projects.

Earnings Potential

Cartographers themselves will tell you that their rewards are more often aesthetic, or come from knowledge that the end product will be of use to another person, than they are financial. Few, if any, have been known to make their fortune. As a graduate trainee, you could expect a starting salary between £18,500 and £22,000, progressing over three to five years to about £22,000 to £30,000, and rising with experience and responsibility to £35,000 to £48,000.

Further Information

British Cartographic Society
www.cartography.org.uk

(click on publications *to take you to* careers in cartography*)*
Society of Cartographers
www.soc.org.uk

Unigis UK
www.unigis.org

Ordnance Survey
www.ordnancesurvey.co.uk

goGeo
http://gogeo.io

Remote Sensing and Photogrammetry Society
www.rspsoc.org.uk

Ordnance Survey Ireland
www.osi.ie

Catering Manager

What is Involved?

As a catering manager, you would most likely work in the rapidly expanding food service management, or contract catering sectors of British industry. This is made up of companies of all sizes, who win contracts to manage the catering needs and related services of a whole range of organisations. It can involve feeding people at work, catering in schools, colleges and universities, hospitals and healthcare or any other companies who prefer to call upon the experts, so that they can get on with taking care of their core business. Food service management companies are now developing their services to include catering for members of the public in such outlets as leisure centres, department stores, airports, railway stations, public events and places of entertainment. Alternatively, you could work in one specific restaurant, hotel or other food outlet, in which case you might be termed a restaurant manager.

In either case, you would be expected to ensure satisfaction with the quality of food and service, manage the whole operation efficiently and profitably and know how to deal with people, both staff and public. The bigger the organisation, the less likely it is that you would be required to cope with front-line welcoming and table organisation; you would concentrate your energies on recruitment, motivation, training, the arrangement and supervision of shifts, quality control, hygiene, health and safety and controlling budgets. Whatever the context, standards would feature high on your priorities.

Opportunities for Training

Opportunities exist at every level, with a range of training routes for school leavers or university graduates. Relevant previous experience or qualifications usually ensure that you are able to join the profession a few rungs higher on the career ladder.

You could go into the business straight from school, perhaps via an Apprenticeship or a craft course, and develop your career up to a managerial position. Alternatively, you could continue your studies to higher national diploma (HND), foundation degree or degree level or you could join a company management training scheme.

Requirements for Entry

For degree entry, you would need at least two A level/Advanced Higher, three Higher or equivalent qualifications, together with a good spread of GCSE/S Grade passes 9-4/A*-C/1-3. The HND route usually requires one A level/Advanced Higher, two Higher or equivalent qualifications. A foreign language would be very useful. You may be able to join a company scheme with A level/Advanced Higher, Higher or equivalent, but a degree or HND would be more usual.

Experience in the industry, at however humble a level, would always be proof of your interest and commitment.

Kind of Person

Above all, you should be highly motivated, with a keen interest in food and drink. You would need a smart personal appearance, the ability to communicate effectively with customers and staff and the confidence to operate in a very public setting. You would have to remain calm under pressure and have the flexibility to cope with the occasional crisis in the kitchen. Physical fitness and the stamina to keep going for many hours a day would be important.

Broad Outlook

By 2018, the hospitality workforce is set to grow by a third to 2.4 million people, including an additional 200,000 managers. It is forecast to increase by a further 3.5% every year until 2020. Over the past decade, student interest has shifted firstly from hospitality to travel and tourism and more recently to events management. This means that a career in catering management may be less fashionable than some other areas but that employment opportunities are plentiful.

As the catering sector grows, so do the career opportunities available. It is not just about preparing and serving food, although these are vital jobs for the success of the sector. Areas that you could work in include: catering services, corporate events and functions, domestic services, facilities management, food production, human resources, marketing, residential services, sales, service development and support services.

Once you have sufficient experience, you could open your own restaurant or set up a contract catering business.

Related Occupations

You might also consider: restaurant manager, hospitality/hotel manager, facilities manager, events manager, chef or leisure services/fitness centre manager.

Impact on Lifestyle

In contract catering, your working hours could be reasonably regular; as a restaurant manager, however, you would have to work late into the evening and could expect to be busiest at weekends and during public holidays. You may work on a split shift system and you may find that, rather than having fixed hours, you have to keep working until the last customer leaves.

Earnings Potential

Junior managers usually earn between £18,000 and £23,000, while more experienced managers could expect £25,000 to £40,000. Some senior managers would receive in the region of £50,000 to £70,000. You may be offered live-in accommodation in some restaurant manager posts. If you can set up and run a successful restaurant or catering business, you should be able to achieve higher financial rewards.

Further Information

Hospitality Guild
www.hospitalityguild.co.uk

Institute of Hospitality
www.instituteofhospitality.org

British Hospitality Association
www.bha.org.uk

People 1st
www.people1st.co.uk

Irish Hospitality Institute
www.ihi.ie

Chartered/Company Secretary

What is Involved?

This is not secretarial work in the normally accepted sense. As a chartered secretary, you would play a central role in the administration and management of an organisation. Your work would include advising the directors/trustees of their legal obligations, administering finances, communicating with stakeholders, preparing agendas, taking minutes of meetings and maintaining the statutory records. You would need a wide knowledge of the law, accounting and business organisations.

As a bridge between the management board, stakeholders and other organisations, you would need to be fully aware of every aspect of your organisation, including the nature of the business and its overall direction, the functions of employees and the current finances.

Opportunities for Training

While it is not essential for you to become a member of the Institute of Chartered Secretaries and Administrators (ICSA), you would find this valuable, especially if you were working as a company secretary. You would, for example, be legally qualified to file the annual report with Companies House and you would be able to supply financial information to the Stock Exchange.

The ICSA Chartered Secretaries Qualifying Scheme (CSQS) comprises two levels, each with four modules. You may need to study all eight modules or, depending on your existing qualifications, you may be exempt from some.

You can study for the CSQS via a variety of routes, including self-study, distance-learning, part-time, or full-time on a collaborative Masters course at a partner university.

Assessment for each module is by examination and exams are held in June and November each year.

Requirements for Entry

While this area of work is open to graduates of all subjects, or even non-graduates, specialisms in law, business/management or accountancy/finance may be preferred and may offer some exemptions from the professional examinations.

As most company secretary positions demand a professional qualification or significant professional experience, it is very unlikely that a recent graduate would have direct entry into the role. Pre-entry experience is therefore desirable and also strongly recommended.

You might, for example, first qualify as a lawyer or accountant with the aim of becoming a company secretary later; you might consider a full-time diploma course leading to a full or partial ICSA qualification. For most people, formal training in company secretarial work starts after a few years of administrative work experience. Suitable experience could include areas such as pensions, personnel, accounts, credit control, purchasing, insurance, sales administration or office management.

Kind of Person

You would need to be good at administration as this is the core of the work. You would be co-ordinating departments and would therefore need to be good at prioritising and seeing the overall picture. Your management responsibilities would require you to be tactful and discreet. You would also be dealing with financial and legal matters, requiring you to be numerate and able to work under pressure to comply with legal deadlines.

Minute-taking would require the ability to write clearly and accurately, while explaining technical matters to a non-expert audience would demand excellent speaking skills. This is a very responsible job demanding the highest standards in professional integrity.

Broad Outlook

Given that there is a legal requirement for every company in the UK to have a company secretary, there should be plenty of scope to work in this area. Not all company secretaries are chartered - they could have a legal or accountancy qualification instead - but the ICSA qualification is a broad one and can be adapted to a wide variety of administrative work in charities, local government, educational institutions and health organisations. You could go on to become a company director or chief executive.

Related Occupations

You may wish to consider: accountant (professional), solicitor, barrister/advocate, civil service fast streamer, civil service executive officer or human resources manager.

Impact on Lifestyle

This is an office-based job and you could expect to work usual office hours unless there is a deadline to meet, which could mean working unsocial hours. There may be some evening meetings to attend. You would be expected to observe a strict code of personal and professional conduct.

Earnings Potential

There are no fixed national scales, and actual rates of pay may vary, depending on the employer and where you live. Typical starting salaries range from £35,000 to £55,000, rising to £70,000 to £100,000 or higher with five years' experience. At senior level, salaries generally range from £90,000 to £180,000. A top company secretarial job in a FTSE 100 company comes with a basic salary ranging from £170,000 to £335,000 plus a substantial bonus.

Further Information

ICSA: The Governance Institute
www.icsa.org.uk

ICSA: The Governance Institute Ireland
www.icsa.org.uk/ireland

Worshipful Company of Chartered Secretaries and Administrators
www.wccsa.org.uk

Companies House
www.gov.uk/government/organisations/companies-house

Chemical/Process Engineer

What is Involved?

As a chemical or process engineer you would apply mainly engineering principles to produce and control the chemical plant and machinery needed to manufacture chemicals, plastics, synthetic fibres, pharmaceuticals, petroleum products, certain food and drink products and medical gases. You would need considerable skill to control reactions which can be highly unstable and where factors such as temperature, pressure, flow rate, heat removal and concentration of reactants must all be taken into account. Your work would often revolve around turning a small-scale laboratory project into a large-scale, economically viable, safe and reliable industrial process.

Apart from this area of new product development, you might work in plant design and construction, in production management or in more general management, technical sales or exports.

According to the *Why not Chemeng* website, "The challenge for chemical engineers in the 21st century is to protect water supplies and the environment, develop clean energy solutions and end the suffering of the millions affected by incurable diseases."

Opportunities for Training

Several UK universities offer degrees in chemical engineering. These can last three years for a BEng or four years for an MEng (or a year longer in either case for a sandwich course giving practical experience in industry). In order to become a chartered chemical engineer, you would need to complete at least four years of academic study. The MEng would meet this requirement, whereas you would need to add another year of more specialised study, known as a 'matching section', to top up a BEng qualification.

You would then need, in either case, to follow your degree with a number of years of approved work experience known as the period of Initial Professional Development (IPD). The BEng degree can take you to incorporated engineer status (see our separate article on engineering qualifications in the introduction).

Requirements for Entry

You are likely to need two or three A level/Advanced Higher, three or four Higher or equivalent qualifications. These should include chemistry and maths and preferably another science subject, together with at least five GCSE/S Grade passes at 9-4/A*-C/1-3 to include maths, English and a science. Some universities run a foundation course for students who do not have the required science qualifications.

Kind of Person

You would need a strong practical interest in science, with meticulous attention to detail and a logical and methodical approach to problem solving. You would need good communication skills, as you would be required to discuss detailed proposals with other chemists and technologists and to explain technical issues to people who do not have your knowledge and expertise.

You are likely to need good IT skills as computers are used extensively in the design of chemical plants. You would need to work both under your own initiative and as part of a team. You are likely to be working in some sort of industrial, research or business environment and so would need to have relevant management and business skills.

Broad Outlook

There are normally very good job opportunities for chemical engineers and there is reasonable expectation that steady growth in demand will build again around the world once the recession that started in 2008 is finally behind us. According to Cogent, the Sector Skills Council for this industry, a recent skills need assessment identified one in four vacancies as hard to fill, with not enough young people entering the profession. A major challenge for 2020 and beyond is to develop transformative technologies, such as carbon capture and storage, in order to make a significant improvement in reducing carbon emissions.

Related Occupations

You might like to consider another specialism as an engineer, such as mechanical engineer, electrical engineer, electronic/electronics engineer or civil engineer. Alternatively, you may prefer to work in the scientific field as a pharmacologist, pharmacist, metallurgist, biotechnologist or biochemist.

Impact on Lifestyle

Whilst you may have set hours of work, you are likely to be required to work irregular hours, should you be asked for example to manage 24-hour petroleum or chemical production processes or to meet a tight deadline. You may find yourself working under pressure from time to time. If you are working in a laboratory or a chemical plant, you may sometimes need to wear protective clothing. You may need to relocate in order to find the job that you really want and you could be expected to travel, for example to negotiate construction contracts, act as a consultant or attend conferences and meetings.

Earnings Potential

Salaries vary according to location, sector, size and the nature of the organisation's business, and are dependent on chartered status. According to the 2016 salary survey conducted by the Institution of Chemical Engineers (IChemE), chemical engineering is a well-paid profession to go into – although the job market is highly competitive. New graduates can expect to earn around £30,000. This can increase to £45,000 to £57,000 for chemical engineers in their early 30s, and to £51,000 to £66,000 by their late 30s. Chemical engineers over 50 can expect to earn between £74,000 and £85,000.

Further Information

Institution of Chemical Engineers
www.icheme.org

Engineering Council UK
www.engc.org.uk

Cogent: Skills for Science-based Industries
www.cogentskills.com

British Chemical Engineering Contractors Association
http://bceca.co.uk

Why not Chemeng?
www.whynotchemeng.com

Engineers Ireland
www.engineersireland.ie

Chiropractor

What is Involved?

As a chiropractor, you would be working in a complementary healthcare profession that specialises in the diagnosis, treatment and overall management of conditions related to mechanical dysfunction of the joints, particularly those of the spine, and their effects on the nervous system. Treatment consists of a wide range of manipulative techniques designed to improve the function of the joints, relieving pain and muscle spasm. Your manipulation would have to be highly skilled and very specific, directed at individual joints in order to reduce strains and improve mobility in one area without disturbing another. You would support this treatment with individual counselling and advice about each patient's lifestyle, work and exercise, in order to help in managing the condition and preventing a recurrence of the problem. The work is similar in some ways to that of an osteopath or physiotherapist but with much greater emphasis on manual treatment, including spinal manipulation or adjustment. Your work may involve taking x-rays as part of the diagnostic process.

Opportunities for Training

You must be registered with the General Chiropractic Council (GCC) before you can call yourself a chiropractor. The GCC training standard means that you must graduate from an accredited institution before being accepted onto the register. There are currently three institutions offering suitable courses at undergraduate and postgraduate levels: the Anglo-European College of Chiropractic in Bournemouth, the McTimoney College of Chiropractic in Oxfordshire and the Welsh Institute of Chiropractic at the University of South Wales.

The five-year Master of Chiropractic, for example, covers in-depth training in a variety of subjects, including life sciences, biomechanics, clinical medicine and differential diagnosis. You would also undergo practical training in adjustment and supervised clinical training, where you would have hands-on practice in treating patients. After qualifying, you may have to undertake a year's structured training with a qualified practitioner in order to gain the diploma in chiropractic. Finally, you must undertake continuing professional development as a requirement for re-registration on an annual basis.

Requirements for Entry

For entry to an accredited course, you would normally need at least two or three A level/Advanced Higher, three to four Higher or equivalent qualifications, preferably including biology and chemistry. Some courses may require GCSE/S Grade passes 9-4/A*-C/1-3 in English and maths plus science subjects. You must be at least 18 before you can start a course.

Kind of Person

You would need a keen interest in human biology and in chemistry, together with a certain amount of physical endurance, as the manipulative skills required can be hard work at times. Good communication and problem-solving skills would be essential when dealing with a wide range of patients, all expecting a high standard of professional care from you. This would involve you in listening to each patient and then explaining your diagnosis. You would probably be working as a self-employed practitioner, so would need to be approachable and someone in whom patients could have confidence. In addition, you would need to be well organised and to have sufficient commercial skill to run your own business.

Broad Outlook

Employment prospects have improved recently as this is an area of medicine that is growing and there should be room for more practitioners to establish themselves. Most chiropractors set up as independent consultants, or possibly as part of a group with other practitioners of complementary medicine. You would have to work for at least a year as an assistant to an established chiropractor before you could set up your own practice. You would not be directly employed in the NHS, although some treatment may be commissioned by GP practices.

Related Occupations

You may be interested in investigating other options in complementary medicine, such as osteopath, homoeopath, reflexologist, acupuncturist or aromatherapist. Alternatively, you might be interested in other therapy-based professional roles in the medical field, such as physiotherapist, occupational therapist, radiographer or speech and language therapist.

Impact on Lifestyle

Being self-employed means that you would have to work hard to get yourself established and to build a reputation. This may include working long hours in the evenings and at weekends.

Earnings Potential

As a newly qualified practitioner working as an associate in private practice, you might be paid a percentage of the fees that you generate for the practice, along with a small retainer while your client list increases. Typical starting salaries range from £22,000 to £40,000.

Predicting salaries later in a career can be difficult as most practitioners are self-employed. Earnings will depend on the number of patients seen and the location of the practice. Financial rewards can be very good. Salaries in the region of £50,000 to £70,000 are not uncommon, with the potential for even higher earnings. The British Chiropractic Association quotes a recent survey suggesting that earnings within five years of graduation can be as high as £100,000 per year.

Further Information

British Chiropractic Association
www.chiropractic-uk.co.uk

General Chiropractic Council
www.gcc-uk.org

Royal College of Chiropractors
www.rcc-uk.org

McTimoney Chiropractic Association
www.mctimoney-chiropractic.org

Scottish Chiropractic Association
www.sca-chiropractic.org

Chiropractic Association of Ireland
www.chiropractic.ie

Civil Engineer

What is Involved?

As a civil engineer, you would design and manage the construction of bridges, roads, tunnels, pipelines, dams, sewage plants, railways, power stations and major buildings. You would be involved with aspects of the national infrastructure, including transport networks and energy and water supply systems. You would use your knowledge of the properties and behaviour of materials to create imaginative and aesthetically pleasing designs, which meet all relevant safety and durability requirements within specified budgetary constraints.

You would oversee construction projects and this would involve detailed planning and co-ordination with other professionals, including surveyors and architects, together with checking that the actual construction work is being carried out according to specifications. You would liaise in particular with site engineers, who are concerned with the day-to-day activity on site, monitoring such issues as construction methods, delivery of materials, supply pipes and cables and the marking out of the foundations.

Opportunities for Training

In order to become a chartered civil engineer, responsible for research, design and development, you would need to spend at least four years in undergraduate study, followed by postgraduate study and supervised experience. The initial requirement can be achieved by taking a four-year degree course that leads directly to an MEng. Alternatively, you could take a three-year degree course leading to a BEng and follow this with a year of more specialised postgraduate study. To become an incorporated engineer, responsible more for the efficient day-to-day management of projects, you could take the BEng route and follow this with further study and on-the-job training. Another route to incorporated engineer status would be a two- or three-year foundation degree or Higher National Diploma (HND), followed again by further study and relevant experience.

A number of construction companies sponsor undergraduates for some of their time at university, offering work experience and/or sandwich placements.

Requirements for Entry

In order to be accepted for an MEng in civil engineering, you are likely to need three A level/Advanced Higher, four Higher or equivalent qualifications, including maths and physics, together with at least five GCSE/S Grade passes at 9-4/A*-C/1-3. Entry requirements for the BEng are usually slightly lower but would still normally include maths and physics at A level/Advanced Higher, Higher or equivalent. HND entry usually requires study of maths and physics to A level/Advanced Higher/Higher, with a pass in at least one of these subjects.

Kind of Person

As a civil engineer, you would need to be creative as well as practical and good at problem solving. You should have a good grasp of both maths and the principles of design. You would need to be a team player. On site, you could find yourself in charge of many people and your leadership skills would be very important. Good communication skills would also be needed, as you would be dealing with a wide variety of people who would need to be very clear about your instructions.

Broad Outlook

Civil engineers can take advantage of work opportunities in both the private and public sectors, often changing jobs to gain more professional experience. They tend to specialise in areas such as roads and bridges, oil and gas rigs and pipelines, power stations, docks and harbours or public health and sewerage. There are courses run by the Institution of Civil Engineers for on-going professional development. UK civil engineering qualifications are internationally recognised and there are many opportunities to work on projects abroad. You could eventually become a director or partner in a civil engineering firm. Alternatively, you could join the armed services, become a university lecturer or set up as a consultant.

Civil engineering projects were severely affected by the economic downturn that started in 2008. However, the industry is now recovering, boosted by the promise in the 2015 government Spending Review that capital funding of transport projects - including electrification of the Trans-Pennine, Midland Mainline and sections of the Great Western railways - will rise by 50% over the next five years, and by plans to hand £2.3 billion to private developers to build 400,000 new homes in England.

Related Occupations

You might also consider: structural engineer, architect, construction manager, land/ geomatics surveyor, surveyor (general practice) or town planner.

Impact on Lifestyle

When working in the office, you would tend to keep to normal office hours. When working on site or abroad, the hours can be much more unsocial if deadlines need to be met and you could be on 24-hour call in case of problems. Most civil engineers work both in an office and on site. The work on site can be dirty, cold and wet and involve working at heights.

Earnings Potential

The latest EngineeringUK report says the estimated mean salary for civil engineering graduates in full-time employment six months after graduation was £26,000 in 2015 and that the annual mean salary for full-time and part-time employees in civil engineering occupations was £42,500. Salaries are above £100,000 at the top end of the scale.

Further Information

Institution of Civil Engineers
www.ice.org.uk

New Civil Engineer
www.newcivilengineer.com

Construction Skills
www.citb.co.uk/bconstructive

Association for Consultancy and Engineering
www.acenet.co.uk

Engineers Ireland
www.engineersireland.ie

Civil Service Executive Officer

What is Involved?

As a civil servant, you would be one of some 440,000 people in a multi-million pound business. You would most likely work in a department or agency - such as Defence or Health - or in a linked smaller organisation. Whatever your particular role, you would have to work in a non-political capacity for the elected government of the day.

The different parts of the Civil Service have two main functions: to advise government ministers on the pros and cons of particular decisions; and to manage and deliver a range of services to the public, such as issuing driving licences, running jobcentres or paying benefits.

There is such a wide range of jobs across the 170 departments and agencies that it is impossible to describe the work in detail here, although the only entry point currently open to school leavers to work at Executive Officer level is the Civil Service fast track apprenticeship scheme. You would start this at management level, possibly in a role such as Assistant Parliamentary Secretary in a minister's private office. This could include responsibility for a specific area of their portfolio or helping to develop a new policy by working with interested groups and other government departments.

Opportunities for Training

As a fast track apprentice, you would develop a range of skills as you work through a structured training programme lasting at least two years. You would be working towards a level 4 higher apprenticeship qualification calling for study and written assignments as well as your full-time job. You would be given time during your working week for study but you would also need to study during evenings and weekends. At the end of the scheme you would be able to apply internally for graduate career jobs.

Beyond the apprenticeship, training within the departments or agencies is mainly on-the-job, and sometimes there are further tests to be passed before promotion is secured. Your training might be linked to the department in which you work, focusing for example on investigating benefit fraud or carrying out immigration checks.

Requirements for Entry

To apply for the fast track apprenticeship scheme you must be a non-graduate aged between 18 and 21 and you must have at least 5 GCSE passes at grades A* to C, including English language and maths. Apprenticeships in project delivery and digital and technology require two A levels or equivalent. These must be in STEM subjects for the digital and technology specialism.

Should other vacancies arise, you will find that each department and agency sets its own entry requirements, depending on the type and level of work available. You would normally need a minimum of two A level/Advanced Higher, three Higher or equivalent qualifications for a junior manager position. In practice, around half the junior managers recruited in recent years have been graduates.

Kind of Person

At all levels in the Civil Service, you would need to be able to work as part of a team, relate well to others and have a calm, reliable personality. You would also need good organisational skills and the ability to work quickly and accurately under pressure.

You would need to show leadership potential for junior manager or higher appointments, together with the ability to use your initiative, analyse problems and deliver results.

Broad Outlook

This is not a good time to be considering a career in the Civil Service: a recruitment freeze first announced in 2010 has been extended, and government ministers say that the Civil Service will be much smaller in future. Some 90,000 jobs had been cut by 2015, with a further 100,000 jobs expected to disappear by 2020. The freeze on external recruitment covers both permanent and temporary posts and inward secondments from external organisations. The main exceptions to the freeze are the fast stream (see our separate article) and the fast track apprenticeship programme described here.

Competition for any available places is very keen. Before the freeze, there were over 17,000 applicants for 500 vacancies across the general and specialist fast stream programmes. A Civil Service reform plan was published in June 2012, setting out details of the skills, knowledge, behaviours and attitudes that civil servants will need in the years ahead.

There is also a legal requirement that selection for appointment to the Civil Service must be on merit on the basis of fair and open competition.

Related Occupations

You might also wish to consider: European Union official, border force officer, diplomatic service officer, press/information officer, tax adviser, tax professional, economist, surveyor (general practice), health service manager or local government officer.

Impact on Lifestyle

Many civil servants work a basic 37-hour week, which may revolve around flexible start and finish times or even shift work. As you become more senior, you may have to work longer hours to complete reports for ministers if they are needed at short notice.

Earnings Potential

Salaries vary according to department and the location of the post. Salaries for senior civil servants also depend on job performance and bands set by the government. As a guideline, typical starting salaries range from around £21,000 to £27,500, rising after four to five years in post to £29,000 to £40,000. Posts in London often command a higher salary.

The Department for Food, Environment and Rural Affairs quotes a pay scale for an Apprentice on the fast track programme as between £25,363 and £29,063. More generally, the government quotes a minimum starting salary of £19,500 for fast track apprentices.

Further Information

Civil Service Careers
www.gov.uk/government/organisations/civil-service/about/recruitment

Civil Service Fast Track Apprenticeship Scheme
www.gov.uk/civil-service-apprenticeships

Civil Service World
www.civilserviceworld.com

Public Appointments Service, Ireland
www.publicjobs.ie

Civil Service Fast Streamer

What is Involved?

As a civil servant, you would be one of some 440,000 people in a multi-million pound business. You would most likely work in a department or agency - such as Defence or Health - or in a linked smaller organisation. Whatever your particular role, you would have to work in a non-political capacity for the elected government of the day.

The fast stream is an accelerated development programme for graduates, preparing you for careers at the highest levels of the Civil Service. Fast streamers are exposed to a range of placements in government departments and agencies, usually lasting around 12 to 18 months but occasionally up to two years. There are, in fact, several fast streams – ranging from generalist to analytical (economics, statistics, operational research), human resources, digital and technology, science and technology and Europe. You must choose one or more when you apply and must be able to demonstrate that you understand in some detail what is involved.

Opportunities for Training

The fast stream is a leadership development programme, and your initial training would focus on your immediate development needs and on the competencies expected of you at senior management level. The dedicated fast stream learning and development pathway includes a combination of formal training courses and on-the-job learning, regular feedback and performance reviews, a mentor to support you through your development, and the chance for supported study towards a range of professional qualifications.

At the end of your programme you will have developed skills and knowledge in a wide range of important areas, such as people management, commercial awareness, financial management, project and programme management, change management and digital delivery.

Requirements for Entry

The majority of fast streamers are recruited from any degree discipline (the exceptions being those entering the streams for statisticians, economists, social research and science and engineering). A 2:2 honours degree is the minimum entry requirement (2:1 for economists and some other streams). The recruitment process is extremely thorough and places greater emphasis on future potential than past achievement.

In general, most posts in the fast stream are open to UK nationals, Commonwealth citizens, European Economic Area nationals or Swiss nationals or, in some circumstances, Turkish nationals. Whatever your nationality, you must have a legal right to work in the UK. Diplomatic Service posts are open only to UK nationals.

Recruitment procedures involve a number of demanding psychometric tests, group exercises and interviews. Practice tests are available via the fast stream website, together with blogs of current fast streamers.

Kind of Person

At all levels in the Civil Service, you would need to be able to work as part of a team, relate well to others and have a calm, reliable personality. You would also need good organisational skills and the ability to work quickly and accurately under pressure.

You would need to show leadership potential for junior manager or higher appointments, together with the ability to use your initiative, analyse problems and deliver results. The fast stream would demand all these qualities and more, especially outstanding intelligence, creative thinking and sound judgement.

Broad Outlook

This is not a good time to be considering a career in the Civil Service: a recruitment freeze first announced in 2010 has been extended, and government ministers say that the Civil Service will be much smaller in future. Some 90,000 jobs had been cut since 2015, with a further 100,000 jobs expected to disappear by 2020. The freeze on external recruitment covers both permanent and temporary posts and inward secondments from external organisations. Given that the main exceptions to the freeze are the fast stream and the fast track apprenticeship programme, which is only for school leavers, the fast stream is currently the only entry point open to graduates.

Competition for any available places is very keen. Before the freeze, there were over 17,000 applicants for 500 vacancies across the general and specialist fast stream programmes. The fast stream is ranked fourth of The Times Top 100 Graduate Employers.

A Civil Service reform plan was published in June 2012, setting out details of the skills, knowledge, behaviours and attitudes that civil servants will need in the years ahead. There is also a legal requirement that selection for appointment to the Civil Service must be on merit on the basis of fair and open competition.

Related Occupations

You might also wish to consider: European Union official, border force officer, diplomatic service officer, press/information officer, tax adviser, tax professional, economist, surveyor (general practice), health service manager or local government officer.

Impact on Lifestyle

Many civil servants work a basic 37-hour week, which may revolve around flexible start and finish times or even shift work. As you become more senior, you may have to work longer hours to complete reports for ministers if they are needed at short notice. Many, but not all, fast stream careers are in London. You will be expected to be mobile and ready to work wherever you might gain the best learning opportunities while on the scheme. Fast streamers are increasingly involved in operational and corporate services work away from London headquarters.

Earnings Potential

The average fast stream starting salary is between £25,000 and £27,000, rising after two years to £32,000. If you are promoted, you could earn around £45,000, usually after four or five years.

Further Information

Civil Service Careers
www.gov.uk/government/organisations/civil-service/about/recruitment

Fast Stream Development Programme
www.faststream.gov.uk

Civil Service World
www.civilserviceworld.com

Public Appointments Service, Ireland
www.publicjobs.ie

Clinical Biochemist

What is Involved?

As a clinical biochemist (or chemical pathologist), you would be largely concerned with the use of biochemical investigations to diagnose diseases in which the body's chemistry goes wrong: diabetes, for example, or kidney failure. A major part of your work would be to provide scientific leadership in the pathology laboratory, through the direction of scientific services and the interpretation of test results for the doctor in the clinic or at the bedside. You could attain equivalent status to a medical consultant and become head of a laboratory. Although your expertise would contribute to the management of patients, you would not be medically trained and so could not take clinical responsibility for patients. In other words, you would not be able to treat them.

You might specialise in a particular area, such as toxicology or endocrinology, using sophisticated equipment to carry out tests on body tissues. Like the majority of clinical biochemists, you would most likely work within the National Health Service, the National Blood Service (blood transfusion) or the Public Health Laboratory Service.

Opportunities for Training

Clinical biochemists are graduates, usually with a first or upper second honours degree in a subject like biochemistry or chemistry, and often with a PhD. Virtually every university in the country offers a degree course in biochemistry or one in which biochemistry is a major component.

Traditionally, staff working as clinical biochemists in the NHS have trained through the Clinical Scientist Training Scheme. However, this scheme has now been replaced by the Scientist Training Programme (STP).

On the STP, you would follow a three-year programme leading to a specifically commissioned and accredited master's degree in Blood Sciences and certification of your workplace-based training, with the first year in a range of settings before specialisation.

Requirements for Entry

You would normally need an upper second or better BSc Honours degree in a relevant pure or applied science. A second degree and/or research experience in your chosen field or equivalent evidence of scientific and academic capability is desirable.

To gain entry to a degree course in this field, you would need A level/Advanced Higher/Higher or equivalent passes in biology and chemistry, together sometimes with maths or physics. You would also need a broad platform of GCSE/S Grade passes at 9-4/A*-C/1-3, including English and science subjects.

Kind of Person

You would need to have a strong interest in science and in laboratory procedures. If you do not enjoy your practical science lessons at school, this is probably not the career for you. Patients' lives could depend on your accuracy and efficiency in carrying out tests and interpreting results. You would need to have a logical and methodical approach to your work. Although you would be primarily based in a laboratory, you would be working as part of a team of professionals. You would need to make clear explanations of your findings and opinions, which would demand good communication skills.

Broad Outlook

The major changes introduced in 2011 into scientist training in the NHS make it difficult to comment on future prospects. Consult the Health Careers and ACB websites to ensure that you have the very latest information.

Many entrants to the profession will already have obtained a PhD, and the training and research experience that this provides can prove invaluable to the work of the clinical biochemist. In larger departments, there may be opportunities to study for a research degree after entering the profession but this may take some years to complete.

It may be possible to advance your career by taking on more responsibility and by gaining wider or more detailed experience. As a senior clinical biochemist, for example, you might have managerial responsibility for a department or section; alternatively, you might consider moving to production, sales or marketing in the pharmaceutical industry.

Related Occupations

You might be interested in working in other science-based fields, particularly those involving biology or chemistry. Such careers as: research chemist or research biologist/bioscientist, doctor (hospital), doctor (general practice), pharmacologist, pharmacist or forensic scientist could be of interest. In researching this career, you need to be clear about the distinction between a clinical biochemist, a medically qualified doctor and a biomedical scientist. Each has a different and essential role and requires different qualifications and training.

Impact on Lifestyle

You are likely to be working regular hours and a 37-hour week, which should not normally include weekend or evening work. However, you may be expected to be on call at times in cases of emergency.

Earnings Potential

Starting salaries for pre-registration clinical scientists in NHS Band 6 are currently £26,565 to £35,577, rising after registration to Band 7: £31,696 to £41,787. Senior manager or consultant posts can offer salaries ranging from £57,640 to £100,431. Additional payments are made for employment in and around London.

Further Information

Association for Clinical Biochemistry and Laboratory Medicine
www.acb.org.uk

Biochemical Society
www.biochemistry.org

National School of Healthcare Science
www.nshcs.org.uk

Royal College of Pathologists
www.rcpath.org

Health and Care Professions Council
www.hcpc-uk.org

Health Careers
www.healthcareers.nhs.uk

Association of Clinical Biochemists in Ireland
www.acbi.ie

Computer Careers

Careers in Computing or Information and Communications Technology (ICT) can be very hard to pin down, not least because the sector is still growing and changing at a rapid pace and, at the same time, employers have a tendency to use different job titles to describe broadly similar types of work. In this section of The Careers Directory we seek to identify and decode some of the more common employment roles you may come across during your career planning.

Should you find yourself studying specific job descriptions, perhaps because you are applying for a particular position, pay careful attention to the key skills and competences sought by the employer, and ask questions at interview to establish clearly what might be expected of you on a day-to-day basis.

The UK cyber workforce has grown by 160% in five years, according to research by the Tech Partnership, and this expansion is set to continue. Among the new jobs, junior positions look likely to grow the fastest, which is excellent news for young people looking to enter careers in tech. You may find it especially useful to explore the study and training programmes currently available. The Tech Partnership accredits, for example, employer-designed degrees in IT Management for Business (ITMB) and Software Development for Business (SDfB). There are currently some 1,250 students in over 20 universities undertaking these 'Gold' degrees, supported by a growing network of more than 90 employers.

The Tech Partnership also offers degree apprenticeships, available in England since September 2015. Over a minimum period of three years, you can earn a trainee salary while studying towards an honours degree in Digital and Technology Solutions. Each programme includes a core focus on technology skills, with additional study options relevant to professional roles such as software engineer, IT consultant, IT business analyst, cyber security analyst or network engineer.

Career Descriptions

Applications Developer
Writes or modifies programs for a variety of technical, commercial and business users. These applications may then be bought off the shelf or tailored to meet the needs of specific clients. The work requires a thorough knowledge of programming techniques and computer systems in order to develop effective programs in accordance with agreed specifications. A degree in computer science, software engineering or information systems can be a useful starting point, although opportunities also exist for those without academic qualifications.

Back End Developer
Carries responsibility for defining and maintaining an IT application and a database stored on a server. Whilst users interact with the 'front end' of an application, all the data they enter is stored in and retrieved from a remote database or 'back end'. Must understand front end technologies and platforms and show proficiency in programming languages such as PHP, Ruby and Python.

Computer Engineer/Scientist
Combines the training of an electronic engineer with an extensive knowledge of software design and implementation; may work in computer design, the creation of individual components for computer equipment, networking design, or integrating software options with the hardware that will drive the applications.

Computer Games Designer/Developer

Creates and produces games ranging from computer, console and arcade games to mobile phone, internet and other applications; might specialise in art and design - deciding on the original concept and creating characters, objects and scenery; in animation - bringing the game to life with computer modelling and animation software; or in programming - creating the code to make the game work. Needs creativity and imagination more than academic qualifications, although many games developers are graduates.

International Game Developers Association (US)
www.igda.org

Database Administrator

Constructs and/or maintains a computerised information system, taking responsibility for its performance, integrity and security. Increasing threats of hacking and virus attack mean that security and disaster recovery have become exceptionally important aspects of the work. Databases often contain highly sensitive information - perhaps hospital patient record systems or a bank's customer account network. There are no set entry requirements, although a degree in computer science, computer systems engineering or information technology could be useful.

Digital Marketing Executive

Also known as: insights executive

Manages brand and product strategies to drive online traffic to an organisation's website, using such techniques as SEO and PPC (see our separate entries regarding these terms); oversees social media strategy, evaluates customer research and constantly reviews new technologies to keep the organisation at the forefront of digital developments.

Forensic Computer Investigator

Investigates cyber or computer-based crime; may be involved with such issues as phishing, hacking and online scams, political and industrial espionage, terrorist communications, possession of illegal pornography, or theft of sensitive commercial information. Could act as a cyber security consultant or work more specifically for the police, security services, a bank, or an IT firm specialising in computer security. There is no single entry route to this rapidly developing career area but a flair for problem solving and a passion for IT are key characteristics.

Computer Forensics World
www.computerforensicsworld.com

Front End Developer

Creates fast, clear, easily understandable website pages and interfaces that make users understand, believe in and care about the data provided. Uses skills in HTML, CSS, and JavaScript to ensure that information coming from the back end (see our separate entry for this) is accurately and attractively displayed, and that users can navigate through it.

Information Systems Manager

Carries responsibility for the computer systems within an organisation, including quality standards and strategic planning; purchases hardware and software, oversees installation and ensures that security procedures and back-up systems operate effectively. Experience of computer operations is normally more important than academic qualifications, although a degree in computer science, software engineering or business management could be extremely useful.

Computer Careers (continued)

Information Technology Consultant
Also known as: business analyst or enterprise-wide information specialist

Works in partnership with clients to help them get the best possible return on their technology investment by integrating information technology systems into their business operations, advising on how to improve the efficiency of systems and overcome problems. Strong communication and problem solving skills are more important than academic qualifications, although a degree in information systems, computer science, software engineering or mathematics could be useful. A postgraduate qualification in information technology might be necessary for a non-computing graduate, showing evidence of both commitment and competence.

Information Technology Sales Professional
Interacts with clients by identifying their specific business needs and applying detailed technical knowledge of products to meet those needs; must be able to provide advice on all aspects of the installation and use of systems and networks, both before and after the sale. A strong sales background and ability to meet targets are more important than academic qualifications, although it is helpful to have some interest in and knowledge of information technology.

Institute of Direct and Digital Marketing
www.theidm.com

Malware Analyst
Also known as: cyber security specialist or web security architect

Works in the field of computer and network security to examine, identify and counter cyber-threats such as viruses, worms, bots, rootkits and Trojan horses. All of these represent malicious code that can infect systems and cause them to behave in unexpected ways. Malware can compromise the integrity of a computer or network and can steal proprietary data such as financial records. A malware analyst must be thoroughly conversant with both interpreted and compiled programming languages, and must possess a keen understanding of both reverse-engineering and software development.

Infosec Institute (US)
www.infosecinstitute.com/jobs/malware-analyst.html

Mobile Applications Developer
Designs and creates apps for smartphones, tablets and other portable computing devices. Must have strong working knowledge of all available platforms - particularly Android and iOS - and experience in such areas as C++, Objective-C, wireless networks, PHP, MS/SQL, Adobe, Java, HTML, cloud storage and Flash.

Multimedia Designer
Combines design skills and technical knowledge, using text, data, graphics, sound, animation and other digital and visual effects, to create content for internet sites, electronic games, online learning materials, advertising and interactive television. Although there are no set academic entry requirements, most entrants are graduates. A degree or postgraduate qualification in an art and design-related subject such as graphic or multimedia design can be particularly useful.

Creative and Cultural Skills
http://ccskills.org.uk/careers/advice/any/design/digital-multimedia-design

Network Engineer
Also known as: hardware engineer or network designer

Installs, maintains and supports computer communication networks within an organisation or between organisations. Actual duties in this highly technical role depend on the size and type of the network, which can range from linking a few workstations locally to a global area network with international links. Several entry routes exist, including an apprenticeship in computing or a degree in computer science, electronics or computer systems engineering.

Pay-Per-Click (PPC) Executive
Devises and implements PPC advertising campaigns on key platforms such as Google AdWords and Yahoo AdCentre to drive visitor traffic to a website. In addition to constructing campaigns, the work involves bidding on keywords and analysing and drawing insight from third party analytics data.

Pen Tester
Sometimes known as an 'ethical hacker', works as a network security consultant trying to break into or find possible exploits in different computer systems and software. Runs tests and completes assessment reports for clients. May specialise in the security of wireless networks, databases, software development or company secrets. Must combine creativity and imagination with an outstanding level of technical knowledge and hands-on experience.

Pentest
www.pentest.co.uk

Programmer
Writes code - the step-by-step instructions that direct computers to process information - to create or modify software applications. Works from a flow chart that shows diagrammatically how information will flow through the computer and any peripheral equipment. Must be meticulous, logical and competent in more than one major programming language (C, C++, Java), often acquiring skills through a degree in a subject such as computer science, information technology or software engineering.

Search Engine Optimisation (SEO) Expert
Ensures that an organisation's brands and websites build high visibility, ranking and traffic as a result of searches on Google, Bing, Yahoo and other search engines. SEO also goes beyond websites to reach the target audience across all platforms and user experiences, including mobile apps, social media, video, blogs and retail portals. Usually works alongside web content, social media and digital marketing professionals to ensure that everything that appears online is SEO-friendly.

Computer Careers (continued)

Social Media Manager

Implements an organisation's strategic marketing on social media by creating and distributing relevant and consistent content in order to attract and retain a clearly-defined audience. The goal is usually to develop brand awareness, generate inbound traffic and cultivate leads and sales. May write a blog, respond to comments, answer questions and actively participate in the online community to connect with potential customers and advocate the brand.

Institute of Direct and Digital Marketing
www.theidm.com

Software Engineer

Also known as: application programmer, software architect or system programmer/ engineer

Creates the original system-level programs needed to enable computers to carry out a very wide range of functions. These programs (or software) could include complex automation control for industry, accounts packages for bookkeeping or sophisticated business management systems. Often works on the basis of specifications laid down and agreed with a client, usually via a systems analyst. May work alone on small projects, or as a member of a team of software engineers for large projects. Having written the software, liaises with a software tester to make sure everything works properly, and with a technical author to write up installation instructions and user manuals. Would normally have a computing, software engineering or related degree, together with knowledge of languages such as Java, .Net, HTML, Perl, Ruby on Rails and Python.

Software Tester

Also known as: test analyst or software quality assurance tester

Tries to anticipate all the ways in which an application or system might be used and how it could fail. Doesn't necessarily program but needs a good understanding of code. Prepares test scripts and macros, and analyses results, which are fed back to the software developer so that fixes can be made. May also be involved at the early stages of a project in order to anticipate pitfalls before work begins.

Systems Analyst

Also known as: product specialist, systems engineer, solutions specialist or technical designer

Investigates problems related to the use of computers in business and other organisations. Having been called in to analyse a particular system, begins by talking to the client to understand exactly what is required, then prepares a feasibility study to see whether the organisation's present system can be adapted to meet the newly identified need. If it cannot be suitably modified, advises on a new system to overcome the problem. May also design the new system or call in a software engineer to take the specification and turn it into a working solution. Needs to combine commercial and technical awareness with a good understanding of people. Would normally have a computing, software engineering or related degree, plus several years' experience.

Technical Support Manager
Also known as: helpdesk support, operations analyst or problem manager

The professional trouble shooter of the ICT world, may work for a hardware manufacturer or supplier, solving the problems of business customers or consumers, but may equally work for an end-user company, supporting, monitoring and maintaining workplace technology and responding to users' requests for help. Needs wide-ranging technical knowledge, patience, tact and excellent communication and listening skills.

Telecommunications Engineer

Operates in such sectors as internet, mobile and wireless communications, data networks, and programming and security for telecommunications. Current issues include cloud computing, software defined networking and network function virtualisation. Strong problem solving abilities and excellent communication skills are essential, together with a degree in a subject such as electronic and communication engineering, telecommunications, computer science, physics, mathematics or information technology.

Institute of Telecommunications Professionals
www.theitp.org

Institution of Engineering and Technology
www.theiet.org

User Experience/Interface (UX/UI) Developer

A specialist in human-computer interaction, seeks to understand user needs and produce concepts, solutions or designs that people want to use. The aim is to enhance user satisfaction by improving the usability, accessibility, and pleasure provided in the interaction between the user and the product, using tools such as Balsamiq Mockups to create interactive wireframes and Silverback to record usability testing sessions.

Balsamiq Mockups
https://balsamiq.com

Silverback
http://silverbackapp.com

UX Mastery
http://uxmastery.com

Computer Careers (continued)

Web Analytics Executive

Pulls together and interprets key data from all areas of an organisation's online activities, including organic search engine traffic, paid traffic, social media metrics and e-marketing analytics. Must be able to draw conclusions from the data collected and reference it to customer experience online, customer engagement, conversion rates to sales/enquiries, conversion rates to email newsletter signups, social media signups and so on.

Web Content Manager

Also known as: online content manager/producer

Develops and maintains the information that appears on an organisation's website, working with a project team to coordinate the site content and make sure it caters to the needs of the target audience, and using a web content management system to analyse usage statistics. There is no single route into this career, although a background in journalism, marketing, public relations or communications might be useful. Previous experience of writing content in some form, not necessarily online, is usually essential.

Web Developer

Also known as: web designer, web producer, multimedia architect or internet engineer

Sets up, runs and maintains websites for companies, organisations or individuals. The websites might be used for such purposes as publicity, marketing or buying and selling on the internet, so starts by discussing in some detail the precise needs of the client, advising on such matters as graphics, text and sound, together with possible links to other sites. If the company or organisation has its own intranet (an internal version of the internet), discusses how this could best be linked to the web. Would be expected to advise on the cost of the project, and either design and program the website pages or supervise others to do this. Once the design is agreed and the site is up and running, ensures that it is kept up to date and any problems are dealt with. Might work on a freelance basis as an independent consultant or be employed full-time. There is no single route to becoming a web developer. Experience and talent can be as important as qualifications, although there are many relevant courses available at different levels of entry.

Further Information

Skills Framework for the Information Age
www.sfia-online.org

Chartered Institute for IT
www.bcs.org

National Computing Centre
www.ncc.co.uk

Tech Partnership
www.thetechpartnership.com

British Interactive Media Association
www.bima.co.uk

UK Web Design Association
www.ukwda.org

Apprenticeships
www.getingofar.gov.uk

Certified Internet Web Professional
www.ciwcertified.com

Institution of Analysts and Programmers
www.iap.org.uk

World Wide Web Consortium
www.w3.org

Irish Computer Society
www.ics.ie

Lero: Irish Software Research Centre
www.lero.ie

Irish Internet Association
www.iia.ie

Breaking Jobs in ICT

In the fast-moving world of ICT, it is not unusual to come across job titles that would not have registered at all in previous editions of this *Careers Directory*, despite our best efforts to keep abreast of new developments. Trying to distinguish newly-emerging technologies from trendy buzzwords can be a dangerous guessing game, and there's no guarantee that we'll identify the most enduring career directions, but we're more than willing to have a go at providing an ABC (and more) of what appear to be the hottest jobs in ICT for 2018. Inevitably, some fields will falter, while others grow to become the next big thing. The key is to remain alert and ready to develop new skills as new opportunities emerge.

Augmented/Virtual Reality Developer

Once the sole province of computer games developers, augmented/virtual reality (AR/VR) is predicted by experts at Goldman Sachs Research to become the next major computing platform. They expect AR/VR to become an $80 billion market by 2025, roughly the size of the desktop PC market today. The technology has improved considerably since earlier launch attempts and is already transforming such sectors as house buying, healthcare and education. AR - which overlays digital information onto the physical world - and VR - which immerses the user in a virtual world - seem certain to reshape existing ways of doing things.

Google is a major player in the VR field with its Cardboard and Daydream projects, currently being used as a storytelling tool by the *New York Times*, and under development at YouTube and at Lucid, producer of the world's first affordable point and shoot VR camera.

Here's a list of skills considered essential by Lucid: Objective-C, C++, Computer Vision, C, computer graphics, mobile application development, OpenGL ES, C#, OpenGL, DirectX, WebGL, and digital image processing.

Another company working in VR is Samsung, with its Gear 360 camera designed to record virtual reality videos for the Gear VR headset. The Galactica rollercoaster at Alton Towers, for example, uses Samsung VR headsets to give the impression that you're flying through space.

Microsoft, meanwhile, is pouring considerable development funding into AR research with its Hololens AR headset. This wearable technology projects holograms into the real world.

The company says that it is looking for software engineers with excellent technical problem-solving, design, coding, and testing skills; native development in C++ design and coding, with strong debugging skills; and two+ years of relevant software design and development experience.

Blockchain Engineer

There is growing demand for engineers and developers familiar with the blockchain, the core technology behind bitcoin, and experienced in cryptography, distributed systems and hash algorithms.

There are currently over 200 companies and open source projects seeking to apply blockchain technology to applications such as trading platforms, secure identification cards, self-executing contracts, and many applications in financial services.

The technology is not that difficult to understand, according to one developer, but it is new and in some ways more like advanced mathematics than programming. It begins with understanding how decentralised architecture works and combining the roles of software architect and cryptography expert.

If you wish to pursue a career in blockchain engineering, you will need experience in Python, bitcoins and distributed systems.

Cognitive Computing/Machine Learning Specialist

Cognitive computing (CC), an initiative developed by IBM with its Watson program, aims to mimic the functioning of the human brain and make human-style problems computable. It addresses complex situations that are characterised by ambiguity and uncertainty. In dynamic, information-rich, and shifting situations, data tends to change frequently, and it is often conflicting; the goals of users evolve as they learn more and redefine their objectives. To respond to the fluid nature of users' understanding of their problems, CC offers a synthesis not just of information sources but of influences, contexts and insights. To do this, systems often need to weigh conflicting evidence and suggest an answer that is 'best' rather than 'right'. While some artificial intelligence systems like Facebook's facial recognition software use machine learning and image recognition, they only function for their designed purpose and do not create a deeper human engagement that reasons through data to determine what matters to a person. CC seeks to sidestep the human intervention into machine programming and learning.

Specialised applications are now developing around Watson and related technologies, bringing with them a range of new career opportunities. SparkCognition, for example, is using machine learning, big data analysis, modelling, and other cognitive-related technologies to better understand security threats. WayBlazer is focused on consumer travel, and @Point of Care, one of a number of healthcare-related Watson partners, allows doctors to access on a mobile platform peer-reviewed content on specific diseases.

IBM is currently helping universities develop cognitive-related course materials. Data curation is a key element, it says, adding that you don't build a cognitive system without thinking of a body of documents or websites. A job listing with IBM Watson Health group says that candidates should be hands-on in their approach to technology. This includes unstructured data, statistical extraction of entities, machine learning, natural language processing, and search.

Machine learning, by the way, is defined as a field of study that gives computers the ability to learn without being explicitly programmed. It explores the study and construction of algorithms that can learn from and make predictions on data, building a model from example inputs in order to make data-driven predictions or decisions.

Computer Security Incident Response Specialist

Cyber security specialist is already a recognised career option but the increasingly sophisticated nature of cyber attacks and the ability to use new technologies such as machine learning algorithms to analyse, understand and counter those threats has fundamentally changed the nature of the job, and has given rise to the emerging specialism of security information and event management (SIEM).

SIEM combines a number of functions into a single system, including identifying trends in cyberspace with regard to adversary tactics, techniques, and procedures; using standard hacking methodologies to test infrastructures; proactively researching emerging cyber threats; performing testing, research and investigation of new technologies to improve detection, response, intelligence, mitigation and coordination; and applying an analytical understanding of hacker methodologies and tactics, system vulnerabilities and key indicators of attacks and exploits.

Skills needed include a knowledge of networking fundamentals (all OSI layers), protocols and packet analysis, encryption and tokenisation technologies, and experience in writing PL/SQL or SQL scripts.

GPU Cluster Engineer

While the CPU (central processing unit) is often considered the brains of the PC, it is increasingly being enhanced by another component: the GPU (graphics processing unit), sometimes described as the PC's soul.

The GPU goes far beyond basic graphics controller functions, and is a programmable and powerful computational device in its own right. Its advanced capabilities were originally used primarily for 3D games, but now its power is being harnessed more broadly to accelerate computational workloads in areas such as financial modelling, scientific research and oil and gas exploration.

GPUs are optimised for taking huge batches of data and performing the same operation over and over very quickly, unlike PC microprocessors, which tend to skip all over the place. This is because a GPU is composed of hundreds of cores that can handle thousands of threads simultaneously, while the CPU is composed of just a few cores with lots of cache memory that can handle a few software threads at a time.

GPU computing improves application performance by offloading compute-intensive portions of the application to the GPU, while the remainder of the code still runs on the CPU. This advantage is vital to companies like Facebook and Experian that deal with enormous data sets.

Facebook's Big Sur runs the social networking company's machine learning servers and is heavily reliant on GPU clusters, which can be more efficient than conventional CPUs for such tasks. Information services company Experian, which helps people to check their credit report and protect against identity theft, and helps businesses to manage credit risk, prevent fraud, target marketing offers and automate decision making, also uses GPU clusters.

At the same time, the Ford Motor Company - which is seeking to redefine the car as 'a networked computing platform upon which an ever-evolving set of applications is being designed' - is looking for GPU engineers to work on its driverless car programme. The extensive list of minimum skills needed includes: experience with GPU, parallel programming tools and language extensions, together with a broad array of programming skills, among them C/C++, Perl, Python, Java, OpenGL, OpenCV, CUDA, MATLAB, and more. A degree in Engineering, Sciences, Mathematics or a similar field is also essential.

You can learn about recent developments in GPU computing by visiting the GPU Computing News community on Facebook at:
www.facebook.com/gpucomputing

Internet of Things Architect

The Internet of Things (IoT) seeks to connect everything with everything, thereby integrating the physical world into computer-based systems. The aim is to improve accuracy, efficiency and economic benefit by embedding 'things' - devices, vehicles, roads, buildings and other objects - with software, sensors and network connectivity to collect and exchange data, allowing them to be sensed and controlled remotely. Each 'thing' is uniquely identifiable through its embedded computing system but is able to inter-operate within the existing Internet infrastructure.

In other words, the IoT is about taking all the information gathered by all the sensors in the world, analysing it in real time and applying it in other ways. For example, a new flyover might be built using smart concrete, equipped with sensors to monitor stresses, cracks, and warping. This can alert highways authorities to potential structural issues before they cause a catastrophe, while the same sensors can detect, say, ice on the road and communicate the information to the GPS in your car. Once your car knows there's a hazard ahead, it will automatically slow down. Similarly, if traffic flow is congested, the car will seek an alternative route. This form of machine-to-machine (M2M) communication enables the IoT to turn information into action.

One innovative company recently advertised for what it calls an 'IoT solutions architect'. Among other skills, applicants should have experience in managing delivery of complex solutions involving IoT, M2M, cloud, security, professional services, and SaaS (Software as a Service). In addition to strong technology marketing and analytical skills, candidates must possess the financial management skills needed for forecasting, pricing, and margin analysis.

Further information

To find out more about career opportunities in computing, visit the website at:
www.thetechpartnership.com/tech-future-careers

Construction Manager

What is Involved?

As a construction manager, you would be responsible for running a construction site or a section of a large project. You might also be known as a site manager, site agent or building manager. Your work would include developing a strategy for the construction of the project, planning ahead to anticipate problems and solve them before they happen, making sure all processes are carried out safely, reporting on the progress of the project and motivating the workforce to get the best out of them. You would be responsible for liaising with the architects and planners, for carefully assessing the specifications and site plans. You would consult engineers, surveyors, quantity surveyors and estimators, checking costs of labour, supervision and materials before producing time schedules, agreeing labour force requirements and placing orders. You would be in control of the site throughout the construction process.

Opportunities for Training

There are several possible training routes. You could, for example, take a three- or four-year degree in a relevant subject such as construction, building, construction or building management, building studies or technology; you could take a full- or part-time higher national certificate or diploma (HNC/D) in a similar subject; or you could start as a technician with a national certificate or diploma. Sandwich courses are available, which give the opportunity for practical paid experience during your degree. There are also opportunities for sponsorship during your degree course, usually with the larger construction companies. Following your academic training, you could work towards professional qualifications awarded by the Chartered Institute of Building or the Chartered Association of Building Engineers.

You may be interested in the new degree apprenticeship in construction, on which you split your time between university study and the workplace and are employed throughout - gaining a top level qualification while earning a wage and getting real on-the-job experience.

As with other apprenticeships, the cost of tuition is shared between government and your employer, meaning that you can earn a full bachelor or even master degree without paying any fees.

The professional qualification 'Chartered Builder' is increasingly important for career progression. Details are available on the Chartered Institute of Building website.

Requirements for Entry

The degree route would normally require two or three A level/Advanced Higher, four Higher or equivalent qualifications often including passes in maths and/or physics, together with at least five GCSE/S Grade passes 9-4/A*-C/1-3, including English, maths and a science subject. For the HNC/D, one or two A level/Advanced Higher, three Higher or equivalent qualifications, or a national certificate/diploma would be necessary.

Kind of Person

You would need to apply all your knowledge of construction techniques to ensure that each project is completed to time, on budget and safely. You would have to be able to motivate people and would need excellent communication skills. You would also have to be able to stay calm when things don't go quite as planned. Other people would expect to rely on your judgement. Your decisions would need to be based on your knowledge of technical, legal and health and safety factors but above all on practical common sense and experience. You may find yourself working under pressure when, for example, schedules are slipping or materials fail to arrive.

Broad Outlook

The demand for construction managers depends to a great extent on the state of the construction industry and the picture in 2017 is starting to look encouraging, as the sector recovers from the severe downturn that started in 2008. Indeed, the UK construction industry has turned around to become one of the fastest-growing sectors in the economy, offering new hope for construction managers in the years to come.

Related Occupations

You might consider other construction- and property-related careers, such as: building control officer/surveyor, building services engineer, civil engineer, quantity surveyor, architect, architectural technician/technologist, town planner, surveyor (general practice), estate manager/land agent, estate agent, rural practice surveyor or auctioneer/valuer.

Impact on Lifestyle

Whilst your basic hours of work are likely to be around 40 hours a week, you could expect to be working longer hours than this when you are on site. The hours of work on building sites tend to be particularly long during the summer, when there are a lot of daylight hours, but much shorter in the winter. At times, you may be expected to work in the evenings and at weekends. In addition you can expect to be working outside in all kinds of weather, and would need to wear protective clothing such as a hard hat when on site. Most of your working day would be spent on site or even travelling from site to site. Some managers move from one location to another as projects are completed and new ones start. Some are able to reach the site by travelling every day; others live away from home during the week and return home at weekends.

Earnings Potential

As a graduate, you could expect to start on a salary of about £23,000 to £27,000, depending to some extent on where in the country you are working. This can be raised by allowances for being on site or for travelling. Experienced construction managers can expect to earn between £40,000 and £65,000, rising to around £75,000 for a senior manager. Salaries tend to be higher in London.

Further Information

Careers in Construction
www.citb.co.uk/careers-in-construction

Chartered Association of Building Engineers
www.cbuilde.com/home

Chartered Institute of Building
www.ciob.org

Bconstructive
www.citb.co.uk/bconstructive

Construction Industry Council
http://cic.org.uk

Construction Industry Federation, Ireland
http://cif.ie

Cosmetic Scientist

What is Involved?

As a cosmetic scientist you would be involved in the research and development of cosmetics, hair care, perfume and toiletry products, ensuring not only that they do what they are intended to but above all that they are safe to use for the consumer.

During the development process a product goes through many different stages requiring a range of skills. Depending on the size of the project and the company, you may only work at one of these stages or you may see a product through from concept to the production line and post launch.

Although science-based, this job requires a lot of creativity, an eye for colour and a nose for smell. You will often work at a fast-moving pace to ensure deadlines are met and products are launched on time. You may liaise with the marketing department to interpret new trends and you may be required to answer questions and trouble-shoot problems relating to the formulation once it reaches the production line.

Opportunities for Training

In order to be a cosmetic scientist you normally need to study a science subject at university. However, some companies will employ A level or equivalent school leavers at technician level and provide suitable in-house or external industry training.

Suitable university courses include chemistry, chemical engineering, biology and pharmacy. You could then follow your chosen degree by taking a Diploma in Cosmetic Science, which will give you an integrated knowledge of the fundamentals of cosmetic science and the industry. This is available by distance learning, with units written and assessed by experts in the industry. The course is in a modular format and the material can be accessed online once you are enrolled. For some units, specially designed activity kits enable you to undertake important practical work in your own home.

Topics covered include: foundations in chemistry, physiology, biochemistry and microbiology; the key functional roles of development, production, packaging and marketing; auxiliary services such as stability testing, microbial preservation, quality assurance, legislation, safety assessment, performance evaluation and market research; and specific product categories such as hair, skin and oral care, colour cosmetics, aerosols and perfumes.

There is also a Principles and Practice of Cosmetic Science course, targeted at scientists who have been working in the industry for a few years and are looking to move on to more managerial or supervisory roles.

Two universities offer cosmetic science as a degree course: De Montfort University and the University of the Arts, London.

Requirements for Entry

Most universities will want you to have at least two A levels (or three Higher grades if you're in Scotland), and five GCSE/S Grade passes at 9-4/A*-C/1-3. Each university sets its own entry requirements, and some might ask for higher grades than others, so make sure you look around.

Kind of Person

A cosmetic scientist must be multi-disciplinarian, creative and with excellent attention to detail and good sensory perception. Students need excellent laboratory skills, good time management and team-working skills, good written and oral communication skills and an inquiring mind.

Broad Outlook

Despite some of the larger companies moving their manufacturing overseas the UK cosmetics industry is thriving.

As consumers live longer and take more interest in their appearance, the market for cosmetic products is continuing to grow and the demand for innovation within the industry is great. This growth creates opportunities for cosmetic scientists to work on projects involving not just performance actives (materials that have a targeted activity on the function of the skin, such as anti-ageing or protecting; vitamins, peptides and anti-oxidants all fall in to this category) but also to work in growing niche markets, such as organic and fair trade products.

The European cosmetics market represents almost one third of the global market, with total sales for the European Union plus Norway and Switzerland at €72 billion and European exports to the rest of the world totalling €36.2 billion. In 2015, direct and indirect employment in the European cosmetics industry was approximately two million people in some 4,500 companies.

Related Occupations

You might also consider: perfumer, fragrance evaluator or pharmacologist.

Impact on Lifestyle

In most parts of the industry you would work a fairly typical 9am to 5pm day from Monday to Friday. In production or quality control, you may need to work on a rota basis as the production line is likely to be in 24-hour operation. You would need to wear protective clothing when dealing with some hazardous substances and at other times you may be required to wear anti-contamination clothing in a scrupulously clean environment.

Earnings Potential

Newly qualified cosmetic scientists can earn around £20,000 and as they gain in experience they can get paid over £50,000 a year. There are also opportunities to move into management positions or change direction to work in sales or marketing.

Further Information

Society of Cosmetic Scientists
www.scs.org.uk

Distance Learning in Cosmetic Science
www.scsdlc.com

Cosmetic, Toiletry and Perfumery Association
www.ctpa.org.uk

Cosmetics Europe
www.cosmeticseurope.eu

Countryside/Nature Conservation Officer

What is Involved?

As a countryside/nature conservation officer, you would be an environmental specialist responsible for advising on issues concerned with protecting and conserving the countryside. You would ensure that conservation laws are being observed and would take steps to enforce them if necessary; you could be responsible for managing a site of special scientific interest or for designating a new one; or you may assess the environmental impact of proposed major construction developments. While you might spend some time outside on site surveys, you would be largely office-based, reading and writing reports, consulting maps and charts, preparing talks or checking details of legislation.

Opportunities for Training

Although there is no set training route, you would be unlikely to secure a post without a relevant degree and even a postgraduate qualification. Possible degree subjects would include ecology, environmental science, geology, geography, conservation and countryside management, biology or estate management. There is fierce competition for jobs, so part-time and voluntary experience is very important. You should take every opportunity to show your commitment by undertaking voluntary projects and you should check degree courses for the amount of fieldwork and other practical experience they offer. A postgraduate qualification at MSc or PhD level in conservation, ecology or land management would also be advisable.

Joining a professional body such as the Chartered Institute of Ecology and Environmental Management (CIEEM) would give you both professional recognition and access to training and networking opportunities.

Requirements for Entry

Degree entry requirements would vary depending on your choice of both subject and university. However, you would normally need a minimum of two A level/Advanced Higher, three Higher or equivalent qualifications and five GCSE/S Grade passes at 9-4/A*-C/1-3. In order to be accepted for postgraduate study, you are likely to need first class or upper second honours in your first degree.

A full driving licence would almost always be essential.

Kind of Person

You may find yourself having to negotiate with people who are opposed to your ideas, so you would need to show diplomacy and tact in your approach to them. At the same time, you would have to have confidence in your point of view and powers of persuasion to make your case clear. This may involve communicating complex scientific or technical information to non-specialists. You could be required to write reports and to speak at public meetings. You would need to be prepared for criticism of your work from people who do not understand your point of view or your recommendations. You would find yourself working as part of a team but you would need to be able to work unsupervised and to manage your own time. A real commitment to, and knowledge of, preserving the environment would be essential.

Broad Outlook

There are jobs for countryside conservation officers with government agencies such as Natural England or Scottish National Heritage, with local government and with organisations such as The National Trust. However, there is very strong competition for jobs and each advertised post often has a large number of applicants. You may well need to move around the country and to apply for a large number of jobs in order to secure a suitable post. Some positions are on short-term contracts or are purely seasonal, and you may have to gain experience with one or more of these before finding a full-time position. There would be opportunities to progress to managing a team of conservation officers or to pursue a specific interest, which could lead you into research, lecturing or specialist consultancy work.

Related Occupations

You might also consider: countryside ranger/warden, ecologist, environmental consultant, forest/woodland manager, town planner, landscape architect, rural practice surveyor, marine biologist/marine scientist, recycling officer, research biologist/bioscientist, cartographer, geologist/geoscientist, microbiologist or zoologist.

Impact on Lifestyle

You would nominally work a normal week of around 40 hours, Monday to Friday. You may, however, have to attend evening and weekend meetings and you would have to work whatever hours it takes to write up a report in the required time.

Earnings Potential

As a countryside conservation officer working for a government agency, you would be likely to have a starting salary of around £20,000, rising with experience to around £30,000. Senior positions may command salaries of around £34,000. Local government salaries are likely to be similar but charitable organisations often start at lower levels, perhaps around £15,000.

Further Information

Land Based and Environmental Careers
www.lantra.co.uk/Careers

Conservation Volunteers
www.tcv.org.uk

Countryside Jobs Service
www.countryside-jobs.com

Chartered Institute of Ecology and Environmental Management
www.cieem.net

Natural England
www.gov.uk/government/organisations/natural-england

Natural Resources Wales
http://naturalresources.wales

Scottish Natural Heritage
www.snh.gov.uk

Northern Ireland Environment Link
www.nienvironmentlink.org

Field Studies Council
www.field-studies-council.org

Department of Arts, Heritage and the Gaeltacht, Dublin
www.ahg.gov.ie

Countryside Ranger/Warden

What is Involved?

As a countryside ranger or warden, your job would be to protect, manage and develop a particular area of countryside. This might be something like a wildlife habitat or a site of special scientific interest. Your role would also involve helping the public to enjoy that particular area of countryside. You are likely to be working somewhere like a national park, an area of outstanding beauty or a nature reserve.

Your job might include patrolling the area to look for repairs that need doing or developments that could be achieved to enhance the site. You may carry out the necessary work yourself or organise teams of people. You could become a specialist in a particular area relevant to your area of work. In addition to the outdoor activities, you might also work in an information centre or an office, producing information booklets or planning exhibitions and site visits to explain the flora and fauna and geographical features of your site.

Opportunities for Training

Countryside management is a high-qualification, training-conscious industry, with nearly two-thirds of employed workers having degrees, Higher National Certificates/ Diplomas or equivalent professional qualifications. While opportunities are available for non-graduates through routes such as Apprenticeships and National Diplomas, there is a tendency for graduates to apply for jobs at all levels, including the most basic.

Apprenticeships exist at both intermediate and advanced level in environmental conservation; access and recreation; rivers, coasts and waterways/flood risk management; or dry stone walling. You will need to check which schemes are available in your local area.

By joining the Countryside Management Association (CMA), you would be able to attend regional and national training and study days, and gain professional accreditation through a programme of continuing professional development.

Requirements for Entry

While there are no specific entry requirements for many of the training schemes, competition for places is strong and you should have a good standard of education. You would probably need at least four GCSE/S Grade passes at 9-4/A*-C/1-3 or equivalent, including English, maths, a science subject and another academic subject.

Many applicants, as noted above, have a degree or HND in a relevant subject such as ecology, biology, environmental science, land management, agriculture, leisure and recreation, geography or geology. You would need to show evidence of part-time or voluntary work in a countryside or conservation field and you would probably need to be able to drive.

Kind of Person

You would need to be physically fit and prepared for hard practical work. Your employers would be looking for evidence of a genuine interest in the countryside. You would probably be dealing with the public, who may need you to explain aspects of the site or the work. For this you would need a pleasant and tactful manner.

You may be expected to speak in public, giving presentations to publicise your area of work. Depending on where you work, you may need to have knowledge of the law relating to countryside rights and to health and safety issues. Your personal, practical skills and willingness to learn are likely to be as important as your academic achievements.

Broad Outlook

The environmental conservation industry is expected to continue expanding in the future but it is estimated that there are 200,000 volunteers and a mere 50,000 paid staff. Included in this number are some 5,700 countryside rangers or wardens. Competition for full-time jobs is intense and there is almost always an expectation of considerable voluntary or part-time experience before you apply. There are limited opportunities for promotion, although it is possible - depending on your qualifications and experience - to move into some of the related occupations listed below. You may need to be prepared to move around the country in order to find a suitable vacancy.

Related Occupations

You might like a job in a related field such as arboriculturist, ecologist, environmental consultant, estate manager/land agent, recycling officer, countryside/nature conservation officer, forest/woodland manager, horticultural manager, microbiologist or marine biologist/marine scientist.

Impact on Lifestyle

Your job as a countryside ranger is likely to involve working in the evenings and at weekends. You might be working in a fairly remote countryside area, which could be quite isolated. You may find the work tiring, as it can include walking many miles or handling heavy equipment. You will be exposed to the elements at all times of the year.

Earnings Potential

Countryside rangers are usually paid between £18,000 and £25,000, with senior rangers or site managers earning up to £30,000. A vehicle may be provided for use at work but you would also need your own transport.

Further Information

Land Based and Environmental Careers
www.lantra.co.uk/Careers

Conservation Volunteers
www.tcv.org.uk

Countryside Jobs Service
www.countryside-jobs.com

Countryside Management Association
www.countrysidemanagement.org.uk

Apprenticeships
www.getingofar.gov.uk

National Trust
www.nationaltrust.org.uk

Groundwork
www.groundwork.org.uk

Forestry Commission
www.forestry.gov.uk

National Parks and Wildlife Service
www.npws.ie

Dental Technician/Technologist

What is Involved?

As a dental technician/technologist, you would be involved in the design and construction of appliances prescribed for their patients by dental surgeons. These would include dentures, crowns and bridges and orthodontic appliances such as braces designed to correct misalignment of the teeth. You would most likely work in a commercial dental laboratory, using a wide range of materials - metal alloys, gold or porcelain for crown and bridge work, acrylic or metal for braces, plastic or chrome cobalt for dentures - to meet the specific requirements of each prescription. The work requires great precision and technical skill but only rarely involves actually meeting the patient for whom you are ultimately working.

There are four specialist areas: prosthodontic technicians design and make dentures; conservation technicians specialise in crown and bridge work; orthodontic technicians make braces to correct tooth positions; maxillo-facial technicians (sometimes also known as maxillofacial prosthetists) work in hospital oral surgery, ophthalmic, cancer and burns units, helping to reconstruct the faces of patients damaged by accident or disease.

You might carry out work for a number of local dentists or even offer a postal service for dentists from a wider area. Alternatively, you might work in a hospital, supporting oral and maxillofacial surgeons.

Opportunities for Training

In order to work as a dental technician/technologist, you must be registered with the General Dental Council.

There are three possible routes to qualification:

- study full-time for a BTEC level 3 diploma, foundation degree or BSc degree in dental technology and apply for a technician post once you have successfully completed the course

- work as a trainee in a commercial laboratory or dental practice and study part-time for an approved qualification. Traineeships often take four to five years

- complete a relevant degree with at least a 2:1 classification and apply for a place on the graduate-entry NHS Scientist Training Programme (STP). If successful, you will be employed in a fixed-term, salaried training post and will study towards a masters degree qualification in Clinical Science (Maxillofacial Technology).

Whichever way you train, you will cover subjects such as dental anatomy, materials and basic lab techniques, complete and partial denture prosthetics, conservation and restoration, orthodontic appliances and dental bridge fabrication.

Requirements for Entry

Two or three A levels or equivalent are normally required for BSc degree entry; while one A level or equivalent is needed for direct entry to the Foundation Degree, which will normally take 2 years full-time or 3 years part-time.

For the BTEC diploma you will normally need four GCSE passes (9-4/A*-C) or equivalent, including English language, maths and a science.

Kind of Person

The work you would be involved in is highly skilled and you would need to be practical, with a high level of manual dexterity and some artistic flair. You would need a keen eye for detail, the ability to concentrate on what is often very precise work and sufficient scientific understanding to follow detailed technical instructions. You may work alone or as part of a team. Good eyesight with or without glasses and good colour vision are important.

Broad Outlook

There is a shortage of skilled dental technicians, which should mean that finding a job is relatively straightforward. Most of the 8,000 dental technicians in the UK work in commercial laboratories but there is also scope in the NHS, in individual dental practices or in the armed services. There may be opportunities to work abroad or to set up your own laboratory once you have the required experience.

Related Occupations

You might also consider: dental hygienist/therapist, dental nurse, dentist, medical/clinical technologist or orthotist/prosthetist.

Impact on Lifestyle

You would probably have a normal working week of 37 to 39 hours in the NHS, slightly longer in a commercial laboratory. If you specialise in maxillofacial work, you may expect to be called out at any time in cases of emergency.

You may have to be reasonably flexible about where you work, for many laboratories are concentrated in the larger population areas.

Earnings Potential

As a newly qualified dental technician in the NHS, you would be paid in Band 5 on a scale ranging from £22,128 to £28,746. Promotion to the specialist grade could take your earnings to £35,577 at the top of the scale, while a further appointment as an advanced dental technician could increase your salary to a maximum of £41,787. Additional allowances are paid for appointments in and around London, ranging from 20% of basic salary for Inner London, to 15% for Outer London and 5% for the London Fringe. Earnings in the private sector are generally likely to be higher, depending on where you live and the hours you are prepared to work.

Further Information

Dental Laboratories Association
http://dla.org.uk

Dental Technologists Association
www.dta-uk.org

General Dental Council
www.gdc-uk.org

Inspiring Dental Education and Advice
www.ideacareers.co.uk

Institute of Maxillofacial Prosthetists and Technologists
www.impt.co.uk

Health Careers
www.healthcareers.nhs.uk

Dental Council of Ireland
www.dentalcouncil.ie

Dentist

What is Involved?

As a dentist, you would be responsible for the dental health of a group of clients, examining, diagnosing and treating patients in line with your professional judgement. Your work would include fillings, removing teeth and fitting bridges or crowns. When necessary, you may refer patients for specialist treatment such as orthodontics.

Alternatively, you might choose to work in a hospital and specialise in a particular area such as oral surgery - which could include repairing damage to the jaw caused by accident or disease and also corrective surgery to repair birth defects. This could also include carrying out more complicated bridgework or surgery to gums that cannot be performed by a general dentist. Another area is orthodontics, which is concerned with straightening teeth. In hospital there is a hierarchy of dentists that works up to a consultant level as with doctors. The majority of dentists work in general practice, on their own or as part of a group. You could also work in the armed forces, as a company dentist in a large organisation or as a community dentist in a clinic. There is some scope for specialising in work with animals, including dogs, cats and horses.

Opportunities for Training

You would have to take a degree (BDS or BChD) before you could register with the General Dental Council and start to work as a dentist. This is a five-year course, which combines theoretical subjects such as anatomy, physiology and dental materials science with the practical and clinical skills needed to treat patients. In addition, you would need to learn about anaesthesia and radiology, how to design and fit dental aids as well as relevant aspects of dental law and ethics. Most dental students start practical work on patients in the second or third year of study, although some courses offer integrated courses with clinical work in the first year.

Requirements for Entry

Competition for places at dental schools is very fierce and you would have to offer three very good A level/Advanced Higher, five Higher or equivalent qualifications to get in. While some schools require three A level/Advanced Higher, Higher or equivalent qualifications to be in science subjects, the minimum is usually chemistry plus another science subject or maths. A few dental schools allow students without the right subjects to take a pre-dental year, although this would severely limit your choice of school. In addition to academic success, you should have a strong interest in the subject and should arrange some work experience with a dentist before you apply.

You may also have to take the UK Clinical Aptitude Test (UKCAT), which is used in the selection process by a consortium of medical and dental schools.

The test helps universities to make more informed choices from amongst the many highly-qualified applicants who apply for their medical and dental degree programmes.

Kind of Person

Dentists need to have good interpersonal skills, to be interested in, and able to communicate with, all types of people. Patients may be worried about the visit and it is important that the dentist is friendly and can help them to relax. All dentists need to be able to work as part of a team with a number of different people - dental nurses, receptionists, hygienists or other medical staff in hospital. Dentistry requires an interest in science, good eyesight and manual dexterity. Working in general practice also involves some business and marketing skills.

Broad Outlook

Most dentists choose to work as family general dental practitioners (GDPs). The first step is to undertake vocational training (VT), which is supervised training, working in an approved practice. Following satisfactory completion of the VT period, dentists usually enter an established practice as an associate, that is as a self-employed dentist, responsible for the treatment that they provide, but working in a practice owned by someone else. Later on, a dentist may often become a practice owner (principal), by becoming a partner, buying a practice or establishing a new practice. There is no formal GDP career structure, so you can further your knowledge at your own pace and follow the particular dental specialisms that are of interest to you.

An increasing number of dentists have in recent years been providing general dental care independently of the NHS. This may be under a private contract between dentist and patient where the dentist's fees are determined by things such as the time spent, materials used and the complexity of the procedure. Alternatively dentists may offer their patients treatment under dental insurance and capitation schemes.

Related Occupations

You might consider: doctor (general practice), doctor (hospital), biomedical scientist, pharmacist or pharmacologist. Look at: dental hygienist/therapist, dental technician/technologist or dental nurse if you want to specialise in oral care.

Impact on Lifestyle

In general practice, you could be quite flexible about the hours you work, although NHS dentists often have to offer emergency cover on a rota basis. Dentists in hospital may have to work unsocial hours and be prepared to be on call.

The work can be physically very tiring as it involves a lot of standing and bending of the spine.

Earnings Potential

Most GDPs are self-employed and earnings vary according to the services they provide. In the NHS, during your foundation year of work after leaving university, you would currently earn £31,696. After that, as a self-employed contractor working at least in part for the NHS, you could typically expect to earn between £60,000 and £120,000 depending on your working arrangements. Salaried dentists, who work mainly with community dental services, earn between £39,070 and £83,258. Consultants in dental specialities are paid on the same scales as other hospital consultants and earn between £76,001 and £102,465, dependent on length of service and payment of additional performance-related supplements.

Further Information

Inspiring Dental Education and Advice
www.ideacareers.co.uk

British Dental Association
www.bda.org

General Dental Council
www.gdc-uk.org

UK Clinical Aptitude Test
www.ukcat.ac.uk

Dental Council of Ireland
www.dentalcouncil.ie

Dietitian

What is Involved?

As a dietitian, you would need a fascination with food and health, together with the ability to translate medical advice and scientific findings about food into practical diets that people can understand. You may work as part of a healthcare team in a hospital or in the community, offering advice on a well-balanced diet to ensure healthy living. In a hospital or GP's clinic, you may be helping patients with problems such as difficulty in swallowing or checking that the meals provided are nutritionally balanced and appropriate for each individual. You may run clinics in outpatients departments for people who are overweight, people with eating disorders or those who have to live with diabetes, food allergies or other conditions. You might also be involved in health promotion activities or talking to groups such as pregnant women or those with young children.

In the food industry, you might provide specialist advice to manufacturers or trade associations. You would analyse food products and check information leaflets to ensure that the content is correct and nutritionally sound.

Opportunities for Training

You must have an approved degree or postgraduate qualification in dietetics or (human) nutrition and dietetics before you can start work as a state-registered dietitian. Your course must be approved by the Health and Care Professions Council.

Degree courses are generally full-time and take four years. All courses include practical training in a hospital or community setting. In addition to nutrition and dietetics, you would study physiology and biochemistry, medicine and pharmacology, psychology and social science, some microbiology and food science, with statistics and research methods to help with your final Honours project.

The two-year postgraduate courses are for students with a relevant first degree in a science subject.

Requirements for Entry

For entry to a dietetic degree, you would usually need five GCSEs (9-4/A*-C) or equivalent, including maths and English, plus three A levels or equivalent, including chemistry and at least one other science-related subject (which could include maths). Check with course providers for exact entry details because alternative qualifications, such as an Access to Science course, may also be accepted.

For an approved postgraduate course, you would usually need an honours degree in a life science subject (covering topics such as human physiology and biochemistry). Course providers will advise you further about the relevance of your first degree.

You may have an advantage if you have some paid or voluntary experience that demonstrates your interest in and understanding of this area of work.

Kind of Person

Your role as a dietitian would require tact and perseverance to convince people who are ill that, by changing their diet, they can reduce their symptoms and put themselves more in control of their illness.

You would need to be able to interpret scientific and medical information so that your patient can understand it. In order to give advice, you must be aware of how a person's personal circumstances can affect their lives and how your dietary recommendations might need to be adjusted to make them workable. You would have to accept your patients' lifestyles and religious or cultural beliefs without passing judgement.

Broad Outlook

With increased interest in healthy living and growing awareness of the importance of well balanced diets, the prospects for dietitians look extremely promising. Most jobs are currently to be found in the NHS but, if you want to do research, you'll need to look around and be prepared to move. Other opportunities include work in the food industry, in retail chains such as supermarkets, acting as a nutrition adviser, or in product development and marketing for food companies producing specialist dietary products.

Related Occupations

If your main interest is in food and nutrition, you might also consider: food scientist or technologist, nutritional therapist or hospitality/hotel manager and catering manager. If you want to work with people on health-related issues, you might prefer to explore alternative careers such as nurse, pharmacist, radiographer, speech and language therapist or occupational therapist.

Impact on Lifestyle

An NHS dietitian works a 37.5-hour week, which can include some weekend work or hours on call.

Your job may require you to work with vulnerable groups of people and, as a result, you would need to declare any criminal record. You would also need to complete a health declaration. Problems in either of these areas may not stop you from completing a university course but they may not allow you to become State Registered, which means that you would not be able to practise at the end of your course.

Earnings Potential

As a newly qualified dietitian in the NHS, you would be paid in Band 5 on a scale ranging from £22,128 to £28,746. Promotion to the specialist grade could take your earnings to £35,577 at the top of Band 6, while a further appointment to dietetic team manager could increase your salary to a maximum of £41,787. Additional allowances are paid for appointments in and around London, ranging from 20% of basic salary for Inner London, to 15% for Outer London and 5% for the London Fringe. Earnings in the private sector are generally likely to be higher, depending on where you live and the hours you are prepared to work.

Further Information

The Association of UK Dietitians
www.bda.uk.com

Health Careers
www.healthcareers.nhs.uk

Health and Care Professions Council
www.hcpc-uk.org

Irish Nutrition and Dietetic Institute
www.indi.ie

Diplomatic Service Officer

What is Involved?

As a member of the diplomatic service, you would be working for one of the major departments of the civil service. You would be primarily involved with representing British interests abroad and advising government ministers on aspects of foreign policy. The service is based in London, with high commissions in Commonwealth countries and embassies in other countries around the world, together with missions to international organisations such as the European Commission and United Nations. During the course of your career, you might work in several different areas of the service, including commercial, information, consular, immigration, political assessment and liaison and general administrative or managerial duties. You would normally spend much of your career working abroad, with tours of duty of two to four years.

Opportunities for Training

The first few years of your career in the service would normally be spent at the Foreign and Commonwealth Office in London, initially learning the broad outline of diplomatic work and then acquiring the knowledge and skills for the specialisation in which you are going to work. For some postings, full-time language training would be provided as part of a continuous programme of preparation for working in a particular country. All staff would have the opportunity to learn the local language before taking up an appointment.

As a graduate with at least a second class honours degree, you could compete for selection to the Fast Stream Development Programme.

Requirements for Entry

You must be a British citizen and have been resident in the UK (apart from temporary periods of travel, or study abroad) for at least two of the ten years preceding your application. Competition for places is intense and the majority of successful applicants are graduates with good honours degrees. In the past, arts graduates have predominated but science, business, economics and technological degrees are increasingly welcome.

It is not essential to speak a foreign language, but knowledge of certain 'hard' languages such as Arabic, Cantonese, Farsi, Japanese, Korean, Mandarin or Russian, or having a general aptitude for languages, can be useful.

Because of the security vetting procedures, the recruitment process may take up to nine months.

Kind of Person

Because of the nature of the work, you would be expected to have a keen interest in international issues and recognise Britain's unique role in world affairs. You should be a natural team player; confident, friendly, calm and reliable in your dealings with others, particularly with those you do not know. You should be keen to travel and prepared to visit and live in some of the less developed parts of the world. Much of your work would require a good organisational approach and the ability to work to precise and demanding standards as well as to think on your feet.

Broad Outlook

The traditional view of the civil service offering a job for life with good promotion prospects is much less true today than it might once have been. The diplomatic service could be said to have been less vulnerable to this change, with prospects remaining bright for those with the right qualities and attitudes. There may be opportunities to work in related government departments, such as the Department for International Development.

Regular appraisal of your work and detailed assessment of your performance would give you a clear picture of your progress and of the prospects for your future career development. A civil service reform plan was published in June 2012, setting out details of the skills, knowledge, behaviours and attitudes that civil servants will need in the years ahead.

Related Occupations

If you have the qualities demanded by the diplomatic service, with high levels of integrity and excellent communication and organisational skills, you could aspire to high level positions elsewhere in the civil service, in industry or in export/import organisations. You might also find a role in the media.

Impact on Lifestyle

The majority of your service would be in overseas locations and you would need to uproot your family, adjust to new climates and cultural systems, make new friends and leave others behind. You would need to be adaptable, to see changes as exciting challenges and to build up your contacts within and outside the service. If you have children, you would need to help them cope with an interrupted family life and adjust their education to your travels.

Earnings Potential

The average fast stream starting salary is between £25,000 and £27,000, rising after promotion, usually after four or five years, to around £45,000, and eventually climbing to around £51,000. These salary ranges apply to London-based posts because this is where you would begin your fast stream Diplomatic Service career.

When stationed abroad, you would be entitled to a range of payments on top of your basic salary to cover the local cost of living, in addition to rent-free accommodation, educational allowances for your children and various fare-paid allowances for travel to and from the UK. Your salary would compare very favourably with the main professions and would rise with promotion and the relative importance of your work.

Further Information

Civil Service Careers
www.gov.uk/government/organisations/civil-service/about/recruitment

Fast Stream Development Programme
www.faststream.gov.uk

Foreign and Commonwealth Office
www.gov.uk/government/organisations/foreign-commonwealth-office

eDiplomat
www.ediplomat.com

Dispensing Optician

What is Involved?

As a dispensing optician, you would supply and fit glasses and other optical aids but you would not be trained to carry out eye tests or treat disorders of the eyes. You would be qualified to interpret the prescriptions you are given by an optometrist or ophthalmic surgeon and then make an order for the glasses to be made up by a prescription house. You could also fit contact lenses after additional training.

You would most likely work in private practice in a high street retail outlet, ensuring that clients get the correct glasses or lenses for their needs and lifestyle. You would need to spend time with each patient, taking precise facial measurements and discussing with them the optimal balance between the prescription requirements and their own feelings about appearance, comfort and the conditions in which the glasses or contact lenses are to be used. You would also ensure that the final choice fits securely and matches the prescription.

Opportunities for Training

You must be registered with the General Optical Council (GOC) before you can work as a dispensing optician. In order to achieve this, you will need to complete a course approved by the GOC and pass the Professional Qualifying Examinations from the Association of British Dispensing Opticians (ABDO).

The GOC has approved three routes, which means you can qualify by taking one of the following:

- a two-year full-time diploma course, followed by one year working under supervision

- a three-year day release course (if you are in suitable employment)

- a three-year distance learning course, including a four-week residential block with ABDO (if you are in suitable employment)

Approved training programmes are offered by City, Anglia Ruskin and Glasgow Caledonian Universities, plus Bradford, City and Islington and ABDO Colleges.

If you want to develop your career once you are qualified and experienced, the University of Bradford offers a career progression course enabling you to graduate with a degree in optometry in approximately 12 months.

Requirements for Entry

You would need at least five GCSE/S Grade passes at 9-4/A*-C/1-3, to include English, maths or physics and another science-based subject. Certain course providers require two A level/Advanced Higher, three or four Higher or equivalent qualifications and some specify science subjects such as biology, physics, chemistry and/or maths. It is essential to check prospectuses before you apply.

Kind of Person

You must like people and you must be able to deal with them tactfully and confidently. In addition, you would be required to understand the information contained in prescriptions and to operate a number of scientific instruments. You would be to some extent selling frames and accessories, so you would need to know which styles are in fashion and which colours are available. A smart appearance, patience and a sense of humour would all be helpful.

Broad Outlook

As one of around 5,700 registered dispensing opticians in the UK, you are most likely to find a job in private practice, but you could also work in hospitals, in teaching, as a consultant to a lens manufacturer or as a representative selling ophthalmological instruments.

Your career prospects will vary depending on the sector you work in and the size of the business. With experience, you could progress to an assistant manager post or become self-employed, possibly working in partnership with optometrists.

Once you have qualified and gained some professional experience, you may go on to take further professional training to specialise in a particular area or to add to your portfolio of skills. The best-known advanced course is the Contact Lens Certificate, which qualifies you in the supply and fitting of contact lenses.

Registration with the GOC is recognised in many other countries, which means that working overseas could also be an option.

Related Occupations

You might be interested in other professions concerned with visual problems or disorders, such as optometrist or orthoptist. You might also consider therapeutic professions in the medical field, such as audiologist, occupational therapist, speech and language therapist or dietitian.

Impact on Lifestyle

Most dispensing opticians work a five-day week, but in a high street shop you would certainly find yourself working on Saturdays and possibly one or two evenings a week.

Earnings Potential

There is no set scale for dispensing optician salaries. Trainees working full-time can earn about £15,000 to £18,000. This should increase on registration to around £20,000 to £25,000 and can rise according to experience and responsibility to £28,000 to £36,000. Practice managers can earn up to £45,000. You may earn a salary much higher than this if you can establish a business as a self-employed dispensing optician.

Further Information

General Optical Council
www.optical.org

Federation of Ophthalmic and Dispensing Opticians
www.fodo.com

Association of British Dispensing Opticians
www.abdo.org.uk

Irish Association of Dispensing Opticians
www.iado.ie

Doctor (General Practice)

*W*hat is Involved?

As a doctor in general practice, usually known as a general practitioner or GP, you would be the first point of contact for most patients, providing a complete spectrum of medical care in the community, diagnosing and treating illness, disease and infection. You would need an extensive knowledge of medical conditions in order to assess a problem and decide on a course of action.

*O*pportunities for Training

All medical students in the UK must complete either an undergraduate course leading to a Bachelor of Medicine and Surgery, or a four-year graduate entry programme. Courses tend to fall into three different categories: *traditional, integrated* and *multi professional.* For the *traditional* courses, you would begin your training with two years of 'pre-clinical' work, involving study of the basic medical sciences. This is followed by the 'clinical' course, of approximately three years, during which you work in hospital wards under the supervision of consultants. *Integrated* courses, now offered by the majority of medical schools, combine the pre-clinical and clinical phases, meaning that you can expect to see patients right from the beginning of your training. The medical schools which focus on *multi-professional* learning organise their programme to ensure that students of two or more professions learn the same content side by side.

Most medical schools also offer students the opportunity to take an extra year (sometimes two) in the middle of their medical training to study a subject of interest, leading to a BSc honours degree. At some schools this intercalated degree is available only to high achievers, whereas at others it is built into the curriculum.

Two-year foundation schools (known as F1 and F2) then require you to demonstrate your abilities and competence against set standards and in a variety of settings. After the foundation years, you will have full registration with the General Medical Council (GMC) and will be eligible to apply for training in general practice. This stage takes around three years to complete, split between supervised training in a GP practice for 12 to 18 months and working in a hospital for 18 to 24 months.

Finally, you will be awarded a Certificate of Completion of Training, enabling you to join the Royal College of General Practitioners and the GMC GP Register, and to apply for an appropriate medical appointment.

*R*equirements for Entry

Individual medical schools set their own requirements, making it essential that you consult prospectuses and/or contact the schools directly to seek clarification where needed. The majority require A level or equivalent in chemistry, and some biology as well. If you do not have these subjects, it is possible to undertake an additional pre-medical year at some universities. This is essentially a preliminary course in chemistry, physics and biology.

In addition to exceptionally demanding academic entry standards, most schools have adopted the UK Clinical Aptitude Test (UKCAT) to help them select the best candidates. A much smaller group uses the Bio Medical Admissions Test (BMAT). Competition for places to read medicine is very intense.

*K*ind of Person

You must be dedicated and prepared for an enormous amount of hard work, absorbing vast amounts of technical information while developing highly tuned listening and communication skills. Practical ability and manual dexterity are also important. You would need to deal with a wide range of people, to be tolerant of their weaknesses, pain and fear and to help them when they are at their most vulnerable. At times you would need to show emotional resilience as you may be faced with making rational and objective decisions in difficult and distressing circumstances. Others must be able to trust you and depend on you to keep calm in a crisis.

Broad Outlook

Until fairly recently, it was common for a GP to join a practice and remain there until retirement. Nowadays there is a trend towards greater flexibility. While it is still possible to work towards a partnership in a practice, you might prefer to work as a salaried doctor or as a stand-in locum. This means you do not take on the same responsibilities and are not involved in such non-medical matters as the administration of the practice. You can also diversify your career development by pursuing an interest in a particular area, such as substance misuse, epilepsy, endoscopy, safeguarding children, palliative care or sexual health.

Related Occupations

You may be interested in other medical-based professions such as doctor (hospital), dentist, optometrist, physiotherapist, radiographer, pharmacist, pharmacologist, osteopath or nurse.

Impact on Lifestyle

The hours can be very long and anti-social, particularly in the early years. The training takes a long time, which means that you would be working hard for little financial reward for much longer than in many other careers. You need to be prepared for shift work and to have the determination to continue even when you are tired and over-worked. On the positive side, doctors are generally among the most valued, highly regarded and trusted members of any community.

Earnings Potential

In the most junior hospital trainee post (F1) the basic starting salary is £27,000. This increases in F2 to £30,000. For a doctor in specialist training the starting salary is £36,461 rising to £46,208. Many GPs are self-employed and hold contracts, either on their own or as part of a Clinical Commissioning Group (CCG). The profit they make will vary according to the services they provide for their patients and the way they choose to provide these services. Salaried GPs who are part of a CCG earn between £56,525 and £85,298 dependent on, among other factors, length of service and experience.

Further Information

British Medical Association
www.bma.org.uk
General Medical Council
www.gmc-uk.org
Biomedical Admissions Test
www.admissionstestingservice.org/for-test-takers/bmat/about-bmat
UK Clinical Aptitude Test
www.ukcat.ac.uk
Medical Specialty Training
http://specialtytraining.hee.nhs.uk
Royal College of General Practitioners
www.rcgp.org.uk
Royal Medical Benevolent Fund: The Doctors' Charity
www.rmbf.org
Irish Medical Organisation
www.imo.ie

Doctor (Hospital)

What is Involved?

As a hospital doctor you would examine, diagnose and treat patients referred by a general practice doctor or by another health professional. You may specialise in medicine (working in areas such as cardiology, dermatology, geriatrics, neurology ophthalmology or paediatrics); pathology (investigating the cause of disease and its effect on patients); psychiatry (working with patients experiencing mental health problems) or surgery (caring for patients before, during and after operations). Other specialisms include anaesthetics, obstetrics, gynaecology, radiology and oncology.

Opportunities for Training

All medical students in the UK must complete either an undergraduate course leading to a Bachelor of Medicine and Surgery, or a four-year graduate entry programme. Courses tend to fall into three different categories: *traditional*, *integrated* and *multi professional*. For the *traditional* courses, you would begin your training with two years of 'pre-clinical' work, involving study of the basic medical sciences. This is followed by the 'clinical' course, of approximately three years, during which you work in hospital wards under the supervision of consultants. *Integrated* courses, now offered by the majority of medical schools, combine the pre-clinical and clinical phases, meaning that you can expect to see patients right from the beginning of your training. The medical schools which focus on *multi-professional learning* organise their programme to ensure that students of two or more professions learn the same content side by side.

Most medical schools also offer students the opportunity to take an extra year (sometimes two) in the middle of their medical training to study a subject of interest, leading to a BSc honours degree. At some schools this intercalated degree is available only to high achievers, whereas at others it is built into the curriculum.

Two-year foundation schools (known as F1 and F2) then require you to demonstrate your abilities and competence against set standards and in a variety of settings. After the foundation years, you will have full registration with the General Medical Council (GMC) and will be eligible to apply for specialist training. The area of medicine you choose will determine the length of training required before you can become a senior doctor. In general surgery, for example, the training takes eight years.

Finally, you will be awarded a Certificate of Completion of Training, enabling you to join the GMC specialist register and to apply for an appropriate medical appointment.

Requirements for Entry

Individual medical schools set their own requirements, making it essential that you consult prospectuses and/or contact the schools directly to seek clarification where needed. The majority require A level or equivalent in chemistry, and some biology as well. If you do not have these subjects, it is possible to undertake an additional pre-medical year at some universities. This is essentially a preliminary course in chemistry, physics and biology.

In addition to exceptionally demanding academic entry standards, most schools have adopted the UK Clinical Aptitude Test (UKCAT) to help them select the best candidates. A much smaller group uses the Bio Medical Admissions Test (BMAT). Competition for places to read medicine is very intense. You would need to show that you have a genuine interest in the subject and if possible demonstrate relevant paid or voluntary work experience.

Kind of Person

You must be dedicated and prepared for an enormous amount of hard work, absorbing vast amounts of technical information while developing highly tuned listening and communication skills. Practical ability and manual dexterity are also important. You would need to deal with a wide range of people, to be tolerant of their weaknesses, pain and fear and to help them when they are at their most vulnerable. At times you would need to show emotional resilience as you may be faced with making rational and objective decisions in difficult and distressing circumstances. Others must be able to trust you and depend on you to keep calm in a crisis.

Broad Outlook

Many hospital doctors aspire to become a consultant, responsible for their own work and for supervising the work and training of all doctors in their team. Under the current training structure, you could become a consultant eight years after graduating, although most consultants train for longer than this, as extra experience and research is often advantageous for competitive posts. Progression through the different grades involves study and continuous professional development in the form of assessment and examinations. The number of jobs at all levels of service is determined by current and future service need.

Related Occupations

You may be interested in other medical-based professions such as doctor (general practice), dentist, optometrist, physiotherapist, radiographer, pharmacist, pharmacologist, osteopath or nurse.

Impact on Lifestyle

The hours can be very long and anti-social, particularly in the early years. The training takes a long time, which means that you would be working hard for little financial reward for much longer than in many other careers. You need to be prepared for shift work and to have the determination to continue even when you are tired and over-worked. On the positive side, doctors are generally among the most valued, highly regarded and trusted members of any community.

Earnings Potential

In the most junior hospital trainee post (F1) the basic starting salary is £27,000. This increases in F2 to £30,000. For a doctor in specialist training the basic starting salary is between £37,000 and £48,000. Some posts progress further to £52,000. Doctors in the specialty doctor grade earn a basic salary of between £37,547 and £70,018. Consultants can earn between £76,001 and £102,465, dependent on length of service.

Further Information

British Medical Association
www.bma.org.uk
General Medical Council
www.gmc-uk.org
Biomedical Admissions Test
www.admissionstestingservice.org/for-test-takers/bmat/about-bmat
UK Clinical Aptitude Test
www.ukcat.ac.uk
Medical Specialty Training
http://specialtytraining.hee.nhs.uk
Royal Medical Benevolent Fund: The Doctors' Charity
www.rmbf.org
Irish Medical Organisation
www.imo.ie

What is Involved?

As a dramatherapist, you would use improvisation, mime and other dramatic techniques to support people who are experiencing physical, psychological, psychiatric or social problems. You could be working with people of any age, including those with autistic tendencies, those with mental health problems, those living with HIV or AIDS, those in prison or children who have been abused. You would be applying your knowledge and experience of drama to promote healing, open up new experiences and improve the quality of life for each individual.

Opportunities for Training

You could become a dramatherapist either through an 18-month full-time or three-year part-time postgraduate course at one of five centres across the UK. The courses, based in Derby, London (Central School of Speech and Drama), London (Roehampton) and Cambridge (Anglia Ruskin), combine a strong practical element with theoretical and academic study.

All of the institutions offering the course approach it differently, although common components would normally include:

- Experience and competence in a broad range of drama and theatre skills, approaches and techniques including performance work
- Understanding and awareness of relevant psychological, psychotherapeutic and anthropological principles and practices
- Participation in an ongoing, experiential dramatherapy training group
- Knowledge of related therapies such as art, music, dance/movement and play
- Supervised dramatherapy practice
- Continuous assessment and written work
- Personal development/therapy

These courses lead to a qualification approved by the Health and Care Professions Council (HCPC), accredited by the British Association of Dramatherapists (BADth), and recognised by the Department of Health.

Only successful completion of courses with HCPC approval and BADth accreditation can lead to full membership of the British Association of Dramatherapists. To become a full BADth member, proof of registration with the HCPC is needed. Student membership is available whilst training.

The course providers sometimes offer short courses for prospective students.

Requirements for Entry

The entry criteria to any of the courses would normally include a first degree in drama or a psychological health-related subject or appropriate professional qualification/ degree, equivalent of one year's full-time experience working, paid or voluntarily, with people with specific needs (for example mental ill health, learning disabilities), experience of practical drama work and good interpersonal skills. Selection is usually by interview and audition, with applicants coming from all over the world.

Kind of Person

As a drama and movement therapist you would be working with a wide range of clients, some of whom could have very difficult and deep-seated problems. Respect for each individual would be vital. You would have to be strong - mentally, emotionally and physically - since you could be working in a variety of demanding environments. You would need to be totally committed to your work, able to enthuse your clients and talented enough to demonstrate dramatic techniques. Resilience would be another valuable quality, together with the ability to cope with both success and apparent failure.

Broad Outlook

There is no formal promotion pattern within dramatherapy and prospects will depend upon your personal drive and opportunities occurring within an employing institution. You could work as a dramatherapist in hospitals, schools, youth work, prisons, community centres and in private consultancy. You could work full-time or part-time. You might decide to specialise in one particular area of work or go on to train as a course leader. You may work on a freelance basis, building up your reputation through effective practice over a period of several years.

Related Occupations

Other occupations which might interest you could include: art therapist, music therapist, actor, occupational therapist, psychiatric nurse, psychotherapist, social worker, speech and language therapist or teacher.

Impact on Lifestyle

Given the very demanding nature of dramatherapy, you would have to be totally committed to your work. You would almost certainly be expected to work within a wide variety of work environments. You should be prepared to give up time in the evenings and at weekends for some sessions.

Earnings Potential

Payment would vary widely, according to the type of work and whether the sessions were with individuals or with groups. As a freelance dramatherapist, you might charge £190 to £350 per day. Detailed advice on a suitable fee structure can be obtained from the British Association of Dramatherapists. Within the NHS, you would normally start in Band 6, on a scale ranging from £26,565 to £35,577. This could rise to £41,787 at the top of Band 7. Additional allowances are paid for NHS appointments in and around London, ranging from 20% of basic salary for Inner London, to 15% for Outer London and 5% for the London Fringe.

Further Information

British Association of Dramatherapists
www.badth.org.uk

Dramatherapy Network
http://dramatherapy.net

Dramatherapy Ireland
www.dramatherapyireland.com

Economist

What is Involved?

As a professional economist, you could be one of a small group of advisers working for the government, a financial institution or a very large organisation. Alternatively, you might be part of a specialist consultancy. Your work would involve analysing information about what is happening in world financial and employment markets in order to identify significant trends or other points that might influence future policy or strategy. You might study, for example, the ways in which labour markets determine wages and unemployment, why some countries take a bigger share of the world market than others or the role of government in providing goods and services.

Your work might vary considerably according to the sector in which you are working but certain tasks would be similar in any employing organisation:

- You would research data from every relevant source and analyse it using mathematical, statistical and logical tools, particularly computer-based simulations

- You may focus on macro-economic issues - concerned with large economic units such as nation states - or micro-economic issues - concerned with the financial characteristics of firms, industries or households, and the way individual elements in an economy (such as consumers or commodities) behave. A typical macro-economic task might be to forecast the GDP (gross domestic product) of the USA in the coming year, whilst at the micro-economic level you could be concerned with predicting the demand for furniture in South East England over the next quarter

- You would produce a report based on your research and analysis.

Opportunities for Training

To work as a professional economist, you would need a good (first or upper second class) honours degree, usually in economics although a joint degree may be acceptable as long as economics forms the major part. You may find it useful or even essential to continue your studies with a postgraduate award before seeking employment. Similarly, you should consider joining a professional organisation such as the Society of Business Economists or the Royal Economic Society in order to receive their journals and attend their programme of events. The Government Economic Service (GES), the largest single employer of economists in the UK, recruits over 150 graduates each year through its fast stream programme. There is also a Diplomatic fast stream for economists with the Foreign and Commonwealth Office.

Requirements for Entry

To take an honours degree in economics you would need two or three A level/ Advanced Higher, four Higher or equivalent qualifications, usually including maths. You would also need a minimum of five GCSE/S Grade passes at 9-4/A*-C/1-3, including maths and English. A good honours degree would be essential for admission to a relevant postgraduate course.

Kind of Person

You would need to enjoy analysing data, to be comfortable with figures and able to communicate your findings to non-specialists. Logic and accuracy are also very important, as are advanced computing skills. You would need to work as part of a team, to meet deadlines for producing reports and to be quick thinking during meetings. As your role would usually be that of an adviser, you must be prepared to accept that your recommendations might not always be acted upon.

Broad Outlook

A degree in economics provides you with the ability to apply economic principles and models to a range of issues whilst understanding the wider driving forces shaping social policy. You could join the GES as an assistant economist, rising to economic adviser usually within four or five years, although public spending cuts mean a significant decrease in the number of GES vacancies at present. The Bank of England is another major employer, followed by other banks and financial institutions, large companies, consultancies and other organisations. With experience, you could progress to senior levels or choose to become a self-employed freelance consultant.

Related Occupations

You might also consider: accountant (professional), actuary, chartered/company secretary, civil service executive officer, civil service fast streamer, diplomatic service officer, financial adviser, investment analyst, operational researcher/management scientist, statistician or stockbroker.

Impact on Lifestyle

Economists are office based and tend to work regular office hours, although deadlines can mean evening and weekend work from time to time. You may be involved in travel abroad depending on your employer.

Earnings Potential

Salaries vary between employers and even between civil service departments but, as an example, the fast stream starting salary in London is between £25,000 and £27,000, rising in year three to £32,000. Pay increases after that are based on performance. If you're promoted, you may earn over £45,000 after four to five years. Successful senior economists can expect to earn around £60,000 to £80,000, although a few earn considerably more. Economists working in banking, financial services, industry and consulting sectors are usually better paid, with reported salaries up to £350,000 alongside good benefits packages.

Further Information

Royal Economic Society
www.res.org.uk
Society of Business Economists
www.sbe.co.uk
Government Economic Service
www.gov.uk/government/organisations/civil-service-government-economic-service
Why Study Economics
www.whystudyeconomics.ac.uk
Royal Statistical Society
www.rss.org.uk
Careers in Statistics
www.statslife.org.uk/careers
Bank of England
www.bankofengland.co.uk
Civil Service Fast Stream Development Programme
www.faststream.gov.uk
Irish Economy
www.irisheconomy.ie

Electrical Engineer

What is Involved?

As an electrical engineer, you would be largely concerned with generating and supplying electrical power, although you might branch into the closely related field of electronic engineering, where you would be more involved with designing and making machines that use electricity. Electrical engineers work mainly with large power applications, generating and harnessing electrical power. You could be researching more efficient power generation systems, developing alternative energy sources or planning the future development of the electricity supply network.

In the move away from burning fossil fuels to generate electricity, your work might involve designing an improved wind turbine, re-examining the advantages and disadvantages of nuclear reactors or exploring ways of harnessing the power of the oceans.

Opportunities for Training

There are a number of universities offering degrees in electrical engineering either as a single subject or in combination with electronic or manufacturing engineering, management, languages or other subjects. It is important to read prospectuses carefully and to ensure that your final choice is accredited by the Institution of Engineering and Technology. In order to become a chartered engineer, focusing on research, design, development and management, you would need to complete four years of academic study. Your degree should be an accredited four-year Master of Engineering (MEng) or three-year Bachelor of Engineering (BEng) qualification. You would have to follow the BEng with an extra year of specialised study, known as a matching section, in order to progress to chartered status. In either case, you could take a sandwich course, which would include a year working on an industrial placement. After graduating, you would need to complete a period of approved work experience in order to achieve chartered status. If you want to be more involved with the day-to-day management of production processes as an incorporated engineer, you could take the BEng route and follow it with a period of formal training.

Requirements for Entry

For degree entry, you would need at least two A level/Advanced Higher, three Higher or equivalent qualifications, usually including maths and physics, together with a broad platform of GCSE/S Grade passes at 9-4/A*-C/1-3. There are foundation courses available at some universities for students who do not have the required passes in maths and physics. The MEng route usually requires higher grades (or more UCAS points) than the BEng.

Kind of Person

Electrical engineers work in a rapidly developing environment and you would need to be creative, imaginative and prepared to keep up-to-date with changes in your field. You should have a logical and practical approach to solving complex scientific problems. A useful indicator at this stage could be how much you enjoy maths, design and technology and science (especially experiments with wires and batteries) at school. In addition to your scientific skills, you are likely to need good communication skills. You would probably be working as a member of a team and may need to communicate with a wide range of people, not all of whom would have your technical knowledge and skills. You may be involved in some form of cost management, so some awareness of financial or business management would be helpful.

Broad Outlook

The UK engineering and technology sector has undoubtedly been affected by the global recession that started in 2008, but companies driven by innovation and the creation of technological advantage are finding that prospects are rapidly improving. For example considerable growth is forecast in the three main clean technology sectors - solar photovoltaics, wind power and biofuels - as part of the urgent need to improve operational performance, productivity or efficiency while reducing costs, inputs, energy consumption, waste and pollution. Such issues, even in uncertain economic times, provide the prospect of positive career opportunities for electrical engineers.

Chartered engineer status is recognised throughout Europe and there are other chances to work all over the world.

Related Occupations

You might also consider: electronic/electronics engineer, civil engineer, mechanical engineer, manufacturing engineer, chemical/process engineer or aeronautical/ aerospace engineer, materials scientist/engineer, metallurgist, physicist, medical physicist, biotechnologist, geophysicist or computer engineer/scientist.

Impact on Lifestyle

You may be working set hours and a five-day week. However, you are also likely to work overtime and under some pressure when you have a tight deadline to meet. There might be occasions when you are rushing to solve a problem or finish a product ahead of a competitor. You may need to wear protective clothing in some environments. You could be required to travel for your job, both in the UK and overseas.

Earnings Potential

You could expect to earn around £24,000 to £30,000 straight after you graduate. Once you are chartered, your salary is likely to rise considerably and should range from £45,000 to £65,000. Average earnings for incorporated engineers are, according to the Engineering Council, around £45,500.

Further Information

Institution of Engineering and Technology
www.theiet.org

Engineering Council UK
www.engc.org.uk

Engineering Opportunities Online
www.engopps.com

Engineering UK
www.engineeringuk.com

Royal Academy of Engineering
www.raeng.org.uk

Semta: Engineering Skills for the Future
http://semta.org.uk

Engineers Ireland
www.engineersireland.ie

Electronic/Electronics Engineer

What is Involved?

As an electronic(s) engineer, you would be concerned with designing or making equipment that uses low power electric current. Your work would be likely to have a large impact on the way that people live their lives in the modern world, and could range from communications satellites through to the smallest smartphone or lightest tablet. As society demands ever more sophisticated technological development, you could be among the team of people exploring new possibilities in robotics, artificial intelligence and the information superhighway. There is considerable overlap with electrical engineering (see our separate article on this subject) or you might specialise in areas such as communications, computing, software, control, informatics or manufacturing.

Opportunities for Training

There are a number of universities offering degrees in electronic engineering either as a single subject or in combination with electrical or manufacturing engineering, management, languages or other subjects. It is important to read prospectuses carefully and to ensure that your final choice is accredited by the Institution of Engineering and Technology. In order to become a chartered engineer, focusing on research, design, development and management, you would need to complete four years of academic study. Your degree should be an accredited four-year Master of Engineering (MEng) or three-year Bachelor of Engineering (BEng) qualification. You would have to follow the BEng with an extra year of specialised study, known as a matching section, in order to progress to chartered status. In either case, you could take a sandwich course, which would include a year working on an industrial placement. After graduating, you would need to complete a period of approved work experience in order to achieve chartered status. If you want to be more involved with the day-to-day management of production processes as an incorporated engineer, you could take the BEng route and follow it with a period of formal training.

Requirements for Entry

For degree entry, you would need at least two A level/Advanced Higher, three Higher or equivalent qualifications, usually including maths and physics, together with a broad platform of GCSE/S Grade passes at 9-4/A*-C/1-3. There are foundation courses available at some universities for students who do not have the required passes in maths and physics. The MEng route usually requires higher grades (or more UCAS points) than the BEng.

Kind of Person

You would be working in an area of rapid change and advance and would need to keep up-to-date with the latest developments, and indeed to be one step ahead of the opposition. You are likely to be continually learning and solving problems in new and creative ways. You would need to have good analytic and logical skills to apply to problems. You should enjoy maths, physics and design and technology lessons at school, as these point towards the types of problems that you would be working on. In addition to your technological skills, you would also need to be able to work on a project as a member of a team. You would need good communication skills as you may be required to make presentations to people who do not share your technical knowledge. You could require a sound business sense, as you might be involved with feasibility studies to assess whether a project is worth starting or completing.

Broad Outlook

The UK engineering and technology sector has undoubtedly been affected by the global recession that started in 2008, but companies driven by innovation and the creation of technological advantage are finding that prospects are rapidly improving. In the next few years considerable growth is forecast in the three main clean technology sectors - solar photovoltaics, wind power and biofuels - as part of the urgent need to improve operational performance, productivity or efficiency while reducing costs, inputs, energy consumption, waste and pollution. Such issues, even in uncertain economic times, provide the prospect of positive career opportunities, while the medical technology, wireless, consumer and transport sectors also look very promising.

Related Occupations

You might also consider: electrical engineer, civil engineer, mechanical engineer, manufacturing engineer, chemical/process engineer, aeronautical/aerospace engineer, materials scientist/engineer, metallurgist, physicist, medical physicist, biotechnologist, geophysicist or computer engineer/scientist.

Impact on Lifestyle

Although you may have specified hours, you are likely to have occasions when you are working under considerable pressure to meet a tight deadline or to keep ahead of the opposition and this may require you to work overtime. In addition, you are likely to need to read a lot and to keep up to date with developments in this field. You may be required to travel to conferences or meetings in order to liaise with other specialists or to advise or solve the problems of clients.

Earnings Potential

Salaries vary from company to company, with some sectors attracting higher salaries due to demand. Your starting salary as a newly graduated electronic engineer is likely to be in the range £24,000 to £30,000. With qualifications and experience, this should rise to between £45,000 and £65,000. As a highly experienced electronic engineer, you could earn in excess of £75,000 per annum. Average earnings for incorporated engineers are, according to the Engineering Council, around £43,300.

Further Information

Institution of Engineering and Technology
www.theiet.org

Engineering Council UK
www.engc.org.uk

Engineering Opportunities Online
www.engopps.com

Engineering UK
www.engineeringuk.com

Royal Academy of Engineering
www.raeng.org.uk

Semta: Engineering Opportunities for the Future
http://semta.org.uk

Engineers Ireland
www.engineersireland.ie

Environmental Health Practitioner

What is Involved?

As an environmental health practitioner, your job could include ensuring that the food we eat is safe and of good quality, improving housing conditions, safeguarding standards of workplace health and safety, or creating a better environment. You can choose to be a generalist or to specialise in a particular area. You might be employed by a major supermarket chain to manage food safety and hygiene, by a housing association to advise on housing standards, or by a local authority to deal with noise nuisance or environmental pollution. In the public sector, you would be empowered to make unannounced visits to such places as shops, factories and offices, leisure facilities, abattoirs, restaurants and hospitals; you could issue warnings, give advice on how to correct problems or even serve notices of closure if you were to find a situation which contravened the law.

Opportunities for Training

You would need to complete a first degree or postgraduate course accredited by the Chartered Institute of Environmental Health (CIEH). There are currently several universities offering accredited courses, on a full- or part-time basis.

Many of these courses include the statutory practical work experience necessary for qualification, but it would be possible for you to do your work experience after graduation. You would need to register with the Environmental Health Registration Board (EHRB) and pass the professional exams set by the CIEH in order to obtain your Certificate of Registration.

Once qualified, you will need to keep up to date with new developments throughout your career. The CIEH offers a range of short courses and workshops to help your professional development. After five years of professional practice, you can apply to the CIEH for Chartered Environmental Health Practitioner status.

The training is similar in Scotland but you would register with the Royal Environmental Health Institute of Scotland.

Although they may vary slightly, all accredited courses cover essentially the same ground, including the five key areas of environmental health - food safety, housing, environmental protection, occupational health and public health. Just as important is the emphasis placed on developing your skills in general management, communication, negotiating, analysis and evaluation. You'll learn how to intervene and how to go about ensuring legal compliance.

Requirements for Entry

The minimum entry requirements for an undergraduate degree course in environmental health or science (BSc) would be 64 UCAS points with science at AS/A2 or equivalent, or 80 UCAS points without science. The course would last three or four years. Alternatively, you could qualify for entry to a two-year postgraduate course in environmental health (MSc) after completing a first degree in a relevant science subject.

Kind of Person

A concern for the environment and for the welfare of your fellow citizens would be very important. You would need excellent communication skills, balancing sympathetic understanding with the need to explain your findings and decisions clearly and firmly, since you would be talking to people of widely differing backgrounds, sometimes in difficult situations. You would also have to be able to express yourself very clearly in your written reports. You might not always be welcome (or at least your findings might not be), so you would need to be resilient, scrupulously fair, and willing to back your judgement. You should be able to assimilate and understand a large amount of scientific, technical and legal detail and, while you would be working on your own quite a lot, you should also be a willing member of a team.

Broad Outlook

A clearly defined promotion structure within local government leads to senior, principal and chief officer posts in environmental health. It may be necessary to move to other authorities to gain more experience, breadth of work and promotion. There are increasing opportunities for experienced environmental health practitioners to diversify into other fields in central government, consultancies and the private sector.

Related Occupations

You might also consider: food scientist or technologist, forensic scientist, health and safety inspector and trading standards officer.

Impact on Lifestyle

You would normally work a standard five-day week, but you should be prepared to put in extra hours in the evening or at weekends in an emergency. The work would involve a good deal of travelling and you might well have to move to another area of the country for promotion. Some of the places you would have to visit might be unpleasant, such as abattoirs, and you might encounter some hostility, so you would have to be mentally and physically tough. It is not a job for those of a squeamish disposition.

Earnings Potential

A newly qualified environmental health practitioner could expect to earn around £25,000 to £35,000. With experience and promotion, you could earn around £70,000 as a director of public health. Pay scales in the private sector would be generally higher, particularly if you reached managerial status. Despite the present economic situation, there is still a national shortage of environmental health practitioners and demand for qualified individuals remains high.

Further Information

Chartered Institute of Environmental Health
www.cieh.org

Environmental Health Registration Board
www.ehrb.co.uk

Royal Environmental Health Institute of Scotland
www.rehis.com

Environmental Health Careers
www.ehn-jobs.com

Environmental Health Association of Ireland
www.ehai.ie

Estate Agent

What is Involved?

As an estate agent, you would specialise in the buying and selling of property, including house, commercial, industrial and land sales. You would normally act for the seller (vendor), taking a percentage of the selling price as commission when you have completed a successful sale. You might also deal with the letting and management of properties. As an agent involved with buying and selling houses, you would be known as a negotiator. In this capacity, you would visit the client's house, advise on a suitable selling price and then try to find a suitable buyer by marketing the property and contacting your database of potential buyers. If a buyer is not willing to pay the full purchase price, you would negotiate with both sides to reach an acceptable agreement. Often more than one prospective buyer could become involved and you would have to negotiate on your client's behalf.

Opportunities for Training

Much training is in-house and on-the-job. You may be able to work towards qualifications awarded by the National Federation of Property Professionals (NFOPP), a body brought about by the recent merger of the National Association of Estate Agents (NAEA) with the National Association of Valuers and Auctioneers, the Association of Residential Letting Agents, and the Institution of Commercial and Business Agents.

The NFOPP Technical Award in Sale of Residential Property is a nationally recognised level 3 qualification, which shows that you have the knowledge to undertake your job successfully. You can progress to the level 4 Certificate in the Sale of Residential Property, which will meet the qualification criteria to apply for Fellow Membership of the NAEA.

Some estate agents are qualified chartered surveyors. In order to qualify, you would need to complete a degree or diploma accredited by the Royal Institute of Chartered Surveyors (RICS). It is also possible to take a degree course in a relevant subject, such as estate management or building and land surveying and valuation.

Another option might be to begin your career as an estate agent through a property services apprenticeship. Check the website to find relevant apprenticeships in your home area.

Requirements for Entry

There are no specific qualification requirements to become an estate agent, although you would normally need three A level/Advanced Higher, four Higher or equivalent qualifications for admission to a RICS-approved degree course.

Whilst academic qualifications are always helpful and applicable, personal qualities and abilities are the most important aspect. Increasing legislation means that estate agents require a good knowledge of relevant law and it can help to be able to show clients or potential employers that you are a professional with a good knowledge of the business.

Kind of Person

You would have to like meeting all sorts of people and be good at negotiating and communicating. Buying or selling a house is often the single most important financial transaction that people make. The housing market is complicated, often involving 'chains' of buyers and sellers, deals often fall through and as a consequence feelings can run high. You would need to be a tactful and sympathetic person to cope with this. You would also need to be a good salesperson.

Broad Outlook

The housing market has had an extremely difficult time after the recession that started in 2008, with a massive drop in sales, widespread redundancies, falling house prices and potential buyers finding great difficulty in securing mortgage finance. Over the past four years the market has been extremely buoyant, however, and it has staged a remarkable recovery. If you pursue a career in estate agency, you must accept that this is a field that fluctuates and that your prospects and your pay will tend to rise or fall in relation to the volume of sales you generate.

Related Occupations

You might also consider: building surveyor, surveyor (general practice), rural practice surveyor, property developer, auctioneer/valuer or estate manager/land agent.

Impact on Lifestyle

You would probably be expected to work during some evenings and on Saturdays at weekends. You would be out of the office a great deal, going to see clients and showing them around houses, other property or land. The workload tends, however, to be seasonal and to fluctuate.

Earnings Potential

This can be up to you. Starting pay is usually around £17,000 to £20,000 but you would often receive commission, so the more houses you sell the more you would make. At senior level, salaries range from £25,000 to £60,000 plus. Working hard, networking and getting your name and face known would all be important here. You would be dealing closely with solicitors, banks and other lending organisations and it would be to your advantage to build up personal contacts. If you progress to become a partner, you could earn significantly more depending on the success of the agency and the state of the economy at the time.

Further Information

NAEA/Propertymark (National Association of Estate Agents)
www.naea.co.uk

Royal Institution of Chartered Surveyors
www.rics.org

Propertymark (National Federation of Property Professionals)
www.propertymark.co.uk

Property Services Apprenticeships
www.gov.uk/guidance/property-services-apprenticeships

Society of Chartered Surveyors Ireland
www.scsi.ie

Events Manager

What is Involved?

In the ever more competitive world of business and commerce, events, conferences and corporate hospitality days are being used to promote and increase awareness of products, stimulate customer loyalty and reward staff. As an events or conference manager, you would be in charge of the overall organisation of an event, including the venue, the catering, the staffing and the reception arrangements. You might be employed by a large organisation or company, or by a particular venue, or by a specialist company brought in to do the job. Your work could involve a good deal of travel and would certainly mean that you had contact with a wide variety of people, both clients and your own staff. You would discuss and agree what the organisation wanted and what size budget would be at your disposal.

You would need to be aware of all the facilities required to ensure that delegates gain the maximum benefit from each event under your control.

Opportunities for Training

There is no single route into events or conference management but many entrants would have experience of working in hotels or restaurants, or perhaps in a managerial position in such areas as personnel (human resources), leisure, marketing or tourism. You could also work your way up through the ranks. Training would usually be carried out on-the-job. The Association of Conferences and Events runs short courses and can provide lists of companies and venues, together with other useful information.

Requirements for Entry

While there are no particular educational qualifications required, increasing numbers of graduates are being employed. Almost any subject would be acceptable, although you might give particular consideration to courses in hospitality management or leisure and tourism, or to others including elements of business studies, marketing or modern languages.

For entry to a degree course, you would normally need a minimum of two A level/ Advanced Higher, three Higher or equivalent qualifications, together with five GCSE/S Grade passes at 9-4/A*-C/1-3, or equivalent. Courses usually last three or four years and many would be described as 'sandwich courses', which means that they incorporate periods of industrial experience. There are also Foundation degree Award (FdA) and Higher National Diploma (HND) courses, which are usually a year shorter than corresponding degrees. For FdA/HND entry, you would need one or two A level/ Advanced Higher, two or three Higher or equivalent qualifications, together with five GCSE/S Grade passes 9-4/A*-C/1-3.

You could gain useful experience by organising events and activities in your personal or social life. Paid or unpaid work as a steward at large events or exhibitions can also be a good way of building contacts in the industry.

Kind of Person

You would need excellent communication skills to deal with a wide variety of people. The ability to persuade others to your point of view would be particularly valuable. A good head for business and an understanding of how particular companies work would stand you in good stead. You would need to be tough, both mentally and physically, as the work would probably involve you in long hours, weekend and evening work. You would need to be a good organiser, concerned with getting all the details right while juggling several priorities at any time. You would be on show, so a smart appearance would be important.

Broad Outlook

Events and conference management is being seen more and more within the hospitality industry as an important tool for commercial and business success. It is, however, very much at the mercy of the national economic climate. Competition for the top jobs is intense but the rewards can be substantial. As a successful manager, you could progress to setting up your own company or go on to a senior managerial position.

Related Occupations

You might also consider: advertising account executive, hospitality/hotel manager, catering manager, leisure services/fitness centre manager, market researcher, marketing executive or public relations executive.

Impact on Lifestyle

You would have to be prepared to work long hours, at the weekends and in the evenings, sometimes in order to meet deadlines and sometimes to conduct actual events or conferences. There would almost certainly be quite a lot of travel involved.

Earnings Potential

There is a considerable range in earnings, since the type of work involved varies so widely. As a graduate trainee, you might expect to start on a salary of around £18,000 to £25,000, increasing to £27,000 to £45,000 once you gain experience and can demonstrate success. At a more senior level, you might earn £50,000 to £80,000 per annum. You may receive additional income through commission payments. *Event* magazine conducts a regular salary survey (which recently found, for example, that 12% of those polled earned more than £70,000) and also profiles a number of existing events managers as part of its student hub.

Further Information

Association of Conferences and Events
www.ace-international.co.uk

Event magazine
www.eventmagazine.co.uk

Hospitality Guild
www.hospitalityguild.co.uk

Association of British Professional Conference Organisers
www.abpco.org

Business Visits and Events Partnership
www.businessvisitsandeventspartnership.com

Event and Visual Communication Association
www.evcom.org.uk

Association of Event Organisers
www.aeo.org.uk

Fáilte Ireland
www.failteireland.ie

Facilities Manager

What is Involved?

As a facilities manager, sometimes known as a business services, support services or contracts manager, you would make sure that buildings and the facilities within them meet the needs of the people who work there. You might work in the public or private sector, with a range of duties that would normally include responsibility for:

- general upkeep and maintenance
- refurbishment, renovation and office moves
- health and safety standards and other legal requirements
- energy efficiency
- catering, cleaning, parking and waste disposal
- budgets and records of payments
- contracts with suppliers
- security
- office equipment and IT systems

You might work for a facilities management company contracted to manage facilities for a number of organisations. On the other hand, you might have a facilities management brief within a single organisation.

Opportunities for Training

The British Institute of Facilities Management (BIFM) offers qualifications ranging from levels two, three and four up to postgraduate level seven. These offer a career development path from entry level through to senior consultancy.

The level five qualification, for example, is aimed at those who deal with specialised and complex functions at middle or senior management level, while level six is aimed at facilities managers with high levels of responsibility who wish to develop their strategic skills.

If you have an undergraduate or postgraduate degree accredited by the Royal Institution of Chartered Surveyors (RICS), you can become a chartered surveyor within the Facilities Management Faculty. To do so you must successfully complete the Assessment of Professional Competence offered by RICS, a structured training programme lasting around two years.

Alternatively, you may be able to start training via an Apprenticeship programme.

Requirements for Entry

You would normally need a combination of relevant experience and qualifications. This might include technical skills related to buildings and property, in addition to broad management experience. For example, you might combine a knowledge of building services engineering or IT installation with management experience gained in hospitality, security or the armed forces.

There are no absolute requirements for entry but you might find it useful to offer a foundation degree, HND or degree in facilities management, a related qualification in construction, engineering, management or business studies, or a professional qualification in, say, surveying, accountancy or estate management.

Kind of Person

You would need to be able to develop good working relationships with a wide range of people. You should have good organisational, problem solving and decision making ability, together with excellent spoken and written communication skills. The ability to manage a varied and complex workload is equally important, allied to technical knowledge of building services, IT skills, strong numeracy and the ability to understand financial data and control a large budget.

Broad Outlook

Skills shortages in facilities management mean that prospects look good for practitioners who can develop innovative ways of reducing costs while keeping staff motivated. You may start as an assistant manager focused on a single operation, such as catering, cleaning or maintenance, before progressing to managing a department and subsequently taking charge of all operations. It is also possible to specialise in consultancy and some facilities managers go on to set up their own consultancy business. You may need to move in order to gain experience in a variety of operations and to develop your career.

Sustainability is currently an important topic in facilities management, as organisations seek to promote a positive image in terms of environmental and ethical policies.

Related Occupations

Depending on your specific interests, you might also consider: building services engineer, building surveyor, catering manager, health service manager, housing manager or surveyor (general practice).

Impact on Lifestyle

Working hours are generally 40 per week, although longer hours may sometimes be required to meet project deadlines or to cover emergencies. Some roles may require shift work in order to cover 24-hour operations. Meetings and visits may sometimes necessitate out-of-hours working.

Earnings Potential

According to the most recent salary survey on the BIFM website, some 42% of facilities managers polled earn between £61,000 and £75,000 a year. A quarter of consultants earn £91,000 a year or more.

Entry-level roles are more likely to start at around £20,000 to £26,000.

Further Information

British Institute of Facilities Management
www.bifm.org.uk

Royal Institution of Chartered Surveyors
www.rics.org

Apprenticeships
www.getingofar.gov.uk

BIFM Ireland
http://bifmireland.org.uk

Farm Manager

What is Involved?

As a farm manager, you would oversee the running of a farm as an efficient and profitable business. You might work for the owner of a large estate or for a big commercial organisation and the exact nature of your work would depend on the size of the business and the type of farming involved. Broadly speaking, you would be likely to work in one of three areas:

- An arable enterprise would see you producing crops such as wheat, potatoes, sugar beet, linseed, flax, lavender or turf. You might choose to specialise in the rapidly expanding business of organic production, avoiding the use of artificial fertilisers and pesticides on your land
- The livestock sector would involve you in the production of pigs, beef, dairy cattle, sheep and poultry or, more rarely, deer and ostrich. Here you would have the opportunity to work with animals both outdoors and indoors and to plan breeding programmes
- A mixed farm would offer you a combination of both arable and livestock elements

While your work may involve you being outside in all weathers, you would spend at least some of your time in an office, planning ahead, dealing with staffing issues, keeping records and managing the accounts. You would be responsible for the financial success of the farm, making sure that whatever you produce arrives at the right market at the right time and sells for the best possible price.

Opportunities for Training

You would normally have a degree or foundation degree in agriculture or agricultural business management from university or agricultural college, or a vocational qualification at level 4, together with considerable relevant experience. Courses usually last three or four years and course content varies enormously, often being specifically geared to arable or livestock farming as outlined above.

You may be able to get started as an assistant farm manager through an advanced level Apprenticeship scheme.

Requirements for Entry

At least two A level/Advanced Higher, three Higher or equivalent qualifications are required for entry to degree courses. Chemistry is often specified; biology and geography are regularly mentioned. For foundation degrees, the entry level is usually slightly lower. Check with individual course providers for exact details. You would need considerable work experience and you would find it difficult to survive without a driving licence.

Kind of Person

In the rapidly changing world of modern agriculture, you may find that business management and IT skills are even more important than a thorough grounding in farmyard skills and a love of the countryside. Farming can be highly unpredictable as weather conditions change, crops lose their market value or animals become sick. As a manager, you would need to be adaptable, unflappable and able to rearrange plans at very short notice. Good communication skills would be essential for working with staff, advisers, suppliers and customers.

Broad Outlook

Farming has been going through difficult times in recent years and this could affect the number of managerial jobs available. As they diversify into less traditional activities to 'add value' and increase profitability, farm businesses will be looking to use traditional resources, such as land, labour, buildings and equipment, for uses over and above livestock, milk and crop production. You could improve your overall prospects by trying to apply innovative thinking to the process of moving away from intensive production towards such areas as leisure pursuits, organic farming and conservation.

Related Occupations

You may wish to consider: agricultural adviser/consultant, agricultural biologist, agricultural chemist, agricultural inspector, agricultural/land-based engineer, animal nutritionist, horticultural manager, landscape architect, estate manager/land agent, forest/woodland manager, countryside ranger/warden, rural practice surveyor, soil scientist or fish farmer. You could move into other commercial aspects of agriculture, such as technical sales or contracting. With the increase of tourism in the countryside, you could specialise in the management of tourist facilities.

Impact on Lifestyle

Many people view agriculture as an industry that offers long hours for poor reward. You should find in reality that, while there are rarely any set hours and you are expected to vary your workload according to the changing demands of the seasons, farming is becoming increasingly 'market aware', calling for flexible, innovative and enthusiastic people who are well rewarded for their commitment. Running a farm tends to become a way of life and early mornings, late evenings and weekend commitments can often be part of the lifestyle.

Earnings Potential

There is no official salary scale for farm managers. An assistant or trainee farm manager can expect to start on around £22,000. This should rise fairly quickly to around £28,000. As an experienced farm manager, you might earn in the region of £60,000. Senior posts, including those in a consultancy or advisory role, can pay in excess of £70,000. You could have a car and a house on the farm as part of your employment package and you may even be able to participate in a profit-sharing scheme.

Further Information

Land-based and Environmental Careers
www.lantra.co.uk/careers

Apprenticeships
www.getingofar.gov.uk

Department for Environment, Food and Rural Affairs
www.gov.uk/government/organisations/department-for-environment-food-rural-affairs

Institute of Agricultural Management
www.iagrm.org.uk

Innovation for Agriculture
www.innovationforagriculture.org.uk

Land Based Colleges Aspiring to Excellence
www.landex.org.uk

Farmers Weekly magazine
www.fwi.co.uk

Irish Farmers' Association
www.ifa.ie

Fashion Designer

What is Involved?

As a fashion designer, you would work with others in designing and making clothes and accessories. There are three areas of fashion design: 'haute couture', 'designer ready-to-wear' and 'high street fashions'. Haute couture is the top end of the market, where individually designed clothes are made for exclusive clients. The fashion houses involved - Armani, Dior, Calvin Klein, Chloe, for example - all display their latest collections at glitzy shows and it is often these designs that influence what the rest of us wear over the next season. Designer ready-to-wear clothes are produced by the haute couture fashion houses and are emblazoned with their all-important designer label or logo. These are usually limited runs of the design, sold in specialist boutiques. Most fashion garments are sold in high street stores, including French Connection, Marks and Spencer, Debenhams and TopShop. Fashion is one of the largest industries in the UK, employing more than 555,000 people and contributing significantly to British exports.

You could work in the dominant womenswear market or you could choose to focus on the growing menswear and childrenswear segments. Other possible areas include accessory design, millinery, shoe and sportswear design or you could even specialise in costume design for film, TV and theatre work.

Opportunities for Training

With over 250 fashion degrees and higher national diplomas (HNDs) currently available in the UK, you would need to research training courses carefully before making a final choice. A good starting point could be a one- or two-year foundation course in art and design, allowing you time after school to explore a range of options in creative design and to develop a suitable portfolio of your work. Courses should take you through all the stages from an initial design idea to a prototype garment. You may find it useful to work through the list of universities and colleges who are members of the British Fashion Council. The Council recognises these institutions as offering high quality training in fashion. Their courses represent the total breadth of fashion courses, from womenswear and menswear to knitwear and lingerie, sportswear and accessories.

You may find an on-the-job training place with a design studio but you would need to be sure that you would focus on design rather than on manufacturing garments.

Requirements for Entry

Most institutions offering degree and HND courses require five GCSE/S Grade passes at 9-4/A*-C/1-3 or equivalent, preferably with maths and English, together with relevant AS/A level/Advanced Higher/Higher or equivalent qualifications including an art-related subject, and/or the completion of an art foundation course. You must be able to present a portfolio of work, with evidence of good drawing skills and a lively interest in fashion. Work experience is important and it would be helpful to demonstrate that you have made up a garment, taken photographs or assembled your own fashion scrapbook.

Kind of Person

You would need a real passion for fashion, with a love of clothes, textiles, colour, texture and pattern. Good drawing skills would be essential, together with the ability to communicate your ideas to buyers or manufacturers and the practical ability to make up sample garments. You would need to work as part of a team, to be able to use fashion-specific IT packages and to have some knowledge of the business constraints of budgeting and costing. For haute couture, in particular, you would need to be exceptionally creative and determined to succeed.

Broad Outlook

Competition in fashion design is intense and success can be as dependent on getting a lucky break as on having talent, drive and irrepressible determination. You may want to gain experience by working in the UK or abroad, possibly for low pay in a very junior position, in the fashion centres of London, Paris, Milan and New York. The majority of actual jobs in the UK are at the high street end of the market and may be somewhat removed from the glamour associated with star names. If your ultimate career aim is to set up and run your own label, you will find it useful to develop such skills as pattern cutting, textile technology, production management and studio management.

Related Occupations

You may wish to consider other *design* areas such as: footwear designer, textile designer, interior designer, industrial or product designer, jewellery designer or graphic designer. Alternatively, you might wish to consider other fashion options such as: retail merchandiser, photographer, fashion buyer or journalist.

Impact on Lifestyle

Fashion design could well become dominant in your life as you work through the night to meet deadlines for fashion shows and rearrange holidays to fit work schedules. Inspiration can come at any time and you would need to capture ideas before they disappear again.

Earnings Potential

You could expect to start on about £18,000 to £23,000 a year, probably based in London. Depending on your talent and opportunities, you could be earning in the region of £45,000 to £85,000 after ten years and, if you become a top design director, you might earn £100,000 or more.

You may choose to work on a freelance basis, in which case your earnings would depend totally on how hard you work and how successful you are in selling your designs.

Further Information

British Fashion Council
www.britishfashioncouncil.com

Creative Skillset
http://creativeskillset.org/creative_industries/fashion_and_textiles

Chartered Society of Designers
www.csd.org.uk

Apparel Search
www.apparelsearch.com

UK Fashion and Textile Association
www.ukft.org

Style Bible
www.stylebible.com

Not Just a Label
www.notjustalabel.com

Financial Adviser

What is Involved?

As a financial adviser, you would help individual clients choose financial products and services. These might be investments, savings or pensions, possibly linked with mortgages and insurance. You would take a comprehensive view of each client's financial situation, exploring their short-, medium- and long-term goals as well as a wide range of possible financial needs.

A key element of the work is to build a relationship based on trust, so that clients feel confident in your ability to help them make plans for their future and decide how to make the best use of their money.

You could work in one of two ways: as an *independent* financial adviser (IFA), you would consider all retail investment products or providers available to meet each client's needs, providing unbiased and unrestricted advice; as a *restricted* adviser you would focus on a limited range of products or on products from one or a limited number of providers.

You must make clear from the outset whether you offer independent or restricted advice, and you would need to follow strict financial industry rules and guidelines, designed to make sure that you act fairly and that you are properly qualified.

Opportunities for Training

You must undertake industry-recognised training that meets regulatory standards set by the Financial Conduct Authority. For work related to the retail investment market, this means at least a Level 4 approved qualification, such as the:

- Diploma in Regulated Financial Planning from the Chartered Insurance Institute
- Diploma in Investment Planning from the Chartered Banker Institute
- Diploma for Financial Advisers from ifs University College
- Investment Advice Diploma from the Chartered Institute for Securities and Investment

Most employers provide training and pay for exams, but you would usually be expected to study outside working hours, with many courses offering distance learning opportunities.

There is also a Level 4 Higher Apprenticeship in Providing Financial Advice (England and Wales only), a degree in Financial Services, Planning and Management at Manchester Metropolitan University, and a degree in Banking Practice and Management with ifs University College.

Requirements for Entry

While there are no formal academic entry requirements, the most prestigious employers would require a degree or at least A level/Advanced Higher, Higher or equivalent qualifications, together with evidence of numeracy. Many people starting as financial advisers are graduates in business studies, accountancy or similar subjects, although this is not an essential requirement. Some people become financial advisers after gaining experience in clerical positions, although this could take some time because of the level of maturity expected by clients.

Kind of Person

This is a job for a 'people' person. You would have to be good at communicating - both listening carefully to your clients' requirements and being able to explain your proposed solutions to their financial needs. You would meet all sorts of people and you would need to inspire confidence in them. You would need to be numerate and have an understanding of financial products and the legal or taxation implications of making certain investment decisions. Good IT skills are essential. Honesty is vital, both in terms of explaining the extent of your independence and of treating personal information confidentially. You would normally be expected to dress smartly and conventionally for this type of work.

Broad Outlook

Financial advice is an area undergoing rapid change. The sector has had some bad publicity in recent years but its image has changed with tighter regulation, greater transparency and the introduction of compulsory training.

You might work for an independent financial advice company, a financial planning firm, a broker, a larger investment firm, insurance provider or bank, a specialist pension consultancy, or as a self-employed adviser. Opportunities are nationwide. Because of the regulatory aspects of financial advice, most jobs are UK-based, serving UK consumers.

Related Occupations

You may consider: accountant (professional), banking executive, insurance broker, insurance underwriter, paraplanner, stockbroker, tax adviser, investment fund manager or investment analyst.

Impact on Lifestyle

Generally financial advisers are office based, working normal office hours. However, you might be expected to visit clients in their homes and this could involve having to see them in the evening or at weekends.

Earnings Potential

There are no set salary levels and earnings can vary considerably. As a graduate, you might expect to earn around £22,000 to £30,000 in your first year and considerably more later if you exceed your targets. You could achieve very high earnings as an experienced and successful independent adviser.

Further Information

Personal Finance Society
www.thepfs.org
Association of Professional Financial Advisers
www.apfa.net
Institute of Financial Planning
www.financialplanning.org.uk
Chartered Banker Institute
www.charteredbanker.com
Chartered Insurance Institute
www.cii.co.uk
The London Institute of Banking & Finance
www.libf.ac.uk
Chartered Institute for Securities and Investment
www.cisi.org
Chartered Financial Analyst Society of the UK
www.cfauk.org
Institute of Bankers in Ireland
www.iob.ie

Firefighter/Fire Officer

What is Involved?

As a firefighter or fire officer, you would be working as part of a team to save people and property from fire and other hazards. While you would certainly be involved in the often dangerous and stressful process of actually fighting fires, you would also be responsible for making the general public aware of fire hazards, visiting public and commercial premises to advise on fire regulations and safety standards and responding to other emergency calls. These may range from floods to road, rail and air crashes or working with other emergency services at sites of major disasters. You would be trained in first aid so that you could administer immediate help before the arrival of the emergency medical services.

As a more senior officer, you might organise the response of your service to call-outs and you might attend major incidents to co-ordinate the work. At other times, you could be reviewing the operating policies of your brigade or organising the training of the firefighters under your command.

Opportunities for Training

As a new recruit, you would take part in a full-time induction training programme, which will introduce fire safety standards and protective measures, fire prevention and safety education work. This lasts between 12 and 16 weeks (18 weeks in Northern Ireland).

To prepare for the practical side of firefighting, you would train in areas such as: fire behaviour and firefighting, basic rescue techniques and entering smoke-filled rooms, fitting protective clothing and using breathing apparatus, handling foam and other types of fire extinguishers, using ladders, hoses, knots and other equipment, first aid, and health and safety.

When you have successfully completed your induction training, you would join a fire station for a probationary period of up to two years. During this time you would work alongside experienced firefighters and your performance would be continually assessed.

An Integrated Personal Development System (IPDS) is now being used across the fire service, enabling you to be involved in continually updating and developing the skills you need for your job.

Requirements for Entry

There are no formal entry requirements, although some brigades may require specific GCSE/S Grade passes, and you would have to pass a series of psychological and physical tests. There is no separate entry scheme for candidates with higher level qualifications but you should be able to pass training and promotion exams relatively more quickly.

You must be at least 18 before you can join the Fire Service, fully fit and able to meet national fitness standards in lung capacity and upper body strength. Good vision in both eyes is essential and you should have normal colour vision.

Kind of Person

You must be able to work as part of a highly disciplined team but with the capacity to respond to challenges by showing initiative when needed. You would be required to accept the brigade dress code and restrictions on your personal appearance.

Handling specialist equipment calls for a variety of practical skills and you must be able to react calmly but quickly in dangerous situations. Good communication and interpersonal skills are vital. You would need to be physically strong to carry your equipment and mentally resilient in view of the sometimes harrowing situations you would encounter.

Broad Outlook

There is fierce competition for Fire Service positions and there are always many more applicants than vacancies, although there is scope in rural areas to work as a part-time 'retained' firefighter.

All new entrants start on the same grade and promotion is strictly on merit. You could rise to the rank of station commander through internal promotion but would need to move to different areas to obtain more senior appointments.

Related Occupations

You might also consider: army officer, Royal Air Force officer, Royal Navy/Royal Marines officer, merchant navy officer, police officer, security officer or ambulance paramedic.

Impact on Lifestyle

Firefighters work a shift system, which means both day and night time working and work at weekends. Occasionally, you may be required to work overtime but can expect on average to have two days off each week. The work can be highly stressful and physically demanding, often involving work in very uncomfortable situations, such as at height or in enclosed spaces. Being out in all weathers and exposed to danger from collapsing buildings, vehicle fumes and explosions is part of the job.

Earnings Potential

As a trainee firefighter, you would start on a salary of £22,237, rising to £29,638 when competent. A watch manager earns up to £36,381 and a station manager up to £42,154. There is also a London weighting allowance and there are agreed overtime rates for all grades.

Further Information

Contact the recruitment department of your local fire service.
UK Fire Service Recruitment
www.fireservice.co.uk/recruitment

Skills for Fire and Rescue
www.sfjuk.com/sectors/fire-rescue

Chief Fire Officers Association
www.cfoa.org.uk

Fire Officers' Association
www.fireofficers.org.uk

Fire Brigades Union
www.fbu.org.uk

Fire Service College
www.fireservicecollege.ac.uk

Institution of Fire Engineers
www.ife.org.uk

Fire Ireland
www.fire-ireland.com

Food Scientist or Technologist

What is Involved?

As a food scientist, you would examine the chemistry and biology of manufactured foods from the raw materials through to the final product. As a food technologist, you would use food science and other technological expertise to turn raw materials into finished products for the consumer, often with the aid of sophisticated equipment. You might work for a food-processing company, for a large supermarket chain, for the civil service or for the environmental health service, ensuring that food products are safe to eat and economical to produce, that they taste good and look inviting. You could be testing products in a laboratory to monitor chemical and microbiological changes during cooking and storage; you could be developing new products to meet changing consumer demands; you may be creating low-fat, ready-to-eat meals for airlines; you may be experimenting with new ways of preventing fruit from rotting. While there is considerable overlap between the two types of work, you would be more likely to work in a laboratory as a food scientist and in a food production establishment as a food technologist.

Opportunities for Training

There are many institutions in the UK offering Food Science, Food Technology or closely related subjects at degree or foundation degree level. Some of the courses are sandwich-based, giving you a chance to combine your academic study with practical experience in the industry. It is also possible to train on the job, without a higher education qualification, possibly starting on an Apprenticeship. There may be opportunities to specialise in areas such as meat and poultry processing, baking technology or brewing.

If you are interested in working abroad, some courses offer study in Europe as part of the course. You would be expected to continue to study throughout your working life in order to keep up to date with new developments in the food market.

Requirements for Entry

You should be thinking of studying chemistry plus at least one subject from food science, maths, biology or physics as a grounding for a degree or foundation degree. Most universities require three good A level/Advanced Higher, four Higher or equivalent qualifications for degree entry, including chemistry. The foundation degree route would normally require one A level, two Higher or equivalent qualifications.

It is possible to work as a technician in food and drink production if you have four GCSE/S Grade passes 9-4/A*-C/1-3 in English, maths, biology and chemistry or an equivalent qualification.

Kind of Person

You would need a genuine interest in food and drink, coupled with a meticulous approach to detail and hygiene when you are conducting trials or laboratory tests on food. You would also need good communication skills and the ability to work as part of a team. Knowledge of food safety law is required, to ensure that you work within relevant health and safety regulations.

Broad Outlook

Food and drink is a large, expanding and changing industry, with new jobs being created all the time. There is a wide range of possible employers, from food or drink manufacturers, large retailers or supermarket chains to Government research establishments, local authorities or universities.

To gain promotion in a large organisation, you would need to develop specialised skills relevant to the company and to demonstrate the broad qualities sought for management responsibility. You may find it necessary to change employers a few times in order to develop your career. There is currently a shortage of new graduates joining the industry, which employs some 400,000 people across the UK and says it will need 109,000 new recruits by 2022.

Related Occupations

You may be interested in working in the food industry as a dietitian, biochemist, biotechnologist, microbiologist, environmental health practitioner or chef.

Impact on Lifestyle

You would most likely work a typical 35- to 40-hour week. Some manufacturing companies may have a 24-hour production programme, in which case you would work shifts in order to supervise and test the quality of the food during production. This may include some weekend work.

Meticulous hygiene requirements would mean that you would at times have to wear special clothing, including a hat or hairnet, gloves and even a mask.

Earnings Potential

As a graduate food scientist or technologist, you should start earning in the region of £25,000 to £28,000. This should rise to £30,000 to £45,000 with experience and to £65,000 or more for a senior managerial position, depending on the size of the organisation, your responsibilities and your qualifications.

Further Information

Tasty Careers in Food and Drink
http://tastycareers.org.uk

Apprenticeships
www.getingofar.gov.uk

Department for Environment, Food and Rural Affairs
www.gov.uk/government/organisations/department-for-environment-food-rural-affairs

Food and Drink Federation
www.fdf.org.uk

Institute of Food Science and Technology
www.ifst.org

The National Skills Academy for Food & Drink
http://nsafd.co.uk

Irish Agriculture and Food Development Authority
www.teagasc.ie

Institute of Food Science and Technology Ireland
www.ifsti.ie

Forensic Scientist

What is Involved?

As a forensic scientist, you would be working at the meeting point between science and the law, examining and analysing minute particles of materials in the search for physical traces which might be useful for establishing or excluding an association between someone suspected of committing a crime and the scene of the crime or victim. Such traces commonly include blood and other body fluids, hairs, textile fibres from clothing, materials used in buildings such as paint and glass, footwear, tool and tyre marks, flammable substances used to start fires and so on. Much of your work would be carried out in close co-operation with the police and would make a very valuable, at times critical, contribution to the process of the law. You are likely to be involved with cases of arson, burglary and fire and murder investigations. You might also be concerned with car accidents or cases involving drugs. You would work in a laboratory, possibly analysing samples of DNA, and occasionally visiting the scenes of crimes.

Opportunities for Training

There are two main elements in the training required to become a general forensic scientist. The first involves academic courses, and the second on-the-job training, usually with one of the main suppliers of primary services to police. You would need a good honours degree in a relevant subject in order to become a forensic scientist and progress to senior level. There are some universities offering degrees in Forensic Science either as single or joint honours but it is possible to start training with a good degree in a subject such as chemistry, biochemistry, pharmaceutical chemistry, biology or metallurgy, followed by a one- or two-year postgraduate course in forensic science. There is no one academic route recommended by the Chartered Society of Forensic Sciences, nor one that will guarantee you a job in this oversubscribed field. The Society's website lists courses that have undergone its accreditation process, and this could be a good starting point for your research. The Royal Society of Chemistry (RSC) also accredits Forensic Science degrees. Look for courses recognised as suitable for admission to Associate Membership of the Society (AMRSC).

Requirements for Entry

For entry to a relevant science degree, you would need A level/Advanced Higher, Higher or equivalent qualifications in chemistry and another science subject, with some universities specifying maths or biology. There is a rapidly growing number of forensic science degree courses available and admission offers can be higher than for other chemistry- or biology-based courses. A pre-entry postgraduate qualification is increasingly desirable as competition for career opportunities is intense. A relevant PhD or MSc in forensic science, for example, may increase your chances of being shortlisted for interview.

Kind of Person

You would need a strong interest in science and a methodical and analytic approach to problem solving. At times you would be required to make very detailed examinations of the scene of an incident. The tests that you carry out would call for accuracy and a sound understanding of maths. In addition to your scientific and analytical skills you would need to express yourself clearly both verbally and in written reports. You may be required to stand up in court and give evidence, in which case you may have to face cross examination. You are likely to become an expert in one particular area of forensic science and would, therefore, work fairly independently but always as a team member. Finally, you would have to cope with crime scenes, which can be very unpleasant.

Broad Outlook

This is a fiercely competitive area of work. Employment in the sector has grown at an unprecedented rate over the past ten years, due largely to advances in technology such as the National DNA Database, and an increased reliance on forensic techniques by police forces. While there are about 5,000 people working in the UK forensic science industry, there are currently some 1,500 forensic science graduates being produced each year by UK universities, chasing around 200 vacancies.

The majority of forensic scientists in England were employed by the Forensic Science Service (FSS) in England and Wales, by specific police forces in Scotland and by regional government in Northern Ireland. The government closed the FSS in 2012 and its work is now contracted to private companies. These may specialise in providing primary forensic science services to the police, or focus on specific areas of forensic science such as fire investigation. There is now a proposal to re-establish the FSS and you should check the websites below for news of the latest developments.

Related Occupations

You might be interested in other careers with a scientific base such as research chemist, pharmacologist, chemical/process engineer, metallurgist, biochemist or pathologist.

Impact on Lifestyle

You may be called out to a crime scene at night or at weekends, and this could clearly have an impact on your social life. Apart from being available on an on-call rota of this sort, you could expect your normal working week to be around 40 hours spread over five days. Some of the scenes of crime you attend may be distressing, so this is not a career for the faint-hearted.

Earnings Potential

As a general guide, bearing in mind that actual rates of pay may vary, depending on your employer and where you live, starting salaries for trainee forensic scientists typically range from £19,000 to £21,000. An MSc or PhD in a relevant subject may enable you to start higher on the salary scale. With two to three years' experience, salaries increase to £25,000 to £35,000. Typical salaries at senior levels are around £50,000 plus.

Further Information

Chartered Society of Forensic Sciences
www.csofs.org

Forensic Science Northern Ireland
www.justice-ni.gov.uk/topics/forensic-science/forensic-science-northern-ireland

LGC Forensics
www.lgcgroup.com/sectors/forensic-science

Cellmark Forensic Services
www.cellmarkforensics.co.uk

Skills for Justice
www.sfjuk.com/sectors/forensic-science

Forensic Science Ireland
www.forensicscience.ie

Forest/Woodland Manager

What is Involved?

Forestry is defined as the science and practice of managing forests and woodlands but modern multi-purpose forestry is about far more than just growing trees for timber. Your work as a forest manager could embrace everything from planting and managing large coniferous forests to creating and tending small broadleaved woodlands; from raising young trees in nurseries to felling and delivering timber to wood-using industries. Timber production still underpins the work but your remit would be much broader, including managing woods and forests to offer multiple benefits for people, wildlife and the environment in general. Forests can provide havens for wildlife, can screen and enhance the landscape, filter the air and cater for many types of recreation.

You would usually commence your career as a technical manager or supervisor, known in the industry as a forester. You would plan and control forest operations and ensure that the forest environment is protected and enhanced. You might also manage public recreation and access. There are chances to specialise in wildlife conservation, recreation, training, research, harvesting, marketing and processing. You would probably spend about three days a week out in the forest and the rest of the time in an office.

Opportunities for Training

There are several possible training routes. You would normally need a degree, postgraduate qualification or a foundation degree or higher or national diploma in forestry (ND/HND). An Apprenticeship could also enable you to work your way up to a similar level. A degree would take three or four years to complete and ND/HND two or three years. You should obtain relevant work experience before starting any of these courses. You may find it useful to work towards full membership of the Institute of Chartered Foresters, which carries with it recognition of your experience and success in passing their examinations.

Requirements for Entry

For entry to a forestry degree, you should have at least two A level/Advanced Higher, three Higher or equivalent qualifications in science subjects and five GCSE/S Grade passes 9-4/A*-C/1-3. The HND would require at least one A level/Advanced Higher, two Higher or equivalent qualifications and GCSE/S Grade passes 9-4/A*-C/1-3 in maths, English and a science subject; for the ND you would need similar GCSE/S Grade passes. A full driving licence would be essential.

Kind of Person

You would need to be interested in the successful development and economic viability of forests, in their conservation and their environmental roles. You would have to be fit and to enjoy working outdoors. You would need good team skills, the ability to organise the schedules of those working for you and to communicate effectively with colleagues and members of the public.

Broad Outlook

The UK is one of the few places in the world where the tree cover is actually expanding as more and more trees are planted with the advent of community forests and the National Forest. Recent government initiatives in the expansion of leisure facilities in both private and public forests, coupled with grants to encourage the use of more land for forestry, have increased employment possibilities. Nevertheless, competition is keen and gaining work experience is vitally important. More than 30,000 people work in the forestry sector in Britain, including some 3,000 employed by the Forestry Commission. Others work in private estates and the wood-processing industry, other forest management companies and timber harvesting companies.

Most UK career opportunities are in rural areas in Scotland, Wales and northern England. Openings exist with national and local government agencies, forest management companies, private estates, land agency firms, timber companies and independent consultants. There are forestry opportunities in New Zealand, Canada and the USA. Volunteer forestry workers can also be employed by charities working in underdeveloped countries. There are opportunities for postgraduate work and research in forestry with universities and the Forestry Commission.

The increase in environmental awareness and outdoor recreation has highlighted the need for professionally trained foresters and arboriculturists capable of managing Britain's woodlands and trees.

Related Occupations

You might also consider: arboriculturist, countryside ranger/warden, ecologist, environmental consultant, fish farmer, fisheries officer, horticultural manager, landscape architect or rural practice surveyor.

Impact on Lifestyle

You may have to work long hours, especially in commercial forests to meet contract deadlines. The Forestry Commission has an official 42-hour week, although that may include evening and weekend work. You are likely to be based in a very rural and possibly quite remote environment.

Earnings Potential

The Forestry Commission graduate development programme, which lasts two years, offers a starting salary of £24,000. This should rise to £30,000 to £35,000 with experience and £55,000 to £70,000 for more senior positions. Private estates tend to pay rather less than the Forestry Commission but there may be additional benefits, such as accommodation and transport.

Further Information

Forestry Commission
www.forestry.gov.uk

Institute of Chartered Foresters
www.charteredforesters.org

Royal Forestry Society
www.rfs.org.uk

Forest Service Northern Ireland
www.daera-ni.gov.uk/topics/forestry

Woodland Trust
www.woodlandtrust.org.uk

Coillte
www.coillte.ie

Freight Forwarder

What is Involved?

In today's global economy, we buy our everyday needs from all around the world: smartphones from China, furniture from Sweden, televisions from Japan and computers from the USA. We also sell our own goods all over the world. As a freight forwarder, you would be part of the international industry that uses ships, planes, trucks and railways to transport these goods to their markets around the globe.

You might work as a freight forwarding agent, assisting exporters or importers by collecting and delivering between them and the shipping line or airline, buying space on sailings or flights, handling documentation and dealing with HM Revenue and Customs. Alternatively, you might work for an airline, a shipping company, a road transport operator or a courier, dealing in high volumes of small and urgent packages. See also our separate article on 'Logistics Manager'.

You would need a clear knowledge of the advantages and disadvantages of all types of transport and of the handling techniques at ports, railway stations, road transport terminals and airports worldwide.

Opportunities for Training

While there is no single recommended training route, there are many relevant higher national diploma (HND) and degree courses in international trade, business and logistics management. These can lead to a fast-track development programme within some of the larger freight organisations. The British International Freight Association (BIFA) provides training leading to qualifications recognised both inside and outside the industry, including Air Cargo Security, Dangerous Goods, Freight Forwarding and International Trade, and Customs Procedures. Other relevant qualifications are offered by the Chartered Institute of Logistics and Transport, the Freight Transport Association and the Institute of Export.

Requirements for Entry

For degree course entry, you would normally need two or three A level/Advanced Higher, three or four Highers or equivalent qualifications, together with a good platform of GCSE/S Grade passes 9-4/A*-C/1-3. HND entry would normally require one A level/ Advanced Higher, two Higher or equivalent qualifications. There are no specific subject requirements but subjects such as economics, foreign languages and geography could be useful. You should try to spend some time on a relevant work experience placement before making an application.

Kind of Person

The main qualities required would include an analytical mind with a practical side to it, as you could be constantly called upon to unravel problems such as goods going astray, suffering damage or failing to connect with a container ship or cargo plane. You would need to examine the fine detail without losing sight of the wider picture. You must be willing to assume independent responsibility, to communicate clearly and decisively, to insist on getting the facts, to negotiate and be adaptable and to cope with all these stresses and frequent changes. Excellent communication skills, both verbal and written, would be vital to carrying out your tasks, in which efficiency of operation, speed of turn-around time and the availability of return freights would be essential.

Broad Outlook

The world has had to cope since 2008 with the first global decline in international trade for many decades, with particular attention being focused on the reluctance of banks to finance large contracts. Falling exports have inevitably had an impact on career opportunities in freight forwarding, although there is still a great demand for the movement of goods around the world and the UK economy is now enjoying a strong recovery. The UK and other European states tend to be losing market share to the Asian gateways, Singapore and Hong Kong.

Many people come into the freight industry by accident but then stay for a life-long career. There are some 1,500 freight-forwarding offices in the UK, from large companies (with 30 or more branches) down to single-outlet operators. All the pointers suggest that this is an industry facing significant change, leading many freight forwarders to extend their range of services to include warehousing, sorting, order picking, packaging and goods assembly.

Related Occupations

You might also consider: logistics/supply chain manager, passenger transport manager, shipbroker, transport planner, marketing executive, insurance broker, insurance underwriter or tour operator.

Impact on Lifestyle

The freight industry operates 24 hours a day, seven days a week. It could make major demands on your time, especially if you are in regular contact with people living on the other side of the world. Your hours of work could be long and irregular and you may be expected to travel extensively.

Earnings Potential

A typical starting salary for a graduate management trainee is around £20,000 to £25,000, rising with experience to £26,000 to £30,000. Other salaries are difficult to gauge but many experienced freight forwarders earn around £40,000 to £50,000.

Further Information

Chartered Institute of Logistics and Transport
www.ciltuk.org.uk

Institute of Chartered Shipbrokers
www.ics.org.uk

British International Freight Association
www.bifa.org

Careers in Logistics
www.careersinlogistics.co.uk

Freight Transport Association
www.fta.co.uk

Institute of Export
www.export.org.uk

Irish International Freight Association
www.iifa.ie

Geologist/Geoscientist

What is Involved?

As a geologist or geoscientist, you would study the structure, evolution and dynamics of the planet Earth and its natural mineral and energy resources. You would investigate the processes that have shaped the Earth through its 4.54 billion year history in order to unravel that history and reveal its direct relevance to modern society. By mapping the distribution of rocks exposed at the Earth's surface, looking at how they are folded, fractured and altered by geological processes and determining their ages and field relations, you could produce the geological maps and databases which are the basic tools underpinning the use of all geological resources. You might analyse how energy resources such as oil and gas, coal and uranium are formed and where they may be found, or you might be involved in the search for sources of geothermal energy. You may be employed in exploration and surveying on land and sea, using aerial or satellite photography and electro-magnetic measurements (remote sensing). If you were to specialise in engineering, you might advise on the best locations for the construction of mines, roads, buildings and bridges. As an *environmental geologist*, you would give advice on contaminated sites and sites used for waste disposal. You might also advise on the effects of past activities, such as subsidence resulting from earlier mining, or on ongoing processes such as coastal erosion.

Opportunities for Training

To pursue a professional career, you would need an MSc or MGeol degree in geology or geoscience. Most students follow a broadly based course, although you could concentrate on a particular aspect such as environmental geology or geophysics. Fieldwork plays a vital part in most courses and you should be prepared to spend time out of doors to undertake group expeditions lasting from a few days to one or two weeks. Increasingly, students wishing to become geoscientists go on to take a postgraduate qualification, such as a PhD, concentrating on a particular area of interest to employers (e.g. petroleum geology, geophysics or hydrogeology). The Geological Society runs an accreditation scheme for geoscience degrees and successful completion of an accredited course can be the first stage of becoming a chartered geologist (CGeol).

Requirements for Entry

For degree entry, you would normally need two or three A level/Advanced Higher, three or four Higher or equivalent qualifications. Science and technological subjects, especially chemistry, physics, biology, mathematics and engineering, are preferred and a foreign language can be useful.

Kind of Person

You would need good spatial awareness and practical skills to use sophisticated instruments and you would have to possess good IT skills. You would sometimes work alone and sometimes as part of a team; you would need to be fit and healthy, since you may be working in physically challenging environments anywhere in the world. Any colour blindness could be a serious problem. Good communication skills would be essential for writing reports, making presentations and participating in discussion with professional colleagues.

Broad Outlook

Many geology graduates enter professions directly related to their degree. Popular roles include exploration and production, water supply, environmental engineering and geological surveying. Typical employers include the oil, gas and petroleum sector and environmental consultancies and civil engineering companies. Overseas work can be a common feature, while some experienced professionals may also become self-employed consultants.

Statistics collected from recent geology graduates show that just over half of those surveyed were in full-time paid work six months after graduation. The majority of these were employed as scientific research, analysis and development professionals (26%) with a further 15% in engineering and 13% employed as other professionals and in associate professional and technical occupations.

A high percentage of geology graduates choose to undertake full- or part-time further study. The majority opt for a vocational MSc such as Petroleum Geology, Engineering Geology or Geochemistry whilst others choose the PhD route.

Related Occupations

You might also consider: engineering geologist, marine biologist/marine scientist, geochemist, geophysicist, hydrogeologist, land/geomatics surveyor, surveyor (general practice), energy engineer, petroleum engineer, civil engineer, structural engineer, mining engineer, hydrographic surveyor or cartographer.

Impact on Lifestyle

Most professional geologists spend at least part of their working career doing fieldwork, sometimes in remote areas in difficult conditions. You could be land-based, in mining operations or take part in underwater drilling operations. Temperatures can be extremely high in desert areas in the day and very low at night. In locations like Alaska you would experience sub-zero conditions and very short daylight hours. You would need a wide range of safety equipment and protective clothing to cope with each situation.

Earnings Potential

Typical starting salaries range from £28,000 to £35,000, depending on the level of qualification on entry. Earnings usually increase significantly following completion of necessary training. At senior level, salaries are rarely less than £50,000 and may climb to more than £80,000 to £130,000 plus benefits. Salaries vary considerably by sector, employer's business and location, and level of qualification. Positions based offshore or in risky or remote locations are often compensated in their salary. The highest salaries are in major oil companies, but some consultancies pay well too.

Further Information

British Geological Survey
www.bgs.ac.uk

Geological Society
www.geolsoc.org.uk

Geologists' Association
www.geologistsassociation.org.uk

Rockwatch
www.rockwatch.org.uk

Petroleum Exploration Society of Great Britain
www.pesgb.org.uk

Institute of Geologists of Ireland
www.igi.ie

Graphic Designer

What is Involved?

As a graphic designer, you would add a dimension of visual flair to the words and pictures making up magazine and newspaper layouts and covers, advertisements, posters, book jackets, sales brochures, catalogues, websites and product packaging. Graphic design is about drawing and presentation skills and about the ability to handle colours, lettering and patterns. Increasingly too, because of the development of design software, it is about a high degree of computer literacy. You might work on a wide range of projects or you could become a specialist in, for example, typography (print), illustration, packaging, corporate identity or magazine design.

You would often be expected to suggest a number of designs and colour combinations for consideration, possibly modifying layouts, typestyles and overall emphasis according to the wishes of your client or art director. Branding and house style, costing/budgeting, delivery dates and media to be used would all need to be agreed before your design work is finalised and handed over for printing or publication.

Opportunities for Training

There are no required qualifications but a good starting point would normally be to take an art foundation course before going on to a further course of training at an art school or university. A foundation course would give you a broad introduction to working in different areas of design and would provide the opportunity to build up a portfolio of your best work before you choose a specialised degree, foundation degree or higher national diploma (HND) course. In Scotland, the foundation would be the first year of a four-year course.

As a graphic designer, you will need to be skilled in using a variety of software packages, such as InDesign, QuarkXPress, Illustrator, Photoshop, Autodesk 3ds Max, Acrobat, Director, Dreamweaver, CorelDRAW, Paintshop and Flash. If you are involved in media design, you may be required to learn about TV special effects systems. Some employers will fund participation on training courses, but many freelance and self-employed designers have to fund their own development.

Requirements for Entry

Entry to foundation courses can be from GCSE/S Grades or A level/Advanced Higher, Higher or equivalent qualifications, with great importance placed on a current portfolio of your own artistic work. The courses last one or two years full-time and can be found at sixth form colleges, further and higher education colleges, art colleges and some universities.

Entry to an HND course would normally require a minimum of four GCSE/S Grade passes and one or two A level/Advanced Higher, Higher or equivalent qualifications. The course would usually last two years, with the possibility of conversion to a degree course.

Kind of Person

You would need to be artistically creative and imaginative. You would also need to have good technical and drawing skills and the ability to visualise a design concept. You would need to be able to understand the technical aspects of printing and, if applicable, multimedia systems. Computer skills would be essential, as graphic design is almost always based on specialist design software. You would need to communicate well with your clients, to listen carefully to their ideas and suggestions and be able to explain your own design concepts. In addition, you would need some understanding of budgeting and costing when preparing your plans.

Broad Outlook

Britain has the largest number of higher education courses in graphic design in Europe, which means that entry to the profession is competitive. However, there are more openings in graphic design than in any other area of design - in advertising agencies, design studios, in-house company departments and consultancies as well as in the freelance sector. Most agencies and studios are based in the larger cities, with a particular concentration in the London area. There is growing demand for designers specialising in television and video graphics and in website design.

Related Occupations

You might also consider: advertising creative, animator, photographer, artist/illustrator, exhibition/display designer, interior designer, computer games designer, multimedia designer, user experience/interface (UX/UI) developer, front end developer or web developer.

Impact on Lifestyle

You may have a contract that states your hours will be nine to five, Monday to Friday. At times, however, you would be expected to be flexible and work longer than this if there is a tight deadline to meet. You may find yourself travelling to visit clients and having to meet them at times that are convenient to the client rather than to you. As a junior designer, you are likely to find yourself working in an open plan environment with other designers.

Earnings Potential

There is a wide range of starting salaries depending on your age and experience, but you can expect to earn around £16,000 to £22,000 when you first start. This can rise with experience to around £25,000 to £50,000 for a senior designer, and to £65,000 and above for a creative director. There are good opportunities for experienced designers to work freelance, in which case your salary would depend on your skills, your ability to market yourself and the hours you are prepared to work.

Further Information

Creative and Cultural Skills
http://ccskills.org.uk/careers/advice/any/design/communication-design

Design Week
www.designweek.co.uk

Chartered Society of Designers
www.csd.org.uk

The Ideal Candidate
http://idealcandidate.represent.uk.com

D&AD
www.dandad.org

Innovation Bank
www.britishdesigninnovation.org

Institute of Designers in Ireland
http://idi-design.ie

Health and Safety Inspector

What is Involved?

As a health and safety inspector, you would visit a wide variety of workplaces and other sites, including building sites, farms, factories, fairgrounds, schools and hospitals, to ensure that all aspects of relevant health and safety law are being upheld.

You would most likely work as part of the Field Operations Directorate of the Health and Safety Executive (HSE), although some inspectors are employed by local authorities. In seeking to protect the welfare of the workforce and the general public, you would have the power to arrive at premises, unannounced, to examine equipment and machinery, manufacturing processes and working methods, and write up a full report. Local authorities are responsible for enforcement in offices, shops and other parts of the services sector.

If you find evidence of unsafe practice, you would make recommendations for change to the employer and you would have the sanction, in extreme cases, of issuing a prohibition order - closing the premises until the required improvements are made - or even taking the employer to court. You would work alone for much of the time, although you would be part of a small team of six to eight inspectors, and you would have a fair degree of freedom to organise your own work within the overall limits set by your principal inspector.

Opportunities for Training

The HSE training programme offers a clearly defined, three-year training period, including practical training on the job. You would attend intensive, in-house courses as well as studying for a level 7 postgraduate diploma in Occupational Safety and Health.

Health and safety inspectors within local authorities usually undergo a similar period of training. Irrespective of the setting, all inspectors must attend frequent courses in order to update their knowledge on new developments in health and safety.

Requirements for Entry

You would generally be expected to come into the profession with at least a 2:1 honours degree or equivalent qualification. You should have completed a year or two of work experience.

The subject of your degree would not be crucial, although applied sciences, engineering, environmental health and food technology are the most relevant. Entry to a degree course would normally require two or three A level/Advanced Higher, three or four Higher or equivalent qualifications. A full driving licence would be essential.

Kind of Person

An interest in people's welfare would be important. This is a very responsible job and you would need to be confident and tough enough to back your own judgement in potentially awkward situations. Good communication skills would be vital (particularly in the realms of tact and diplomacy), as you would be dealing with a wide variety of people at all levels of employment, and you would need to write clear and detailed reports.

You might have to present your findings in a court of law. You would need to be able to assimilate large amounts of knowledge (some of it quite technical) and apply this in practical situations. You would need good powers of observation and would have to pay great attention to detail.

Broad Outlook

There is always a demand for health and safety inspectors, although the overall number employed by the Health and Safety Executive is not very large and there is fierce competition to fill vacancies, with approximately 3,000 applicants for 60 places in a typical year. You might like to specialise in one particular area or branch out into the field of policy making.

Inspectors are also employed by large organisations to advise on health and safety matters, while some experienced inspectors start up their own advisory consultancies or work on a freelance basis. Promotion can be gained into management positions.

Related Occupations

You might also consider: environmental health practitioner, occupational hygienist, facilities manager, health and safety adviser, quality assurance manager, operational researcher/management scientist, human resources manager or trading standards officer.

Impact on Lifestyle

You would normally work a standard five-day week, but you should be prepared to put in extra hours in the evening or at the weekend in cases of emergency. As well as being involved in a fair amount of travel, you might have to move around the country in order to gain further experience and/or promotion. You would also have to be prepared to visit some rather unsavoury places - possibly cold, wet, dangerous or noisy - and sometimes wear protective clothing.

Earnings Potential

Salaries for trainee inspectors based in the HSE begin at around £26,500, while salaries for inspectors who have completed their training and have three to five years' experience range from £35,000 to £50,000. At senior levels, those with either increased responsibility or knowledge of a particular specialist area can earn up to £70,000. Annual increments are dependent upon performance.

Further Information

Health and Safety Executive
www.hse.gov.uk

Chartered Society for Worker Health Protection
www.bohs.org

British Safety Council
www.britsafe.org

Department for Work and Pensions
www.gov.uk/government/organisations/department-for-work-pensions

Institution of Occupational Safety and Health
www.iosh.co.uk

European Agency for Safety and Health at Work
https://osha.europa.eu

Health and Safety Authority Ireland
www.hsa.ie

Health Service Manager

What is Involved?

As a health service manager, you could work in the private or public sector, although you would be more likely to operate within the public National Health Service (NHS). Depending on your qualifications and experience, your post may be operational or based around policy-setting, planning or strategic development. Health service management is such a large and varied sector that your role could be that of an administrator running a doctor's surgery or that of a chief executive controlling a large hospital with a budget of many millions of pounds.

Opportunities for Training

Most health service managers are experienced healthcare professionals who move into managerial positions after achieving state registration in their specialised area. As a new graduate in England, you could join the NHS Graduate Management Training Scheme. Split into general, financial, informatics and human resources management, the scheme offers a two- to three-year structured training programme. Trainees on the general management scheme are given the opportunity to gain postgraduate qualifications in healthcare or general management. On the financial management scheme, you would study for professional accountancy qualifications (e.g. Chartered Institute of Public Finance Accountancy); on informatics for the PG Dip Health Informatics; and on human resources for Chartered Institute of Personnel and Development (CIPD) qualifications. Scotland, Wales and Northern Ireland administer their own management training schemes.

Requirements for Entry

You could join the NHS at a clerical level without any formal qualifications and work your way up. For the NHS graduate management training scheme, you would need a 2:2 degree in any subject or an equivalent professional qualification in a health or management-related discipline. A good way of checking that you meet the requirements is to try the NHS 'match-me' tool, an online self-assessment questionnaire.

Kind of Person

You would need excellent communication skills, the ability to lead through example and to influence others through persuasion and negotiation. Other qualities listed by the NHS include: conceptual skills - seeing the implications of actions and decisions; analytical skills - using and interpreting data and facts; impact and influence - making informed decisions, justifying your position and persuading others; taking action - planning your work, setting priorities and dealing with problems in a flexible and proactive way; numerical skills - understanding and applying figures.

Broad Outlook

The NHS in England is a £120 billion-a-year-plus business. It sees 1 million patients every 36 hours, spending more than £2 billion every week. If the NHS were a country, it would be around the 30th largest in the world. Entry to the NHS management training scheme is very competitive but successful completion should mark you out as a high flyer with considerable potential.

Private sector healthcare continues to expand, with some private providers now having their own management training schemes.

Related Occupations

You might also consider: chartered/company secretary, civil service executive officer, civil service fast streamer, local government officer, accountant (professional) or human resources manager. Alternatively, you could begin by qualifying as a nurse, radiographer, physiotherapist, speech and language therapist or other healthcare professional.

Impact on Lifestyle

Advances in medical technology, tough expenditure targets, a high political profile and rising public expectations mean that, at the higher levels, this can be a very demanding job. You may need to move around the country to broaden your experience and seek promotion.

Earnings Potential

As a management trainee, you would currently start on around £23,000, rising to around £34,000 on completion of your training scheme, and with the prospect of future earnings of £70,000 to £96,000 as an executive director or £120,000 plus as a chief executive. If you are already working as a healthcare professional, you may be able to retain your existing salary while working through the management training programme. A project manager would currently earn from £26,565 to £35,577, a human resources team manager £31,696 to £41,787and a professional manager (clinical) from £40,428 to £58,217. Additional allowances are paid for appointments in and around London, ranging from 20% of basic salary for Inner London, to 15% for Outer London and 5% for the London Fringe. Earnings in the private sector are generally likely to be higher.

Further Information

Institute of Healthcare Management
www.ihm.org.uk

NHS Graduate Management Training
www.nhsgraduates.co.uk

NHS Education for Scotland
www.nes.scot.nhs.uk

Academi Wales
https://academiwales.gov.wales

Health and Social Care Leadership, Northern Ireland
www.leadership.hscni.net

NHS Jobs
www.jobs.nhs.uk

BMI Healthcare Jobs
https://bmihealthcarejobs.co.uk

Skills for Health
www.skillsforhealth.org.uk

Health Careers
www.healthcareers.nhs.uk

Health Management Institute of Ireland
www.hmi.ie

Homoeopath

What is Involved?

As a homoeopath, you would be working in a branch of complementary medicine based on the 'like cures like' concept, in which minute doses of a medicine that could produce similar symptoms in a healthy person are used to stimulate the body's own natural healing powers. You would examine a patient's whole physical, emotional and social state and look closely at those aspects of their lifestyle, including diet, posture, exercise and relationships, which could be contributing to their symptoms. The idea is that you would develop a clear picture of your patients and would match your remedy to each individual, encouraging them to take a major role in helping themselves. You could choose to specialise in homoeopathic treatment of animals.

Opportunities for Training

There are several bodies offering different training routes for homoeopaths. The Society of Homoeopaths, for example, lists a number of training centres in the UK offering courses lasting three years full-time and four years part-time. The courses are structured in four main ways:

- Part-time courses - four years, usually meeting for 10-15 weekends each year or for a similar number of two-day blocks mid-week

- Part-time courses with initial correspondence course - four years, with the first one or two years available through a correspondence course. The clinical education aspect would make your physical presence essential in the later stages

- Full-time courses - three years, with attendance typically for three days each week, during three terms each year

- Degree courses - similar to diploma courses but with additional academic components, often in the wider field of health studies

All routes would take you to the same status as a licensed homoeopath. You could become a registered member by completing a course successfully, practising for at least a year and presenting cases for inspection by the society. The Faculty of Homoeopathy, on the other hand, promotes training online, at four centres in the UK and four overseas, but only if you are already a qualified healthcare professional, such as a doctor, dentist, vet, pharmacist, podiatrist or nurse.

Requirements for Entry

You would normally need five GCSE/S Grade passes 9-4/A*-C/1-3 and three A level/ Advanced Higher, four Higher or equivalent qualifications, preferably including biology or human biology, chemistry and physics, for entry to a course accredited by the Society. However, life and work experience are as important and may be acceptable in place of examination passes.

Late entry is common, especially if you have already met the registration requirements of a conventional healthcare profession and wish to join the Faculty as outlined above.

Kind of Person

You would need excellent interpersonal skills, particularly when it comes to listening and explaining. You should have a genuine desire to help people (or animals), be confident and emotionally stable yourself and able to treat your patients with objectivity. You would need to assess conditions, offer clear advice and be able to recognise when a patient needs referral to a conventional practitioner. As you are likely to be self-employed, you would need sufficient commercial awareness to run your own business.

Broad Outlook

Complementary medicine has expanded rapidly in the last twenty years and homoeopathy has steadily acquired respect and recognition, although acceptance by the NHS is currently under review. You may work in private hospitals or clinics or, at least at present, in the NHS with patients recommended to you by their GPs.

Demand continues to increase, with opportunities throughout the UK.

Related Occupations

You may choose to qualify first as a conventional healthcare professional such as doctor (general practice), dentist, veterinary surgeon, pharmacist, podiatrist/chiropodist, nurse or health visitor. Alternatively, you may wish to consider other specialisms in complementary medicine such as aromatherapist, osteopath, chiropractor, herbalist or naturopath.

Impact on Lifestyle

As most homoeopaths are self-employed, you could enjoy considerable flexibility both in the hours you choose to work and the places you work in. On the other hand, there are few promotion prospects, fluctuations in demand for treatment and the costs to consider of maintaining a therapy room and associated expenses.

You may find that patients are most keen to see you when they are not themselves at work, keeping you busy in the evening and at weekends.

Earnings Potential

Your income would depend on how many people you see and how much you charge. Earnings vary considerably, usually based on charges of between £50 and £250 per session. Fees in London and the South East of England are likely to be higher than in most other parts of the UK. Many homoeopaths work part-time and may earn around £6,000 a year in the early stages, rising to around £30,000 when established.

Further Information

Society of Homoeopaths
www.homeopathy-soh.org

Homoeopathic Medical Association
www.the-hma.org

Alliance of Registered Homeopaths
www.a-r-h.org

British Homeopathic Association
www.britishhomeopathic.org

Faculty of Homoeopathy
www.facultyofhomeopathy.org

Irish School of Homoeopathy
www.ish.ie

Irish Society of Homoeopaths
www.irishhomeopathy.ie

Horticultural Manager

What is Involved?

There are two main branches of horticulture: commercial and amenity, sometimes referred to as production and non-production horticulture respectively.

As a commercial horticultural manager, you would be involved in the production for sale of fruit, vegetables, glasshouse crops, mushrooms, herbs, pot plants, shrubs, trees, bulbs and flowers. Your role as a manager would include deciding what to grow, bearing in mind the land available, local growing conditions and your knowledge of the market. You would also have to ensure that you recruit the right staff, buy the seeds, plants and other materials needed for the next crop cycle, keep detailed planting and cropping records, control your finances and deliver consistent product quality to your customers at competitive prices. All this would usually be in addition to the day-to-day practical necessities of planting, weeding, pruning, spraying, harvesting and so on.

As an amenity horticultural manager, you would be responsible for planning and maintaining large public parks, sports grounds, private estates and green spaces in towns and cities. Your role as a manager might include determining how to make your park or garden attractive and accessible, supervising the work of gardening staff, controlling the budget for park maintenance, publicising your amenity and keeping abreast of plants that are currently in vogue. You would also normally want to be actively involved with the practicalities of digging, sowing, lopping, grass-cutting and so on.

Opportunities for Training

There are many possible training routes, ranging from degree and postgraduate courses through specialist qualifications offered by the Royal Horticultural Society or the Royal Botanic Gardens to part-time vocational qualifications.

Degree courses in horticulture normally take three years full-time or four years if they include a 'sandwich' of industrial experience. They may specialise in commercial or amenity horticulture, so it is important to read prospectuses carefully before you apply. All courses would normally include the underlying science of horticulture, crop characteristics, growing techniques and marketing and finance. Higher national diploma (HND) and foundation degree courses cover similar ground at a more practical level and over a shorter period of time.

Requirements for Entry

For a degree course, you would normally need two or three A level/Advanced Higher, four Higher or equivalent qualifications in one or two sciences, especially chemistry and biology; for the HND route, one or two A level/Advanced Higher, two to three Higher or equivalent, would be required. For either route, your application should ideally be supported by periods of work experience in horticultural or agricultural organisations. There are no entry requirements for some of the specialist qualifications.

Kind of Person

You would need to be physically robust, very interested in the cultivation of plants, good at teamwork and willing to put up with irregular hours depending on the seasons of the year and the weather. You would need a strong sense of priorities in meeting essential deadlines and a firm grasp of production costing, aided by good numeracy and book-keeping/accounting skills and a reasonable level of computer literacy. Communication skills would be essential in dealing with clients and suppliers and in clearly explaining your requirements to staff.

Broad Outlook

Opportunities are forecast to increase in commercial horticulture. Ever-growing technological demands are creating an ongoing requirement for higher-level skills in information and production technologies as well as the ability to understand and operate complex production systems. There is also a demand for business management and marketing abilities.

The amenity side has been less positive in recent years, with local authorities in particular cutting back staffing levels. However, Lantra, the UK sector skills council for land-based and environmental industries, predicts that what it calls the green space sector will need at least 11,000 new people between now and 2020, with almost one-third at graduate level or above. Some 12% of employers currently complain that skills shortages make it hard to recruit suitable applicants.

Related Occupations

You might also consider: agricultural adviser/consultant, agricultural research scientist, ecologist, environmental consultant, landscape architect, farm manager, floral designer/florist, forest/woodland manager, countryside/nature conservation officer or countryside ranger/warden.

Impact on Lifestyle

You would normally work a theoretical 39-hour week but you might at times have to tailor your hours to fit the demands of particular growing seasons. Many people in horticulture like to start work early in the morning to make the most of daylight hours. Sports grounds and public gardens are often busiest at the weekend. In setting up your own nursery or garden centre, enormous efforts and sacrifices would be essential, with often a seven-day week, in order to meet strong weekend demand.

Earnings Potential

As a junior manager, you would start at between £18,000 and £22,000, rising to £30,000 to £60,000 as a senior manager within a well-established company. The rewards for owner managers can be considerably greater.

Further Information

Lantra
www.lantra.co.uk
Royal Botanic Garden, Kew
www.kew.org
Royal Botanic Garden, Edinburgh
www.rbge.org.uk
Chartered Institute of Horticulture
www.horticulture.org.uk
Royal Horticultural Society
www.rhs.org.uk
Agriculture and Horticulture Development Board
http://horticulture.ahdb.org.uk
Grow Careers
www.growcareers.info
Management Development Services Ltd (MDS)
www.mds-ltd.co.uk
Royal Horticultural Society of Ireland
www.rhsi.ie

Hospitality/Hotel Manager

What is Involved?

Hotels vary enormously in size and scope but your job as a manager would include ensuring that the day-to-day running of the establishment is well organised and efficient and that guests enjoy using your services. You might have responsibility for accommodation, food and drink, conferences, special events and leisure facilities, hence the use in the business of the broader term hospitality. You could be in overall control of every department, with a number of assistants, or you might have to manage several of these responsibilities yourself, especially in a smaller hotel.

Opportunities for Training

There is no single training route for hospitality management and you do not always need academic qualifications. You may decide, for example, to gain experience at a lower level and work your way up, or you may enter the industry from an allied occupation such as human resources, accountancy or restaurant management. If, however, you want to obtain direct entry to a management trainee scheme, you would do well to consider a relevant higher national diploma (HND) or degree course. Look out also for foundation degrees, which are similar to HNDs, covering the hospitality framework.

The HND in Hospitality Management would take two or three years, while a similar degree would take three or four years to complete. To develop your skills when in employment, you could consider the part-time diplomas and specialist certificates offered by the Institute of Hospitality.

Another way in to this type of work could be through the Apprenticeship programme, such as the level 3 advanced apprenticeship in Hospitality and level 4 higher apprenticeship in Hospitality Management.

Requirements for Entry

To enter a hospitality/hotel management degree course, you would need two or three A level/Advanced Higher, three or four Higher or equivalent qualifications, together with a minimum of five GCSE/S Grade passes 9-4/A*-C/1-3. Entry to an HND course would require a minimum one A level/Advanced Higher, two Higher or equivalent qualifications, together with four GCSE/S Grade passes 9-4/A*-C/1-3. It is vital to check each institution's entry requirements and it would help to obtain work experience before applying.

Kind of Person

You should be able to communicate effectively with other people, both staff and guests, and take a keen interest in their welfare and comfort. You would need to be tough, both physically and mentally, to cope with long hours and the need to be constantly available for decision making and problem solving. You should also be well versed in IT, with acute business awareness, good organisational skills and the ability to deal with financial matters. A smart appearance would be essential and knowledge of foreign languages would certainly be an asset.

Broad Outlook

Although competition for hospitality manager positions is intense, the industry usually has no shortage of opportunities on offer. Much importance is placed on experience and proven performance. Managers of small hotels can be promoted to jobs in larger or more prestigious establishments, or to responsible jobs in the administration of chains of hotels. Working for a hotel chain could lead to travel or work abroad. You may need to move several times to develop your career, while there is always the prospect of using your experience to set up your own guest house or hotel.

According to the UK Hospitality Digest, the industry will create some 300,000 new jobs by 2020. While some experts disagree with this figure, the sector is clearly in an expansionary mood, as the UK economy recovers from recession, and new hospitality outlets are opening every day.

The Hospitality Guild website offers a personality test which you can use to match your profile with relevant career opportunities.

Related Occupations

You might also consider: events manager, leisure services manager/fitness centre manager, marketing executive, human resources manager, public relations executive or restaurant manager.

Impact on Lifestyle

As a hotel manager you would be expected to work long hours, including regular evening and weekend commitments. If you worked in a small hotel or owned your own establishment, you would probably have to accept that the work could sometimes even spread over 24 hours, with considerable implications for your family and social life. Accommodation is often provided as part of the job but that can make it difficult for you ever to be completely off duty.

Earnings Potential

There is a wide range of salaries, according to the size and type of hotel you would be working in and the level of management responsibility you achieve. Some managers can receive profits or performance bonuses, and there could be financial advantages to living in (although there could be obvious disadvantages as well). You might start as a trainee manager on about £20,000 to £23,000. This could rise to around £25,000 to £40,000 as an assistant general manager and £60,000 to £100,000 plus for an experienced manager in a top international establishment.

Further Information

Hospitality Guild
www.hospitalityguild.co.uk

Institute of Hospitality
www.instituteofhospitality.org

British Institute of Innkeeping
www.bii.org

Apprenticeships
www.getingofar.gov.uk

British Hospitality Association
www.bha.org.uk

Jobs in Hotels
www.jobsinhotels.co.uk

Irish Hospitality Institute
www.ihi.ie

Human Resources Manager

What is Involved?

Your job as a human resources (HR) or personnel manager would focus on getting the best from the people who work in your organisation, from selecting the right people in the first place to managing them effectively when they are in post. The exact nature of your work would depend on what your organisation does, whether it is in the private or public sector, how large it is and whether it has strong union representation.

However, common issues would include understanding what your organisation needs in terms of workforce skills and experience, planning future recruitment and training and devising policies for health and safety, equal opportunities, communication, training and development, pay and conditions of employment. You might also design procedures to measure performance, handle complaints, maintain discipline and keep employee records.

You could operate as a generalist across all of these areas or you could choose to specialise in a topic such as health and safety, employee relations or recruitment and selection.

Opportunities for Training

You would normally develop your skills on the job. Many employers would also expect you to take qualifications offered by the Chartered Institute of Personnel and Development (CIPD), and may pay towards your study.

If you are new to HR, or if you are a personnel administrator looking to progress, you can take the level three foundation certificate in Human Resources Practice. With more experience, you could take the level five intermediate certificates in Human Resource Management and Human Resource Development. CIPD Advanced level qualifications are at level 7 (level 11 and 9 for Scotland and Ireland respectively), equivalent to a postgraduate level qualification.

Requirements for Entry

A degree, foundation degree or higher national diploma (HND) would be a good starting point. Any subject would be acceptable but business studies, law or psychology could be particularly relevant and may give some exemption from the professional qualifications awarded by the CIPD.

You would normally need two or three A level/Advanced Higher, three or four Higher or equivalent qualifications, together with five GCSE/S Grade passes 9-4/A*-C/1-3, for degree course entry. HND entry would require at least one A level/Advanced Higher, two Higher or equivalent qualifications, together with similar GCSE/S Grade passes.

Relevant experience is always regarded as important, and a postgraduate qualification could be useful.

Kind of Person

You should be genuinely interested in the way people work and behave. In order to succeed, you would have to be able to deal with many different situations in a fair and even-handed way, balancing the needs of each individual employee against the overall interests of the organisation. Tackling issues such as discipline or redundancy can be extremely stressful.

Excellent communication skills, both oral and written, would be necessary, together with willingness to work in a team, both as a leader and member. Tact, discretion and an understanding of the need for complete confidentiality when dealing with people's personal details would be essential.

Broad Outlook

Competition for the available vacancies, especially for inexperienced graduates, continues to be very keen. Indeed, some employers indicate that they have a higher percentage of applications for HR work than any other function.

All kinds of organisations employ HR professionals, including banks, local government, health services, further and higher education institutions, airlines, hotels, retail organisations and manufacturing industries. The nature of the HR profession has undergone some change during recent years, with movement away from staff welfare and administration-centred activities towards strategy and planning. HR departments are now expected to add value to the organisation they support.

You might start out as a trainee manager and work your way up the ladder in one organisation or move to a larger one with more scope. With sufficient experience, you might set up your own business, offering specialist recruitment, training or other services. You could have the opportunity to travel, if you work for a multi-national organisation.

Related Occupations

You might also consider: careers adviser/guidance counsellor, occupational psychologist, office manager or recruitment consultant.

Impact on Lifestyle

You would normally work the usual office hours from Monday to Friday, though you might have to work overtime at certain times, for interviewing or attending meetings. Weekend work would be unusual.

Earnings Potential

Salaries within HR vary considerably between employers. They can be influenced to some extent by location but also by industry sector, level of responsibility, seniority and particular function. According to the CIPD Careers Guide, a graduate level HR officer can expect to earn on average £25,950. With the right skills and motivation, you can expect swift progression early on. HR managers earn on average £39,783 and HR directors average £73,682. However, when bonuses are taken into account, HR business partners can earn over £70,000 and HR board directors can earn upwards of £150,000.

Further Information

Chartered Institute of Personnel and Development
www.cipd.co.uk

Recruitment and Employment Confederation
www.rec.uk.com

Personnel Today
www.personneltoday.com

Chartered Institute of Personnel and Development (Ireland)
www.cipd.co.uk/global/europe/ireland

Hydrographic Surveyor

What is Involved?

Working as a hydrographic or marine surveyor, you would be concerned with mapping the vast expanse of the earth's surface that is underwater. You might measure and chart the seabed or survey underwater for mineral resources, gas and oil deposits. You could get involved with land reclamation schemes, with dredging or with defining international boundaries. You might also survey ports, oceans, channels and inland waterways.

Another area in which you could become involved is the search for hazards to shipping, such as rocks or wrecks, strong currents and tides. You would be likely to use advanced technological equipment, including sonar scanning, to obtain information about the seabed and aerial or satellite photography for mapping and charting. In common with all measurement at sea, precise positioning is essential and you would use a range of systems, from lasers for short-range, very high accuracy work to global satellite navigation systems for positioning throughout the world's oceans.

Most of the processing and presentation of the data collected at sea is undertaken using computers. In many cases survey data can be processed on board ship, providing immediate access to the end product charts and maps. Certain types of survey data processing would require access to large computing resources and very elaborate processing software.

Opportunities for Training

You would normally train on the job in areas such as seamanship and instrument handling. Before working offshore, you must usually undertake a basic offshore safety and emergency training course. This usually includes fire fighting, helicopter underwater escape training, first aid and safety at sea.

For chartered membership of the Royal Institution of Chartered Surveyors (RICS), completion of an accredited degree or postgraduate qualification and a minimum of two years' planned training and experience are required for the Assessment of Professional Competence (APC). Graduates with non RICS-accredited degrees need to complete an additional period of training and experience to meet the requirements of the APC.

There is also a Royal Navy entry route, with training available at the Flag Officer Sea Training Hydrography and Meteorology (FOST HM) School in Devonport.

Requirements for Entry

You would normally need three A level/Advanced Higher, four Higher or equivalent qualifications to enter an accredited degree in a surveying discipline, together with five GCSE/S Grade passes 9-4/A*-C/1-3, including English and maths.

You would find it helpful to have a driving licence and RYA powerboat qualifications.

Kind of Person

You would need to be quite technically minded in order to operate and understand all the sophisticated equipment involved. The use of computers is also an important aspect of this work. You would need to be physically robust and able to cope with being at sea in all kinds of weather. You may be out on a boat for extended periods of time.

Whilst some of your time would be spent out on location, you would also need to be prepared to work in an office, usually with a computer, analysing data and writing up and explaining the results of your surveys. You are likely to be part of a team and at times this could be an international team of professionals. As you may be working in confined conditions on a boat for several days at a time, you would need to be tolerant of others.

Broad Outlook

Many of the opportunities in the private sector are associated with the offshore oil and gas industry, which is exploring ever-deeper waters for hydrocarbon reserves, and there are a number of specialist marine survey companies. Many of the companies and organisations concerned with marine survey operate on a worldwide basis. The Royal Navy recruits graduates as Hydrography, Meteorology and Oceanography Warfare Officers.

With considerable experience, you could set up your own freelance consultancy and bid for survey contracts all over the world.

Related Occupations

You might be interested in another specialist career in surveying, such as minerals surveyor or land/geomatics surveyor, or in another career involving the sea, such as hydrogeologist, oceanographer or marine biologist/marine scientist. Alternatively, you might consider a career as a Royal Navy/Royal Marines Officer, cartographer, geochemist, geologist, geophysicist or meteorologist.

Impact on Lifestyle

You would need to be prepared to work at sea in hostile environments when the weather is rough, or even when it is extremely hot. You are likely to have to spend extended periods of time away from home, which could sometimes make family and social life difficult.

Earnings Potential

A typical graduate starting salary would be around £18,000 to £25,000, plus an allowance of £70 to £110 for each day spent offshore. In a full year, you would spend between 140 and 180 days at sea, earning an additional £10,000 to £17,000. The base salary for a party chief is around £40,000, with £100 to £170 for every day offshore, which is usually around 150 days per year, so earning potential could reach around £70,000. If you choose to join the Royal Navy as a hydrographic surveyor, your salary would be set by the normal officer pay scales. Sub-lieutenants currently receive £31,741 to £34,180, rising to £40,690 to £47,127 for lieutenants. Salaries rise significantly on further promotion and officers receive additional allowances for such things as flying, serving in submarines or being at sea. A Captain currently earns £84,878 to £93,304.

Further Information

Hydrographic Society
www.ths.org.uk
Royal Institution of Chartered Surveyors
www.rics.org
Society for Underwater Technology
www.sut.org
International Federation of Hydrographic Societies
www.hydrographicsociety.org
Royal Navy Careers
www.royalnavy.mod.uk/Careers
Society of Chartered Surveyors Ireland
www.scsi.ie

Industrial Chemist

What is Involved?

As a newly qualified chemistry graduate, you could decide to work in such industries as chemicals and pharmaceuticals, food and drinks, oil refining or agricultural chemicals and polymers. Alternatively, you could become an analyst in the water industry, join one of the environmental protection agencies or enter the general graduate employment market.

You could go into research and development in industry. Research is normally carried out in teams with other scientists, seeking to discover new chemical entities such as a new enzyme, drug or a plastic. Development is more about turning research knowledge into commercially valuable products to meet customers' needs. This requires skills beyond chemical knowledge, such as marketing, economics, safety and management.

You could go into production management, ensuring that the manufacturing process is run efficiently and cost-effectively, and that chemical plant operatives are given suitable leadership and that production schedules are maintained.

Alternatively, you could opt for UK or export sales or you could provide techno-commercial support for a range of your company's products. In most of these cases, your insight and understanding of chemistry would be of great advantage.

Opportunities for Training

Many universities have degree courses in chemistry, biochemistry, pharmacology and similar subjects and these usually take between three and four years of full-time study. It is also possible to read chemistry as a joint honours degree with a range of different subjects. For example, it might be useful to read chemistry and a foreign language, which could be beneficial for working on chemical exports, or perhaps chemistry and law for organising legal agreements to make sure new discoveries are protected by patent and are economically viable. You will see some degrees described as MChem or MSci. These are extended programmes that last four years, whilst BSc courses last three years. The first two years are usually identical to those of the Chemistry BSc course at the same institution. Students then take different routes in year 3 or 4.

Courses vary immensely, but a basic stipulation is that the additional year included in MChem/MSci courses must contain more advanced material than the BSc, rather than just a greater quantity. The extended programmes are designed to prepare students for direct entry into professional practice or provide a basis for progression to a PhD.

Requirements for Entry

A level/Advanced Higher or Higher qualifications in chemistry and ideally in maths or another science are likely to be required for entry to a chemistry degree. However, if you choose to combine chemistry with a very popular subject, such as law, you may need to obtain higher grades than are required for chemistry alone. It is possible for students without these qualifications to take a foundation course before starting their degree, either at a university or a college of further education. The entry requirements for the MChem/MSci courses are generally a little higher than those for the corresponding BSc courses.

Kind of Person

In order to be successful as a chemist, you would need to have a technically enquiring mind. You would want to know why chemical reactions occur and what the effects of these changes might be. Chemistry is an investigative science, so you would need to have an analytical approach to problem solving. You would be required to be extremely accurate in measuring and recording your results.

In addition to such scientific and intellectual abilities, you would need to be able to communicate orally and in writing with a wide range of other people. You are likely to be working as part of a team and may find yourself supervising production workers, technicians or sales staff.

Broad Outlook

The chemical industry was severely affected by the economic downturn that started in 2008 but has returned to sustained growth in in the past couple of years and is committed to delivering by 2030 a 50% increase in the gross value it contributes to the UK economy. Positive prospects may be found in fields considered vital for the future, such as addressing climate change, providing energy, securing food and water or developing new technologies in healthcare, communication and security.

Should you decide that you want to continue with postgraduate study, it is sometimes possible to get your research funded by your company once you start. Depending on the type of career you choose to pursue, you could find yourself working in a chemical production plant, a laboratory or an office.

Related Occupations

You might consider other careers in the field of chemistry, such as chemical/process engineer, pharmacologist, forensic scientist, biochemist, microbiologist or pathologist.

Impact on Lifestyle

Although you are likely to work office hours mainly during the week, you may at times need to work late and in production management to cover shift work. You may have tight deadlines to meet, a report may be needed to brief a senior director or a piece of research may require you to work extra hours to complete it. In addition, you would be expected to keep up to date with the numerous developments in your subject, which would involve reading scientific and technical literature in your own time.

Earnings Potential

As a scientist who has recently graduated, you might expect to earn £22,000 to £30,000 initially, rising with experience to £30,000 to £45,000. This could increase to £65,000 and beyond in some industries when you start to take on managerial responsibilities.

Further Information

Royal Society of Chemistry
www.rsc.org

Society of Chemical Industry
www.soci.org

Chemeurope
www.chemeurope.com/en

Chemistry and Industry magazine
www.soci.org/Chemistry-and-Industry

Science, Engineering and Manufacturing Technologies Alliance
http://semta.org.uk

Institute of Chemistry of Ireland
www.chemistryireland.org

Industrial or Product Designer

What is Involved?

As an industrial or product designer, you could design almost any sort of product from toys, toasters, television sets or washing machines to bicycles, cars and even spacecraft. You would be given a design brief and would have to consider not only the aesthetic appeal of the product but also its viability in terms of cost, materials used, ease of manufacture, safety and marketability. You would quite often be working in a team of designers but, even if you were working alone, you would be in constant consultation with other professionals, such as engineers, manufacturers, computer experts and marketing managers, as well as with your client.

You would prepare plans (often computer-generated) with models for inspection and discussion, and would have to be prepared to modify them as necessary. You would normally be based in a design studio or workshop. Some industrial or product designers have extensive knowledge of engineering and manufacturing techniques, and many tend to concentrate on particular technical areas of design work.

You may also be involved in packaging design, specialising in finding ways of making products look attractive while you protect them until they are safely in the hands of the consumer.

Opportunities for Training

While it is not essential, the best-established training route is a degree, foundation degree or higher national diploma (HND) in a design-based subject. The usual way into this is via a foundation course in art and design (general year in Scotland). Universities and art colleges offer many relevant courses, with varying titles but often classified under a heading such as 'three-dimensional design', 'computer-aided design' or 'product design'. The Institution of Engineering Designers publishes on its website a list of accredited courses.

Requirements for Entry

For entry to a one-year art foundation course in England or Wales, you would need a good portfolio of work, relevant A level/Advanced Higher, Higher or equivalent qualifications, together with five GCSE/S Grade passes 9-4/A*-C/1-3. You could then progress to your chosen HND or degree course. In Scotland, the first year of a four-year degree is broadly similar to the foundation course.

Some universities and colleges place a greater emphasis on the technological aspects of industrial/product design and may require passes in maths or physics, so you must check prospectuses very carefully. Equally, some admissions staff for art and design courses could accept you purely on the strength of an exceptionally good portfolio of work.

Kind of Person

You would need a high degree of artistic, creative talent but this would have to be matched with an appreciation of the various constraints, particularly those of attractive appearance and good function versus cost of production and materials. You should be able to persuade others of your point of view, but you should also be able to take criticism and suggestions for improvement, and be happy working as part of a team.

You should have a good grounding in maths and an understanding of basic engineering principles and properties of engineering materials. A high level of computer proficiency would be essential to take advantage of the design software tailor-made for this field. Poor colour vision would limit your potential in industrial/product design but would not necessarily be a complete barrier.

Broad Outlook

As manufacturers have become more conscious of the marketability of good design, so the demand for industrial and product designers has increased, particularly for those with specialised knowledge of technology. Some large companies have their own design departments, while others employ design consultancies. Experienced designers also work on a freelance basis, having set up their own businesses. UK industry was severely affected by the economic downturn that started in 2008, but sustained recovery is now under way and is creating new opportunities for product designers.

Related Occupations

You might also consider: automotive engineer, architect, ceramics designer, furniture designer, manufacturing engineer, mechanical engineer, graphic designer, interior designer or set designer.

Impact on Lifestyle

Designers employed by a company usually work normal office hours, but you would need to be prepared to work in the evenings and at the weekend if there were deadlines to be met. If you work as a freelance designer you would have to face the possibility of financial insecurity until you become established.

Earnings Potential

Earnings vary a great deal, depending on the nature of the work, location and type of employer. Trainees working in-house could start at around £20,000 to £25,000, with those in consultancies getting more. Experienced designers and freelancers can typically earn around £33,000 to £55,000, while a senior consultant could earn in excess of £70,000.

Further Information

Creative and Cultural Skills
https://ccskills.org.uk/careers

Institution of Engineering Designers
www.institution-engineering-designers.org.uk

Design Council
www.designcouncil.org.uk

Chartered Society of Designers
www.csd.org.uk

Design Business Association
www.dba.org.uk

Directory of Design Consultants
www.designdirectory.co.uk

Institute of Designers in Ireland
www.idi-design.ie

Insurance Broker

What is Involved?

As an insurance broker, you would be an independent expert helping clients decide what sort of insurance cover they need, where to look for it and how much they should pay for it. You would use your knowledge and experience to assess risks thoroughly and accurately, and to find the appropriate policy or policies. You must put the interests of your client first, even though it is the insurance companies who pay you commission for the business you put in their direction. The range of insurance products is expanding all the time and it is possible to insure virtually anything, from cars, ships and aeroplanes to pets, pianists' hands and even the risks associated with a country's politics. You would have to know who to contact among over 700 insurance companies. This could include Lloyd's, a London market consisting of individuals or syndicates offering insurance cover, but not all brokers are authorised to do this.

You would normally be able to deal instantly with straightforward cases, such as motor insurance, but more complex risks would involve you in compiling a detailed report to present to the underwriters. You would use the report to negotiate cover with the insurers and obtain a quotation for your client. For very large risks, such as ships and aircraft, the risk is spread among a number of insurers, with each underwriter accepting only a small percentage of the risk. You would then have to contact many different insurers to obtain full cover for your client.

Opportunities for Training

Your training would be a mixture of on-the-job learning and study for insurance industry qualifications, possibly through a company's structured training scheme. If you advise clients on life assurance, health insurance, mortgage protection insurance or pensions, an appropriate qualification must be gained first, as these are regulated functions. There are examinations set by the Chartered Insurance Institute (CII) and the British Insurance Brokers Association (BIBA). The CII has a Broker Academy, which is essentially a 'one stop shop' training and development facility for insurance brokers, offering qualifications, learning and revision materials, access to face-to-face training, online learning and assessment facilities, membership of the CII and its dedicated Faculty of Broking. If you deal with complex and specialist risks in the London Insurance Market (sometimes known as being a 'Lloyd's broker'), you should pass the Lloyd's and London Market Introductory Test (LLMIT).

Requirements for Entry

Whilst there are no specific educational requirements, many organisations prefer graduates or A level/Advanced Higher, Higher or equivalent students for their trainee broker positions. However, a great deal of emphasis is placed on personal characteristics, making it possible to join a broking firm as a school leaver and progress to a post with quite considerable responsibility. You may be able to train via the Apprenticeship scheme. For entry to a degree course, you would need two or three A level/Advanced Higher, three or four Higher or equivalent qualifications.

Kind of Person

You would need good communication skills, both oral and written, since you would be dealing with a wide variety of people and often explaining complex matters. The information in a report must be presented to the underwriter logically and clearly, with great attention to detail. When approaching underwriters, you would require confidence and good negotiating skills. Numeracy would also be important. Another essential quality would be honesty, together with discretion, since you could be dealing with confidential and sensitive issues. You would benefit from an outgoing personality and business flair. In particular, you would need an analytical mind and the ability to assimilate large amounts of information. Much of your work would be on computer, so good IT skills would be essential.

Broad Outlook

The development of online, self-service insurance portals is changing the nature of broking - freeing brokers from much of the administrative side of managing relationships with clients and allowing them to concentrate on offering new products and services. The market is also becoming more international, which could indicate that good language skills and geographic mobility would open up a wider range of opportunities for career development and promotion.

Related Occupations

You might also consider: insurance underwriter, accountant (professional), actuary, loss adjuster, stockbroker, banking executive or financial adviser.

Impact on Lifestyle

Broking can be very demanding and at times frustrating when things go wrong and, despite hard work, a deal is lost. You would have to be persistent and calm even when underwriters are being uncooperative or clients impatient. You would usually work normal office hours during a five-day week, but you would need to be prepared to work in the evenings or at the weekend to meet particular clients.

Earnings Potential

You could expect to earn around £22,000 to £26,000 as a graduate trainee. Salaries may be performance-related and can vary significantly depending on the size and nature of the firm. With a few years' experience, you should be earning in the range £40,000 to £80,000. At the top end of the scale, a top broker in the City of London could earn well over £100,000 plus bonus. Additional benefits can include company car, private medical insurance and pension scheme, often non-contributory. The graduate training scheme at Lloyd's offers a starting salary of £27,000, with an increase of £1,000 after six, twelve and eighteen months and a bonus at the end of the programme.

Further Information

Chartered Insurance Institute
www.cii.co.uk

British Insurance Brokers Association
www.biba.org.uk

Apprenticeships
www.getingofar.gov.uk

Lloyd's of London
www.lloyds.com

Discover Risk
www.discoverrisk.co.uk

Insurance Institute of Ireland
www.iii.ie

Insurance Underwriter

What is Involved?

As an insurance underwriter, you would work for one of the major insurance companies or Lloyd's of London, assessing the extent of any given risk and deciding whether your organisation should accept it and on what terms. You would have to determine the appropriate premium for the risk, setting an amount high enough to reflect the potential loss that could result but low enough to attract the business away from any competitors.

In order to carry out these tasks, you would have to build up a thorough understanding of the risks you handle. In the early stages of your career, the risks you underwrite would be those for which there are well-established statistical data and for which rating guides are available. However, with more complex or more unusual risks, you would rely on your skill and experience to assess and rate risks appropriately.

You could specialise in, for example, large-scale risks in marine or aviation insurance or you could focus on smaller-scale but hugely valuable sectors such as motor car, life or property insurance. Lloyd's itself is an insurance marketplace, where underwriters and brokers meet to agree terms on what might be very straightforward or highly unusual or complicated risks.

Opportunities for Training

Training for insurance underwriters is usually in-house, under the supervision of experienced underwriters, or by moving from department to department to learn how premiums are charged, and claims checked and paid out. You can study by day release, evening classes or distance learning for the Associate examination of the Chartered Insurance Institute (CII), which is not essential but could be extremely valuable when seeking promotion. If you work for Lloyd's of London, you would be expected to sit the Lloyd's and London Market Introductory Test and the Certificate in Risk Management. The development of regulation under the Financial Conduct Authority has greatly increased the importance of appropriate qualifications and continuing professional development.

Requirements for Entry

While you can start as an underwriting trainee with A level/Advanced Higher, Higher or equivalent qualifications, you will find that many training programmes are aimed at graduates. As there is no school or degree subject which would fully equip you for an underwriting career, employers are unlikely to specify any particular course of study. However, subjects such as business studies, economics, law, science and engineering can be helpful, as can some interest in biology, physiology or medical matters for life underwriting. Some universities offer degrees in insurance, business studies or financial services with modules giving partial exemption from the CII Associate examinations. It may, on the other hand, be possible for you to enter as a trainee or junior underwriter through a level 2 apprenticeship or level 3 advanced apprenticeship in Providing Financial Services, following the General Insurance pathway.

Kind of Person

You would need to be decisive and capable of justifying your decisions with logical and sound argument. Given that you would often be dealing with extremely confidential information about an individual or organisation seeking insurance protection, you must be able to handle these details with the utmost discretion. For the more unusual risks, the ability to think and solve problems creatively could be extremely valuable. You would need a logical, analytical and retentive mind and the ability to take into account many different factors before making decisions. You would need to feel confident when dealing with numerical and statistical data, and would need to communicate clearly with actuaries, insurance technicians and other members of your team. It would be vital to be able to write up contracts covering the terms and conditions of your underwriting agreements.

Broad Outlook

The insurance industry has changed in recent years and many companies now have call centres and websites to deal with straightforward risks, cutting out some of the traditional work of the underwriting department. There are still, however, good career opportunities in over 700 insurance companies, including household name groups, small specialist insurers and Lloyd's of London.

Related Occupations

You might also consider: insurance broker, actuary, accountant (professional), banking executive, loss adjuster, statistician, stockbroker, surveyor (general practice) or financial adviser.

Impact on Lifestyle

Underwriting can be a very intense way of life, with a huge responsibility to get your quotations right and avoid unacceptable levels of loss. This calls for courage and confidence and the ability to accept worry and stress when large claims are made. Otherwise normal office hours should apply with very little disruption of your family and social life, although you may have to work unsocial hours if you need to be available to answer the more unusual call centre enquiries.

Earnings Potential

A typical starting salary for a graduate trainee would range from £24,000 to £26,000. This should increase with experience, increased responsibility and successful performance to £40,000 to £100,000. Professional underwriters at Lloyd's of London, who are different from 'underwriter members', can earn over £300,000.

Salaries can vary between employers and regions, and may include benefits such as subsidised mortgages and discounted insurance.

Further Information

Chartered Insurance Institute
www.cii.co.uk

International Underwriting Association of London
www.iua.co.uk

Lloyd's of London
www.lloyds.com

Apprenticeships
www.getingofar.gov.uk

Discover Risk
www.discoverrisk.co.uk

Association of British Insurers
www.abi.org.uk

Institute of Risk Management
www.theirm.org

Insurance Institute of Ireland
www.iii.ie

Interior Designer

What is Involved?

Interiors are big business. As an interior designer, you could be hired to create a desirable ambiance in a pub, club or restaurant to attract big-spending customers. You could be working with a chain of DIY stores to market a new range of wallcoverings, paint effects or soft furnishings. You could be adding a touch of designer style to private homes. In work that is often highly technical, you would liaise with your clients (or their architects) about design schemes to take account of the purpose of the space involved, the needs of the people using it, their budgets and timescales. Your brief may include curtains, carpets, furniture, lighting, fixtures and fittings.

This would involve design sketches, mock-ups, samples of fabrics and colour schemes and sourcing items such as light fittings. You would then oversee your projects, which would involve liaising with contractors. Closely associated specialist design work is also available in film, television and theatre set design; exhibition and display design; and any other interior space, from an aeroplane to a department store. You could work freelance, for an interior design consultancy, within an architectural practice or for a large hotel or store group or furniture manufacturer.

Opportunities for Training

Most entrants have a formal qualification in art and design. There are numerous degree courses in Interior Design, Interior Architecture or Spatial Design, which are available either as specialist courses or as part of other art and design courses. There are also foundation degrees, Higher National Certificates/Diplomas and postgraduate courses. The British Institute of Interior Design lists relevant courses on its website, although it does not offer any sort of recommendation or formal recognition.

Requirements for Entry

To obtain entry to an art and design course, you would usually have completed a foundation course in art and design (general year in Scotland). The foundation courses in England and Wales take two years for students aged 16 with five GCSE/S Grade passes 9-4/A*-C/1-3, or one year for students aged 17, who might also have an A level/Advanced Higher, Higher or equivalent qualification in a relevant subject. In most cases, a good portfolio of your best artistic work is more important than exam passes. Progression to a degree course would then be via interview, at which your portfolio would be carefully examined by the staff and questions asked.

Kind of Person

As a designer you would not have as much of a free hand as you would as an artist. You would have to meet your clients' needs and wishes, which can sometimes be difficult for creative people, and you would need to be tactful and persuasive but be prepared to compromise when it is wise to do so. You would need good drawing skills and must be able to communicate your ideas to the client. Team working skills would also be important, together with a willingness to meet deadlines.

You would need to be practical as well as creative, have a technical understanding of the materials you are working with and the sensitivity to assess their suitability for use. You would need a keen interest in fashion and an eye for colour, texture and pattern.

Broad Outlook

Interior design is seen as a glamorous profession and demand for jobs outstrips supply, although there is always a place for good creative talent. Most entrants start as an assistant in order to learn the practical aspects of the work, which can be for the company sector or for private clients. Self-employment is an option for experienced and established designers.

Related Occupations

You might also consider: architect, artist/illustrator, exhibition/display designer, fashion designer, furniture designer, graphic designer, industrial or product designer, landscape architect, set designer, textile designer or retail merchandiser.

Impact on Lifestyle

As an interior designer, you would be working both in a studio and on site as well as visiting clients in their homes. Designs have to be prepared, discussed and changed; furniture, fittings, fabrics and colour schemes have to be agreed...which is all very time consuming and calls for much patience, charm and diplomacy.

Although the work tends to be done in regular office hours, there are always deadlines to meet and contractors to engage and supervise, which could involve working evenings and weekends. Then there is the problem of finding time to assess work, produce written quotations, compete for prestigious contracts with hotels, restaurants, new housing estates, time-shares, property, land developments, holiday chalets and furnished flats, without which business would grind to a halt.

Earnings Potential

Earnings would vary widely, depending on your talent, your location and who you are working for. Starting as an assistant designer, you could expect to earn between £20,000 and £26,000. This should rise with experience to £30,000 to £70,000, and you could earn considerably more if you manage to make a name for yourself. Freelance designers charge anything from around £25 per hour upwards.

Further Information

British Institute of Interior Design
www.biid.org.uk

Chartered Society of Designers
www.csd.org.uk

Design Nation
www.designnation.co.uk

Careers in Design
www.careersindesign.com

Creative and Cultural Skills
http://ccskills.org.uk/careers

Institute of Designers in Ireland
www.idi-design.ie

Interpreter

What is Involved?

As an interpreter, you would be a highly skilled linguist specialising in the spoken word. You could be involved in simultaneous or consecutive interpreting, usually translating into your mother tongue from one or several other languages. Simultaneous interpreters generally work from a soundproof booth at multi-language conferences, listening to speeches through headphones and relaying an instant translation into a microphone; at smaller meetings, for one or two people and certain court proceedings, direct whispering may replace the technology. Consecutive interpreting occurs when the speaker pauses at intervals to allow you to translate what has been said into the target language. You might need to take notes in order not to forget anything that the speaker has said.

You would be expected to have a broad understanding of the cultural, technical, professional or practical issues under discussion, with the requisite vocabulary in the target language to convey what is necessary. Linguistic skills alone would not be enough.

Opportunities for Training

You would normally need a degree in interpreting or in languages followed by a postgraduate course. Your training should give you language laboratory practice in interpreting techniques, experience of technical vocabulary, note-taking and memorising exercises and practical work experience. You may be expected to work towards recognised vocational qualifications in interpreting and you would usually need to join and pass the examinations of professional organisations such as the International Association of Conference Interpreters (AIIC), the Chartered Institute of Linguists (CIOL) and/or the Institute of Translation and Interpreting (ITI).

The Diploma in Public Service Interpreting is a qualifying examination for membership of the National Register of Public Service Interpreters. This is for interpreters working in the context of public services, such as court hearings, police interviews, other legal contexts, health and government-related services.

Requirements for Entry

You would need two or three A level/Advanced Higher or three or four Higher passes (or equivalent) for degree entry, including one or more foreign languages. At least a year of your course should be spent in another country. The vocational qualifications route does not require any formal academic qualifications and could prove attractive if you have advanced linguistic skills, cultural awareness or technical knowledge but do not want to go to university. You would have to provide evidence of your ability in the form of recordings and simulated performance.

Kind of Person

Interpreting would require you to be alert, confident, capable of spontaneous reactions and articulate enough to communicate ideas rather than exact translations. You must have total mastery of your mother tongue and of one but preferably more foreign languages, together with a thorough knowledge of the institutions, culture, attitudes and practices in the countries where your languages are spoken, normally acquired through residence there. You would also need, for much of the work, a flair for technical subjects and a readiness to keep up to date with new developments. A good memory, the ability to concentrate for extended periods and a clear speaking voice would all be essential.

Broad Outlook

Starting up as an interpreter is not easy. The competition is intense and only the really skilled succeed. Few organisations employ full-time interpreters and, if they do, it is normally on short contracts. It is much more common for interpreters to be freelance. This would give you a great deal of freedom but it could take several years to establish your reputation and build up a network of contacts.

You could operate in international organisations such as the European Union, the United Nations and its agencies, NATO or aid agencies; you could work in law courts and conferences as well as in multinational corporations and companies. Public services employ interpreters for liaising with ethnic communities, or in legal work in court when a person does not understand the English language adequately.

Related Occupations

You might also consider: translator, teacher (secondary), TEFL/TESOL teacher, secretary linguist, tour operator, journalist, solicitor or diplomatic service officer.

Impact on Lifestyle

The implications for your domestic life are considerable, since you would be expected to travel extensively, sometimes at short notice. Conferences often take place in the evenings or at weekends and the work can be extremely tiring. Given the unpredictable nature of the work, you may need to supplement your income with other activities, such as teaching or translating.

Earnings Potential

There are relatively few salaried jobs for interpreters, and the best paid jobs tend to be based outside the UK. Freelance rates vary widely, from £100 to £500 or more per day depending on the setting, type of interpreting required, location, your experience and the level of demand for your languages. You may also be able to claim travel time and costs.

Agencies and telephone interpreting are increasingly being used to reduce costs, particularly in the public sector.

It is often difficult to sustain a steady income from interpreting, unless employed by one organisation as a conference interpreter.

Further Information

Institute of Translation and Interpreting
www.iti.org.uk

Chartered Institute of Linguists
www.ciol.org.uk

International Association of Conference Interpreters
http://aiic.net

European Commission Directorate General for Interpretation
http://ec.europa.eu/dgs/scic/index_en.htm

National Register of Public Service Interpreters
www.nrpsi.org.uk

Irish Translators' and Interpreters' Association
www.translatorsassociation.ie

Investment Analyst

What is Involved?

As an investment analyst, you would study the performance of companies on the stock markets of the world in order to advise your clients or employers on good new investment opportunities, or to warn them of any growing weaknesses in performance, which could undermine their existing investments. You would initially work in a team under the supervision of a qualified senior analyst. Typically, you would study company accounts, relevant newspaper articles or announcements, information on the Internet and statistical data on past performance. You would also visit companies to discuss their profit forecasts and the development of their trading activities.

This information would then be collated and written up in report format for your clients or managers, with your recommendations to buy, hold or sell the stocks concerned. You could advise investment banks or fund managers of pension funds or you could deal directly with companies needing advice on investment, including stockbrokers who wish to help their own clients. The roles of investment analyst and fund manager are quite similar but the fund manager would make buying decisions after considering the research/advice of the investment analyst.

Opportunities for Training

Almost all entrants are graduates, often with a professional qualification in a related field and with experience of a specialist market sector. You would normally train on the job and may be expected to obtain the Investment Management Certificate (IMC), which is assessed by the CFA Society of the UK, or the Chartered Institute for Securities and Investments Institute (CISI) Certificate in Investments. With experience, you could progress to the Chartered Financial Analyst (CFA) qualification, the CISI Diploma or the Certified International Investment Analyst qualification of the Association of Certified International Investment Analysts (ACIIA).

You can study for these qualifications by distance learning or by a mixture of distance learning and classroom-based study.

Requirements for Entry

You would normally need a degree or professional qualification for which typically two or three A level/Advanced Higher, three or four Higher or equivalent qualifications would be required in the first place. Postgraduate qualifications are not necessary, although some firms may favour applicants with a Master in Business Administration (MBA) award. Pre-entry experience can be highly beneficial, for example an internship, work experience or vacation work in a financial institution.

Kind of Person

You would need to be strongly interested in the stock market and financial news and prepared to keep up to date with trends and developments. Numerical and statistical skills would be vital to deal with the huge amount of financial data you would have to analyse, summarise and assess for future trends. You would need reasonable IT skills, as you would be using computers for much of your work. Sound judgement would be essential, with the ability to see behind the headlines and not to be swept into recommending excessively speculative investments.

A grasp of international politics and geography would be necessary to recognise the possible impact of war, conflict or other economic and financial problems on levels of world trade. It would also be helpful to earn the trust and respect of managers whose company results you are analysing, given that your recommendations could have a huge impact on their future trading. You would be expected to dress smartly and conventionally.

Broad Outlook

The global economic crisis of 2008 was blamed by most commentators on reckless investment in high-risk sectors by professionals who should have known better. Consequently, investment analysis, normally one of the most sought-after careers by the most ambitious graduates, lost much of its allure. The recent return of sustained market confidence means that many firms are keen to restore their recruitment levels and regain their traditional appeal.

Related Occupations

You might also consider: corporate investment banker, economist, investment fund manager, insurance underwriter, actuary, accountant (professional), statistician, stockbroker or financial adviser.

Impact on Lifestyle

Although this is an office-based career, stock markets are global and financial news arrives on a 24-hour basis. This can mean working irregular hours at times and keeping in touch with clients and colleagues around the world by telephone, fax and email every day.

Your performance would be continuously assessed, so you would need to be alert to significant news and to move fast in channelling this to clients. You would need to travel abroad to assess the soundness of some overseas companies and to hold meetings with overseas clients. Considerable disruption of your social and family life could occur at times in keeping pace in this highly demanding career field.

Earnings Potential

A typical starting salary for an entry-level graduate position in London is £30,000 to £40,000, with the addition of bonuses of 20% to 100%. Earnings would be lower in other parts of the UK. After five to eight years, salaries would normally rise to £65,000 to £100,000 plus large bonuses. Typical salaries at senior levels can be £120,000 to £150,000 with bonuses of up to 200% of salary.

Further Information

CFA Society of the UK
www.cfauk.org

London Stock Exchange
www.londonstockexchange.com

Chartered Institute for Securities and Investment
www.cisi.org

Association of Certified International Investment Analysts
http://aciia.org

Association for Financial Markets in Europe
www.afme.eu

Financial Conduct Authority
www.fca.org.uk

Irish Stock Exchange
www.ise.ie

Journalist

What is Involved?

As a newspaper journalist working for a local or national newspaper you would gather information and write reports about relevant people, places, events, politics, sport or crime. As a magazine journalist working for the ever-increasing number of magazines from the world of business, computing, sport, fashion, art and leisure, you would find many similarities with your newspaper journalist colleagues, although you might spend less time chasing news stories and more writing specialised feature articles. The process of recording interviews, researching information, writing up copy and sub-editing is largely the same. As a broadcast journalist working for national and local radio and television companies, you would be involved in researching, writing and presenting programmes and you may also have to operate studio equipment. As an agency journalist you would supply news, stories and photographs to magazines, newspapers and television stations.

Journalism in the 21st century is rapidly changing, with new publishing platforms meaning that reports are sourced, written and broadcast at faster speed than ever before. Where magazines and newspapers once had daily, weekly and monthly deadlines, every moment is now a deadline for publishing on the web. All journalists need to know how to work across all publishing platforms, in print, online and broadcast. In the course of one day a multimedia journalist can be expected to write a blog, film a short video piece for web publication and file an in-depth 500-word report for print. Versatility is key.

Opportunities for Training

There is no standard entry route into journalism. The National Council for the Training of Journalists (NCTJ) regulates training for newspaper work, offering possibilities linked to 'direct entry' or 'pre-entry.' Direct entrants usually follow a two-year training contract, working as journalists while studying part-time; pre-entry means following an accredited full-time course before finding a job. If you are sure that you want to make a career in journalism, you can take an NCTJ-approved post-A level/Advanced Higher, Higher, degree or postgraduate course.

The NCTJ is also involved with training for broadcast and magazine journalism, and there are courses accredited by the Periodicals Training Council within the Professional Publishers Association. Training for broadcast journalism focuses rather more on ad hoc provision organised by individual companies, although there are courses accredited by the Broadcast Journalism Training Council.

Requirements for Entry

The majority of journalists enter as graduates but not necessarily with a degree in journalism. You need to have a strong command of English, good communication skills and to be interested in people and news. Previous experience can often prove to be as valuable as academic achievement. Being on the editorial staff of your school/college magazine or undergraduate newspaper can show this, as can working as a volunteer on your local hospital or campus radio station or work-shadowing a journalist. It is important to build up a portfolio of your writing and any published articles to give evidence of your work.

Kind of Person

You would need to be familiar with computers and modern methods of communication and to meet deadlines. If you struggle to hand in your homework on time, consider whether you're really likely to succeed in the heat of the newsroom! You would need to be self-confident and persistent, to relate well to others and to be willing to work hard, often at unsocial hours. Any interests you have such as sport, fashion or a hobby may also be useful.

Broad Outlook

Despite the number and range of newspapers and magazines, competition for jobs and promotion is fierce and success is achieved solely on merit. There are always more candidates than places available and a constant stream of fresh young graduates serves to remind even experienced journalists that they are only as good as their last story.

Some freelance journalists become well established before embarking on their own and selling articles to newspapers and magazines. Others only write the occasional article and are not dependent on journalism for their income.

Related Occupations

You may be interested in other jobs in this field such as author/creative writer, technical author, commissioning editor, lexicographer, press/information officer, advertising account executive, public relations executive or broadcasting/media researcher.

Impact on Lifestyle

You may work irregular hours, often at weekends and evenings, and when a story breaks you have to be there. It is a job many people would like to do, and those in it have to be dedicated. Magazine journalists are more likely to work regular hours, although deadlines can still require staying on the job until your material is ready to print.

Earnings Potential

The starting salary for a trainee reporter on a local/regional paper may be as low as £15,000 to £16,000, although you can expect rises of £2,000 to £3,000 as you progress through training. Experienced journalists can earn from £22,000 a year to over £50,000, while the highest paid journalists and national newspaper editors can earn over £100,000.

There is wide variation between regional papers and national newspapers.

Different rates apply for broadcast and magazine journalism. The BBC Journalism Trainee Scheme offers a one-year contract paying £20,800 (non-London) or £25,205 (including London weighting), plus some travel and accommodation expenses.

Further Information

National Council for the Training of Journalists
www.nctj.com
Journalism
www.journalism.co.uk
BBC Journalism Trainee Scheme
www.bbc.co.uk/careers/trainee-schemes-and-apprenticeships/journalism/jts
Professional Publishers Association
www.ppa.co.uk
Broadcast Journalism Training Council
www.bjtc.org.uk
National Union of Journalists (including Ireland)
www.nuj.org.uk
Creative Skillset
http://creativeskillset.org

Land/Geomatics Surveyor

What is Involved?

As a land/geomatics surveyor, you would be primarily concerned with the accurate measurement of the natural and built environment, the description and classification of features, the analysis and collation of relevant data and the presentation of data in forms required by users such as architects, civil engineers, property developers, planners, solicitors, environmentalists, geologists, archaeologists, geographers and map makers. Your work would be an essential preliminary to virtually all planning, property development and construction, major engineering and other projects relating to the natural environment and urban infrastructure.

You would learn about the traditional survey methods of triangulation and traversing, and would use them when appropriate, but you would come to rely more and more on satellite geodesy and computerised mapping and Geographic and Land Information Systems. Your detailed surveys would often be based on plotting from aerial photography and the use of sophisticated computer-driven plotting equipment.

Opportunities for Training

Land surveying is part of the geomatics faculty of the Royal Institution of Chartered Surveyors (RICS). There are various routes to full RICS membership but the most likely in this case would be to take an accredited degree or postgraduate course in land surveying or a similar subject with a land or geomatics option. Your course should introduce you to the major methods of measuring and recording data, from levels, theodolites and simple maps to techniques involving the modern technology outlined above. An introduction to positioning and navigation using the Global Positioning System (GPS) would also be given and a residential field course would ensure that you could apply your knowledge to real-world tasks. On completion of your accredited course, you would be eligible to move to the two-year RICS structured training stage with an employer, concluding with an interview known as the Assessment of Professional Competence (APC).

Postgraduate courses in more specialist areas are also available, including subjects such as geodetic surveying, environmental management and earth observation, hydroinformatics and geographical information science.

Requirements for Entry

You would normally need three A level/Advanced Higher, four Higher or equivalent qualifications to enter an accredited degree in a surveying discipline, together with five GCSE/S Grade passes at 9-4/A*-C/1-3, including English and maths.

Kind of Person

Your job would involve the interpretation and analysis of data, requiring you to be observant and comfortable with numerical work. There would be extensive use of computers, so you would need to be confident in using the relevant software packages. You would need to be well organised and ordered in your approach to work as you would be collecting data from a number of different sources, often at enormous expense. You would usually work as a member of a team, particularly on larger projects. This might involve you in managing and coordinating the work of members of your team. In addition to liaising with fellow professionals, you might have to explain quite complicated and technical information to clients with little previous knowledge. You would need to be physically fit, as you are likely to spend a lot of time out on site or in open countryside.

Broad Outlook

The demand for land surveyors depends to a great extent on developments in construction and civil engineering and it must be said that the picture from 2008 to 2013 was far from encouraging, when the housing market weakened and demand for industrial, office, retail and leisure facilities declined considerably. Now the UK construction market is seeing a rise in demand after several subdued years. This upsurge is creating pressure across an industry which failed to invest in attracting new talent or in the training of existing employees at the height of the economic downturn. The good news is, therefore, that there is reason for optimism, with workloads, profits and employment all forecast to deliver growth over the next 12 months and it is now the responsibility of the industry to invest in training and technology to ensure that it capitalises on these opportunities.

You may be able to work abroad, or to branch out into areas such as archaeological surveying. Land surveyors are employed in certain government departments, large construction and civil engineering companies and local authorities. There are also increasing opportunities to work in private practice or as an independent consultant.

Related Occupations

You might also consider: surveyor (general practice), hydrographic surveyor, quantity surveyor, rural practice surveyor, building surveyor, engineering geologist, environmental consultant, geologist/geoscientist, town planner, architect, cartographer or civil engineer.

Impact on Lifestyle

This is unlikely to be a nine to five job. Whilst there would be times when you are based in an office with regular hours, you would also be expected to go out to sites. When on location, you could be in a remote area, which might take a long time to reach.

Earnings Potential

The average graduate salary is around £22,000, rising to around £30,000 to £40,000 on reaching chartered status. With seniority and experience, you should be able to earn £45,000 to £75,000 a year. Salaries in the commercial fields tend to be greater than those in the public sector and surveyors working in cities earn more than their rural counterparts.

The RICS Rewards and Attitudes Survey 2017 reports a continuing gender pay gap, with male property professionals earning an average of £11,000 more than their female counterparts.

Further Information

Royal Institution of Chartered Surveyors
www.rics.org

Faculty of Architecture and Surveying, Chartered Institute of Building
www.ciob.org

Chartered Institution of Civil Engineering Surveyors
www.cices.org

Survey Association
www.tsa-uk.org.uk

Society of Chartered Surveyors Ireland
www.scsi.ie

Landscape Architect

What is Involved?

As a landscape architect, you would work to preserve the natural scenery and ecology of an area while creating attractive settings for construction projects such as housing developments, roads, parks, play areas, offices or industrial buildings. You might also work on preserving parts of the coastline, rescuing derelict factory sites or restoring disused pits and quarries. You could specialise in countryside issues or you could focus on urban projects. Whatever the particular project, you would hold discussions with your clients to find out what the job is about, make visits to the site to carry out surveys and then draw up plans and projected costs.

Once these have been agreed, you would visit the site from time to time to check that the landscaping work is progressing smoothly. In order to produce workable design solutions, you would need an understanding of topics such as civil engineering, surveying, geology, horticulture and earth-moving techniques. Indeed, you would usually be part of a team including architects, civil engineers, town planners and construction technicians.

Opportunities for Training

There are two possible routes to qualification: a degree in landscape architecture or postgraduate study after taking a degree in a related subject, such as architecture, horticulture or botany accredited by the Landscape Institute. The higher degree can be taken straight away or, on a full- or part-time basis, after you have spent some time in related work.

Being a Chartered Member of the Landscape Institute (CMLI) is the recognised professional qualification in landscape architecture. To achieve this chartered status, you must first attain licentiate membership by completing your first degree or postgraduate course and then gain at least two years' approved practical experience on the Pathway to Chartership (P2C) before taking the Institute's professional practice examination.

Requirements for Entry

The minimum requirements for degree entry would normally be two A level/Advanced Higher, three Higher or equivalent qualifications, plus supporting GCSE/S Grade passes at 9-4/A*-C/1-3, which should include English and either maths or a science. The Landscape Institute regards subjects such as art, biology, botany and geography as particularly relevant, although you should check with university prospectuses to be sure of exact entry requirements. You would also be expected to show a portfolio of artwork, including landscape designs, to provide evidence of your creative potential. For entry to a postgraduate course, you would need a good first degree.

Kind of Person

You would need a genuine concern for the environment, an understanding of conservation issues, creative vision, good drawing ability and excellent communication skills. You would almost certainly use a computer for your design work and would need a reasonable standard of IT literacy. Good organisational and negotiating skills would be very important for working as part of a team. Inspecting construction sites can be demanding physically, so you would need to be reasonably fit.

Broad Outlook

Like the construction industry generally, landscape architecture has highs and lows reflecting the state of the national economy. After the recession of 2008, building temporarily slowed down considerably and with it opportunities for architects of all kinds. Present economic development and growing emphasis on sustainable development, however, offer the prospect of increased demand for landscape architects.

About half of all landscape architects work in private practice for small firms or consultancies. Other major employers include local authorities and government agencies such as the Environment Agency, Natural England, Scottish Natural Heritage, the Countryside Council for Wales and environmental charities such as Groundwork.

There is a formal career structure in the public sector, with corresponding security, but many landscape architects prefer to move to private practice when they have some experience, in order to develop their ideas more freely.

Related Occupations

You might also consider: countryside/nature conservation officer, environmental consultant, surveyor (general practice), forest/woodland manager, horticultural manager, town planner, civil engineer, architectural technician/technologist or architect.

Impact on Lifestyle

You would need to be prepared to go on site in all weathers but you would usually spend less than a quarter of your time outdoors. Far more of your time would be taken up with deskwork and meetings. Landscape architects working in private practice are likely to spend quite a lot of time travelling, undertaking commissions around the country.

In the public sector, you would normally work a basic 37-hour week, whereas private practice is more likely to include long and irregular hours, often involving evening and weekend meetings with clients.

Earnings Potential

According to the Landscape Institute, the most common salary range for chartered members is £30,000 to £49,999. Just over 61% of those responding to the latest survey indicate that their salary falls within this range.

More than three-quarters of licentiate members say their salaries are between £20,000 and £29,999.

While many public-sector landscape architects have seen reductions in their team, department or organisation in the past 12 months, there are signs of strong employment rates and indications of growth in salaries in the private sector.

Further Information

Landscape Institute
www.landscapeinstitute.org

British Association of Landscape Industries
www.bali.org.uk

Society of Garden Designers
www.sgd.org.uk

Irish Landscape Institute
www.irishlandscapeinstitute.com

Legal Executive

What is Involved?

As a chartered legal executive in England and Wales (there is no direct equivalent in Scotland), you would be a qualified lawyer, working alongside solicitors and barristers, and would be involved in a specialist area of the law. For example you could choose to specialise in civil litigation, company and business law, conveyancing, criminal law, family law or probate.

You may well find yourself as the main point of contact for clients concerned about their legal affairs and may have an administrative or managerial role within a legal practice. Your day-to-day work would be similar to that of many solicitors and you could continue to train, should you wish to do so, until you qualify as a solicitor.

Opportunities for Training

To qualify as a legal executive lawyer, you must register with the Chartered Institute of Legal Executives (CILEx) as a student member and complete two stages of training:

- Level 3 Professional Diploma in Law and Practice - an introduction to the main areas of law and legal practice (after five units you will have achieved the Level 3 Certificate in Law, with the full Level 3 Professional Diploma after 10 units)
- Level 6 Professional Higher Diploma in Law and Practice - specialist higher-level study of law, equivalent to degree level

You can study by day-release, evening classes or distance learning.

On average it takes four years of part-time study to pass both levels of examination, giving you Membership of CILEx. However, if you have a recognised law degree or postgraduate law qualification, you could qualify in around nine months through the CILEx Graduate 'Fast-track' Diploma. In order to become a fully qualified chartered legal executive lawyer, you would also need to complete up to five years of qualifying employment. This can include carrying out work of a legal nature under the supervision of a solicitor, senior chartered legal executive, barrister or licensed conveyancer.

You may be able to enter the profession via a level 3 Advanced Apprenticeship or level 4 Higher Apprenticeship in Legal Services, as there are some common units with the CILEx level 3 qualification.

Requirements for Entry

You would need at least four GCSE/S Grade passes at 9-4/A*-C/1-3 or equivalent. These must include English and at least another two academic subjects. However, there is strong competition for places in legal practices, so you may need more than these minimum stated requirements. Many successful applicants are graduates, including Law graduates. You can make valuable contacts by doing holiday work in a solicitor's office or in a local court. This should show that you have a genuine interest in and knowledge of this sort of legal career.

Kind of Person

You would meet a wide range of people in your job, so you would need the ability to communicate effectively at all levels. You would be required to express yourself fluently and persuasively, both verbally and in writing, with a clear understanding of technical legal terms.

At times you would have to work under pressure and you would have to analyse and solve problems as and when they arise. It would be important that you have good attention to detail. You would be working in an office, possibly dealing with several different cases at the same time, and would need to have good organisational and administrative abilities.

Broad Outlook

There are opportunities for chartered legal executives to run their own departments, and to manage other executives, administrative staff and junior solicitors. The CILEx training route may also be used as entry to the final stages of the qualification scheme for a solicitor.

Chartered legal executive lawyers can become partners in law firms alongside solicitors, barristers, conveyancers and patent attorneys.

Changes to the eligibility and application criteria for the judiciary mean that chartered legal executive lawyers can now become District Judges, Deputy District Judges and Tribunal Chairmen.

Related Occupations

You may be interested in other careers in the legal field such as barrister, barristers'/advocates' clerk, licensed conveyancer, paralegal, patent attorney, solicitor or shorthand writer/court reporter.

Impact on Lifestyle

Although you would be working in an office, your hours may at times be long when you have a deadline to meet or when there is a large volume of work to complete. In addition, you would need to be prepared to use your free time in the early years to study for your exams.

Earnings Potential

There is no recommended minimum salary for trainee legal executives but the CILEx Salary Survey 2015 report indicates that starting salaries typically range from £13,000 to £29,000 in the north of England, and from £15,000 to £30,000 in the south. Your salary is likely to rise with experience and increasing responsibility to £35,000 to £55,000, and even more for a senior Fellow. Salaries vary greatly depending on employer, location and type of work, with those in the City, particularly in commercial litigation, normally very high. This salary diversification looks set to continue increasing.

Many employers help out with course or examination fees while you are working for them.

Further Information

Chartered Institute of Legal Executives
www.cilex.org.uk

CILEx Careers
www.cilexcareers.org.uk

All about Law
www.allaboutlaw.co.uk

Skills for Justice Career Pathways
www.skillsforjustice-cp.com

Apprenticeships
www.getingofar.gov.uk

Leisure Services/Fitness Centre Manager

What is Involved?

As a leisure services manager, you would be responsible for the efficient operation of a leisure and sports complex or centre. You would ensure that the whole organisation runs smoothly on a day-to-day basis, that there are sufficient suitably-trained staff on the premises, that safety procedures are in place and that the customers are enjoying themselves. You would be in charge of the sports coaches and instructors, together with office, catering and maintenance staff, and you would be dealing with every aspect of running the centre, including financial control and book-keeping, the recruitment of staff and the organisation of timetables and special activities (such as school holiday courses and tournaments).

You might have some face-to-face involvement with customers, dealing with complaints and possibly doing some sports coaching yourself, if you are suitably qualified. Leisure and sports centres vary widely in size and scope, with the largest quite possibly encompassing indoor and outdoor facilities, such as swimming pools, gymnasia and fitness centres, badminton, squash, tennis and basketball courts, football and cricket pitches. They may also include dance floors, saunas, and children's activity centres, and there will almost always be cafés, usually with bars too. Some centres specialise in outdoor and adventure pursuits, such as rock-climbing and canoeing.

Opportunities for Training

While there are several possible routes to a responsible position of this kind, employers are increasingly looking to appoint graduates with professional qualifications and relevant experience. A good starting point would therefore be a degree in sports and leisure studies or sports science or a degree in another subject followed by a postgraduate course.

You could then study on a part-time basis for the certificates and diplomas of the Chartered Institute for the Management of Sport and Physical Activity. An alternative would be to start at a lower level and study part-time for degree and professional qualifications. You may also be able to get into the leisure industry through an Apprenticeship scheme. The range of Apprenticeships available in your area will depend on the local jobs market and the types of skills employers need.

Requirements for Entry

Degree course entry would normally require two or three A level/Advanced Higher, three or four Higher or equivalent qualifications, together with five GCSE/S Grade passes at 9-4/A*-C/1-3. You should check course details carefully because they vary a great deal and may not contain the right elements for you. A talent for sport, and proven success, would be an advantage and the ability to drive could be useful. Lifeguard qualifications and first aid training might also be looked for.

Kind of Person

You should be well-motivated, organised and efficient, in order to make sure that the centre functions smoothly at all times. If there is a problem, you should be able to deal with it or delegate someone else to do so. You should have a good sense of business, in order to promote the centre and attract new customers, and you should be able to cope with financial matters where necessary.

Good communication skills, both verbal and written, would be extremely important and you should enjoy being both a leader and member of a team, so that your staff will respect you and enjoy working with you. You should also be enthusiastic and knowledgeable about sport, enjoying the contact with the customers, and helping them to enjoy what the centre has to offer.

Broad Outlook

Leisure and sports centres have proliferated over the past few years, all over the country, and are usually very popular. Opportunities to progress to senior management positions have generally kept pace with the growth in leisure provision. There is scope for managers to be promoted to bigger centres, or to take up administrative and managerial posts with local authorities in their sports and recreation departments. We are likely to see a growing number of local authorities outsourcing their sports and leisure facilities to the private sector.

Related Occupations

You might also consider: marketing executive, PE/PT teacher/instructor, public relations executive, retail manager, professional sportsperson, sports administrator, sports and exercise psychologist, sports physiotherapist, swimming coach/teacher or sports coach.

Impact on Lifestyle

By the very nature of the industry, you would have to expect to work some weekends and in the evenings, as well as normal office hours. Usually a rota would be worked, in order to share out the unsocial hours. You should also be prepared to work additional hours whenever necessary. You may have to move around the country to find a new post as you develop your career.

Earnings Potential

Salaries vary widely, according to the size and location of the centre (with higher pay in London), and between the public and private sector. There are national pay scales for those employed by local authorities. In general, starting salaries range from around £18,000 to £27,000, rising with promotion and increased responsibility to around £35,000 to £55,000. In the private sector, you may also receive a bonus related to targets, such as membership retention or attracting new members.

Further Information

Chartered Institute for the Management of Sport and Physical Activity
www.cimspa.co.uk

Sport and Recreation Alliance
www.sportandrecreation.org.uk

Apprenticeships
www.getingofar.gov.uk

SkillsActive - Sector Skills Council for Active Leisure and Learning
www.skillsactive.com

UK Active
www.ukactive.com

Leisure Jobs
www.leisurejobs.com

Ireland Active
www.irelandactive.ie

Librarian/Information Manager

What is Involved?

As a librarian, you might just as likely be known as an information manager or scientist, since the management, storage, retrieval and presentation of information would be at the core of your job, and the amount and variety of information, both in content and form, would be absolutely huge. Gone are the days of the stereotypical librarian, surrounded by mounds of dusty or dog-eared volumes, fussily telling readers to "shush"! Books, periodicals and printed catalogues are still of vital importance but information now comes via a great many other media, including the internet, CD-ROM, video and DVD, making your work as a librarian increasingly diverse.

You might be based in a public library, with plenty of contact with readers and responsibility for a wide variety of topics; you might specialise in a particular field (possibly medical or legal) and work for a learned or professional organisation; you might like the idea of working in an academic library in a university or other institution of higher education.

Whatever type of library you chose, the basic principles of your work would be the same: to make sure that your acquisitions are up to date and meet the needs of your clients; to organise the material in the most accessible way; to help users find the information they require, if necessary researching and acquiring new material for them. You might also, in a public library, organise events to promote the library and encourage new readers.

Opportunities for Training

A pre-entry postgraduate qualification accredited by the Chartered Institute of Library and Information Professionals (CILIP) is essential. A postgraduate diploma or MA/MSc in librarianship, information science, or information management is required unless your first degree is in librarianship or information studies. Some universities will take experienced library professionals without a degree on to their postgraduate courses after an interview or enter you on to a postgraduate diploma course. Early application for postgraduate courses is advised.

In order to qualify for chartered membership of CILIP, you must undertake further training as part of a continuing professional development (CPD) programme, and demonstrate evidence of appropriate skills gained through professional practice. Most members gain chartered membership two or three years after graduating.

Requirements for Entry

The minimum entry requirement for undergraduate degree courses is two A level/Advanced Higher, three Higher or equivalent qualifications, together with five GCSE/S Grade passes 9-4/A*-C/1-3, though in practice many courses will be looking for more than this. The courses usually take three or four years full-time or four or five years part-time. Postgraduate courses take one year full-time or two or three years part-time. Up to one year of library experience is normally required for entry to postgraduate courses.

Kind of Person

You should have excellent communication skills, since you would be dealing with a wide variety of people and would need to understand what they want and how to direct them to the information they require. In any library, a high level of computer literacy would be important, together with a methodical approach and excellent record keeping. Wide-ranging general knowledge and active intellectual curiosity would be clear assets in this type of work, together with specialised knowledge if you are working in an academic library.

Broad Outlook

As a librarian/information professional, you would be at the heart of the information revolution. This does not necessarily indicate a huge shortage of suitably qualified people but it does acknowledge that library work is changing rapidly. Indeed, your career development may depend on how willing you are to embrace new methods of storing and accessing information and to move between different employment sectors in order to broaden your experience. There is a particular shortage of librarians with scientific or technical backgrounds.

In the current climate of austerity and spending cuts, there is a concern that local authorities may seek to close a substantial number of public libraries. In the past six years, for example, 343 libraries have closed and some 8,000 jobs - a quarter of the workforce - have disappeared, and CILIP fears another 340 closures over the next five years.

Related Occupations

If you like the sound of librarianship/information management, you might also be interested in: antiquarian bookseller, archivist, bookseller, indexer, lexicographer, museum keeper - art gallery curator or teacher (secondary).

Impact on Lifestyle

Your working hours as a librarian would depend very much on where you are based. You might well have to work on a shift basis, including evenings and weekends, particularly in the public library service or in university libraries. On the other hand, you might have a term-time only contract in a school library. There is considerable potential for part-time working or job-sharing. You may have to move around the country to develop your career.

Earnings Potential

Earnings vary massively from job to job and you are advised to consult CILIP for detailed salary guidelines. In public libraries, for example, the current recommended salary scale is £19,800 to £24,500 for a newly qualified librarian, rising to £24,000 to £30,000 after two to five years and to £45,000 to £55,000 for a head librarian. The director of a higher education library might expect to earn £57,000 to £75,000.

Further Information

Chartered Institute of Library and Information Professionals
www.cilip.org.uk

Society of College, National and University Libraries
www.sconul.ac.uk

Library Jobs
www.lisjobnet.com

School of Information and Communication Studies, Dublin
www.ucd.ie/sils

Library Association of Ireland
https://libraryassociation.ie

Licensed Conveyancer

What is Involved?

As a licensed conveyancer in England and Wales, you would be a specialist property lawyer, trained and qualified in all aspects of the law dealing with property transfer. You could act for buyers, sellers and lenders in the process of transferring the ownership of a house, flat, commercial property or piece of land from one person to another, otherwise known as conveyancing.

Your work would be office-based and would involve conducting searches into the ownership of properties, their leasehold or freehold status, likely planning changes, rights of way, checking the new owner's liability for unsound building structures and repairs, planned changes to roads and highways and local factory and property developments. You might work for a licensed conveyancer, solicitor, local authority, bank or building society, provided that an appropriately qualified conveyancer or solicitor is head of the legal department.

Opportunities for Training

In order to qualify, you would need to work for at least two years in a legal environment, gaining practical experience of conveyancing. At the same time, you would have to pass the foundation and final examinations of the Council for Licensed Conveyancers (CLC). You could study for these by part-time attendance at a college or university or through distance learning. The topics covered would include all aspects of conveyancing law and practice, law of contract, land law, landlord and tenant agreements and accounts.

Having successfully completed the examinations and practical training, you would be eligible to apply for a limited licence, allowing you to offer conveyancing services through your employer. After a minimum period of three years at this level, you could apply for a full licence and become a partner in a firm or even set up your own business as a sole practitioner.

Requirements for Entry

You would need to have at least four GCSE/S Grade passes 9-4/A*-C/1-3 or equivalent which must include English and three other approved subjects. However, many applicants have A level/Advanced Higher, Higher or equivalent qualifications as well. A degree in law would give you exemption from many of the qualifying examinations. Conveyancing practitioners in Scotland have a degree in law or a diploma/certificate in legal studies and must be registered with the Law Society of Scotland.

Kind of Person

You would need to be well organised in order to deal efficiently with the large amount of paperwork involved. Attention to detail would be important to avoid potentially costly errors in the documents you are preparing. At times these documents could be quite complex, so you would need to have the patience and perseverance necessary to work your way through them. In addition, you would need good communication skills to explain legal matters to your clients. If you establish yourself as an independent practitioner, you would need the relevant commercial skills to run your own business. The CLC will not approve your licence until it is satisfied that you are a 'fit and proper person' to practise as a licensed conveyancer.

Broad Outlook

This is a relatively new profession, which started in 1987 after the law was changed to end the effective conveyancing monopoly held by solicitors. The number of practising conveyancers is now growing and the qualification is becoming increasingly sought after, both by people wishing to practise on their own account and by employers responsible for providing legal services.

The housing market has been depressed since the recession that started in 2008, with a massive drop in sales, widespread redundancies, falling house prices and potential buyers finding great difficulty in securing mortgage finance. For a number of years before that, however, the market had been extremely buoyant and all the indicators confirm that business is booming again in 2017. If you pursue a career in conveyancing, you must accept that this is a field that fluctuates and that your prospects and your pay could rise or fall in relation to the volume of property transfers.

Related Occupations

You might also consider: estate agent, legal executive, facilities manager, local government officer, paralegal, solicitor, civil service executive officer, accountant(professional), insurance underwriter or insurance broker.

Impact on Lifestyle

You would be working office hours but may well need to work into the evenings and at weekends to meet deadlines. This would be particularly true if you were trying to establish a business and develop your own customer base. You might need to offer a faster, cheaper, more efficient service in order to entice clients away from traditional providers of conveyancing services. The initial training can be expensive and you may wish to seek financial support from your employer to help you through this phase of your professional development.

Earnings Potential

In general, salaries for trainees without experience tend to be around £16,000 to £20,000, while those for qualified licensed conveyancers with at least three years' experience range from £30,000 to £50,000. Employed conveyancers may be salaried or paid on a commission basis. A partner or owner of a conveyancing firm could earn around £60,000.

Further Information

Council for Licensed Conveyancers
www.clc-uk.org

Society of Licensed Conveyancers
www.conveyancers.org.uk

Law Society of Scotland
www.lawscot.org.uk

Local Government Officer

What is Involved?

As a local government officer, you would be part of a huge workforce of over one million people in England alone, working within a network of some 350 local authorities, and covering more than 500 different occupational areas. Your work would address the needs, conflicts and concerns of the local population in a variety of services ranging from education, leisure and environmental protection to trading standards, social services and waste collection. You could be engaged in a range of management challenges relating to any one of these services, working alongside specialist professionals such as architects, surveyors, social workers, teachers and environmental health officers.

Local authorities are led by elected councillors and you would have to implement their policies. You might advise on the initial decision-making process and you would certainly be involved in setting up procedures to carry out decisions, manage systems efficiently and ensure that public money is being spent wisely. You would be expected to report back to councillors on a regular basis. You might work from a large public building such as a county hall or from a smaller office in the area covered by your authority.

Opportunities for Training

There are several different training routes. You could, for example, join as a clerical or administrative assistant and work your way up to officer level by achieving a relevant vocational qualification. Alternatively, you could take a degree in any subject and apply for the National Graduate Development Programme (NGDP), which is specifically designed to create a new generation of managers with the ability to take on senior roles. Though recruited at a national level, you would join a local authority and would spend two years there, taking on strategic project work, obtaining a postgraduate management qualification and participating in short-term placements with other public and private sector partners. As you progress through the programme, you would gain the capabilities and experience to make an impact on the direction local government might take in the future.

Requirements for Entry

The NGDP aims to attract high calibre graduates with a wide range of abilities and knowledge. You would therefore need at least an upper second class honours degree in any subject. For other opportunities, the skills and experience needed would vary according to the duties and level of responsibility, so you should check the entry requirements carefully for each job. You may find that qualifications to degree standard are required, while in some cases relevant life or work experience will suffice.

Kind of Person

According to the NGDP, you would need to demonstrate the following range of skills and personal characteristics to respond to the challenges of local government administration: teamwork - using your skills to complement others and sharing your talents to achieve a common goal; leadership - inspiring, directing and influencing staff at every level with enthusiasm, energy and assertiveness; analysis - identifying, analysing and interpreting relevant information from a range of sources to develop well-informed solutions; communication - talking, writing and presenting your ideas clearly and logically; organisation - managing your time and priorities to deliver to deadline-driven objectives; IT awareness - understanding the benefits and pitfalls of computer applications within local government; motivation - personal and career drive to achieve success through continued learning, perseverance and proactivity.

Broad Outlook

Sweeping job losses in local government between 2013 and 2015 have continued, with a target of cutting some 1.2 million public sector posts by 2018. Restructuring, delayering, redundancies, recruitment freezes, job sharing and outsourcing all conspire to confirm that this is not the best time to be starting a career as a local government officer. Where vacancies occur, competition is certain to be intense.

Many traditional local government services have been privatised or contracted out in recent years, leading to increased opportunities for switching between the public and private sectors. One growth area, once you have gained sufficient experience, is to set up your own consultancy specialising in areas such as drawing up service specifications, negotiating contracts and monitoring contractor performance.

Related Occupations

You might also consider: civil service executive officer, civil service fast streamer, facilities manager, health service manager, housing manager, human resources manager, social worker or chartered/company secretary.

Impact on Lifestyle

You would normally work a fairly standard 37-hour week, Monday to Friday, although you may be expected to attend some evening meetings. Local government employers often make provision for very flexible working patterns, including flexitime, job sharing and term-time only contracts.

Earnings Potential

As a graduate recruit to the NGDP, you would receive a starting salary of £23,698 plus London weighting if applicable. If you start as an administrative assistant, you would be paid on a scale ranging from around £16,000 to £20,000. This could rise with experience to £30,000 to £40,000. Your entry point would depend on such factors as the grade of the job and your level of responsibility.

Further Information

Local Government Jobs
www.lgjobs.com

Local Government Association
www.local.gov.uk

National Graduate Development Programme
www.ngdp.org.uk

Institute of Administrative Management
www.instam.org

Convention of Scottish Local Authorities
www.cosla.gov.uk

Welsh Local Government Association
www.wlga.gov.uk

Public Appointments Service, Ireland
www.publicjobs.ie/publicjobs

Logistics/Supply Chain Manager

What is Involved?

As a logistics manager, you would specialise in organising and improving the supply chain, the complex sequence of events and decisions which connects sourcing raw materials with manufacturing and the end consumer. You may work for a large organisation, such as a manufacturer or retail company, aiming to get the right quantity of a product to the right place, at the right time, in the right condition and at an acceptable cost.

You might be responsible for the smooth operation of a manufacturing process or for managing a distribution centre. Equally, you may plan a new supply strategy or be involved in production scheduling or vehicle routing. Getting the supply chain exactly right is vital, as late deliveries, over-ordering of stock or miscalculating delivery times could cost your company their competitive edge. You would aim to make things happen 'just-in-time', which means being involved with buying, manufacturing, movement of goods by say road or rail, warehousing and general distribution. All of these areas are interdependent and you would have to co-ordinate them efficiently, making considerable use of IT to process data.

Opportunities for Training

Entry into the industry is usually via a graduate training scheme. There are industrial placements available for sandwich course students and also summer internships for undergraduates. Once in employment, you would receive in-house training and have the opportunity to study for a professional qualification in logistics. Another option would be to start with a company in a more junior role, for example as a transport clerk, before working your way up to supervisory and management levels. There may be relevant Apprenticeships available in your area.

The Chartered Institute of Logistics and Transport offers professional qualifications at junior, middle and senior management levels, with courses covering the development of general management skills, key personal abilities, professional standards, road freight regulations, operations and administration, transport economics, inventory management, movement of people, government transport policy and resource management. Companies may offer full- or part-time training or distance learning, including postgraduate study to MSc level.

Requirements for Entry

The minimum requirements for degree course entry would be two or more A level/ Advanced Higher, three Higher or equivalent qualifications, together with five GCSE/S Grade passes 9-4/A*-C/1-3 including English and maths. There are some degree courses in logistics management but many employers would accept a good quality degree in other subjects.

Kind of Person

To manage, co-ordinate and improve the total supply chain demands high-level managerial skills and the capacity to play a key part in meeting your company's longer-term strategic objectives. You would need to be numerate and able to solve problems, think on your feet and manage people. The ability to use IT packages and electronic communication methods would be vital, not least because, with the growing use of internet shopping, the supply chain is at the heart of developments in telecommunications and e-commerce. Foreign language skills would be a great advantage, since you could be in contact with suppliers or buyers all over the world.

Broad Outlook

Career opportunities in logistics continue to grow. Even during downturns in the business cycle, when companies are cutting costs, the demand for able and experienced supply chain managers tends to remain high. You could expect to achieve managerial level after about five years and could go on to be a director. There should be many opportunities to move to other companies wishing to develop their logistics expertise or you could consider setting up your own consultancy business.

Environmental concerns are creating new areas of opportunity. For example, the supply chain no longer ends with the consumer but includes consideration of how goods can be recycled; you might be involved in ensuring that a distribution centre is energy efficient or in minimising the pollution impact of a large fleet of lorries.

Growth in internet sales is another important driver for career opportunities, with increasing demand from parcel operators for cross dock parcel hubs to service internet orders.

Related Occupations

You might also consider: buying executive, facilities manager, marketing executive, operational researcher/management scientist, passenger transport manager, retail manager, warehouse manager, shipbroker or freight forwarder.

Impact on Lifestyle

As this job is all about deadlines, you would be expected to work extra hours when the occasion demands, especially during emergencies such as transport delays. Logistics management often operates 24 hours a day, seven days a week. It could make major demands on your time, especially if you are in regular contact with people living on the other side of the world. Your hours of work could be long and irregular and you may be expected to travel extensively.

Earnings Potential

The range of typical starting salaries for new graduates is £20,000 to £27,000. Larger companies may pay more, especially on completion of training. It is common for graduates to double their starting salary after five years. On promotion to middle to senior management level, salaries range from £45,000 to £120,000. The Chartered Institute of Logistics and Transport website lists current vacancies together with details of remuneration offered.

Further Information

Chartered Institute of Logistics and Transport (UK)
www.ciltuk.org.uk

Skills for Logistics
www.skillsforlogistics.co.uk

Apprenticeships
www.getingofar.gov.uk

Careers in Logistics
www.careersinlogistics.co.uk

Logistics Manager
www.logisticsmanager.com

Supply Chain Management Institute
www.ipics.ie

Management/Business Consultant

What is Involved?

As a management consultant, your job would be to help companies and organisations improve their success rate by investigating their current structure and work practices, searching out any weaknesses and suggesting or implementing appropriate remedies. This would involve in-depth research, including the consideration of staffing, marketing strategies, growth potential, financial controls and the strength of the competition where appropriate.

In a time of technological change, as now, you might also be called upon to advise on and often oversee the implementation of new methods of working, bearing in mind the implications this would have on existing staffing and traditional work patterns.

Opportunities for Training

There is no single route of training to become a management consultant. Many practitioners come into the work after successful management experience in industry or commerce and, quite often, with a postgraduate qualification such as the MBA (Master of Business Administration).

However, some very large management consultancies do recruit recent graduates and give them intensive in-house training. You can become a member of the Institute of Consulting, the professional body which regulates standards of qualifications and competence.

You might start, for example, with the level 5 qualification in Professional Consulting, which is intended for people considering a move in to the profession from a functional discipline, or for those who wish to obtain an introduction to the skills and knowledge needed. You can then progress to the level 7 qualification and continue to Certified Management Consultant status.

Requirements for Entry

Although there is no educational requirement actually laid down for entry into the profession, it is virtually all graduate. The subject of your first degree could be drawn from a wide variety, followed by management training. There are, however, plenty of degrees in management and related fields or a combination of, say, a modern language and management/business, financial or engineering studies, which could provide a good introduction.

If you like the idea of studying for a degree in management, you should look very carefully at the subjects required at A level/Advanced Higher, Higher or equivalent for entry. Some courses might specify maths beyond GCSE/S Grade levels.

Kind of Person

You would need excellent communication skills, both spoken and written, as you would be dealing with a wide variety of people, at all levels of seniority, and would have to write clear, cogent reports on your findings and recommendations. Some of these would not necessarily be very popular, and you would need tact, resilience and understanding to deal with this. You would almost certainly be working as a member of a team, but should also have considerable independence of mind and the confidence to make decisions based on your own judgement.

You should enjoy problem solving and analysing situations and you should have plenty of stamina, both physical and emotional, as you might be working long hours in order to meet deadlines and you would be making far-reaching decisions. You should be able to work comfortably with a variety of IT systems.

Broad Outlook

Given the ever-increasing pace of change, management consultants often find it necessary or desirable to specialise in different aspects of the work, such as finance, marketing or IT, or in particular types of organisation, such as manufacturing, commercial sales/exporting, retailing or even charities. Competition for places in the best-known management consultancies is very great but, if you make the grade, the potential for promotion is good, particularly with the growth of multi-national companies, and increasing competition and mergers. Some experienced consultants set up their own agencies. The UK consulting market is the largest outside the US, with a current value of around £10 billion, employing some 80,000 consultants.

In common with most other sectors, management consultancy has faced tough trading conditions in the economic downturn. While the commercial environment remains challenging, fee income has now returned to pre-crisis levels.

Related Occupations

If you think you have the skills and qualities to be a management consultant, you might also like to consider: actuary, accountant (professional), economist, financial risk analyst, information technology consultant, operational researcher/management scientist, human resources manager, recruitment consultant or systems analyst.

Impact on Lifestyle

Management consultants are generally called in to do a particular job, and are given a budget and a timescale. This means that you would have to be prepared to work long hours, possibly at the weekend, in order to fulfil your contract. You could also be expected to travel anywhere in the world.

If you were employed by a firm of consultants, your income would be steady but, if you were on a fixed-term contract, you might have to face a certain amount of insecurity from job to job. You would also have to be sure that you could handle the knowledge that your recommendations, based on your professional judgement, could result in people facing unemployment.

Earnings Potential

Earnings vary a great deal but are generally well above average for graduates, depending upon the size and nature of the contract. For senior management consultants the rewards can be very high. As with many competitive professions, it is getting the first job that can be the hardest. Typically, a new graduate would receive a base salary of £25,000 to £35,000, depending on the type of consulting. On progression to a more senior level, the pay rise percentages become considerably higher, ranging from £50,000 with a few years' experience to £250,000 at partner or director level.

Further Information

Institute of Consulting
www.iconsulting.org.uk

Management Consultancies Association
www.mca.org.uk

International Council of Management Consulting Institutes
www.cmc-global.org

Manufacturing Engineer

What is Involved?

As a manufacturing engineer (sometimes known as a production engineer), you would be concerned with all stages of the conversion of raw materials into usable products either for the general public or for other industries. In some instances, your job would be very similar to that of a mechanical engineer but you would be more concerned with broad manufacturing technology. You could be involved with overseeing the production processes and systems involved in making any sort of manufactured goods. As a result, your job is likely to include designing or maintaining complex machinery. You could be using robotics or involved with other computer-driven equipment. Your main concern could be with designing, testing and maintaining the equipment itself or you could be involved with the design and layout of the plant in a factory. In order to present your product(s) to the marketplace at the time, price and quality that the customer expects, you would need a wide range of knowledge and skills, from product design, marketing and accounting to management, economics and finance. You would also need to appreciate the blend of people, machines and materials necessary to impart quality to the manufacturing process.

Opportunities for Training

There are a number of universities offering degrees in manufacturing engineering, sometimes combined with product design or with mechanical engineering. In order to become a chartered engineer, primarily concerned with research, design and development, you would need to complete at least four years of academic study and would usually achieve this via an MEng degree. If you want to be more involved with the day-to-day management of production processes as an incorporated engineer, you could take a three-year BEng degree. You don't always have to choose your specific training route from the start, so you should read prospectuses carefully. See also our separate article on engineering qualifications. There are sandwich courses available for both types of degree; these add an extra year but give the opportunity for a period of work experience, which can be very valuable when you are looking for a job. After graduating, you would need to complete a period of industrial training and responsible work experience before you achieve chartered or incorporated engineer status.

Requirements for Entry

For degree entry, you are likely to need maths at A level/Advanced Higher, Higher or equivalent and usually physics plus another one or two subjects. If maths and physics are not required, they are certainly preferred by universities. In addition, you would need at least five GCSE/S Grade passes at 9-4/A*-C/1-3. You would normally need higher grades for MEng than for BEng admission.

Kind of Person

You would need the ability to learn and develop the multidisciplinary knowledge, competencies and skills relevant to manufacturing so that, on graduation, you would be able to undertake the diverse range of management functions found in industry. You would be involved with the application of computer technologies to integrate management and processes, requiring advanced IT skills, and you would find foreign language skills useful.

You might find yourself giving or taking orders, liaising with others and co-ordinating the work of fellow team members. In addition, you may need to give presentations to senior staff, to explain your ideas and discuss plans with people who do not always have your expertise.

Broad Outlook

UK manufacturing is very much alive and well: ranking 9th in global output, it makes up nearly half (45%) of UK exports, employs 2.6 million people, and accounts for 68% of UK business research and development.

Whilst the expected post-recession upturn has not yet fully materialised, either within the UK or the European Union, future trends paint a very different and more optimistic picture. Reports project that annual global output will more than double in two decades, from $78 trillion to $176 trillion. The UK does not have the capability or the resources to succeed in every emerging technology, but it can excel in such areas as energy-efficient computing, energy harvesting (from the environment), graphene (the thinnest material possible), nanotechnology and digital technologies.

Related Occupations

You might consider: mechanical engineer, automotive engineer, control and instrumentation engineer, electrical engineer, electronic/electronics engineer, materials scientist/engineer, telecommunications engineer, civil engineer, chemical/process engineer, mining engineer, petroleum engineer, robotics engineer or marine engineer. Other possibilities might include analytical chemist, quality assurance manager or cybernetics/systems specialist.

Impact on Lifestyle

Whilst you may have specific hours of work you are also likely to be asked to work overtime on occasion, when there is a deadline to meet or a problem with production. Some production lines run continuously, so you may be required to be on call when problems arise.

Depending on the area of production with which you are involved, you may need to spend at least some time working in a factory or manufacturing area. Occasionally this could be dirty or noisy and you may be required to wear protective clothing.

Earnings Potential

You are likely to earn around £24,000 to £30,000 when you first start work after graduating but this has the potential to rise sharply as you gain experience. Once you are chartered, your salary is likely to rise to around £40,000 to £60,000 and beyond. Average earnings for incorporated engineers are around £43,500.

Further Information

Institution of Mechanical Engineers
www.imeche.org

Engineering Council UK
www.engc.org.uk

Engineering UK
www.engineeringuk.com

Tomorrow's Engineers
www.tomorrowsengineers.org.uk

Manufacturing Institute
www.manufacturinginstitute.co.uk

Make it in Manufacturing
www.manufacturinginstitute.co.uk/ charitable-campaigns

Engineers Ireland
www.engineersireland.ie

Marine Biologist/Marine Scientist

What is Involved?

Working as a marine biologist, you would be concerned with the astonishing diversity of plant and animal life in the world's oceans. Your area of study could include anything from microscopic bacteria to the largest whales. You could concentrate on a specific group of marine organisms or you could look more broadly at marine ecology and the interaction between groups of organisms. You might work in an area such as monitoring fish stocks and developing sustainable methods of harvesting food from the sea; you might be searching for new chemicals for the pharmaceutical industry; you might be measuring the effects of dumping waste in the oceans.

Opportunities for Training

There are 22 universities and colleges offering degrees in marine biology, mostly organising their courses on a modular basis. This structure should give you experience of a range of biological disciplines, such as genetics, ecology, zoology, biochemistry, botany and microbiology. Other modules would be designed to give you a necessary background in marine chemistry, physics and geology and an understanding of how these disciplines interact to explain what is found in the ocean and why. You could also undertake more specialised postgraduate study in marine biology and you may find this essential before you enter the labour market.

You would find that most courses have a large fieldwork component, giving you plenty of opportunity to get your hands wet as you go to sea in a research vessel or collect samples on the shoreline. You may also have the opportunity to gain a diving qualification, which could prove highly useful.

It is possible to take a degree in any of the biological sciences (for example, molecular biology could enhance career prospects), and then go on to specialise in marine biology with a Masters or PhD.

Requirements for Entry

To gain admission to a degree course in marine biology, you would normally need three A level/Advanced Higher, four or five Higher or equivalent qualifications, together with at least five GCSE/S Grade passes 9-4/A*-C/1-3 or equivalent, including English and maths. Some universities specify A level/Advanced Higher, Higher or equivalent in biology and another science subject.

Kind of Person

You should have a keen interest in science generally, with a particular passion for the sea. You would probably be involved in research work and much of this would involve careful attention to accuracy and detail. You would be expected to communicate your results to others, some of whom may not have the same scientific background as you. You should therefore have good written and verbal communication skills. You would almost certainly make extensive use of computers for obtaining, processing and storing data and would therefore need excellent IT skills. Your work would involve you in being out of doors in all sorts of weather, sometimes at sea. For this you would need to be quite fit and robust.

Broad Outlook

Job prospects in this area are not good in the UK, where there are many more marine biology graduates than there are vacancies. There is only a limited amount of research being undertaken and this is often commissioned on short-term contracts.

There is some work in the commercial sector but marine departments tend to be small, with limited promotion prospects. You may find that a specialised postgraduate qualification is essential before you can get started in the labour market.

The University Marine Biological Station Millport (UMBSM), the National Facility for Marine Biology Fieldwork, closed in 2013, following the withdrawal of its annual funding, although it has now reopened as a fieldwork centre for the Field Studies Council.

Related Occupations

You might wish to consider: research biologist/bioscientist, biochemist, ecologist, engineering geologist, environmental consultant, hydrographic surveyor, meteorologist, microbiologist, oceanographer, water quality analyst, geologist/ geoscientist or countryside/nature conservation officer.

Impact on Lifestyle

If you are working in a land-based, laboratory environment you are likely to be working normal office hours. However, you might at times have to go to sea, which would involve working longer hours, in harder conditions and could take you away from home for several weeks. Wherever you work as a marine biologist, you are very likely to get wet at times. Your lifestyle is likely to revolve around short-term contracts, much moving around and a lifetime of learning new skills.

Earnings Potential

Entry-level positions for graduates tend to offer salaries in the region of £19,500 to £24,000, with rates varying considerably depending on the role, type of organisation and sector. The range of typical starting salaries for PhD holders is from £26,000 to £36,000, although reaching the higher end of the scale is dependent on experience. A typical salary at senior level would be £50,000 plus.

Further Information

Marine Biology UK
www.marinebiology.co.uk

Natural Environment Research Council
www.nerc.ac.uk

Centre for Environment, Fisheries and Aquaculture Science
www.cefas.co.uk

Marine Conservation Society
www.mcsuk.org

Marine Biological Association
www.mba.ac.uk

Scottish Association for Marine Science UHI
www.uhi.ac.uk/en/campuses/campus_sams

National Oceanography Centre
www.noc.soton.ac.uk

Institute of Marine Engineering, Science and Technology
www.imarest.org

Field Studies Council Millport
www.field-studies-council.org/centres/scotland/millport.aspx

Marine Engineer

What is Involved?

As a marine engineer, you could be involved in the design, management and maintenance of many different sorts of systems and equipment used in a maritime environment, including:

- Ocean engineering, involving all aspects of the exploration and production of oil, gas and minerals found under the seabed. The range of activities includes oil and gas extraction, mining the seabed for minerals, and development of renewable energy resources.

- Offshore engineering, involving the design, construction, commissioning and operation of fixed and mobile offshore platforms and their associated systems. Designers and operators have to find ways of overcoming the problems presented by winds, waves, currents and the nature of the seabed, while dealing with high pressure, high temperature and corrosive fluids and gases.

- Seagoing engineering, involving the safe and efficient operation of a vessel's main propulsion machinery, associated equipment and systems. The traditional career path here would be to train with the Merchant or Royal Navy, gaining qualifications and experience at sea. See our separate articles for Royal Navy and Merchant Navy Officer.

Opportunities for Training

To become an Incorporated or Chartered Marine Engineer, you normally start by taking a BEng (Bachelor of Engineering) or MEng (Master of Engineering) degree accredited by the Institute of Marine Engineering, Science and Technology (IMarEST) in a relevant subject, such as marine engineering, marine technology or ship science. BEng courses usually last three years (four years in Scotland); MEng courses are a year longer. The MEng provides a broader engineering education than the BEng. On the other hand, the BEng would allow you to complete your academic studies more rapidly, and to enter industry a year earlier to continue your education in the workplace. See our separate article on engineering qualifications in the introduction.

Your academic education would normally be followed by a period of structured training and experience known as Initial Professional Development.

Requirements for Entry

For degree entry, you would normally need at least two A level/Advanced Higher, three Higher or equivalent qualifications, including maths and usually physics or a subject which includes physics. You would also be expected to have supporting GCSE/S Grade passes 9-4/A*-C/1-3 or equivalent, usually including English. Other useful subjects would include technology and foreign languages. At many universities, students without the necessary background in science and mathematics can take a one-year foundation course.

Kind of Person

Maritime engineering is a practical subject, attracting people who are interested in science and technology and finding out how things work and who have an affinity with the sea. You should have an open and enquiring mind, with a creative approach to problem solving. Teamwork skills are important because co-operation is essential in maritime engineering, particularly for engineers who serve at sea. You would need to be good at numerical reasoning and at using computers for your work. You would also have to be able to explain your thoughts and ideas clearly to other members of the engineering team.

Broad Outlook

Research into the exploration and recovery of minerals from under the seabed is progressing rapidly and enormous engineering expertise will be required to carry out deep-sea operations in a sustainable and environmentally friendly way. Although the size of the UK shipbuilding industry has reduced dramatically over the past 20 years, the sector is presently vibrant and market forces are beginning to work in favour of the remaining shipyards. The emphasis now is on building specialist vessels, particularly for the offshore industry and the Royal Navy, and there is a continuing demand for engineers in this area.

Related Occupations

You might also consider: Royal Navy/Royal Marines officer, Merchant Navy officer, naval architect, aeronautical/aerospace engineer, automotive engineer, mechanical engineer, civil engineer, electronic/electronics engineer, electrical engineer, oceanographer or hydrographic surveyor.

Impact on Lifestyle

Working hours vary from job to job. Your working environment might include an office, shipyard or boatyard, ship, submarine or offshore installation. Many jobs involve a combination of indoor and outdoor work.

If you work in ship design or construction, your job would be shore based. You could also be away from home for long periods, working on ships, submarines or offshore installations. Outdoor work could sometimes be physically demanding.

Earnings Potential

You are likely to start earning around £24,000 to £26,000 when you first graduate and this will rise quite rapidly as you gain experience and take on more responsibility. The average salary of an experienced chartered marine engineer is over £55,000.

Further Information

Institute of Marine Engineering, Science and Technology
www.imarest.org

Sea Vision UK
www.seavision.org.uk/careers

British Marine Federation
www.britishmarine.co.uk

Merchant Navy Careers at Sea
www.careersatsea.org.uk

Irish Maritime Development Office
www.imdo.ie

Maritime Careers Ireland
www.maritimecareers.ie

Market Researcher

What is Involved?

As a market researcher, you might be employed to find out what the public think about a wide range of issues. Manufacturers, politicians, pressure groups and others need to know the public response to various products, advertising campaigns and initiatives. You might work as a freelance, researching for an independent agency or as a member of the research department of a large company.

It would be your job to target an appropriate sample of people, to ensure that the right questions are asked, to collate the results efficiently and to present them in the best possible way. Depending on your circumstances and seniority, you might be involved in interviewing or analysing data and making presentations of your findings. Market research is increasingly being conducted on an international basis, and there might well be scope for travel.

Opportunities for Training

The Market Research Society (MRS) is an official awarding body in the UK for vocational qualifications in this field. As well as running short courses, the MRS offers the Advanced Certificate and Diploma in Market and Social Research Practice and accredits a small number of Master level postgraduate courses. Many companies offer new graduates the opportunity to take part in the MRS professional development scheme.

Several business-related degree, foundation degree and higher national diploma (HND) courses offer options in market research and allied subjects, and there are some postgraduate courses available. Work experience or work shadowing would be an advantage when applying for courses or employment opportunities.

Requirements for Entry

While there are no particular educational requirements laid down for entry into market research, graduates are becoming increasingly in demand. The actual subject of your degree or HND would not be of critical importance, but business studies, economics or other subjects including evidence of numeracy would show that you have the aptitude for coping with numbers and statistics. Psychology or sociology could also be useful, and languages might give you an advantage in certain situations.

The minimum entry requirements for university degree courses are two A level/Advanced Higher, three Higher or equivalent qualifications, together with five GCSE/S Grade passes 9-4/A*-C/1-3. In practice, you should aim to offer more than the minimum. Courses last three or four years. For HND courses, you would need one or two A levels/Advanced Higher, two or three Higher or equivalent qualifications. The courses last for two or three years.

Kind of Person

In order to succeed in market research, you would need excellent communication skills, both spoken and written, as you would be in contact with a wide variety of people. Persuasive skills would also be an asset, and the ability to deal with disappointment in a highly competitive world.

A keen sense of business would be an advantage. You should be able to absorb and analyse data quickly and accurately, and you should have a high level of computer literacy. You should be able to work independently and also as part of a team, and be capable of working under pressure in order to meet deadlines. It would help if you were inquisitive and interested in how people think and behave.

Broad Outlook

In an increasingly competitive business world, the work of the market researcher is becoming extremely important, and agencies concerned with consumer research have proliferated over the past few years. Another growth area has been social research, with increased use of researchers by local and national government.

There is a tendency for market researchers to specialise in either quantitative or qualitative research. The former involves working with statistics and percentages and can deliver quick results; the latter involves analysing opinions, searching for the reasons behind certain percentages. Qualitative research is a longer process, sometimes lasting years.

Competition to enter the profession is fierce but the rewards can be high, with good promotion prospects if you can demonstrate the right levels of drive and determination. Later on, you could set up your own agency or head a large department for a major employer.

Career progression can be very fast. Graduates would expect to be a Research Executive for 18 months, then a Senior Research Executive. Promotion is through merit, with many candidates managing accounts and teams by age 30.

Related Occupations

You might also consider: advertising account executive, economist, marketing executive, operational researcher/management scientist, human resources manager, press/information officer, public relations executive, retail manager, social media manager or statistician.

Impact on Lifestyle

Since many market research campaigns are linked to deadlines, you should be prepared for some long hours, together with working weekends and in the evenings. There would quite likely be travelling involved, maybe abroad. You would need to be tough and be prepared to fight your corner.

Earnings Potential

Salaries vary according to employment circumstances, since many market researchers are freelance. As a graduate, you could expect to start at around £20,000 to £25,000, rising after three to five years to £32,000 to £38,000. A senior executive might earn between £45,000 and £100,000 or more, depending on their track record and degree of managerial responsibility.

Further Information

Market Research Society
www.mrs.org.uk

Social Research Association
www.the-sra.org.uk

Royal Statistical Society
www.rss.org.uk

Kantar Media
www.kantarmedia.com/uk/our-solutions/consumer-and-audience-targeting

Association for Qualitative Research
www.aqr.org.uk

Association of Irish Market Research Organisations
www.aimro.ie

Marketing Executive

What is Involved?

Your role as a marketing executive would be to secure the best possible match between the goods or services produced by your organisation and the perceived needs of your actual or potential clients. This could mean conducting market research to find out what customers want and what they understand about the market. You might then use the results of your research to identify your own and your competitors' short-comings, decide on improvements needed, locate the main target markets in the UK and abroad and then put forward your proposals for the next steps. Typical approaches could include producing new promotional material, revamping your image, repositioning your products and upgrading your packaging. You might propose an advertising campaign, employ a public relations (PR) agency or department to enhance your public image, or introduce more effective distribution facilities. Your work might involve industrial products, consumer goods or services or the public sector.

Opportunities for Training

Although it is possible to start as a marketing assistant and progress through promotion, the majority of entrants join by direct entry on graduate trainee schemes. You could take a degree in marketing or a related subject but you would find that any degree subject is acceptable. You could also take a foundation degree or higher national diploma (HND) in business studies with a marketing specialism. Another method of entering this very competitive field is to start by gaining experience in a related area, such as customer service or market research, and then moving across. In most companies, you would train in-house by working alongside an experienced marketing executive. There are formal qualifications run by the Chartered Institute of Marketing (CIM) in association with the Communication Advertising and Marketing Education Foundation (CAM).

Requirements for Entry

For degree entry, you would need two or three A level/Advanced Higher, three or four Higher or equivalent qualifications, together with a supporting platform of GCSE/S Grade passes 9-4/A*-C/1-3. HND and foundation degree requirements are usually slightly less demanding. A similar level of achievement would be required for direct entry as a marketing assistant. In all cases, evidence of skills in English and maths would be important.

Kind of Person

Above all, you would need commercial flair to recognise and exploit market opportunities. You should have an analytical mind, capable of assessing the essentials of each situation, with a clear understanding of your organisation and the position of its products and services within an ever changing market place. Good communication skills, both written and verbal, would be essential, together with the ability to relay your enthusiasm to others and motivate them to meet your marketing targets.

You would frequently face deadlines and would have to produce marketing briefs for senior management or prepare for negotiations with important clients. Numeracy would play a key role in assessing and analysing costs and estimating the effects of changes in pricing policy. You would need writing skills to produce reports or promotional literature and good IT skills. The ability to speak one or more foreign languages would be valuable.

Broad Outlook

Marketing has been for many years one of the most popular career choices for graduates. To develop your career, you would need to gain relevant experience and key transferable skills. One way of achieving these is by moving between in-house departments or working in a marketing agency/consultancy for several different clients. It may also be advantageous to move companies to obtain more rapid career progression. Marketing is considered to be a good basis for moving into general management, so promotion could eventually lead to a post such as managing director or chief executive. Additional qualifications in marketing would enhance your chances. Marketing is recognised as one of the core activities in manufacturing and service industries, and vacancies are widely available throughout the country. Marketing is closely linked with advertising and public relations and a great deal of interchange between these sectors is possible.

Related Occupations

You might also consider: advertising account executive, advertising creative, charity fundraiser, public relations executive, retail manager, market researcher, statistician, social media manager or logistics/supply chain manager.

Impact on Lifestyle

This is a high pressure careers field, with a constant need to keep in touch with other people and to achieve deadlines and objectives. You would be expected to produce information in reports, analyse new data or travel to clients, at home and abroad, often at short notice, especially when you reach more senior levels of management.

Earnings Potential

Typical starting salaries range from £22,000 to £27,000, rising with experience to £30,000 to £50,000 for a manager and £65,000 to £120,000 for a successful director. Salaries tend to be higher in larger organisations in the professional services and financial and business sectors, compared with those in the public sector, charities and small independent companies.

Further Information

Chartered Institute of Marketing
www.cim.co.uk

Communication Advertising and Marketing Education Foundation
www.camfoundation.com

Institute of Export
www.export.org.uk

Institute of Direct and Digital Marketing
www.theidm.com

Getintomarketing
www.cim.co.uk/more/getin2marketing

Marketing Institute of Ireland
www.mii.ie

Materials Scientist/Engineer

What is Involved?

As a materials scientist or engineer, you would specialise in the physical and chemical properties of the materials used to manufacture products. You would be looking for the highest possible standards of performance and long-term reliability. You might, for example, work in the aerospace industry, developing stronger and lighter alloys for airframes or high temperature alloys for engines. Pressure for reductions in pollution and noise and increases in durability would drive your work forward. Other examples could include selecting the best combination of materials (plastics and metals) for a mobile phone, a replacement hip joint or the parts used in a domestic dishwasher. You would need to know the limitations and advantages of a variety of metal, plastic, ceramic, glass and carbon fibre resources and you would be expected to know how best to mould, extrude, shape and manufacture them. Thousands of different materials are available to deal with such problems as corrosion and rusting, high or low temperatures, vibration, bending, stretching, elasticity, resistance to chemical attack and simple daily wear and tear. The right combination of materials, allied to good design, can greatly enhance the performance, appearance, sales and profitability of a product.

Opportunities for Training

You would normally need a degree in materials science, metallurgy, materials engineering or similar. You should look carefully at the content of each course to find the right one for you, as they can vary widely. There is often the opportunity to include the study of a language and spend some time abroad, or to incorporate a management module; you might also consider a sandwich course, which would take a year longer but would offer a period of paid work placement. Some materials engineering courses are accredited for registration with the Engineering Council and could be the first step towards qualifying as a professional engineer. There is also the option of following a postgraduate materials science course, sometimes with sponsorship from an employer.

Requirements for Entry

For degree entry, you would need two or three A levels/Advanced Higher, three or four Higher or equivalent qualifications selected from physics, chemistry, maths or design and technology, together with at least five GCSE/S Grade passes 9-4/A*-C/1-3. Materials and metallurgy courses are often under-subscribed and at some universities it is possible for students without the right A levels/Advanced Higher, Higher or equivalent qualifications to take a foundation course before starting their degree. To be accepted for a postgraduate course, you would need a good honours degree in a relevant scientific or engineering subject.

Kind of Person

You should be interested and have reasonable ability in mathematics, physics and chemistry, but there is more to being a good materials scientist than that. You should enjoy applying scientific theory to practice, and be able to work accurately at all times. Good communication skills, both spoken and written, would be important, as you would be working as part of a team and would be expected to write up regular reports of your work. A logical approach would be required, although the ability to think laterally could be an asset in problem solving. You should also have a high level of computer skills. You may need good eyesight and colour vision for some aspects of the work.

Broad Outlook

The pace of scientific and technological change seems ever increasing, and you should have no difficulty in finding work in many areas of materials science as the UK economy recovers from the 2008 economic downturn. Opportunities arise with private employers, at home or abroad, in research and development, quality control, and management. You could also work for universities or government-owned organisations such as the National Physical Laboratory. Promotion could be within an organisation to a senior position, while some experienced materials scientists establish their own private consultancies or diversify into technical writing, teaching or sales and marketing.

Related Occupations

You might also consider: biomedical scientist, aeronautical/aerospace engineer, automotive engineer, chemical/process engineer, civil engineer, control and instrumentation engineer, electrical engineer, electronic/electronics engineer, management/business consultant, metallurgist, industrial chemist or product designer.

Impact on Lifestyle

In most parts of industry, you would work a fairly typical nine to five day from Monday to Friday. In production or quality control, however, you may need to work on a rota basis as the production line is likely to be in 24-hour operation. You would need to wear protective clothing when dealing with some dangerous substances and at other times you might be required to wear anti-contamination clothing in a scrupulously clean environment.

Earnings Potential

Pay scales vary widely between companies but generally you might start at around £22,000 to £28,000, with progression as you became more experienced and undertake more responsibility to around £50,000 to £60,000. Some materials scientists can earn appreciably more than this, particularly if they go into management. Salaries tend to be higher in what are considered to be 'leading edge' technologies, such as telecommunications and biomedical engineering.

Further Information

Institute of Materials Minerals and Mining
www.iom3.org

Materials Careers
www.iom3.org/information-school-and-college-pupils

Engineering and Materials Education Research Group
www.materials.ac.uk

Materials Classroom
http://classroom.materials.ac.uk

National Physical Laboratory
www.npl.co.uk

Engineers Ireland
www.engineersireland.ie

Mechanical Engineer

What is Involved?

As a mechanical engineer, you would be concerned with applying engineering principles and rules to all sorts of machines and their components. This means that you could be dealing with anything from the largest manufacturing equipment down to the nuts and bolts used in production. Depending on your interests and your level of qualification, you could become involved in design, manufacture, research, development, management or marketing or a combination of these.

Broadly speaking, you would focus more on research, design and development if you pursue your education, training and experience through to chartered status; you would be more involved with production processes as an incorporated engineer. See our separate article on engineering qualifications for a more detailed analysis of these issues.

Opportunities for Training

Training as a mechanical engineer would lead you into one of the broadest areas of engineering. There are many universities offering degrees in mechanical engineering and there is a wide variation in the types of courses and specialisms offered within these degrees, so it is a good idea to check the prospectuses carefully before applying. It is important to ensure that your degree is an accredited course recognised by the Institution of Mechanical Engineers. There are four-year courses, usually leading to an MEng qualification, which can take you to chartered engineer status.

Alternatively, there are three-year courses, usually leading to a BEng qualification, which can take you to incorporated engineer status. It is possible to add a further year of specialised study, known as a matching section, to enable you to progress to the chartered route. There are also sandwich courses, which include a year spent in industry gaining practical work experience, and you should find many opportunities for sponsorship.

Requirements for Entry

Most universities would either prefer or require you to have A level/Advanced Higher, Higher or equivalent in maths and physics, together with five GCSE/S Grade passes 9-4/A*-C/1-3, including maths and English.

Kind of Person

Your job would probably involve understanding and solving complex engineering problems. For this you would need a practical and logical mind that might need to show creative approaches to problems. You are likely to find yourself using maths and statistics in your work and you would make extensive use of computers, including specialised and sophisticated software packages.

You are likely to find yourself working as part of a multi-disciplinary team, which means that you would need to be able to communicate with a variety of people. These could be fellow engineers, who would share your technical expertise and understanding, or non-technical specialists in other fields, who would expect you to explain your ideas clearly to them. You could also find yourself managing a team of people working on a project. In addition, you may need to take into account the costs and budget of a project, so you would need some business skills.

Broad Outlook

UK manufacturing is very much alive and well: ranking 9th in global output, it makes up nearly half (45%) of UK exports, employs 2.6 million people, and accounts for 68% of UK business research and development.

Whilst the expected post-recession upturn has not yet fully materialised, either within the UK or the European Union, future trends paint a very different and more optimistic picture. Reports project that annual global output will more than double in two decades, from $78 trillion to $176 trillion. The UK does not have the capability or the resources to succeed in every emerging technology, but it can excel in such areas as energy-efficient computing, energy harvesting (from the environment), graphene (the thinnest material possible), nanotechnology and digital technologies.

Mechanical engineering can provide a good starting point for a career in management because it is a wide-ranging subject area that requires and develops a number of different technical, people management and business skills. There are opportunities for mechanical engineers in just about all areas of industry and in many other fields of employment. Many mechanical engineers decide to develop additional skills, for example in business, in order to become involved with larger projects and take on greater responsibility. Good commercial awareness is essential for career development, as well as developing people management skills, given that you may be required to lead teams or manage projects.

Related Occupations

You might consider: manufacturing engineer, automotive engineer, control and instrumentation engineer, electrical engineer, electronic/electronics engineer, materials scientist/engineer, telecommunications engineer, civil engineer, chemical/process engineer, mining engineer, petroleum engineer, robotics engineer or marine engineer. Alternatively, you might consider science-based options such as: cybernetics/systems specialist, medical physicist, metallurgist, geophysicist, oceanographer or biotechnologist.

Impact on Lifestyle

You might be working set office hours or you might be expected to work long hours or on a rota system if you are involved with industrial production. You are likely to have to work extra hours from time to time in order to meet deadlines, when you could find that you are working under some pressure. Working towards chartered status can involve several years of further study after you have completed your degree course.

Earnings Potential

You could expect to start earning around £22,000 to £28,000 when you first graduate and you should see your salary rise to around £40,000 to £55,000 within a few years. The average annual earnings for experienced chartered engineers are around £68,000 and for incorporated engineers around £49,500.

Further Information

Institution of Mechanical Engineers
www.imeche.org
Engineering UK
www.engineeringuk.com
Engineering Council UK
www.engc.org.uk
Tomorrow's Engineers
www.tomorrowsengineers.org.uk
Manufacturing Institute
www.manufacturinginstitute.co.uk
Engineers Ireland
www.engineersireland.ie

Medical/Clinical Technologist (working in medical physics)

What is Involved?

As a medical/clinical technologist, you would work in a healthcare environment, maintaining and servicing complex, specialised equipment used to diagnose and treat patients. Specific roles could include:

- Critical Care Technologist - providing support to intensive care or high dependency units, especially with equipment to maintain circulation, respiration and renal support function
- Medical Physics Technologist - assisting clinical and scientific staff in the construction of medical devices; also calibrating x-ray and other electro-medical equipment
- Nuclear Medicine Technologist - using radioactive pharmaceuticals in diagnosis and therapy by administering radioactive agents and imaging their distribution using gamma cameras
- Radiotherapy Technologist - performing quality control on radiotherapy dosimetry equipment and treatment units, and computing radiation treatment plans
- Vascular Technologist - performing and interpreting studies such as ultrasound imaging and blood-flow waveform analysis on patients with arterial and venous disease
- Technologist in Equipment Management - maintaining and servicing electro-medical equipment to ensure both performance and safety
- Rehabilitation Engineer - providing bio-mechanical assessment and the custom manufacture of aids such as wheelchairs and speech synthesisers for individual patients
- Renal Dialysis Technician - responsible for the safe and efficient working of renal dialysis equipment (haemodialysis, peritoneal dialysis, and water treatment) both in hospital and in the patient's home

Opportunities for Training

Training for this career area changed dramatically during 2012 with the implementation of the NHS Modernising Scientific Careers programme. You can now enter medical/clinical technology at undergraduate level through the Practitioner Training Programme (PTP) or through the graduate entry route of the Scientist Training Programme (STP). Check the Health Careers website for details of the latest developments.

For the PTP, you would take an accredited BSc in Healthcare Science (Medical Physics or Clinical Engineering). This is a three-year programme, which combines academic study with practical experience gained in the NHS. At STP level, you would need to search for STP vacancies in clinical engineering, medical physics or imaging.

Requirements for Entry

The minimum entry requirement for the PTP is typically a good range of 9-4/A*-C grade GCSEs plus a minimum of two A levels or equivalent, including a science subject. This is, however, just a guide. You must check with individual universities to confirm their exact requirements.

For STP training places, a 2:1 in a relevant science degree is the minimum required. Each NHS organisation advertising STP vacancies decides which degree subjects are relevant.

Kind of Person

You would often liaise with scientists and doctors, and would have direct contact with patients. You must show great attention to detail, and have the ability to reassure patients who may be uncomfortable with extremely complex machinery.

Broad Outlook

Hospitals are using an increasingly wide range of cutting-edge technology in such areas as radiotherapy, bioengineering and laser procedures, and there is growing demand for people to check the performance and gauge any environmental effects of this equipment.

Clinical technologists are graded according to seniority. In the lower grades, the work is more routine, while higher grade posts involve more decision-making and responsibility for managing and training others. Progression through the grades is not automatic but is gained by applying for higher grade vacancies.

Related Occupations

You might be interested in other science- or technology-based careers such as biochemist, biomedical/clinical engineer, biomedical scientist, electrical engineer, electronic/electronics engineer, medical physicist, molecular biologist, pharmacologist or radiographer.

Impact on Lifestyle

You would normally work a 37.5-hour week, with some shift working on a rota basis to provide 24-hour cover to support clinical services. Working conditions try to ensure that, while you might sometimes work unsocial hours, you are not working excessive hours. Some of your work could involve handling hazardous chemicals and substances, so you may at times need to wear protective overalls, gloves, glasses and a mask.

Earnings Potential

Qualified healthcare science practitioners in the NHS currently start in Band 5, on a scale ranging from £22,128 to £28,746. Earnings can rise to £35,577 for a specialist at the top of the scale and to £41,787at the top of the advanced scale. Additional allowances are paid for appointments in and around London, ranging from 20% of basic salary for Inner London, to 15% for Outer London and 5% for the London Fringe. Earnings in the private sector are generally likely to be higher, depending on where you live and the hours you are prepared to work.

Further Information

Institute of Physics and Engineering in Medicine
www.ipem.ac.uk

Health Careers
www.healthcareers.nhs.uk

Society of Critical Care Technologies
www.criticalcaretech.org.uk

National School of Healthcare Science
www.nshcs.org.uk

British Nuclear Medicine Society
www.bnms.org.uk/careers

Academy of Clinical Science and Laboratory Medicine, Ireland
www.acslm.ie

Medical Physicist

What is Involved?

As a medical physicist, you would be a specialist within a hospital clinical science group, applying science and technology for the benefit of the sick. Although your education and training would be different from that of a doctor, you could still be intimately involved in assessing and treating illness and disability. Close collaboration between a medical physicist and a doctor can achieve much more than either in isolation. You would work in many different medical fields, with a mixture of research, development and routine services to patients.

The main areas are nuclear medicine, radiotherapy, radiology and various aspects of physiological monitoring and investigation, but other specialities range from anaesthetics to urology. You could, for example, be responsible for establishing correct doses of radiation for treating malignant tumours, without causing unnecessary damage to other body tissues, and for ensuring that therapeutic and diagnostic radiographers use radiation equipment safely. You might also devise and erect special monitoring equipment, which can record patients' progress during or after surgery.

Opportunities for Training

Guidance on training has been complicated in recent years by the gradual implementation of the Department of Health Modernising Scientific Careers programme, which offers two entry points into clinical engineering: the Practitioner Training Programme (PTP) or the Scientist Training Programme (STP). You can check on the latest developments via the Health Careers and Institute of Physics and Engineering in Medicine (IPEM) websites.

For the STP, you could start with an IPEM-accredited degree (MEng if you plan to qualify later as a chartered engineer) in a relevant engineering discipline, aiming for at least a 2:1. You could then apply for a place on the NHS Scientist Training Programme for Medical Physicists and Clinical Engineers. This would lead to an MSc in your chosen area, combined with vocational training in a hospital department. Finally, you would apply to the Health and Care Professions Council for state registration.

The alternative under the new programme is to enter at undergraduate level through the NHS PTP route. This would involve an accredited BSc Healthcare Science degree specialising either in clinical engineering or medical physics. These are three-year programmes which combine academic study with practical experience gained in the NHS.

The IPEM Clinical Technologists Training Scheme, developed with the Association of Renal Technologists on behalf of the Register of Clinical Technologists, is a degree programme supporting the regulation of clinical technologists by the Health and Care Professions Council.

Requirements for Entry

Entry to most relevant degree courses would require two to three A level/Advanced Higher, three to five Higher or equivalent qualifications, together with a good platform of GCSE/S Grade passes 9-4/A*-C/1-3. Since there is a shortage of applicants, grade requirements in some universities are not high but all departments would be looking for good grades in physics and maths. For postgraduate study, you would usually need a first degree passed with first or upper second class honours. You should check with individual universities the entry requirements for the new Healthcare Science degrees.

Kind of Person

You would be working in a field that is developing fast, so you would need to keep up to date with new discoveries and advances in technology and a very strong interest in physics, maths and technology. Getting your calculations and measurements right could be critical to the patient. You would need to have an interest in and be at ease with patients. You would be expected to work as part of a team of clinical science professionals, so you would need to communicate clearly and to explain your diagnoses or recommendations.

Broad Outlook

Career prospects in the NHS should become clearer when the MSC programme is fully established. In the meantime, check the IPEM website for the very latest statements on discussions to maintain the professional status of medical physicists.

In the current structure, your career could develop to a point where you are in charge of a scientific department or a major departmental sub-division. The most senior medical physicists have equivalent status to medical consultants. You could also seek employment in the healthcare industry, where your career would be less structured than in the NHS.

Ongoing training and professional development would be an essential part of your career as a medical physicist. The IPEM provides a formal continuing professional development (CPD) programme for all its members, aimed to support and enhance your career progression. You may decide to specialise in an area such as magnetic resonance imaging, medical computing, ultrasound or physiological measurement.

Related Occupations

You might also consider: audiologist, doctor (general practice), doctor (hospital), physicist, radiographer, electrical engineer, electronic/electronics engineer, clinical biochemist, medical/clinical technologist, pharmacologist, optometrist or biomedical/ clinical engineer.

Impact on Lifestyle

You would normally expect to work a 37-hour week in the NHS but might be expected to work extra hours to cover emergencies. You might need to attend lectures or conferences in order to complete your studies, which could be outside your normal working hours, as would keeping up to date on new developments in medical physics.

Earnings Potential

Starting salaries for clinical scientists in the NHS Band 6 are currently £26,565 to £35,577, rising in Band 7 to £31,696 to £41,787. Senior manager or consultant posts can offer salaries ranging up to £100,431. The practitioner training programme starts in Band 5 on £22,128 rising to £28,746. Additional payments are made for employment in and around London.

Further Information

Institute of Physics and Engineering in Medicine
www.ipem.ac.uk
Institute of Physics
www.iop.org
Health Careers
www.healthcareers.nhs.uk
Association of Clinical Scientists
www.assclinsci.org
Health and Care Professions Council
www.hcpc-uk.org
Irish Association of Physicists in Medicine
www.theiapm.ie

Merchant Navy Officer

What is Involved?

As an officer in the merchant navy, you would work for a fleet which operates all over the world, consisting largely of ferries, container ships, passenger ships, survey ships and oil tankers. Additionally, some ships operate as auxiliary vessels for civilian and Royal Navy operations such as updating charts of shipping lanes. The person in charge of a ship is known as the master or captain. This post carries full responsibility for the ship, the crew, the cargo, passengers, the safety of the ship and everyone on board, and for navigating the ship to where it needs to go. The person in charge of a ship's engineering and technical systems is the chief engineer. This post carries full responsibility for the operation and maintenance of complex electrical and mechanical plant and associated control systems. As a ship's officer, you would have responsibility for a range of tasks in the deck, engineering or electro-technical department. There are also some dual officer roles, covering more than one department. You may also control the work of ratings, who perform a wide range of technical and non-technical jobs and have a lower level of responsibility.

Opportunities for Training

Training for deck and engineer officers follows a similar pattern of college- or university-based and shipboard training. The actual number and duration of these 'phases' differs depending on whether you train as a deck or engineer officer. A foundation degree/Scottish professional diploma sits at the heart of a three-year training programme that will qualify you as a junior officer, giving you Officer of the Watch (OOW) certification, the first stage of your professional seafaring qualifications.

Individual shipping companies or training organisations will sponsor you to undertake the course. They may decide which college/university you attend and you will be placed on their ships for the sea-based part of the course. Your sponsoring company will pay your course fees and a salary or training allowance. Some companies may sponsor you on an honours degree in Nautical Science, Navigation and Maritime Science or Mechanical and Marine Engineering, depending on your seafaring route. There are alternative training routes if you already have a degree.

Requirements for Entry

For the foundation degree route, you would need a total of 48 UCAS points in unspecified subjects at A level or equivalent (80 to 112 points for the Honours degree), plus good grades at GCSE/S Grade or equivalent in mathematics, English, a science-based subject and at least one other. You will also need to satisfy the relevant statutory health and eyesight requirements for seafarers in the UK. The sponsoring companies will give you guidance on any particular requirements they may have. You should be over age 18 to begin the foundation degree/Scottish professional diploma course.

If you have any doubt about your ability to pass the statutory health and/or eyesight requirements, you may find it worthwhile to take the appropriate examination before applying. You can ask the sponsoring companies or contact the Maritime and Coastguard Agency (MCA) to establish the details of the requirements and how they may affect you.

Kind of Person

You must be prepared to accept responsibility not only for making important decisions yourself but also for inspiring confidence in the crew. You would need the knowledge, leadership, communication and team-working skills to keep complex systems running in extremes of temperature and weather, to demanding schedules and within safety and efficiency requirements. You would need to be able to cope with living, possibly for several months at a time, in a confined space far from friends and family.

Broad Outlook

Ships carry over 80% of world trade and sea-borne trade is forecast to increase substantially by 2020, which should mean that prospects are generally good. This is despite the fact that fewer crew will be required for the larger and more technically advanced ships of the future.

There are good opportunities for both men and women to obtain promotion but further training and examinations are involved, whilst length of service and personal characteristics also play an important part. After retirement from the service, there are civilian employers who look favourably on those with a successful merchant navy career behind them.

Related Occupations

You might also wish to consider: freight forwarder, logistics/supply chain manager, naval architect, passenger transport manager, shipbroker, marine engineer, mechanical engineer, Royal Navy/Royal Marines officer or the other uniformed services.

Impact on Lifestyle

Life on board a ship is a 24-hours-a-day operation, seven days a week, 52 weeks a year. The work is divided into shifts called watches, which are typically four hours on watch, followed by eight hours off watch. At busy times this may increase to six hours on watch and six hours off watch.

Leave time is generous, to compensate for time spent on board and away from home. For example, after a voyage of around four months, you could get as much as two months or so off at home. Most ships have excellent facilities for those living and working on them and some provide facilities for officers to be accompanied by their husband or wife.

Earnings Potential

Salaries vary from company to company and there is a small variation between salaries for engineering officers and for deck officers. Training salaries for cadets range from £8,000 to £16,000, with all tuition and on-board food and accommodation included. Shore-based accommodation costs are, however, deducted. Junior officers generally start on £25,000 to £28,000. Progression up to the rank of captain or chief engineer can lead to salaries in the range of £36,000 to £80,000 plus, depending upon the type and size of ship. Salaries on foreign-going ships, spending at least 183 days per year out of the UK, may be tax-free.

Further Information

Merchant Navy Training Board
http://mntb.org.uk
Careers at Sea
www.careersatsea.org
Maritime and Coastguard Agency
www.gov.uk/government/organisations/maritime-and-coastguard-agency
UK Chamber of Shipping
www.ukchamberofshipping.com
Irish Maritime Development Office
www.maritimecareers.ie

Metallurgist

What is Involved?

As a metallurgist, you would be a specialist in the science and engineering of metals, concerned with examining how they behave during use, what we can make them do and how we can use them to our best advantage. There are literally thousands of different metal products with widely different physical and chemical properties. You could work in research to overcome problems of metal failure or corrosion in aeroplanes or motorcars, or on the formulation and quality control of new steels/alloys.

There is considerable overlap between the work of a metallurgist and that of a materials scientist/engineer, as more and more manufactured products use combinations of metals, plastics, ceramics and carbon fibre, which need to fit together and survive impacts, dampness and high or low temperatures whilst meeting the need for attractive product design and commercial viability.

You might specialise in the manufacturing processes of converting metals and alloys into products, or you might concentrate on the extraction of metals from ores or recovery from scrap.

Opportunities for Training

You would normally need a relevant degree and there are several universities offering suitable courses in metallurgy or materials science. Some courses cover a wide range of metals, plastics and ceramics, while others might concentrate on just one material, so it is important to examine prospectuses carefully to make sure that courses cover the areas you expect. Metallurgy can also be studied as a joint honours subject with languages, business, management or economics, for example. You could choose to continue your studies in metallurgy with a postgraduate course at MSc or PhD level.

Requirements for Entry

For degree entry, you would need two or three A level/Advanced Higher, three or four Higher or equivalent qualifications selected from physics, chemistry, maths or design and technology, together with at least five GCSE/S Grade passes 9-4/A*-C/1-3. Metallurgy courses are often under-subscribed and at some universities it is possible for students without the right A level/Advanced Higher, Higher or equivalent qualifications to take foundation courses before starting their degree. To be accepted for a postgraduate course, you would need a good honours degree in metallurgy or a related subject such as mechanical engineering.

Kind of Person

You would need to have a strong interest and proven ability in maths, physics and chemistry. You should enjoy the practical aspects of science, such as your practical laboratory work at school. You would need to have a methodical approach to your work and meticulous attention to precise detail.

You may need deep reserves of patience as you carry out repeated tests on particular metals before discovering an acceptable alloy. You would inevitably use computers in analysing data from test equipment. You would also need to communicate well and to be prepared to seek advice from other experts when necessary. You may need to instruct technicians who are helping in your research, and to communicate clearly with others who do not have your scientific background. The ability to write clear, unambiguous reports would be essential if you work in scientific research.

Broad Outlook

The pace of scientific and technological change seems ever increasing, and you should have no difficulty in finding work in many areas of metallurgy as the UK economy recovers from the recent economic downturn. You might be employed by a steel producer or by an automotive, aeroplane, armaments, shipbuilding or railway engine manufacturer. There are opportunities to work in metallurgical research laboratories and for government science research centres, as well as in university research departments. Many other industries employ metallurgists at all stages of their production processes, including electricity and power companies and the oil and chemical industries. There are good opportunities to work abroad and also to work as an independent consultant.

Related Occupations

You might also consider: biomedical scientist, aeronautical/aerospace engineer, automotive engineer, chemical/process engineer, civil engineer, control and instrumentation engineer, electrical engineer, electronic/electronics engineer, manufacturing engineer, mechanical engineer, management consultant, materials scientist/engineer, industrial chemist or product designer.

Impact on Lifestyle

In most parts of industry, you would work a fairly typical nine to five day from Monday to Friday. In production or quality control, however, you may need to work on a rota basis, as the production line is likely to be in 24-hour operation. You would need to wear protective clothing when dealing with some dangerous substances and at other times you might be required to wear anti-contamination clothing in a scrupulously clean environment.

Earnings Potential

Pay scales vary widely between companies but generally you might start at around £22,000 to £28,000, with progression as you become more experienced and undertake more responsibility to around £50,000 to £60,000. Some metallurgists can earn appreciably more than this, particularly if they go into management. Salaries tend to be higher in what are considered to be 'leading edge' technologies, such as telecommunications and biomedical engineering.

Further Information

Institute of Materials Minerals and Mining
www.iom3.org

Materials Careers
www.iom3.org/information-school-and-college-pupils

Engineering and Materials Education Research Group
www.materials.ac.uk

Materials Classroom
http://classroom.materials.ac.uk

National Physical Laboratory
www.npl.co.uk

Engineers Ireland
www.engineersireland.ie

Meteorologist

What is Involved?

As a meteorologist, you would be a specialist in the science and study of the earth's atmosphere and the interaction of the atmosphere with the earth itself. Meteorology seeks to understand and to predict the behaviour of weather, the climate and the atmosphere in general, from the surfaces of land and sea to the edge of space.

The Royal Meteorological Society, the professional body for meteorologists, lists 27 separate areas where meteorologists work. They range from weather forecasting to climatology and from horticulture to the planning and operation of great engineering undertakings. They include the development of complex mathematical representations of the way the atmosphere works and can be predicted, the manipulation of vast data resources, the design, development and testing of new instruments, and the use of modern communications and data-management systems. There are also close links with sister sciences such as hydrology and physical oceanography.

The Met (Meteorological) Office is the largest employer of meteorologists. It is a government institution involved in research, applied and operational meteorology.

Opportunities for Training

A university degree would be essential. This could be in meteorology but an alternative approach would be to enter meteorology at postgraduate level following a first degree in physics or maths or an associated subject such as computing, environmental studies, physical geography or electronics.

The Met Office has its own college in Devon providing training courses for new entrants and for continuing professional development. With a high level of knowledge and experience, you could become a chartered meteorologist. This professional qualification corresponds to others such as chartered accountant or chartered engineer. While it is not essential, accreditation can satisfy clients and employers that you have reached and continue to maintain a specified level of knowledge and experience and that you are conversant with current best practice.

Requirements for Entry

For a meteorology degree, you would need maths and physics at A level/Advanced Higher, Higher or equivalent level. You should research the exact entry requirements of individual universities. There are some Met Office opportunities for non-graduates, where you would need A level/Advanced Higher, Higher or equivalent passes including maths and/or physics.

Kind of Person

You would need a genuine and enthusiastic interest in the weather and climate phenomena, with a good working knowledge of maths and physics. You would also need to be observant, have good communication skills, enjoy problem solving and have a logical approach to collating data. You must be highly numerate and able to cope with sophisticated computer systems and software.

Broad Outlook

The Met Office is the main employer and has a promotion structure which operates on merit. There are jobs with the Natural Environment Research Council and Agricultural and Fisheries Institutes but, as they only employ a small number of meteorologists, there is less chance of internal promotion. There are some opportunities for working abroad with the Met Office, with British companies or with the United Nations.

There are opportunities for pure research, applied research, operational work, scientific and commercial management, entrepreneurial ventures, teaching and consultancy.

Staff employed in the Mobile Met Unit are attached to the Royal Air Force and may be deployed across the world on military exercises and operations. The Royal Navy's Flag Officer Sea Training Hydrographic, Meteorological and Oceanographic (HM) School trains specialist officers of the Royal Navy for a career in meteorology or hydrography. The training programme provides a thorough understanding of the complex physical environment in which the ships, aircraft, submarines and people of the Royal Navy and Royal Marines operate.

Related Occupations

You might also consider: air traffic controller, environmental consultant, hydrogeologist, physicist, oceanographer or hydrographic surveyor.

Impact on Lifestyle

You may be expected to move your work base from time to time in order to broaden your experience. Indeed, it is a condition of Met Office employment that you agree to work wherever required. Some weather stations are located in remote spots, carefully chosen for their extreme weather conditions. As the earth interacts with the atmosphere around the clock, you may have to work shifts, weekends and sometimes long hours.

Although a few meteorologists appear on television as weather forecasters, most of this work is carried out by professional broadcasters after a short course at the Met Office college.

Earnings Potential

Salaries for graduates at the Met Office start at around £21,000, rising at the next level from around £25,000 to £35,000. Managerial positions attract salaries in the £38,000 to over £60,000 range.

Further Information

Royal Meteorological Society
www.rmets.org

Meteorological Office
www.metoffice.gov.uk

British Antarctic Survey
www.bas.ac.uk

World Meteorological Organisation
http://public.wmo.int/en

Royal Navy Flag Officer Sea Training
www.plymouth.ac.uk/schools/fost-hm-hms-drake

Met Éirann
www.met.ie

Microbiologist

What is Involved?

As a microbiologist, you would study micro-organisms such as fungi, bacteria, viruses or algae, investigating their growth conditions and sources. You would also consider the impact of microbes on the environment and the relationship between microbes and other living organisms. If you choose to specialise in the hospital service, you could practise as a clinical microbiologist, working alongside hospital doctors, general practitioners and environmental health officers in the diagnosis and prevention of disease. Alternatively, you could work as a biomedical scientist, dealing with samples from patients and isolating and identifying the microbes that cause illness (pathogens). See our separate article for biomedical scientist.

You may, on the other hand, choose to develop new products in the food industry or work in a public health laboratory, testing food, milk and water supplies for microbiological contamination. There are other openings in areas such as the pharmaceuticals, cosmetics and oil industries, where micro-organisms can be used to produce chemicals, hormones, antibiotics and enzymes, all of which can be of great benefit to society.

Opportunities for Training

Once you are working as a microbiologist, you will usually receive on-the-job training from your employer in such areas as laboratory techniques and technology, and management/supervisory skills. Some employers may also encourage you to study for a postgraduate qualification or membership of a professional body, such as the Microbiology Society.

Postgraduate training in the NHS Scientific Training Programme (STP) leads to a specifically commissioned and accredited master's degree in Clinical Science (Infection Sciences). On successful completion of the STP, you can register as a clinical scientist with the Health and Care Professions Council.

Requirements for Entry

Most microbiologists are graduates and you would need a good honours degree, preferably in microbiology or in another life science such as biology, biochemistry or biomedical science. For degree entry, you would need A levels/Advanced Highers, Highers or equivalent passes in biology and one other science subject, together with five GCSE/S Grade passes at 9-4/A*-C/1-3 including maths, English and two sciences. Some universities may specify chemistry A or AS level/Higher, Advanced Higher or equivalent qualifications but offers are likely to vary considerably between institutions. It is best to check with admissions departments to be sure of their individual requirements. If you decide to take an HND, you are likely to need a science subject at A level/Advanced Higher or Higher, together with four GCSE/S Grade passes at 9-4/A*-C/1-3 including maths, English and a science subject.

Kind of Person

You would need a strong interest in science, particularly biology, although an interest in chemistry is also useful. You should enjoy the practical side of your science lessons at school and be able to work accurately and in a well organised way in the laboratory. Some types of work include following set procedures with rigorous attention to detail and this needs patience and persistence. You would have to show a responsible approach in carrying out your tests and analyses. Communication skills are very important since you would probably be working in a multi-disciplinary team and would need to explain your work to people who do not share your scientific background.

Broad Outlook

Clinical microbiologists work in diagnostic laboratories and pathology departments in large hospitals and medical schools. It is possible to progress from practitioner to specialist to team manager and then to consultant. Additionally, Public Health England is a major employer of clinical microbiologists and epidemiologists.

Beyond the health services, opportunities exist in food production, in the manufacture of all alcoholic beverages, cheeses and yoghurt, and in the disposal of sewage or of harmful industrial waste.

Related Occupations

You might be interested in other scientific careers such as analytical chemist, biochemist, biomedical scientist, pharmacist, technical brewer, research biologist/ bioscientist, food scientist or technologist or forensic scientist.

Impact on Lifestyle

You are likely to work a 37-hour week. Shift or night work is sometimes necessary in manufacturing plants and on-call work is expected when providing a round the clock service, such as in the NHS. Occasionally you may have to work extra hours to meet deadlines. It is usual to wear protective clothing, which varies according to the work and includes laboratory coats, gloves and eye protection.

Earnings Potential

Pre-registration clinical microbiology trainees usually start in NHS Band 6 on £26,565 to £35,577, before moving to the main practitioner Bands. A consultant or very senior manager can earn up to £100,431 a year. In all cases, additional allowances are paid for posts in and around London. Research and development work in pharmaceutical firms, public health laboratories and medical research council units usually attracts salaries in the range of £28,000 to £40,000.

Further Information

Microbiology Careers
www.microbiologysociety.org/all-microsite-sections/careers

Microbiology Society
www.microbiologysociety.org

Society for Applied Microbiology
www.sfam.org.uk

Royal Society of Biology
www.rsb.org.uk

Society for Industrial Microbiology and Biotechnology
www.simbhq.org

Association for Clinical Biochemistry and Laboratory Medicine
http://acb.org.uk

Institute of Biomedical Science
www.ibms.org

Public Health England
www.gov.uk/government/organisations/public-health-england

Irish Society of Clinical Microbiologists
www.iscm.ie

Midwife

What is Involved?

As a midwife, you would work in the community or in healthcare settings such as hospital maternity units, providing care and support for expectant mothers both during pregnancy and throughout labour and the postnatal period. Apart from delivering babies, you would carry out clinical examinations, provide health education, help mothers and their partners prepare for their parental role and give them advice on feeding their baby. You would also work in partnership with other health and social care professionals to meet the particular needs of people such as teenage mothers, socially excluded mothers, disabled mothers and mothers from diverse ethnic backgrounds. Your priority would be to provide a 'woman-centred' integrated care service, offering choice and continuity of support to mother and child.

Although you would be working as a healthcare professional, you would have a client group who are on the whole very healthy and in need of help and advice only because they are expecting a baby. The birth itself may be at the heart of the process, but midwives provide support to women, their babies, their partners and families, from conception to the first phase of postnatal care.

Opportunities for Training

You could enter the profession directly by undertaking a specialised three-year degree course leading to a midwifery qualification. These courses are provided by a number of universities. You could also take a shortened (18 months) midwifery course after first qualifying as a nurse. Courses combine theory and practice, with periods of university-based study interspersed with supervised work in local hospitals, clinics and the community. The degree route has changed, and now students take government maintenance and tuition loans.

Before you can practise, you must be registered with the Nursing and Midwifery Council and you must maintain a portfolio of evidence of your continuous professional development. This would mean updating your skills and knowledge on a regular basis.

Requirements for Entry

Entry to a degree course would require a minimum of two A level/Advanced Higher, three Higher passes or equivalent qualifications, plus supporting GCSE/S Grade passes. A pass in a science subject may be required. The NHS and universities encourage applications from people with a wide range of academic and vocational qualifications, so it is always worth checking with individual institutions before applying to see if your qualifications meet the required entry standard.

You must also pass a medical test.

Kind of Person

You would be providing professional support and reassurance to a huge diversity of women, during some of the most emotionally intense periods in their lives. You must be kind and caring, flexible and adaptable, prepared to look after all women regardless of their class, creed, economic status, race or age. You would need to be able to stay calm and alert in times of stress and enable women to feel confident and in control. On the rare occasions where something goes wrong, you would have to be ready to react quickly and effectively. Good organisation and record keeping are essential.

Broad Outlook

The Royal College of Midwives is campaigning for many more training places but public spending cuts are currently reducing provision. As a result, competition for entry is intense, although you should have no difficulty in finding work once you qualify. Your first job would probably be within the National Health Service but there are openings within the private sector and some midwives practise independently. There are also opportunities for work abroad, although some countries specify that midwives must have full nurse training. Promotion can come as, for example, head of midwifery services or you might like to take further qualifications and become a midwifery teacher.

Related Occupations

You might also wish to consider: nurse, nursery/early years teacher, dietitian, doctor (general practice), doctor (hospital), health visitor, occupational therapist, physiotherapist, counsellor, social worker, teacher (primary) or teacher (secondary).

Impact on Lifestyle

You must be prepared to work shifts, including nights, weekends and holiday periods. You would also have to respond to emergency calls and you would need your own transport in order to travel between the hospital or clinic and people's homes. You would wear a uniform all the time you are on duty.

Earnings Potential

A newly qualified midwife working in the NHS would start in Band 5, earning from £22,128 to £28,746 a year. After that, allowances are paid for additional skills, overtime, shift working, responsibilities and experience, rising to £41,787 at the top of the scale for a midwife team manager. A consultant midwife can currently earn up to £69,168. Additional allowances are paid for appointments in and around London, ranging from 20% of basic salary for Inner London, to 15% for Outer London and 5% for the London Fringe. Earnings in the private sector are generally likely to be higher, depending on where you live and the hours you are prepared to work.

Further Information

Royal College of Midwives
www.rcm.org.uk

Health Careers
www.healthcareers.nhs.uk

Nursing and Midwifery Council
www.nmc.org.uk

NHS Education for Scotland
www.nes.scot.nhs.uk

Northern Ireland Practice and Education Council for Nursing and Midwifery
www.nipec.hscni.net

Nursing and Midwifery Board of Ireland
www.nmbi.ie/Careers-in-Nursing-Midwifery

Mining Engineer

What is Involved?

As a mining or quarrying engineer, you would ensure the safe and financially sound development of mines and other surface and underground operations. Your main role would be to find the best way to extract raw materials from the ground, using blasting, drilling and excavation methods. You would be involved at all stages of a project: assessing the viability of a site before it is developed, planning the mine's structure, overseeing mining production processes, and managing the final closure and rehabilitation process when mining ceases.

You might also design and manage plants for processing the minerals into metals and saleable concentrates or for recycling metals and related minerals. You would be expected to apply environmental best practice in all of these activities and you may find increasing opportunities to work solely in cleaning up the environment and in conservation. This is a very technologically driven industry and one that tries to balance ever-increasing demands for raw material resources with environmental issues.

Opportunities for Training

You would need a degree, foundation degree or higher national diploma in mining engineering from one of the universities specialising in this area. In order to become a chartered engineer, primarily concerned with research, design and development, you would need to complete at least four years of academic study and would usually achieve this via an MEng degree. If you want to be more involved with the day-to-day management of production processes as an incorporated engineer, you could take a three-year BEng degree. You don't always have to choose your specific training route from the start, so you should read prospectuses carefully. See also our separate article on engineering qualifications. There are sandwich courses available for both types of degree; these add an extra year but give the opportunity for a period of work experience, which can be very valuable when you are looking for a job. After graduating, you would need to complete a period of industrial training and responsible work experience before you achieve chartered or incorporated engineer status.

Requirements for Entry

For a degree course, you are likely to need A level/Advanced Higher, Higher or equivalent passes in two or three subjects selected from maths, physics and chemistry. If these subjects are not actually required, they will be strongly preferred by universities. In addition, you would need five GCSE/S Grade passes (9-4/A*-C/1-3), including English, maths and at least one science subject. You would also be expected to have visited some mines and to have an understanding of the key issues in the industry.

Kind of Person

You should be interested in technology and in keeping up to date with developments in your field. You would need a strong interest in maths and science and it might be helpful to have an interest in geology or physical geography. You would probably be expected to find practical solutions in your work, so you should have a logical and creative approach to problem solving. You are likely to be analysing complex information, and may be required to use computers so you would need IT skills. Some of your work is also likely to require you to show meticulous attention to detail. In addition to your technical skills you will need to communicate well with others. You are likely to be working as a member of a small team. In addition to talking to other engineers, you may be expected to direct the work of others and also to explain your ideas to people who may not have your technical expertise.

Broad Outlook

The major mining companies were riding high on the commodities boom, enjoying record metal prices and record profits. All this came to a halt with the world recession that started in 2008, when metal prices plummeted and expansion plans were put on hold. The major organisations have, however, survived and the global outlook is improving again.

Potential employers range from large multinational organisations, such as the major oil and gas producers, to small companies offering specialised services. Owing to the diversity and geographical spread of the industry, it is not possible to describe an average career in mining and minerals engineering. You could focus exclusively on coal or salt, for example, or you could travel extensively - anywhere from Antarctica to Zambia with spells in the UK - gaining experience of mining for, say, copper, zinc, lead or gold.

Related Occupations

You might also consider: drilling engineer, petroleum engineer, chemical/process engineer, civil engineer, mechanical engineer, energy engineer, nuclear engineer, environmental consultant, hydrogeologist, materials scientist/engineer, metallurgist or geologist/geoscientist.

Impact on Lifestyle

If you want to stay involved in mining operations, you have to go where the mines are. Given that many mines are in remote locations, you can't always live where you would ideally like. You may sometimes work normal office hours in a relatively clean environment but you may equally work highly irregular hours, outdoors or deep underground, in conditions that could be difficult, dirty and at times dangerous.

Earnings Potential

Salary levels vary widely according to employer and sector. In the UK, starting salaries range from £21,000 to £27,000. With five years' experience this can increase to between £30,000 and £45,000. By the age of 40, UK mining engineers generally earn between £50,000 and £75,000. Salaries tend to be higher overseas, with Australia, Canada and the US generally providing the best levels of pay. Salaries in South Africa, on the other hand, are relatively low. More demanding work locations may pay better salaries.

Further Information

Institute of Materials Minerals and Mining
www.iom3.org

Engineering Council UK
www.engc.org.uk

Careers in Quarrying
www.careersinquarrying.co.uk

Engineers Ireland
www.engineersireland.ie

Museum Keeper - Art Gallery Curator

What is Involved?

As a curator or keeper, you would usually manage a section of a large museum or art gallery (exhibiting, for example, paintings/sculpture, archaeological objects, historically important documents and artefacts or furniture), and would be responsible for the acquisition, identification, display and care of the exhibits. This would include seeing that they are kept in appropriate lighting and atmospheric conditions and arranging for any necessary restoration or conservation. You may also find yourself involved in the design of exhibitions and in administrative tasks: including cataloguing, preparing exhibition catalogues, articles and poster displays; giving talks and looking after members of the public.

In a large gallery or museum, jobs can be highly departmentalised and you might specialise in, say, 16th century Italian art, 19th century sculpture, Egyptian artefacts, Greek vases or the paintings of JMW Turner. In a small museum or art gallery, you could be responsible for everything from developing an acquisition policy, working with school groups, preparing a touring exhibition and managing volunteers to raising sponsorship and writing press releases.

Opportunities for Training

There is no formal training route in this very small, competitive and highly academic field. You should have a good degree in a relevant subject area - which could mean anything from history, anthropology or history of art to ceramics, textile design or a science or technology subject - followed by a postgraduate course in museum or heritage studies. Around half the people entering professional and management jobs in museums follow this sort of route. The other half may have no postgraduate qualifications at all, but relevant experience or skills, or may have an academic Masters or PhD qualification, or teaching or marketing qualifications.

Some people take a relevant Masters part-time, while working in a museum or gallery. Leicester University museum studies department, for example, has pioneered a distance-learning programme which has replaced its campus-based part-time courses.

You would need to show your commitment by undertaking voluntary work experience or an internship in a museum or gallery and you would find that some employers run formal schemes leading to recognised vocational qualifications in cultural heritage management. You might find it useful to work over a period of several years towards Associateship and then Fellowship of the Museums Association.

Requirements for Entry

You would normally need two or three A level/Advanced Higher, three or four Higher or equivalent qualifications for degree entry, together with a broad platform of GCSE/S Grade passes at 9-4/A*-C/1-3. For a postgraduate course, you should have a relevant first degree and evidence of your commitment (usually in the form of voluntary experience).

Kind of Person

You would need to have a genuine interest in art and historical artefacts, good organisational skills and the ability to explain and arrange exhibits in an imaginative way for visitors to enjoy. You might well be expected to have very detailed knowledge of a particular subject area. Good communication skills would be essential both for giving talks on your specialism and for writing associated articles and catalogues or even books.

Broad Outlook

This is not an easy career route to follow: there is increasingly intense competition for jobs, the pay would generally be described as poor and the level of qualifications and experience demanded is extremely high. In addition, career progression can be difficult - you would have to be willing to move anywhere in the country to widen your experience and gain promotion - and short-term contracts are often seen as the norm. On top of this, UK museum budgets have been regularly cut over the past six years.

The Museums Association website contains details of current opportunities. Potential employers include independent museums and galleries, universities, local authority museums and galleries and national museums and galleries. There is also some scope for overseas work, especially in Commonwealth countries.

Related Occupations

You may also wish to consider: archaeologist, archivist, auctioneer/valuer, arts administrator, conservator, art restorer/conservator, fine art dealer or antiques dealer.

Impact on Lifestyle

While you would generally work around 36 hours per week, you should expect some weekend commitment in line with the opening hours of the museum or gallery. You may find yourself working late into the evening when a new exhibition is being launched, usually with an opening reception for friends of the museum or gallery or for local councillors and sponsors. As noted above, you would almost certainly have to move home from time to time to pursue opportunities for promotion.

Earnings Potential

Low pay is widely recognised as a major problem, with museum pay falling behind that of comparable sectors. To address this issue, the Museums Association produce regularly updated best practice salary guidelines. The current recommendation for graduate entry is £18,622 to £22,114, or from £22,987 to £27,642 for a candidate with a postgraduate qualification and/or relevant experience. A Director of a large establishment could earn up to £95,000.

Further Information

Creative and Cultural Skills
http://ccskills.org.uk/careers/advice/any/heritage

Museums Association
www.museumsassociation.org

Institute of Conservation
http://icon.org.uk

British Museum Future Curators
www.britishmuseum.org/about_us/skills-sharing/future_curators.aspx

National Museum Wales
www.museumwales.ac.uk

National Museums Scotland
www.nms.ac.uk

Irish Museums Association
www.irishmuseums.org

Musician

What is Involved?

As a professional musician, in classical or popular music, you would play one or more instruments and/or sing. You could be a performer or composer, a teacher working from home or in a school, college or university, an administrator, publisher, record company executive, instrument manufacturer, librarian, broadcaster or journalist. Many musicians combine some of these activities, especially those who both perform and teach. As an orchestral player, you may spend many years with one orchestra or work freelance, taking session work for concerts, recordings, backings and jingles. You could also join the armed forces or the police for service with a regimental or police band.

In popular music, you might combine singing with playing an instrument either as a soloist or in a small group. Your main contact with the public would be through performing, perhaps supported with recordings and videos.

Opportunities for Training

Whatever area of music you choose, there is no standard training programme and no fixed career path. Any performing career would demand very high standards, simply because the competition is so intense. For classical musicians, the specialist music colleges and conservatoires offer three- or four-year degree courses with the emphasis on performance. Alternatively, you could study music to degree level at university, where courses may have more academic content, before taking a postgraduate course to concentrate on technique and performance. Music therapy training is also at postgraduate level.

The armed services train musicians (including string players) for military bands. Recruits are brought in from the age of 16 and are given two-and-a-half years of professional training. There is limited formal training for popular music, although there are some courses. Rock music examination board Rockschool, for example, aims to offer rock musicians the opportunity to gain the same qualifications available to classical musicians. All its graded music exams have original set repertoire, encourage improvisation and have an element of free choice. You should, of course, gain as much performing experience as possible, while trying to get noticed by a recording company.

Requirements for Entry

For degree course entry, you would need at least two A level/Advanced Higher, three Higher or equivalent passes plus supporting GCSE/S Grade passes (9-4/A*-C/1-3), and you would need to have reached an advanced level of instrumental or vocal performance (at least grade 8). To teach in a maintained school, you would need a recognised professional qualification for teaching as distinct from training in music. See our separate article for 'Teacher'.

Kind of Person

Qualities such as artistry, determination and dedication must be combined with general musicianship and technical mastery of your instrument or voice. As a performer, you must be confident in your ability and enjoy being in front of an audience. As a private teacher, you should like working with people and would need good communication skills, patience, perseverance and the ability to run your own business. To work in a school, you must like and understand young people and want to teach them, no matter what their ability.

Broad Outlook

Competition is fierce and the pay is generally below that of other jobs requiring similar levels of skill, training and expertise. To succeed, you must have more than talent alone; you must also have absolute dedication and determination. To get work, you have to be known and this means taking every opportunity - concerts, auditions, awards, bursaries and competitions - to show that you are worth engaging. Even after becoming established, you would find that earning a living as a performer - out of recordings, broadcasts and concerts - is hard work. Many performers combine a performing career with teaching or other work in the community, perhaps as a music therapist.

Pop musicians often start informally as a group of students at school or college, usually with a manager to organise gigs and recording contracts. Some become rich and famous but many others work more or less full-time in pubs, clubs and concert halls.

Related Occupations

You might also consider: arts administrator, community arts worker, lecturer (further education), lecturer (higher education), teacher (primary), teacher (secondary), music therapist, recording/sound engineer or producer (film/television/video).

Impact on Lifestyle

Working hours can be long and irregular, with evening and weekend performances and rehearsals during the day, often linked with extensive travel to concerts or gigs. As a music teacher, you would work more regular hours but would usually be expected to organise evening and weekend events.

Earnings Potential

Top performers command extremely high fees but, for the majority, earnings are moderate. The Incorporated Society of Musicians publishes on its website recommended rates for most types of musical activity. Music teachers, permanent members of major orchestras and musicians in the armed forces are among the few to enjoy the luxury of a regular income, although many musicians make a reasonable living.

Further Information

Careers in Music
www.careersinmusic.co.uk

Incorporated Society of Musicians
www.ism.org

Musicians' Union
www.musiciansunion.org.uk

Association of British Orchestras
www.abo.org.uk

Creative and Cultural Skills
http://ccskills.org.uk/careers/advice/any/music

UCAS Conservatoires
www.ucas.com/ucas/conservatoires

Rockschool
www.rslawards.com

Naval Architect

What is Involved?

As a naval architect, you would be a professional engineer responsible for the design, construction and repair of ships, boats and other marine vessels and offshore structures. You could be involved with merchant ships, passenger ferries, naval warships, offshore drilling platforms or yachts, powerboats and other recreational craft. Given the size and complexity of many of these vessels, you would work as a member of a team containing many specialist engineers. Part of your role as a naval architect would be to integrate their activities and take overall control of a project. You would also have a specialist role in ensuring that the final product is safe, efficient and seaworthy.

Apart from the architectural aspects of ship form and layout, you must be able to use complex mathematical and physical models to ensure that your design is satisfactory technically and that it meets the relevant safety rules and standards. Alternatively, you may specialise in construction, usually taking responsibility for the management of a yard or for sections of it such as planning, production or fitting out. There is a continuous striving to make savings on existing techniques and equipment through the adoption of new processes and practices and by better training for the work force. You would also organise the supply of materials and components, inspection and testing as well as the vital resources of manpower.

Opportunities for Training

You would normally undertake a degree course in Naval Architecture, Marine Technology, Offshore Engineering or Ship Science. The course should be accredited by the Royal Institution of Naval Architects (RINA) and lead to registration with the Engineering Council UK as a Chartered Engineer (CEng) or Incorporated Engineer (IEng). There is also scope to qualify below degree level as an Engineering Technician (EngTech). You must have an aggregate of seven years of education, approved training and responsible experience in industry after reaching the age of 18 years before you can achieve full RINA membership and CEng status.

Requirements for Entry

You should take a broad range of subjects at GCSE/S Grade, covering both the arts and sciences and including maths, physics and English. You should then add three A level/Advanced Higher, five Higher or equivalent qualifications, including good pass grades in maths and/or physics. These studies should lead to qualifications satisfying the entry requirements for either an accredited masters degree (MEng) course if you want to become a chartered engineer, or a bachelor degree (BEng) course if you are intending to become an incorporated engineer. (See the separate article on engineering qualifications in the introduction).

Kind of Person

You would need a creative, practical, enquiring and logical mind, excellent communication skills in speech and writing, mature judgement and evidence of leadership ability. A keen interest in sailing, windsurfing or other maritime pursuits can be extremely helpful. You must have a broad understanding of many different branches of engineering together with advanced skills in computer-aided design.

Broad Outlook

Naval architecture is a truly global profession and you should find that your qualifications and experience will open up career opportunities all over the world as the global economy picks up again. You may become a specialist in one particular aspect of ship design or construction or you may use your professional skills in project management to develop a broader management career, possibly outside the maritime field.

Potential employers include ship and boat builders and repairers, offshore constructors, design consultants and, for the ships and submarines of the Royal Navy, the Ministry of Defence. Major equipment manufacturers also employ teams of engineers, including naval architects, on the design of such products as propulsion systems, auxiliary systems, sub-sea production systems and control systems.

Continuing professional development (CPD) is essential and can be achieved through courses and conferences organised by the RINA and other engineering professional institutions or organisations on new technologies, management systems, communication, business and many other topics.

Related Occupations

You may wish to consider: marine engineer, mechanical engineer, electrical engineer, electronic/electronics engineer, civil engineer, control and instrumentation engineer, Royal Navy/Royal Marines officer, Merchant Navy officer or architect.

Impact on Lifestyle

Achieving CEng status can mean considerable extra work in the years immediately following your degree but this should be a good long-term investment. You may have to travel extensively as you seek to develop your career.

Earnings Potential

While you would probably start on around £25,000 to £28,000, you should see your salary increase with experience to £35,000 to £55,000. Higher earners can make £65,000 to £80,000 a year. Salaries vary between employers according to geographical location and specialisation.

Further Information

Royal Institution of Naval Architects
www.rina.org.uk

Defence Engineering and Science Group
www.gov.uk/government/collections/desg-graduate-scheme

Engineering Council UK
www.engc.org.uk

Institute of Marine Engineering, Science and Technology
www.imarest.org

Ship Builders and Ship Repairers Association
www.ssa.org.uk

Nurse

*W*hat is Involved?

As a registered nurse, you would be working as part of a multi-disciplinary team providing health care in hospitals, specialist clinics and the community. You would specialise in one of four main branches:

In the *adult* branch, your main focus would be patients from the age of 16 upwards. As a *children's nurse*, you might be looking after a very sick baby on a life support machine, a 10-year-old needing urgent surgery to repair a broken leg and a 14-year-old with a damaged liver. As a *mental health* or psychiatric nurse, you would be working with patients suffering from problems such as depression, anxiety, alcohol dependency and severe eating disorders. As a *learning disability* nurse, you would be least likely to work in a hospital and could spend most of your time with patients in their own homes or in residential care centres.

*O*pportunities for Training

You would normally undertake a university-based degree programme, leading to registration with the Nursing and Midwifery Council (NMC). Training usually lasts three years (some degrees take four years) and includes equal amounts of theory and practice. You would gain experience in a variety of care settings, including hospitals, nursing homes and the community.

The three-year course is divided into two distinct parts:

- the first year, the Common Foundation Programme or CFP, is undertaken by all students, regardless of branch choice. It includes core issues and topics, together with experience of a wide variety of care environments

- the second part, the branch programme, concentrates on specific branch subjects and practice placements

You should investigate the area of nursing which you would like to study and ultimately work in, as the choice of branch for the second part usually has to be made upon application. However, some universities enable you to make a more informed choice after you have started.

Alternatively, you may be able to join the NHS as an apprentice or healthcare assistant and eventually study part-time for your nursing qualification.

*R*equirements for Entry

For a degree course in nursing, you would normally need at least two A level/ Advanced Higher, three Higher or equivalent qualifications, together with supporting GCSE/S Grade passes. The more scientific courses may specify science subjects at AS or A level, Advanced Higher or Higher, with biology being the most popular. Admissions officers are usually looking for commitment, motivation and experience as well as academic qualifications, so it is a good idea to get some relevant work experience. Working your way up from starting as an apprentice or healthcare assistant may not require any academic qualifications.

*K*ind of Person

You would need to be very resilient, both physically and mentally, to face the many challenges involved in caring for people who are ill or disabled. You would be constantly interacting with other people, so would need to be good at both talking and listening. You would need to be able to inspire trust and confidence, displaying tact, sensitivity and maturity. At times, you would have to put people at ease in stressful situations. You would also have to work closely with others as part of the healthcare team.

Broad Outlook

For many years, nursing was on the list of recognised shortage professions, with the result that employment prospects were excellent. However, financial problems in the NHS a few years ago led to a recruitment freeze and a survey of universities indicated a shortage of career opportunities for newly qualified nurses. The position has since improved, although competition for posts has intensified and graduates need to be flexible on where they are willing to work.

Related Occupations

You may wish to consider: counsellor, physiotherapist, occupational therapist, radiographer, dietitian or speech and language therapist. Alternatively, you might develop your career as a midwife or health visitor.

Impact on Lifestyle

Depending on your chosen branch, you might have to work on a shift basis, including nights, weekends and public holidays, although not usually more than 37.5 hours per week in total. Employers are usually prepared to discuss all types of flexible working arrangements.

Earnings Potential

Funding arrangements have changed, and now students take government maintenance and tuition loans. Qualified nurses in the NHS usually start in Band 5, on a scale currently ranging from £22,128 to £28,746. Earnings can rise to £35,577 for a nurse specialist at the top of the scale and to over £69,000 for a nurse consultant. Additional allowances are paid for appointments in and around London, ranging from 20% of basic salary for Inner London, to 15% for Outer London and 5% for the London Fringe. Earnings in the private sector are generally likely to be higher, depending on where you live and the hours you are prepared to work.

Further Information

NHS Nursing Careers
http://nursing.nhscareers.nhs.uk

NHS Student Bursaries
www.nhsbsa.nhs.uk/Students/816.aspx

Nursing and Midwifery Council
www.nmc.org.uk

Royal College of Nursing
www.rcn.org.uk

Health Careers
www.healthcareers.nhs.uk

Nursing and Midwifery Board of Ireland
www.nmbi.ie/Careers-in-Nursing-Midwifery

Occupational Therapist

What is Involved?

As an occupational therapist, you would help people overcome difficulties which may be brought about by physical or mental illness, an accident or the ageing process. You would work with clients to help them lead full and independent lives and, where possible, prevent disability. A lot of the work involves dealing with individuals on a one-to-one basis and adapting treatment programmes to suit each person's needs and lifestyle.

You may be involved with helping someone who has had a stroke or a person with an eating disorder return to a normal lifestyle. Alternatively, you could find yourself helping burns victims recover from their injuries, work which may include applying make-up to camouflage any scarring. This rehabilitation can start before the patient leaves hospital and continues once they have been discharged, either in the patient's own home or in the occupational therapy department at the hospital. You might also work with long-stay patients in hospital, helping them maintain contact with 'normal' life, and you may become involved with supporting patients' families.

Opportunities for Training

You would need to be state registered with the Health and Care Professions Council, which means in most cases that you must take a validated three- or four-year degree course in Occupational Therapy. All training courses are about two-thirds academic, covering such areas as anatomy, physiology, psychiatry and orthopaedics, together with the particular skills and techniques used by occupational therapists, the organisation and management of occupational therapy departments and how to provide suitable aids and equipment for patients. The remaining third of the course is clinical and is spent in departments and hospital clinics learning about practical day-to-day occupational therapy. During this time, you would learn to assess and treat patients under the guidance of a registered therapist and then build up to treating your own small caseload under supervision.

An alternative route to qualification is the four-year, in-service, day-release course for people already working as assistants in occupational therapy departments. Accelerated postgraduate courses are also available, enabling graduates of other disciplines to obtain a licence to practise in two years.

Requirements for Entry

You would need a minimum of two A level/Advanced Higher, three Higher or equivalent qualifications, together with at least five GCSE/S Grade passes 9-4/A*-C/1-3. Normally, this requirement includes at least one science subject at GCSE/S Grade, while some courses look for A level/Advanced Higher or Higher biology. Demand for courses can be quite high, which means that applicants often need more than the minimum requirements. It is best to check with admissions tutors to be sure of meeting the entry requirements for particular courses.

Kind of Person

Since the job is very varied and you would have to meet and deal with a large number of people with different problems and needs, you would need to be creative and flexible. Each patient will require their own particular programme to work on and will make progress at their own rate. You will need to be able to gain the confidence of your patients both to find out what their needs are likely to be and to be able to encourage them to keep trying. At times progress can be frustratingly slow and hard work. As well as being able to establish supportive relationships with patients, you would have to be able to explain the treatment clearly and adjust the programme as necessary. You would have to keep good records on each patient and you would need to liaise with other healthcare professionals, sometimes taking part in case conferences.

Broad Outlook

With growing demand for occupational therapy services both in the UK and overseas, there are significant career development opportunities. Traditionally, most occupational therapists have worked in the National Health Service, although there is a continuing trend towards establishing opportunities in other work settings.

As a qualified occupational therapist, you can consider working in different job roles, as a practitioner, researcher, manager, lecturer or consultant. You can choose to work in such fields as social care, mental health, education, learning disabilities or physical rehabilitation. You will have a wide choice of practice specialisms to choose from, including eating disorders, hand therapy and substance misuse. You may wish to specialise in working with children, adults or older people. You can also decide whether you want to work for someone else or for yourself, in the community, in a hospital, or in a university educating future occupational therapists.

Related Occupations

You might consider: counsellor, psychotherapist, social worker or other therapy-based professions in the medical field, such as art therapist, dramatherapist, radiographer, physiotherapist, speech and language therapist or nurse.

Impact on Lifestyle

The work can be demanding, stressful and, at times, frustrating so you need to have commitment and a real desire to help others to achieve their potential. You would have to keep up to date with what equipment or exercises are available to help your patients. Occupational therapists usually work a 36-hour week, although you might sometimes be required to work extra hours.

Earnings Potential

A newly qualified NHS occupational therapist would start in Band 5, on a scale ranging from £22,128 to £28,746. This could rise to £41,787 for a team manager at the top of the scale and up to £83,000 for a consultant. Additional allowances are paid for appointments in and around London, ranging from 20% of basic salary for Inner London, to 15% for Outer London and 5% for the London Fringe. Salaries in the private sector are often linked to NHS levels but may be higher.

Further Information

British Association/College of Occupational Therapists
www.cot.co.uk

Health Careers
www.healthcareers.nhs.uk

Health and Care Professions Council
www.hcpc-uk.org

Association of Occupational Therapists of Ireland
www.aoti.ie

Oceanographer

What is Involved?

As an oceanographer, you would be a scientist concerned with the chemistry, biology, physics or geology of the marine world. This could include studying coastlines, waves and tidal flow, the structure of the seabed, estuaries and coastal waters or organisms that live in the sea. Your work could relate to the pollution of the seas or issues of climate change.

If your main interest is biology, you might study sustainable methods of seafood production; as a marine chemist, you might focus on how pesticides or nuclear waste enter and move through the oceans; if you are interested in physics, you might prefer to study the interaction between the wind and ocean currents; as a geologist, you could study the deposition of sediments in the oceans.

Whatever your principal science, the additional dimension of oceanography would give you a broad range of skills and knowledge relevant to understanding and managing the marine environment.

Opportunities for Training

An ocean science degree would give you a broad overview of all the disciplines of oceanography, so that you can understand how they combine to explain the ways in which the oceans interact with the earth and the atmosphere. Most courses are modular, giving you a chance to specialise if you wish to as your awareness grows. There are also universities offering degrees focusing on a particular area of oceanography, such as marine biology or marine chemistry. For postgraduate study, it is more common to specialise in one of these specific areas of oceanography.

Many degree courses in this area include fieldwork and take around four years to complete. If your course does not include work experience, you could try to arrange this yourself through a marine laboratory. At postgraduate level, there are taught Masters degrees, research degrees and PhD programmes. The Society for Underwater Technology has an educational support fund offering sponsorship awards for certain courses.

Requirements for Entry

For entry to a degree course, you would need at least two A level/Advanced Higher, three Higher or equivalent qualifications, usually including passes in sciences related to your main interest. Some universities specify more than the minimum, so you should research admission requirements carefully. Employers of oceanographers often require postgraduate qualifications.

Kind of Person

You would need a strong interest in science and the sea, with an enquiring mind and a keen attention to detail and accuracy. You would probably need to spend extended periods of time on a boat gathering data. You may need to go down to the seabed in a submarine vehicle or by diving. You would need IT skills to carry out detailed calculations.

Some of your work is likely to be carried out on your own but you would also need to work as part of a team. You may need to write up reports and explain to people what you have found out or what you are aiming to explore. These may be other scientists but could also be people who do not share your technical knowledge, so you would need to be able to communicate clearly.

Broad Outlook

Much oceanography work in the UK is created and funded by the Natural Environment Research Council, often in association with such organisations as the National

Oceanography Centre, the Sea Mammal Research Unit and the Tyndall Centre for Climate Change Research.

You may also find opportunities with the Department for Environment, Food and Rural Affairs, and in industries involved in offshore oil and gas extraction, offshore and coastal construction and marine instrumentation. You could go on to work in teaching and research with universities and other research bodies throughout the world who specialise in aspects of oceanography.

Short-term contracts are common in this area of work. As environmental concerns become more important, there is an increasing number of consultancies being set up, creating more opportunities to work in private practice.

Related Occupations

You might also consider: hydrogeologist, hydrographic surveyor, marine biologist/marine scientist, geologist/geoscientist, meteorologist, research biologist/bioscientist, research chemist, physicist, microbiologist or biochemist.

Impact on Lifestyle

Oceanographers can expect to travel widely and, at the very least, to work alongside colleagues from many nations. You are likely to find yourself working away from home, sometimes abroad or living on ships. When you are working out in the field you would be out in all sorts of weathers, sometimes cold and wet, sometimes basking in bright sunshine! You would generally work normal office hours but when you are at sea you may be expected to work long hours on a rota to finish your project in the time available.

Earnings Potential

Using government research and university rates as examples, you will find that typical starting salaries for recent graduates or MSc candidates range from £18,000 to £20,000 and from £23,000 to £30,000 for PhD candidates. Typical salaries for first time lecturers are £27,000 to £37,000, while experienced senior lecturers can earn £38,000 to £56,000 plus. Oceanographers who work in private industry would be on a similar scale or slightly higher. Consultancy pay can be higher still, although most consultants start on a rate ranging from around £33,000 to £35,000, with pay levels increasing with suitable experience.

Further Information

Natural Environment Research Council
www.nerc.ac.uk
National Oceanography Centre
www.noc.soton.ac.uk
Society for Underwater Technology
www.sut.org
British Oceanographic Data Centre
www.bodc.ac.uk
Marine Technology Education Consortium
www.mtec.ac.uk
Tyndall Centre for Climate Change Research
www.tyndall.ac.uk
Marine Institute
www.marine.ie

Operational Researcher/Management Scientist

What is Involved?

As an operational researcher or management scientist, you would specialise in applying mathematical, statistical, computing and other analytical techniques to help organisations evaluate their operational procedures, improve their efficiency and devise strategies for future development. Operational research (OR) work can be very varied, giving you the opportunity to move around and experience many different business environments, ranging from central government, health, defence or transport to manufacturing industry, retailing, financial services or power, water and telecommunications supply companies. Within these, you might consider areas such as information storage, handling and access, management decision making, manufacturing processes, sales administration, accounting systems, logistics, forecasting or scheduling. In a rapidly developing economy, OR techniques are in great demand to keep organisations efficient, economically viable and competitive.

Your work would often involve visiting the workplace to talk to operational personnel and management in order to establish what changes need to be looked at, what kinds of problems arise regularly to disrupt efficient operation and where information bottlenecks are causing delays in, for example, the delivery of goods or in reordering raw materials. You would then apply appropriate OR techniques, such as mathematical modelling and computer simulations, to analyse the problems and come up with pragmatic solutions for the management team or company board to consider. Finally, you could be directly involved in the installation and testing out of new systems.

Opportunities for Training

Most people employed in OR are graduates and many would have followed courses with a significant mathematical, statistical or computing content. However, opportunities can exist for people from other disciplines and those who move into OR from other professions. Many undergraduate courses in mathematics, statistics, business studies and management include some OR, although it is not always necessary for entrants to the profession to have studied OR. Many employers would look firstly for quantitative, logical and communication skills and then provide any further appropriate training. In fact, graduates are recruited from many disciplines - and most OR groups have members contributing a variety of skills. After graduating, you could either seek employment straight away or follow a postgraduate course. Many significant employing organisations prefer candidates with an MSc in OR and a list of suitable courses can be found on the Operational Research Society website.

Requirements for Entry

For entry to an appropriate degree course, you would normally need to have at least two A level/Advanced Higher, three Higher passes or equivalent, in most cases including mathematics. After successfully completing your degree and demonstrating that you have the required analytical and business interest skills, you could progress to employment or postgraduate study.

Kind of Person

A solid grounding in maths, statistics and computing would be an important asset for a career in OR. However, before launching into data analysis, you would have to assemble and understand the information relating to the problem area. This would often involve in-depth discussions with people at all levels. Good communication skills and business awareness would, therefore, be crucial in winning co-operation, whilst literacy, numeracy and computer literacy would be vital in the execution of your work. You would need an excellent grasp of business operations, with an insight into management controls, communications, production and administration systems. You would have to pay careful attention to detail and you might need strong powers of persuasion to convince managers and directors that your proposals would solve their problems.

Broad Outlook

Whatever the economic circumstances and business environment - recession or growth, confidence or uncertainty - organisations are increasingly calling for better information handling and more informed decision taking. You might be employed by OR or management consultancies, the Government Operational Research Service (GORS), universities, research institutions, the NHS, or in various industries including manufacturing, utilities and transport. This is a field in which you can gain an overall grasp of organisational structures, opening up opportunities for rapid promotion to senior general management levels and even to board level. You could also choose to become self-employed as a management consultant.

The OR Society organises a well-supported Careers Open Day every November, bringing together employers, academics and undergraduate and postgraduate students.

Related Occupations

You might also consider: management/business consultant, economist, ergonomist, financial risk analyst, market researcher, software engineer, systems analyst, statistician or actuary.

Impact on Lifestyle

Your work could involve a great deal of travel in the UK and abroad, with often lengthy periods spent away from home and therefore with some disruption of social and family life. Disentangling complex systems and coming up with better ones would often be accompanied by the pressure of meeting deadlines, writing reports and proposals and making presentations to managers or senior executives.

Earnings Potential

While salary rates vary considerably, GORS offers starting salaries ranging from £20,000 to £45,000, depending on experience, location and department. Elsewhere, typical starting salaries are £20,000 to £28,000, rising to £40,000 to £80,000 at senior level. Salaries tend to be highest in self-employment and consultancy, and may exceed £100,000 for an experienced strategic planning specialist.

Further Information

Operational Research Society
www.theorsociety.com

Learn about OR
www.learnaboutor.co.uk

Association of European Operational Research Societies
www.euro-online.org

Government Operational Research Service
www.operational-research.gov.uk

Analytics Society of Ireland
http://mis.ucd.ie/mssi

Optometrist

What is Involved?

As an optometrist (formerly known as an ophthalmic optician), you would work with patients of all ages, performing eyesight tests and examinations and prescribing corrective lenses or spectacles to those who need them. You might also fit spectacles or contact lenses, and give advice on visual problems. You would be trained to examine the eyes to detect signs of injury, disease, abnormality and defects in vision.

In addition, some general health conditions (such as diabetes) show themselves in the eye and an optometrist is trained to detect these. You would refer patients to other healthcare professionals as appropriate.

Opportunities for Training

To become an optometrist, you would need to pass the General Optical Council (GOC) professional qualifying examination. This has two distinct parts:

- BSc Optometry (sometimes called Ophthalmic Optics), a broadly based scientific degree combining theory with clinical work. The theoretical side includes anatomy and physiology, optics, optometry, pharmacology and the use of drugs, recognition of ocular abnormalities; the practical covers dispensing practice and management and professional studies

- A pre-registration period of training, including work-based assessment and supervision by a registered optometrist, followed by a Final Assessment examination based on the GOC Stage 2 core competencies for optometry. This includes practical examinations and a clinical decision-making section based on pre-written case scenarios

The University of Manchester offers a four-year Masters (MOptom) course, which incorporates the pre-registration year. Students who successfully complete this course are fully qualified and able to register as optometrists. Overall, there are 11 UK universities offering a first degree in optometry and there is a high demand for places.

Requirements for Entry

Most universities require two or three sciences at A level/Advanced Higher, three Higher or equivalent qualifications, some specifying biology as one of them; chemistry, maths and physics are other particularly useful subjects. It is advisable to check entry requirements with the individual institutions. Before applying, you should spend some time on a work experience or work shadowing placement with a qualified optometrist.

Kind of Person

Optometry involves combining expert knowledge with good communication skills, patience and precision to achieve the best possible care for your clients' eyes. You need to be able to understand a complex and precise science and have sufficient mathematical aptitude to make the accurate measurements and calculations needed. The instruments used are delicate and you would need manual dexterity to use them correctly. As there are constant developments in this field, you would need to keep yourself up to date. You would be dealing with people from all walks of life, some of them worried about their sight or the prospect of wearing glasses or lenses. If you intend to work in private practice, you would also need good business sense and management skills. An interest in fashion and colour is helpful.

Broad Outlook

With more than half the UK population having a diagnosed visual defect, there is no shortage of work for the nation's 14,642 registered optometrists. Most work in general practice on their own, in partnership for a small independent firm or in one of the big high street chains. Excellent prospects for self-employment attract many people to the profession. There are also opportunities to work in hospitals alongside eye specialists and their teams. Some optometrists become specialists themselves in a particular field or else assist with eye tests and prescriptions following operations or other medical treatment. There are also chances for research and teaching.

Related Occupations

You may be interested in other professions concerned with maintaining or correcting people's vision, such as dispensing optician or orthoptist. You might also consider other medical related professions, such as speech and language therapist or radiographer.

Impact on Lifestyle

Most optometrists in private practice work a 37.5-hour week, although in some of the large practices you may have to work on a rota system in which days off vary. Saturdays are often busy in high street practices. If you set yourself up in practice you would have to work long and unsocial hours, at least to start with, in order to establish yourself. In the NHS, you would work a 35-hour week, although you may be on call at evenings and weekends. There is considerable scope for part-time work.

Earnings Potential

There is no set minimum salary for the pre-registration year but most practices pay around £17,000 to £21,000. Earnings should rise on qualification to approximately £25,000 to £28,000. The range of typical salaries for a senior optometrist in private practice is generally £45,000 to £54,000. Your earnings potential can be higher if you set yourself up as an independent optometrist, although private practice was badly affected by the recession that started in 2008. Hospital eye service salaries are initially graded in NHS Band 6, ranging from £26,565 to £35,577, with additional payments for specialist skills. A hospital consultant can earn over £83,000 at the very top of the scale.

Further Information

New Dimensions in Optics
www.newdimensioninoptics.org

College of Optometrists
www.college-optometrists.org

Association of Optometrists
www.aop.org.uk

General Optical Council
www.optical.org

Optometry Today
www.aop.org.uk/ot

Association of Optometrists Ireland
www.optometrists.ie

Orthoptist

What is Involved?

As an orthoptist, you would investigate, diagnose and treat defects of binocular vision and abnormalities of eye movement. The work involves seeing patients of all ages, from infants to the elderly. You would form part of the eye care team in a particular location and would generally work closely with ophthalmologists, optometrists and vision scientists.

You would be particularly concerned with eye problems related to ocular motility, binocular vision, amblyopia (lazy eye) or strabismus (squint). Your job would be to diagnose these problems and determine appropriate management. The work might involve vision screening of children in schools and community health centres.

You might also have a role in the management of conditions such as glaucoma, cataract, stroke, retinal disease, and neurological disorders, referring patients where necessary to doctors for further assessment, treatment or surgery.

In addition to conducting clinics for outpatients, you would accompany consultants on ward rounds in hospitals. You could also work in private practice.

Opportunities for Training

You would need to study for a degree in orthoptics approved by the Orthoptists Board of the Health and Care Professions Council. This is available at three universities in the UK: Liverpool, Sheffield and Glasgow Caledonian. The degrees take three years in England, four in Scotland, leading to BSc or BMedSci (orthoptics) qualifications. The first year covers general anatomy and physiology. It gives an understanding of the normal visual system as well as introducing optics and orthoptics. In years two and three, the investigation and management of disorders of vision are taught. In addition, you would learn about ophthalmology and pathology so that you can recognise disorders and diseases of the eye. You would be given practical experience with clinical placements in each of the three or four years of your course. The Glasgow Caledonian course started only in 2012 but meets all the requirements for professional registration.

Requirements for Entry

To take a degree in orthoptics you would need three A level/Advanced Higher, four Higher or equivalent qualifications, including at least one science subject, preferably biology but physics or maths would be very helpful, together with five GCSE/S Grade passes 9-4/A*-C/1-3, which should include English, maths, and physics or dual science. It is advisable to arrange a visit to your local orthoptic department to see what the work involves before applying for a place.

Kind of Person

You would need a keen interest in biology, maths and physics, as well as having good interpersonal skills to deal with the wide range of people you would meet in this work. Some of your patients may be hard to communicate with because they are elderly or young children, so you would need to be patient and creative both in your explanations and to capture their attention. Much of the testing involves skilful measuring and the use of precision instruments. You would be expected to keep accurate records on your patients so you would have to be well organised. As well as working as part of a team, you would also need to be able to work responsibly on your own.

Broad Outlook

Orthoptics is a small profession, with fewer than 2,000 members in the British Isles. The three universities mentioned on the previous page, Liverpool, Sheffield and Glasgow Caledonian, supply the needs of all four UK countries and the Republic of Ireland. Members of the British and Irish Orthoptic Society also work in many other countries around the world.

There is demand both for full-time and part-time orthoptists. The majority of orthoptists are employed in the National Health Service within a set grading structure. Opportunities exist for promotion to Head Orthoptist in clinical practice.

You could also study for a higher degree (MSc, MPhil or PhD) and/or consider a teaching career in orthoptics. The British qualification in orthoptics is respected throughout the world and there are opportunities for working abroad. There is great potential for future research within the orthoptic field and all three universities are actively involved in the development of a large and productive research profile.

Related Occupations

You may be interested in other related professions such as dispensing optician or optometrist. Alternatively, you might like to consider another profession in the medical field, such as doctor (general practice), doctor (hospital), radiographer, podiatrist/chiropodist, speech and language therapist or physiotherapist.

Impact on Lifestyle

Most orthoptists work normal hours from Monday to Friday. Your social and family life would therefore be far less disturbed than that of other health professionals working in hospitals, who have to deal with emergencies and patient care on a 24-hour basis.

Earnings Potential

A newly qualified NHS orthoptist would start in Band 5, on a scale ranging from £22,128 to £28,746. This could rise for a specialist in Band 6 to £26,565 to £35,577 and for an advanced practitioner in Band 7 to £31,696 to £41,787. A head of department could earn up to £69,168. Additional allowances are paid for appointments in and around London, ranging from 20% of basic salary for Inner London, to 15% for Outer London and 5% for the London Fringe. Salaries in the private sector are often linked to NHS levels but may be higher.

Further Information

British and Irish Orthoptic Society
www.orthoptics.org.uk

What do Orthoptists do?
www.liverpool.ac.uk/orthoptics/careers

General Optical Council
www.optical.org

Health and Care Professions Council
www.hcpc-uk.org

Osteopath

What is Involved?

As an osteopath, you would be working as a practitioner in complementary medicine. Your skill would reside in your sensitivity of touch, which you would use to locate the source of problems presented by patients, and the manipulative skills of your hands as you apply the treatments. You would look for such things as tissue tension or variations in the movement of joints as indicators of underlying dysfunction. Using your hands to correct joint and tissue abnormalities, you would make it easier for a patient's body to function normally and use its own recuperative powers more effectively. Beyond diagnosing and treating the structural and mechanical problems of the body, you would look at each patient's diet, lifestyle and mental well being to restore the state of balance within their total bodily function.

You would start by listening to a patient's account of their problem and observing the way they stand, walk, and move. You would then use your hands to discover the underlying causes of pain. Sometimes you may make use of x-rays as well. On finding the source of the problem, you would ascertain that it could benefit from osteopathy and you would carry out treatment using a variety of manipulative techniques. You may need to refer the patient to their doctor or another healthcare professional if you feel the problem is not suitable for osteopathy.

Opportunities for Training

In order to practise as an osteopath you must be registered with the General Osteopathic Council, which means that you must have trained at an accredited osteopathic school. Courses vary from four to five years full-time or five years on a mixed-mode basis. There is also an 18-month course open only to medical practitioners.

All of these osteopathic courses offer BSc or BSc Honours degree programmes. You would learn basic medical sciences, including anatomy, physiology and pathology, in addition to osteopathic philosophy, concepts and techniques.

Requirements for Entry

While they may vary slightly between each school, the usual minimum entry requirements are three good A level/Advanced Higher, four Higher or equivalent passes, two of which should be chemistry and biology, together with five GCSE/S Grade passes 9-4/A*-C/1-3, including English and maths.

Osteopathy is not limited to school leavers. In fact, many practitioners choose osteopathy as a second career later in life.

Kind of Person

You would need excellent communication skills, especially in terms of listening to your patients, teasing out details of their problem and explaining your diagnosis. Having gathered the relevant information, you would need to be able to take a logical problem-solving approach in order to assess the facts and decide on a course of action. You would need a caring attitude, with the ability to put nervous or shy patients at ease.

You should be in good health, with a high level of manual dexterity; osteopathy requires skill and technique rather than muscle power, with men and women having equal success as practitioners. To be self-employed or working for a small practice, you would need good organisational and business skills.

Broad Outlook

Over seven million people a year seek osteopathic treatment and demand is increasing. (There has been a 25% increase in demand since the introduction of statutory self-regulation for osteopaths in the 1990s). With most people feeling that they stand a better chance of obtaining relief for back pain outside conventional medicine, osteopathy is a growing profession. Each patient may require more than one treatment and it may be that some patients choose to come back once or twice a year to ensure that a problem does not recur.

Currently, most osteopaths work on a self-employed basis in the private sector, but there is a growing tendency towards multi-disciplinary environments and there is some integration with the National Health Service. Occupational Health within private and public companies is also a key growth area for osteopathic practice.

Related Occupations

You may be interested in other professions in the field of complementary medicine such as acupuncturist, chiropractor, homoeopath or reflexologist. Alternatively, you might consider a therapy-based profession in the medical field such as physiotherapist or occupational therapist.

Impact on Lifestyle

As a newly graduated osteopath, you would have a number of possible areas of practice to consider: set up on your own; join an established practice; work in association with the NHS; or join a multidisciplinary practice. As with all professions, you should reckon on it taking two to three years to become established and develop a full practice with the financial return that goes with it. Whilst London may appear to offer the greatest opportunity, it also has the largest number of practitioners and the most expensive premises. Setting up your practice further afield, where your premises would cost less and your services should be in greater demand, could make a lot of sense.

Earnings Potential

Since most osteopaths are self-employed, your income could vary considerably and would be determined by your reputation and the hours you are prepared to work. A typical charge is between £35 and £50 per session. You would need to meet a number of professional costs, including the retention fee for your professional body. Other business costs may include rental of your clinic, heating, lighting and any equipment plus wages for a receptionist or administrative staff. The average expected salary for an osteopath in the UK is around £34,000.

Further Information

General Osteopathic Council
www.osteopathy.org.uk

Institute of Osteopathy
www.osteopathy.org

Osteopathic Council of Ireland
www.osteopathy.ie

Patent Attorney

What is Involved?

As a patent attorney, also known as a patent agent, you would have a particular expertise in intellectual property rights, encompassing patents, industrial designs, design rights and related copyright areas. You would work in the patent department of a large industrial organisation, in a private firm of patent attorneys or in a government department. A patent is a right granted to inventors or companies, in return for disclosure of an invention, to stop other people using that invention for a certain period of time (maximum 20 years). In order to secure a patent, a full description of the invention needs to be filed with the Patent Office and you would develop special skills in the long and complex process of securing, maintaining and enforcing patent rights.

Patent attorney work is becoming an increasingly Europe-wide profession and you would be likely to have considerable contact with the European Patent Office in Munich.

Opportunities for Training

While it is possible to represent clients without being registered, you would normally obtain a post as a technical assistant to a patent attorney, either in a firm of attorneys or in an industrial patent department, and study for the examinations leading to entry on the Register of Patent Attorneys. It is usual for a person entering the profession to take four or five years to qualify, with foundation papers usually taken after about a year in the profession, followed by the advanced papers two or three years later. Academic training is available, particularly through Certificate and Master's courses in intellectual property run by Queen Mary University of London, Bournemouth University and Brunel University. These qualifications give exemption from some of the examinations.

Most patent attorneys also become European patent attorneys, taking an examination similar to the advanced patent paper. You must be on the list of qualified practitioners if you wish to act before the European Patent Office. Indeed, the European Commission has recently proposed the introduction of a unitary European patent, which will be granted by the European Patent Office. Once these patents take over from national patents, UK patent attorneys may not be needed. Thus, it may be better to focus attention on qualifying as a European Patent Attorney, not as a UK Patent Attorney. It is also possible to qualify as a patent attorney while working as a solicitor in a legal practice with an intellectual property department.

Requirements for Entry

You would usually need a science, technology or engineering degree, together with advanced writing skills, the ability to acquire legal skills and a reading knowledge of French and German.

Kind of Person

You would need to be a mixture of scientist, lawyer and linguist, with a reasonable level of skill in each of these areas. You must be able to write clearly and unambiguously and you would need a logical, analytical mind, combined with attention to detail and keen powers of recall. You may become heavily involved in litigation in the courts of the UK and other countries and would need personal qualities similar to those required by a solicitor or barrister/advocate. See our separate articles covering these occupations.

Broad Outlook

Career development opportunities are generally good and do not always end simply by being a partner in a firm of patent attorneys or the head of a patents department. Some patent attorneys move to executive or management positions, while others move abroad, particularly to English-speaking countries or to multinational companies who work in English. Some choose to take UK solicitor qualifications as well or even become US attorneys.

You could concentrate on patent work or broaden your scope to work across the whole intellectual property field. Similarly, you might specialise in securing or enforcing intellectual property rights for your clients or employers, or you might branch into related areas such as licensing and contract arrangements based on such rights.

Related Occupations

You might also consider: trade mark attorney, patent examiner, solicitor, barrister/advocate, biochemist, pharmacologist, biotechnologist, physicist or engineering professions for example.

Impact on Lifestyle

You would always be working to meet specific deadlines and the work itself can be very mentally and intellectually demanding. Standard office times would usually apply but the internet makes work away from base increasingly viable, both within and outside normal hours. You could be involved in considerable travel, especially within Europe.

Earnings Potential

For industry and private practice, the starting salary for a science graduate would be from £25,000 to £33,000, with a significant salary increase - to £50,000 to £70,000 - usually following qualification. This should rise with experience to £90,000 to £150,000 in industry and £100,000 to £400,000 for a partner in private practice.

Further Information

Chartered Institute of Patent Attorneys
www.cipa.org.uk

European Patent Office
www.epo.org

International Intellectual Property Institute
http://iipi.org

Intellectual Property Regulation Board
http://ipreg.org.uk

UK Intellectual Property Office
www.gov.uk/government/organisations/intellectual-property-office

Centre d'Etudes Internationales de la Propriété Intellectuelle
www.ceipi.edu

Irish Patents Office
www.patentsoffice.ie

Patent Examiner

What is Involved?

As a patent examiner, you would be employed by the UK Intellectual Property Office (IPO) to examine new patent claims before accepting them as valid for official registration. The patent system provides a stimulus to invention by granting innovators a monopoly (extendable up to 20 years in the UK) for the manufacture and sale of patented inventions. In exchange, the innovator discloses the nature of the invention, allowing others to build upon the discovery and avoiding duplication of research effort.

Your job would be to investigate each application to ascertain that the invention is clearly described and you would conduct a search through UK and foreign patent specifications to ascertain that the invention is truly novel. You would write a report of your initial search results and would use this to determine with the applicant or their agent whether to proceed to the second stage of substantive examination and detailed investigation of the claims made for the invention. Finally, the application would either proceed to grant of a patent or would be refused. If refused, the applicant may appeal to the Courts.

The IPO is based in modern premises on the outskirts of Newport, South Wales.

Opportunities for Training

Training begins with lectures and seminars on various aspects of Intellectual Property law and on the basic skills of the examining job. You would quickly move on to working on live applications alongside other newly recruited examiners, tutored by experienced senior examiners. You would be encouraged to study for a postgraduate diploma in Intellectual Property Law, facilitated by a university and taught in-house, with other training and development opportunities including foreign language training.

To enable you to keep abreast of the latest developments, you would be encouraged to visit laboratories, factories and exhibitions and to participate in seminars.

Requirements for Entry

You would need a degree in a mathematical, engineering or scientific subject. Suitable disciplines would include electrical/electronic, telecommunications, mechanical, civil or chemical engineering, physics, organic chemistry, chemistry, biotechnology, computer science and mathematics. See our separate articles on these subjects for details of degree entry requirements.

Kind of Person

You would need sound scientific and technical knowledge and the ability to exercise this knowledge within the concepts of patent law. You should be prepared for a mixture of the legal, the scientific, the technological and the commercial. You would also need excellent analytical and critical skills, coupled with the ability to express an argument cogently, both on paper and orally. To appreciate the level of innovation in patent applications, you would need a flexible and creative approach to problem solving. The work increasingly involves the use of computers, so you would need good IT skills.

Broad Outlook

The UK Intellectual Property Office has been undergoing a rolling recruitment campaign, with no specific deadlines and all applications considered as and when they are received. Vacancies exist in the following fields: computer science, electronics, electrical engineering, aerospace engineering, mechanical engineering, telecommunications, television video and image processing and semiconductors.

The Patent Examiner career is structured, with opportunities for promotion after two to four years and again after five to nine to Senior Examiner. These promotions are 'non-competitive', meaning that you are promoted when your performance reaches the required level; it is not necessary to wait for a vacancy to occur. More senior positions to Deputy Director and above are, however, competitive.

The overwhelming majority of examiners complete their careers within the IPO, but there are opportunities for training in general management and for gaining experience in other areas of government. There is also the possibility of applying directly or of transferring to the European Patent Office, with headquarters in Munich and branches in The Hague, Vienna and Berlin, but your German and French must be strong as you would be working in a totally trilingual environment. With experience, you could consider opportunities with the World Intellectual Property Organisation in Geneva.

Related Occupations

You might also consider: electrical engineer, electronic/electronics engineer, telecommunications engineer, mechanical engineer, civil engineer, chemical/process engineer, physicist, biotechnologist, mathematician/mathematical researcher, barrister, advocate, solicitor, legal executive, technical author, trade mark attorney or patent attorney.

Experience of patent examining work is regarded as qualifying for corporate membership of the Institution of Mechanical Engineers or the Institution of Engineering and Technology.

Impact on Lifestyle

You would usually work a five-day week from Monday to Friday and you would enjoy the normal benefits of the civil service, with a progressive salary scale, promotion prospects and excellent pension fund. The work itself can be very mentally and intellectually demanding. There would be deadlines to meet and you would have to be sure that your decisions on the validity of a patent could not later prove to be incorrect.

Earnings Potential

Associate patent examiners (new starters) currently earn £27,225. Newly promoted patent examiners currently earn £34,300. Newly promoted senior patent examiners currently earn £52,933. More senior posts are paid at Senior Civil Service rates.

European Patent Office salaries are very competitive, depending on the level of your relevant work experience, and include an allowance for expatriates who do not live in their home country and a household allowance for those who are married and/or have children.

Further Information

UK Intellectual Property Office
www.gov.uk/government/organisations/intellectual-property-office

European Patent Office
www.epo.org

World Intellectual Property Organisation
www.wipo.int

Irish Patents Office
www.patentsoffice.ie

PE/PT Teacher/Instructor

What is Involved?

As a PE/PT teacher or instructor, you would have a specialised role in a school, in the armed services or in the community, perhaps in a health club or fitness centre. Your job would be to help people to develop all-round physical fitness, coordination of hand and eye and awareness of the need for exercise; to develop their strength and endurance, to improve their performance in sports generally and to maintain a healthy lifestyle.

In a school your job would, in the main, be performed outside the classroom in the gymnasium, sports hall or on the playing fields. You must become aware of the special demands which physical education poses in terms of commitment and dedication, especially, as often happens, when PE staff are responsible for the running of the school's major games, with often very demanding fixture commitments.

In the armed forces, yours would be a very specialised function. Royal Navy and Marine instructors develop and supervise PT in training centres and commando units. The Royal Army Physical Training Corps (RAPTC) is responsible for the fitness and training of all soldiers, and its members are all Physical Training Instructors (PTIs). The RAF equivalent also embraces specialist training in parachuting, leadership, outdoor pursuits and survival techniques.

Opportunities for Training

Recognised training is essential for teaching posts in maintained schools. You would need to undertake Initial Teacher Training (ITT) and obtain Qualified Teacher Status (QTS) in England and Wales. Routes are similar in Scotland but are not described in terms of ITT/QTS and courses are geared to the specific needs of the Scottish education system. There are several different ITT routes and you should undertake careful research to determine which one would be the best for you. You can, for example, train to be a teacher while completing a degree. This would be a BA or BSc with QTS or, in some cases, a BEd (Bachelor of Education). An alternative would be to take a first degree, usually in a sports-related subject, followed by a postgraduate certificate in education (PGCE) or by a programme of school-centred initial teacher training (SCITT).

Several other employment-based routes exist, details of which can be obtained from the relevant teaching organisation.

In the armed forces, the Royal Air Force recruits people specifically as physical training instructors, whereas the Army and Royal Navy normally appoint PE specialists internally. For example, a prospective PTI with the RAPTC must first join another regiment or corps and then qualify as a Regimental PTI after an eight-week course at the Army School of Physical Training. In the Royal Marines, you must train as a Marine first and succeed in a general Marine job for at least a couple of years before you can specialise as a PTI.

Requirements for Entry

For entry to teacher training or to a sports-related degree, you would normally need two or three A level/Advanced Higher, three or four Higher or equivalent passes, together with a good spread of GCSE/S Grade passes at 9-4/A*-C/1-3, or equivalent including English, maths and a science.

You would need to be very fit and many courses would look for evidence of sporting achievement.

Kind of Person

You would need to be enthusiastic about sport and all manner of physical activity. You would be expected to comply with the code of conduct set down by the governing body of any sport with which you are involved and you should try to establish professional standards of behaviour. You should be able to motivate and inspire people and would need to be patient with those who are slow to learn or who do not share your passion for sporting activity. Good organisational and communication skills would be essential.

Broad Outlook

With obesity-related diseases becoming more and more frequent, a key government objective is to improve the health of the nation through sport and physical activity. Sport is also important for community development, a tool for engaging with groups including disillusioned adults, young people not in education or training and the general public during major sporting events. Despite perennial funding issues, opportunities in the exercise and health club sector are steadily increasing.

Related Occupations

You might also wish to consider: community development worker, leisure services/ fitness centre manager, outdoor activities instructor, professional sportsperson, sports administrator, sports and exercise psychologist, sports physiotherapist, sports coach or swimming coach/teacher.

Impact on Lifestyle

As a PE teacher, you would be spared most of the daily round of marking and administration but you may be expected to organise and lead a great number of out-of-school activities. You could be involved during the holidays with school trips or visits, such as skiing, water-sports and outdoor adventure activities. In the armed services, you would have to be available for duty at any time and could be called upon to organise or participate in particularly demanding exercises or operations.

Earnings Potential

A Newly Qualified Teacher (NQT) in England and Wales can expect to start on a scale ranging from £22,467 to £33,160 or £28,098 to £38,241 in Inner London. In the armed services, you would be paid on the normal scale for your force, with the starting point determined by your age and qualifications. A physical training instructor in the Royal Air Force, for example, starts on £27,324 plus benefits after training.

Further Information

Get into Teaching
https://getintoteaching.education.gov.uk
Education Workforce Council, Wales
www.ewc.wales
General Teaching Council for Scotland
www.gtcs.org.uk
Association for Physical Education
www.afpe.org.uk
SkillsActive, Sector Skills Council for Active Leisure and Learning
www.skillsactive.com
Armed Services Websites:
www.raf.mod.uk/careers
www.army.mod.uk
www.royalnavy.mod.uk
www.royalnavy.mod.uk/royalmarines
Physical Education Association of Ireland
www.peai.org

Petroleum Engineer

What is Involved?

As a petroleum engineer, you would be working in a specialised field of mining engineering concerned with exploration to find reservoirs of oil and gas in the earth. Once the exploration team has located a suitable source of oil and gas, you would determine how to set about the process of extraction. This would mean that you would liaise with other experts, such as geologists, to decide on the best method of drilling, bearing in mind the overall geography and geology of the area and particularly the types of rock involved. You would also need to consider the likely costs of extracting the optimum quantity from the reservoir. This process is likely to involve you in using computer technology to simulate the extraction process and so decide on the most appropriate equipment and processes needed.

Production, the process of getting the oil out of the ground, would be your specialist area as a petroleum engineer but you would be part of a team of engineers of every sort involved in designing, building, maintaining and running the complex structures and equipment on land or at sea.

Back in the research and development laboratories, you might work with scientists and chemical and mechanical engineers to improve products, create new ones, find new ways to extract oil and make the petroleum industry as environmentally friendly as possible.

Opportunities for Training

You should study for a degree at university, with specialist petroleum engineering courses available at Aberdeen, Leeds, London South Bank, Manchester and Portsmouth. It is also possible to study petroleum engineering as a postgraduate course, possibly focusing on the Centre for Petroleum Studies at Imperial College in London or the Institute for Petroleum Engineering at Heriot-Watt University, both of which have strong links with the industry. In order to become a chartered engineer, you would need to complete an approved four-year MEng course or a three-year BEng degree course plus at least an extra year of postgraduate study. See our separate article on engineering qualifications.

Requirements for Entry

You would normally need A level/Advanced Higher, Higher or equivalent qualifications to study at the universities listed above, including at least two subjects from maths, physics and chemistry. If not actually required, then they will be strongly preferred. You would need a good first degree in science or engineering for admission to one of the postgraduate courses.

Kind of Person

You would need a strong interest in maths, science and technology and should enjoy solving problems. Your work would involve you in using sophisticated computer technology, not only to model the possible drilling options but also to sift through the mass of complex information that needs to be considered. You would be working as a member of a small team, some of whom would have different specialised knowledge. You would need to communicate clearly with other team members and also to take account of their views. At times you may need to be flexible and to modify your proposals to fit in with other people's ideas.

Broad Outlook

The industry faces numerous challenges as it addresses growing energy demand, the need for sustainable operations, declining production from older reservoirs, and new resources in harder to reach and harsher environments.

This continuing demand for oil and gas means that there will always be a need for petroleum engineers to discover new petroleum sources on land or under the sea and to optimise the extraction process. It is important, however, to be realistic about your chances of a career in the oil industry. In any one year, the opportunities are limited and they go to the people with the best qualifications and personal qualities for the work.

Engineers can be found in managerial, technical and non-technical roles in all parts of the petroleum business. Most oil companies operate throughout the world and every area of the industry offers a wide choice of jobs for engineers.

Related Occupations

You might also consider: drilling engineer, mining engineer, chemical/process engineer, nuclear engineer, energy engineer or manufacturing engineer. Alternatively, you may prefer to consider: metallurgist, materials scientist/engineer, geologist/ geoscientist, geophysicist or oceanographer.

Impact on Lifestyle

You are likely to spend a great deal of your time monitoring drilling production on locations as far afield as the North Sea or Alaska. This might involve you working in difficult, dirty or dangerous conditions, perhaps on an oil rig at sea or in arctic or desert conditions. You would, therefore, be expected to travel extensively as part of your job and this could have an impact on your family and social life.

Earnings Potential

You are likely to be well paid, starting on around £30,000 to £37,000 as a recent graduate, although salaries at the higher end of the scale are more likely to be available to those with a relevant PhD. Your salary should rise quite quickly as you gain in experience and achieve chartered status. After 10 to15 years, your earnings should be in the region of £55,000 to £95,000. Location and assignments have a considerable influence on salary. There can be generous benefits packages and overseas allowances, together with bonuses for offshore work. An experienced freelance engineer can earn over £1,000 per day.

Further Information

Energy Institute
www.energyinst.org

Energy Careers and Courses
http://careers.energyinst.org/courses

Institute of Materials Minerals and Mining
www.iom3.org

Engineering Council UK
www.engc.org.uk

Society of Petroleum Engineers
www.spe.org

Engineers Ireland
www.engineersireland.ie

Pharmacist

What is Involved?

Your job as a pharmacist would involve working with drugs and medicines. You might prepare and dispense medicines or you could work in researching and developing medicinal products. Many pharmacists work in the community, in one of the large, multiple retail chains, in an independent pharmacy, in a GP surgery or a health centre. This often means working directly with the public, preparing and dispensing medicines according to doctors' prescriptions and also offering advice. Alternatively, you may work in a hospital dispensing drugs, medicines and other preparations such as special feeding solutions or diagnostic materials. Some pharmacists choose to work in industry and become involved in the manufacture of drugs.

Working with other healthcare professionals in a surgery or health centre is currently one of the fastest-growing specialisms for pharmacists, helping to ensure that patients use their medicines safely and effectively. Pharmacists can provide a first port of call to customers for self care of minor ailments and also help people maintain a healthy lifestyle by providing useful advice. It is also the pharmacist's responsibility to make sure that the pharmacy is well run and that staff are properly trained.

Opportunities for Training

In order to work as a pharmacist, you must be registered with the General Pharmaceutical Council. This means that you will have to undertake a four-year Master of Pharmacy (MPharm) degree at a school of pharmacy, which includes some clinical experience as well as the theoretical study of pharmaceutics and pharmacology. There is also a five-year sandwich course, which includes blocks of practical training. At the end of your degree, you would need to complete one year of pre-registration training and then pass the Royal Pharmaceutical Society's registration exam.

The degree course comprises four main subjects:

- Origin and chemistry of drugs. There is an emphasis on the study of synthetic drugs, although drugs from natural sources are also studied
- Preparation of medicines. This includes pharmaceutics, which is the study of the formulation of drugs
- Action and uses of drugs and medicines. This covers physiology, biochemistry, microbiology, pathology and pharmacology
- Pharmacy practice. This covers the supply of medicines and provision of advice, including the laws and standards applying to pharmacy. It includes managing symptoms, promoting healthy lifestyles and advising on all aspects of drug therapy and medicines usage

Requirements for Entry

For the degree in pharmacy, you would need three good A level/Advanced Higher, four Higher or equivalent qualifications, one of which must be chemistry. Most universities would want or prefer your other subjects to be chosen from maths, biology and physics.

If you do not have the qualifications for the MPharm degree, you may be able to take the two-year pharmacy foundation degree. On completion of this course, you can work as a pharmacy assistant or technician and then apply for entry to the second year of the MPharm.

Kind of Person

You would need a strong interest in science and in medicine, with a logical mind and a methodical approach to your work. Accuracy would be very important, as you would be handling potentially dangerous medicines, and you would need good concentration and organisational ability. In addition, you would have to enjoy dealing with people. You may be working with customers or patients, acting as a link between them and the doctor, and this could involve explaining how their prescribed drugs should be administered and detailing possible side effects. If you choose to work in industry, you would be working as part of a team involved in painstaking research and production processes.

Broad Outlook

The changing nature of community pharmacy makes it difficult to be specific about future prospects. There should be attractive opportunities for qualified pharmacists to work in primary care centres or to operate needle exchange services but traditional community outlets are suffering from growing competition from supermarkets. However, opportunities currently abound in both hospital and industrial pharmacy.

Of all the healthcare professionals, pharmacists have the widest education and training in the use of medicines for the prevention and treatment of disease. Community pharmacists make a key contribution to the safety and effectiveness of medicinal treatment.

Related Occupations

You might consider another profession in a scientific or medical field, such as analytical chemist, doctor (general practice), doctor (hospital), dentist, pharmacologist, research biologist/bioscientist, clinical biochemist or biochemist.

Impact on Lifestyle

Whether you work in a pharmacy, a hospital or in a laboratory, you would be working in clean and sometimes sterile conditions. Hygiene is always important and you may need to wear protective clothing. Pharmacists are among the most accessible healthcare professionals because the public do not need to make an appointment to see them and many shops are open extended hours. You may therefore have to work unsocial hours, which could mean working on a rota or shift system, including evening and weekend cover. Industrial pharmacists usually work regular hours, Monday to Friday.

Earnings Potential

Typical starting salaries range from £22,500 to £35,000, with small chains and independent pharmacies often paying lower salaries. Pay can rise with experience to £40,000 to £68,000. See the Chemist and Druggist Salary Survey for detailed figures.

Newly qualified hospital pharmacists in the NHS start in Band 6 on a salary range from £26,565 to £35,577, with additional allowances paid for posts in and around London.

Further Information

Royal Pharmaceutical Society
www.rpharms.com
General Pharmaceutical Council
www.pharmacyregulation.org
Association of the British Pharmaceutical Industry
http://careers.abpi.org.uk
Chemist and Druggist
www.chemistanddruggist.co.uk
Pharmaceutical Society of Ireland
www.thepsi.ie

Pharmacologist

What is Involved?

As a pharmacologist, you would be involved in the discovery and evaluation of new pharmaceutical drugs and associated treatments needed to arrest or cure human and animal diseases. Your work may be based in a hospital or in a laboratory or office within a pharmaceutical company. Having isolated or synthesised a promising bioactive substance, you would conduct experiments to discover its effectiveness, side-effects and safe dosages.

Later you would work with other medical professionals, pharmacists and doctors, to carry out clinical trials on human beings or animals, when it is considered safe to do so. Most of the life-saving drugs used every day by doctors or vets have been tested out in this way and include thousands of different substances, including antibiotics, anti-malarial medicines and chemotherapy drugs used in cancer treatments.

Millions of lives are, however, still lost each year and the search continues for drugs which will be more effective against AIDS, Alzheimer's and Parkinson's diseases. Pharmacologists will be faced with these challenges for a long time to come, although recent advances in genetic engineering are having a significant impact on the rate of progress in these areas.

Opportunities for Training

You would need a degree in pharmacology, which could focus on pharmacology alone or combine it with another subject, such as biochemistry, immunology, toxicology or cell biology. You might start by reading another subject, such as biomedical sciences or medicine itself, and then decide to specialise in pharmacology during your course. There are some sandwich courses available, which allow you to gain practical experience whilst studying. However you organise it, your degree in pharmacology should cover topics such as the causes of disease, the normal functioning of the body, how drugs work and their development.

Having completed their first degree in pharmacology, many graduates choose to pursue a postgraduate course. This may be either a taught Masters in a specialist subject, such as toxicology or clinical pharmacology, or a research degree leading to a PhD.

To work as a *clinical pharmacologist*, at the interface between the drug and the person, you might first gain a degree in medicine and go on to work with patients in hospital settings, having had specialist training in clinical pharmacology. You would then be able to apply the science of medicines to very real human scenarios.

Requirements for Entry

To gain admission to a degree course in pharmacology, you would need three A level/Advanced Higher, Higher or equivalent passes, usually including chemistry and two from biology, physics or maths. You would also need a good spread of GCSE/S Grade passes at 9-4/A*-C/1-3.

Kind of Person

You would need a keen interest and proven ability in chemical and biological research, particularly in scientific and medical discovery. Whilst you would probably have the opportunity to follow your own interests, you would also be working as part of a closely-knit team.

You would report your findings/experimental results at weekly or monthly meetings, so good verbal and written communication skills would be essential. You would need considerable determination to overcome many of the difficulties likely to arise in this work.

New drugs frequently exhibit side effects and it can take months or even years to monitor the effects on patients in clinical trials. It is here that you would work most closely with pharmacists and other health professionals, in order to avoid making serious and sometimes irreversible mistakes.

Broad Outlook

"There are still many diseases we need to find treatments and cures for, such as AIDS, cancer, cystic fibrosis, malaria. Pharmacologists are going to be busy for a long time," say the British Pharmacological Society.

Pharmacology graduates often enter the pharmaceutical industry; others enter careers including teaching, the scientific or other branches of the civil service, business and publishing. The degree is a good starting point for several positions in pharmaceuticals, such as marketing, medical information and product registration, as well as research.

Your future prospects can be further improved by mobility: in order to advance your career you may find it helpful to work in other European countries and in the USA.

Related Occupations

You might be interested in other medical careers, such as pharmacist, doctor (general practice) or doctor (hospital). Alternatively, you might consider other scientific careers such as analytical chemist, biomedical scientist, clinical biochemist, forensic scientist, toxicologist, research chemist or research biologist/bioscientist.

Impact on Lifestyle

You are likely to work normal hours from Monday to Friday. However, you may need to be prepared to work into the evenings researching a specialist topic or to meet deadlines. There would always be a need to keep up with this rapidly advancing subject and some of your private time in the evening and at weekends would doubtless be spent reading relevant professional journals and scientific publications.

Earnings Potential

Typical starting salaries range from £24,000 to £28,000, rising after 10 to 15 years to between £35,000 and £110,000. Salaries in the pharmaceutical industry tend to be higher than those in universities and public organisations. The possession of a PhD can secure up to 25% extra on your starting salary.

Further Information

British Pharmacological Society
www.bps.ac.uk

British Toxicology Society
www.thebts.org

Association of the British Pharmaceutical Industry
http://careers.abpi.org.uk

Photographer

What is Involved?

As a professional photographer, you would most likely specialise in one particular area of work, such as fashion, newspaper, medical or high street photography. 'Photographer' tends to be a blanket term covering several different occupations in which the common factor is that you would be using a camera to record specialist information. The exact nature of your work, not to mention your work environment, would depend very much on your specialism and would be determined by the subject matter of the photographs being taken. As a medical photographer, for example, you would be likely to work in a hospital; as a newspaper photographer, you would work largely on location, going out to record newsworthy events; as a high street photographer, you would take portraits in a studio but would also go out to cover weddings or to take school photographs. The work would generally involve selecting the right location, setting up the lighting and choosing the appropriate equipment. It is important to decide as early as possible which specialisation interests you most and to develop your career within that area.

Opportunities for Training

Training can be formal or informal, depending on your specialist area. As a medical or newspaper photographer, for example, you would have to take relevant university degree/higher national diploma (HND) courses and sit examinations. On the other hand, your training as an advertising or fashion photographer could be entirely on-the-job, starting with odd jobs in the studio such as messenger work or coffee making.

Colleges offer a range of courses in photography every bit as varied as the range of specialisms in the work itself. There is no guaranteed route to suitable employment from the majority of courses. British Institute of Professional Photography (BIPP) professional photography qualifications are highly regarded and are recognised across the world as a benchmark of excellence. There are three levels of qualification, each reflecting increasing levels of experience, skill and achievement: licentiateship (LBIPP) is the entry level, which represents an established level of skill and competence; associateship (ABIPP) denotes a high standard of craftsmanship and individual creative ability; fellowship (FBIPP) is the highest qualification attainable and recognises distinguished individual ability and exceptional standards of excellence.

Requirements for Entry

Whether you are applying for a job or a college course, a good portfolio is essential to prove your interest and motivation. It is likely to be the main discussion point of your interview. The subject matter should reflect the specialist professional area for which you are applying, so you should avoid such things as holiday snaps, sunsets and family photographs. A dozen or so well-presented prints or transparencies should be enough at this stage. To become a medical illustrator/clinical photographer, training is by a full-time degree in clinical photography including work placements. If you have a first degree in photography, you may be able to take a postgraduate course in clinical photography. There is no absolute educational requirement for press photographer training, although degree/HND level standard is in many cases advisable.

Kind of Person

Most professional photographers are self-employed and you would need a high level of self-confidence, allied to exceptional talent and driving ambition, to survive in such fiercely competitive areas as advertising or fashion photography. Even in a high street studio, you would need good business skills and the ability to communicate effectively. While you need a good eye for colour and composition, qualities such as punctuality, patience and reliability are also important. You should have a high level of interest in digital imaging technology and the use of computers, as photography is rapidly switching over to these developments. As a medical photographer, you would need knowledge of anatomy and physiology.

Broad Outlook

Some areas of photography are exceptionally competitive and overcrowded. It is particularly hard to find an opening in fashion, advertising or press photography and vacancies are rarely advertised. Starting as an assistant and gradually building up a network of personal contacts is often the only way to proceed. Once you are established in the profession, a combination of talent and perseverance can open the door to lucrative contracts. If you crave the security of a structured career path, medical photography may be the route to pursue.

Related Occupations

You may wish to consider: TV and film camera operator, graphic designer, animator, artist/illustrator, journalist, videographer or multimedia designer.

Impact on Lifestyle

The impact of the work on your lifestyle would depend on your specialisation. In press and fashion, you could expect to work long and irregular hours. High street photographers are often busiest at weekends, covering weddings and christenings. Medical and industrial photographers would keep much more regular hours.

Earnings Potential

Freelance earnings would depend on how hard you are prepared to work and how good your pictures are. You may have to start as an assistant photographer on an extremely low starting salary, perhaps earning in the region of £12,000 to £14,000. The usual range of entry level salaries is between £15,000 and £22,000, although successful photographers in fashion, advertising or working for the national press can earn much more. Salaries at the top end of the profession range from £35,000 to £70,000 and considerably more for those few photographers who become household names.

Further Information

British Institute of Professional Photography
www.bipp.com

Creative Skillset
http://creativeskillset.org/creative_industries/photo_imaging

Photo Assist
www.photoassist.co.uk

Institute of Medical Illustrators
www.imi.org.uk

National Council for the Training of Journalists
www.nctj.com

Association of Photographers
www.the-aop.org

Irish Professional Photographers Association
www.irishphotographers.com

Physicist

What is Involved?

As a physicist, you would be looking at the nature of matter and of energy. Your work could cover areas such as light, sound, heat, electricity, magnetism, the planets and the forces of gravity and atomic bonding. You could become involved with atomic physics, electronics, computing the uses of laser optics or quantum physics. Your work could form the basis for much of present and future technology.

Current work in nanotechnology, for example, is predicted to transform our lives over the next two decades to a far greater extent than silicon microelectronics did in the 20th century. Nanotubes - one application of this technology - can behave like metals or semiconductors, can conduct electricity better than copper, can transmit heat better than diamonds and rank among the strongest materials known, yet they are just a few nanometres across.

Opportunities for Training

If you wish to work as a professional physicist, you should look for a four-year (five in Scotland) first degree leading to MSci or MPhys. This would provide for study of physics in greater depth than a three-year BSc and should not be confused with postgraduate MSc courses. Most universities offer the option of switching from BSc to MSci/MPhys and vice versa but you should check prospectuses carefully before applying. Look for a course accredited by the Institute of Physics.

The first three years of the MPhys or MSci degree are broadly in line with the content of a standard BSc but, in the final year, you would undertake a substantial research project and study a range of physics topics in depth, some of which are at the forefront of the discipline.

An additional benefit of studying for an accredited MPhys or MSci is that you will have met the educational requirements for chartered physicist status.

Requirements for Entry

Entry to most degree courses requires two to three A level/Advanced Higher, three to five Higher or equivalent qualifications, together with a good platform of GCSE/S Grade passes at 9-4/A*-C/1-3. Since there is a shortage of applicants, grade requirements in some universities are not high but all departments would be looking for good grades in physics and maths. For postgraduate study, you would usually need a first degree passed with first or upper second class honours.

Kind of Person

You would need to have a very strong interest in physics and you should be able to handle the numerical and theoretical aspects of the subject. You should enjoy the practical laboratory work that you do at school, as you are likely to be involved with analysing and monitoring experimental work in a laboratory. You would need good attention to detail and accuracy in taking measurements and readings. You are likely to use powerful computers to help you with the analysis of results, so you would need a high standard of IT skill.

There are likely to be rapid developments in your field and you would need to keep up to date with these and with new technology as it is developed. You would need to enjoy a challenge and have a logical and creative approach to problem solving.

In addition to your scientific interest and ability, you are also likely to need good communication skills. You would probably be working as part of a team and may need to instruct technicians who are helping you as well as keeping other team members up to date with your work. In addition, you may need to explain your work to others who do not share your academic and scientific background.

Broad Outlook

Your career structure would depend very much on the type of work you undertake. In academic research, for example, a PhD is usually followed by short-term postdoctoral research contracts of up to three years in length. These may be based in laboratories worldwide, so geographical mobility can be helpful for progression. Future promotion would depend on your research achievement, normally measured by the quality and quantity of original papers you publish and by your ability to attract funding. You might then progress to a lectureship and ultimately to a professorial post with management responsibilities. In industrial research, a small, specialist organisation may offer early responsibility and the chance to focus on a specific area of physics, whereas your career development in a larger organisation might take you more towards a managerial or commercial role.

Related Occupations

You might also consider: astronomer/astrophysicist, computer engineer/scientist, systems analyst, telecommunications engineer, electrical engineer, electronic/electronics engineer or mechanical engineer.

Impact on Lifestyle

You would mainly work normal office hours from Monday to Friday, although you might occasionally need to work overtime to meet a tight deadline. In addition, you may have to spend some out-of-work time studying and reading to keep up to date with your subject. You may need to travel to conferences and meetings and could have to move in order to find a suitable job.

Earnings Potential

Data collected by the Institute of Physics (IOP) demonstrate that, while the majority of those who study physics (52.4%) go on to further study (studying for Master and PhD qualifications), those who go into employment earn an annual salary almost £3,000 more than the average for graduates of all subjects.

The data, gathered from almost 6,000 final year graduates from 55 universities between 2006 and 2010, suggest that the average salary for a physics graduate one year after graduation was then £22,500. It is now closer to £26,500.

Respondents who undertook the MSci or MPhys degrees were earning, on average, almost £2,000 more than those who undertook the shorter bachelor degree courses.

Further Information

Institute of Physics
www.iop.org

Institute of Physics in Ireland
www.iopireland.org

Physics on the web
www.physics.org

Physics World
http://physicsworld.com

Bright Recruits
http://brightrecruits.com

Physiotherapist

What is Involved?

As a physiotherapist, you would use movement, exercise, electrotherapy, manipulation and massage to treat pain, injury and damage to the body and to enhance the well-being of the body. In addition, you would have to take into account any psychological, social and cultural factors that would affect your patients' ability to help themselves.

You may work in hospitals or in the community, rehabilitating sick or injured individuals, or helping the elderly or disabled to live as independently as possible. Alternatively, you may work as a specialist sports physiotherapist, repairing and trying to prevent injuries as well as helping people maintain levels of fitness. Animal physiotherapy is another possible area of specialism.

Opportunities for Training

For membership of the Chartered Society of Physiotherapy (CSP) and state registration as a physiotherapist, you would need to take a three- or four-year course leading to an honours degree. The course is a mixture of theory and practical work, with a good deal of time spent working with qualified physiotherapists on placement in a clinical setting. You would at times find yourself training alongside other healthcare professionals, which is good experience for the workplace. Your clinical experience should cover areas such as outpatients, intensive care, rehabilitation, care of the older person, mental illness and work in the community. The academic side would include topics such as anatomy, pathology and psychology. In addition, you would learn the practical skills required in the workplace. If you have an honours degree in a relevant subject (such as a biological science, psychology or sports science), you could qualify as a physiotherapist by taking a fast-track postgraduate course.

Requirements for Entry

The minimum entry requirements are the same as those for all degree programmes. However, competition for places means that conditional offers of a place are often set higher than the minimum. In England, Wales and Northern Ireland, for example, you would normally need three A2 subjects at a minimum of grade C and above (one should be biological science), together with a minimum of five GCSEs at grade C and above. In Scotland, a typical student profile is five SCE Highers at grades AABBB taken at one sitting (minimum of two science subjects). In the Republic of Ireland, you should have an Irish Leaving Certificate with a minimum of four passes in subjects at higher level - two at B grade and two at C grade.

Many physiotherapy schools interview applicants, looking for genuine interest in physiotherapy, work experience involving caring for others and the experience of having watched a physiotherapist at work.

Kind of Person

You would have to establish a relationship with a wide range of people, most of whom would be ill, frightened or in pain. You would need to maintain a cheerful and positive outlook in order to reassure them and then encourage them to help themselves. At times, it would be necessary to be firm to make the patient persevere with difficult or uncomfortable exercises. Patience and tact are also needed, as progress made by patients can be very slow.

As well as getting on well with people, you should be able to give clear instructions so that the patient understands what each exercise requires. At the same time, you must be able to work alongside others as part of a team. You should be well organised and able to maintain detailed records of each patient.

Broad Outlook

More than four million patients a year receive physiotherapy on the NHS, particularly those with a musculo-skeletal disorder such as arthritis or long-term conditions such as cystic fibrosis, or those who have had a stroke. Treatment plays an important role in keeping some people well enough to be able to continue working. There is, however, concern that the continuing effect of the economic downturn of 2008, combined with the provisions of the Health and Social Care Act, is limiting employment prospects and reducing the number of training places. The CSP workforce data model shows that 500 additional physiotherapists will be needed each year up to 2020 to meet demand, whereas training places in England for 2016/17 were actually cut back from 1543 to 1439.

Having completed a period of junior rotations in the NHS, you could choose to stay in the service and progress to the senior grades, move into private practice or specialise in the private sector in areas such as health farms, occupational health or sport.

Related Occupations

You may be interested in other therapy-based professions in the medical field, such as occupational therapist, radiographer or speech and language therapist. If you prefer to consider other sport-related options, you might look at: leisure services/fitness centre manager, PE/PT teacher/instructor, professional sportsperson or sports coach.

Impact on Lifestyle

NHS physiotherapists work a 36-hour week, which can include some unsocial or on-call hours. Physiotherapists in the sport and leisure sector often have to work during evenings and at weekends.

Earnings Potential

A newly qualified NHS physiotherapist would start in Band 5, on a scale ranging from £22,128 to £28,746. This could rise to £41,787 for a team manager at the top of the scale and to over £69,000 for a consultant. Additional allowances are paid for appointments in and around London, ranging from 20% of basic salary for Inner London, to 15% for Outer London and 5% for the London Fringe. Salaries in the private sector are often linked to NHS levels but may be higher.

Further Information

Chartered Society of Physiotherapy
www.csp.org.uk

Association of Chartered Physiotherapists in Animal Therapy
www.acpat.org

The Physiotherapy Site
www.thephysiotherapysite.co.uk/physiotherapy/physiotherapists/a-career-in-physio

Health Careers
www.healthcareers.nhs.uk

Irish Society of Chartered Physiotherapists
www.iscp.ie

Podiatrist/Chiropodist

What is Involved?

Podiatrist is the internationally recognised name for a specialist who cares for feet and chiropodists are gradually changing their title to match. As a podiatrist, you would be responsible for maintaining feet and the lower leg in a healthy condition; you would be qualified to diagnose, advise on and treat problems; you would have the chance to work in a number of different environments - hospitals, clinics and in people's homes, for example - and with a range of different people.

There are five main areas of work:

- General clinics, the starting point for all newly qualified podiatrists. The job involves assessing, evaluating and advising on foot care for a wide range of patients. You listen to a history of the patient's health and hear about any foot problems; you then examine the foot, possibly using specialised equipment, and discuss possible treatments with the patient

- Biomechanics, concerning the very complex structure and function of the foot. Podiatrists working in this area are concerned to preserve this mechanism, restore it when it is damaged and ensure that it is capable of working at its maximum capacity. One of the main areas is orthotics or specially designed insoles, fitted inside shoes to help solve structural problems such as fallen arches or to correct problems with children's feet

- Podopaediatrics or working with children. Many children present with developmental biomechanical problems, leading some podiatrists to develop an in-depth understanding of this area of practice.

- High Risk, concerned with patients who have an underlying illness or condition that puts their lower limbs and/or feet at high risk of damage. Examples include problems with circulation or people who have lost the feeling in their feet or lower limbs

- Surgery, involving routine surgical procedures such as treating in-growing toenails or cutting away soft tissue problems. This may involve the use of local anaesthetics, ultrasonics or freezing techniques. Some podiatrists opt for further study to enable them to work on more invasive surgery

Opportunities for Training

To practise in the NHS, you must be state registered, which means that you must take a recognised degree course. These courses, offered at some 13 universities in the UK, take three or four years to complete on a full-time basis. They are modular in structure, comprising a mixture of theoretical and clinical modules, although the exact format and method of teaching varies between institutions. The theoretical subjects covered during the course include dermatology, anatomy, physiology, pharmacology, biomechanics and pathology as well as local anaesthesia and surgery.

Requirements for Entry

You would need two A level/Advanced Higher, three Higher or equivalent qualifications, one of which should be a science subject (ideally biology or chemistry), although some universities accept PE as an alternative. You should also have at least five GCSE/S Grade passes at 9-4/A*-C/1-3, including English Language and two sciences. It is best to check direct with the university admissions office in each case to be sure of specific requirements.

Work shadowing a podiatrist is strongly recommended and is usually quite easy to arrange.

Kind of Person

Many podiatrists are self-employed and for this you need to have a good business sense, organisational skills and the ability to inspire confidence in your clients. Communication skills are important both in dealing with patients and with co-ordinating with other professionals. In addition, you need to have a keen scientific interest and would need to keep up to date with new developments and techniques.

Broad Outlook

There are good opportunities for work in this area, including private practice and some areas of specialisation. Podiatrists often start their career in the NHS, where they encounter a broad range of problems and patients, before deciding to set up in private practice or to specialise.

The Society of Chiropodists and Podiatrists claims that 83% of students seeking employment secure a job within six months of graduation and 100% within the first year. This compares very favourably with many other graduate employment rates.

Related Occupations

You might also consider: doctor (general practice), physiotherapist, occupational therapist, radiographer, speech and language therapist or nurse.

Impact on Lifestyle

In the NHS, podiatrists usually work a 36-hour week. However, in private practice, where the potential for earning is higher, the hours worked are likely to be longer and more unsocial, especially in the early days of establishing your business.

Earnings Potential

Podiatrists in the NHS usually start in Band 5, on a scale currently ranging from £22,128 to £28,746. Earnings can rise to £26,565 to £35,577 for a specialist and to £31,696 to £41,787 for an advanced practitioner. Additional allowances are paid for appointments in and around London, ranging from 20% of basic salary for Inner London, to 15% for Outer London and 5% for the London Fringe. Earnings in the private sector are generally likely to be higher, depending on where you live and the hours you are prepared to work. Many podiatrists who work in the NHS also run part-time private practices.

Further Information

College of Podiatry
www.scpod.org

Careers in Podiatry
http://careersinpodiatry.com

Alliance of Private Sector Podiatry and Foot Health Practitioners
www.thealliancepsp.com

British Chiropody and Podiatry Association
www.bcha-uk.org

Society of Chiropodists and Podiatrists of Ireland
www.podiatryireland.com

Police Officer

What is Involved?

As a police officer, you would serve the local community by working to protect people and property against crime, detecting offenders and taking a lead in dealing with emergencies. You would start your career, after initial training, as a uniformed constable on the beat. This may be on foot or in a patrol car. You must be prepared to deal with whatever comes along, from attending scenes of accidents, searching for missing people and responding to emergency calls, to making arrests, sorting out street fights, taking statements and attending large public gatherings. The work can mean being outside in all weathers, sometimes in unpleasant and potentially dangerous situations. You would also be involved in some office and court-related work, including preparing reports and taking statements, escorting prisoners and giving evidence. You may find it useful to join a voluntary cadet scheme if there is one in your area.

Opportunities for Training

All new police officers undertake an extensive and professional training programme known as the Initial Police Learning and Development Programme (IPLDP) during their first two years of service. Individual forces are responsible for the local implementation and delivery of IPLDP, with the emphasis upon local community involvement and a flexible timetable. IPLDP is divided into four training phases which cover the completion of the level 3 Diploma in Policing:

- phase 1 - Induction (three to five weeks): general introduction to the organisation with training in first aid, health and safety, officer safety, ICT, race and diversity, human rights and community safety strategy

- phase 2 - Community (two to three weeks): training in crime and disorder reduction and a community placement

- phase 3 - Basic Police Skills (week seven for 28 weeks): workplace practice supported by class-based learning, learning in a 'replicated work environment' and work-based learning under supervised patrol

- phase 4 - Independent Patrol (weeks 35 to 104): combines operational duties with independent and distance learning

Requirements for Entry

You must be a British citizen, a citizen of the EU or other states in the EEA, or a Commonwealth citizen or foreign national with indefinite leave to remain in the UK. Applicants from all backgrounds and ethnic groups are encouraged to apply. The minimum age to apply is 18, and there is no upper age limit. One of the most rigorous elements of the screening process is the physical fitness training. If you pass the initial assessment, you will then have to take a physical fitness test. To pass this, you will need to be reasonably fit and able to run short distances fairly quickly.

There are no height restrictions and no specific educational requirements but you must have good eyesight, including normal colour vision. Glasses or contact lenses may be acceptable but you must have reasonable unaided vision. If you are ambitious, a degree may secure you a place on the national graduate leadership development programme.

Kind of Person

Police work is tough on the body, taxing on the brain, draining on emotion and makes demands of your whole life. You would need to be socially aware, self-disciplined and without prejudice, mature and honest. You would be called on to make instant decisions and may face hostility and danger, so courage and self-confidence are very important qualities. You need to be able to stay calm yet able to weigh up a situation quickly. A sense of humour and a degree of flexibility are advantages. It is particularly important that you have good communication skills and can be assertive but courteous in your contact with the general public.

Broad Outlook

The role of the police force and the problems it faces are ever changing, not least after the 2010 spending review cut police budgets in England and Wales by 20% over five years. Further cuts were expected but the 2015 spending review not only protected existing budgets but also promised to increase counter-terrorism spending by 30%.

The police service is under constant scrutiny to ensure that senior posts are allocated fairly in relation to gender and race.

Related Occupations

You may consider other branches of the police service, including British Transport, UK Atomic Energy and the Ministry of Defence police. Other options might include: fire fighter/fire officer, prison officer, army officer, Royal Navy/Royal Marines officer, Royal Air Force Officer, security officer, trading standards officer or health and safety inspector.

Impact on Lifestyle

As with all the emergency services, your hours of work would often be determined by the circumstances prevailing and you would regularly have to work over weekends and holidays.

Because the police force is locally organised, you are likely in your first few years of service to be based either in the area of your choice or your own home area. Later, promotion may depend upon your willingness to move area and be relocated on a regular basis.

Earnings Potential

Rates of pay vary by force but a typical salary is currently £19,773 to £22,893 when you start, rising to £38,001 at the top of the scale and £39,300 to £42,708 if you gain promotion to sergeant. Inspectors can earn £48,690 to £52,812. Uniform is provided and occasionally help with accommodation or subsidised police housing. Additional allowances are paid for appointments in and around London.

Further Information

Police Recruitment
www.policeuk.com

Police Now National Graduate Leadership Development Programme
www.policenow.org.uk

Police Service of Northern Ireland
www.psni.police.uk

Police Scotland
www.scotland.police.uk

Police Oracle
www.policeoracle.com/careers/how_to_become_a_police_officer.html

National Police Service, Ireland
www.garda.ie

Probation Officer

What is Involved?

As a probation officer in England or Wales, you may work for the National Probation Service (NPS), a statutory criminal justice service that supervises high-risk offenders released into the community, or for one of the 21 private sector community rehabilitation companies (CRCs) that manage low- and medium-risk offenders.

Scotland and Northern Ireland have separate criminal justice systems and different arrangements for the provision of probation services.

Opportunities for Training

Major changes are currently taking place to the training route in England and Wales, and information about the new qualification structure is gradually becoming available on *Train to be a Probation Officer*. The first phase of the new Community Justice Learning framework was introduced in April 2016, with a second phase expected in 2017. CRCs are not required to adopt the same training and qualification systems as the NPS, meaning that you will need to contact them directly for information about what each CRC offers.

The new 15-month Professional Qualification in Probation (PQiP) programme for England and Wales is based around distance learning with some face-to-face workshops and seminars, supported by a line manager and a tutor at one of three universities. You'll be employed on a permanent contract as a Probation Services Officer (PSO) and your fees will be sponsored. Once you've completed the programme, you can apply for a role as a Probation Officer. While training, you will gain experience of working with 'high risk of serious harm' offenders and you'll be fully equipped to deal with all the different kinds of offenders. The goal is to cut offending, protect communities and give offenders the opportunity to become active members of society.

In Scotland, probation officers are known as criminal justice social workers. Entry is via a four-year honours degree in social work approved by the Scottish Social Services Council (SSSC). A two-year postgraduate scheme is available for entrants who already possess a degree in another subject. To work as a probation officer in Northern Ireland, you must be a qualified social worker with some experience of working with offenders.

Requirements for Entry

Access to the new qualification framework will no longer be restricted to those with a relevant Honours Degree. You'll need some relevant experience to join the PQiP programme. This can be gained through either paid or voluntary work in any agency that involves working with the kind of challenging behaviour seen from offenders.

Kind of Person

You would have to deal with offenders, some of whom could be aggressive, violent, distressed or withdrawn. You would need to gain trust and develop a constructive relationship with people from a variety of backgrounds and with a number of problems. Your work would include listening to their stories, resolving conflicts and finding ways to move forward. This would need good communication skills, together with patience, authority and persuasive power. You would be involved with researching and writing reports and letters so written communication would be important. You must be able to speak convincingly in court. You would be working as part of a team and handling a lot of confidential and sensitive information about people, so your integrity would be essential.

Broad Outlook

Needless to say, the probation service has been in considerable turmoil since the publication of the Transforming Rehabilitation reform programme. The National Association of Probation Officers is currently campaigning to defend what it sees as the professional values of the service, and to protest against the impact of the privatisation of 70% of its role.

In this climate of uncertainty, we suggest that you research the latest developments very carefully before making any commitment to train in this area of work in England and Wales.

Related Occupations

You might also consider: social worker, teacher (secondary), psychologist, prison officer, police officer or youth worker.

Impact on Lifestyle

The previous normal working week was 37 hours but this could change within the new NPS/CRC structure. You might need to provide cover at night and at weekends, working on a rota basis, but you would probably be given time off to compensate. You might have to move around the UK to find a suitable job. At times you would be expected to deal with stressful situations, which you could not simply leave in the office and not think about again until the next morning.

Earnings Potential

During the 15-month PQiP training programme, you would be employed as a Probation Services Officer earning £22,039 to £27,373 plus a London Weighting Allowance of £3,889 where this applies. Upon successful completion of the programme, you would be eligible to apply for a permanent position as a qualified Probation Officer on a starting salary of £29,038 plus London Weighting where relevant. Senior officers can earn from £35,024 to £39,818.

Further Information

National Probation Service
www.gov.uk/government/organisations/national-probation-service

Train to be a Probation Officer
www.traintobeaprobationofficer.com

Do-It Volunteering
https://do-it.org

National Association of Probation Officers
www.napo.org.uk

Skills for Justice Community Justice Learning
www.sfjuk.com/community-justice-learning

Work with Offenders
www.workwithoffenders.co.uk

Scottish Social Services Council
www.sssc.uk.com

Probation Board for Northern Ireland
www.pbni.org.uk

Probation Service, Ireland
www.probation.ie

Professional Sportsperson

*W*hat is Involved?

In most professional sports, you would be required to focus single-mindedly on your training, fitness and performance levels, shutting out most other demands on your time and energy. Every aspect of your life, diet, sleep, social relaxation and psychological strength would need to be subordinated to or controlled by the demands of your sport, and your career would become in many ways your principal way of life. A career as a professional sportsperson is frequently short, often ending by 35, especially in physical contact or physically demanding sports, and is vulnerable to termination through injury or loss of form. Dedication of vast amounts of time to training and preparation puts stress on both body and mind, which you would need to learn to control. The ability to work with others in teams is increasingly vital, not just in team sports, but in individualised sports where agents, trainers, dietitians, psychologists and physiotherapists are likely to be constant assistants and companions.

*O*pportunities for Training

If you have the potential to succeed as a professional sportsperson, you could receive help from the following schemes:

- sponsorship schemes run by some universities to provide support for you to carry on training whilst studying

- the Talented Athlete Scholarship Scheme, by which national governing bodies of certain sports select young people in higher or further education to receive access to sporting services

- the Advanced Apprenticeship in Sporting Excellence, aimed at 16- to 18-year-olds who show promise of achieving the highest levels in their sport.

It is vital to realise that, in most money-making sports, ability would be recognised at an increasingly early age, with very young footballers encouraged into academies and schools of excellence by premiership clubs, cricketers absorbed into colts teams by county cricket clubs, rugby players enrolled in apprentice schemes and training set-ups by rugby premiership sides, and other sports having their own schemes for identifying and exploiting talent. Even if you are an outstanding school player, it is unlikely that at 17 or 18 you are going to be able to break into a major sports scene.

*R*equirements for Entry

There are no formal entrance qualifications to professional sport but it is sensible not to neglect your education and to take the opportunity to go on to higher education if appropriate. You could often continue to take part in your sport at university, national or even Commonwealth or Olympic levels. Because of the extremely young age of entry, your parents would need to be supportive in both care and financing, though sponsorship might be available in some sports.

*K*ind of Person

Commitment, talent and a competitive streak seem common to all professional sportspeople. The resilience to overcome disappointment, defeat or injury is essential, along with an ability to adjust to the demands of travel, practice and performance. You would need total dedication to practising and improving your sport, maintaining your fitness at a peak level and monitoring your diet.

Broad Outlook

There are huge sums of money involved in major sports like soccer, rugby, snooker, boxing and tennis, but the high-earning superstars are relatively few in number and it is easy to be misled by appearances. It is certain that sport will continue to attract and entertain huge sections of society in the coming decades, but that may be accompanied by a spreading and thinning of the rewards. The participation of women, especially where there is a growth in their involvement in sports like football, tennis and golf, should open more doors to them in the future. Preparation for a future role as coach, manager, administrator or media analyst is a route followed by many sports performers to guarantee an effective career path.

Related Occupations

You might also consider: sports coach, PE teacher/instructor, physiotherapist, chiropractor, osteopath or leisure services/fitness centre manager

Impact on Lifestyle

As indicated above, the full impact on your life is likely to be all-consuming and intense, taking over many aspects of it. Practice, training, travel away from home in the UK and abroad can all create pressure on family and social life.

Earnings Potential

It is impossible to specify what you might reasonably expect to earn, given the great range of sports and the unpredictability of fitness and performance. The greater the popularity of the sport and the higher the level attained, the greater the rewards you can achieve. In addition, for salaried team players, earnings would include appearance money, fees, advertising and endorsements. For those in less popular sports, a supporting job is often necessary.

As a very rough guide, a professional sportsperson on an Apprenticeship may start on around £100 to £200 per week, with accommodation and subsistence sometimes provided. Earnings for established professionals may start at around £20,000 a year, while the most successful professionals in high-profile sports may earn anything from £100,000 to £13 million a year.

Further Information

SkillsActive
www.skillsactive.com

Sports Coach UK
www.sportscoachuk.org

UK Sport
www.uksport.gov.uk

Skills Active Advanced Apprenticeship in Sporting Excellence
www.skillsactive.com/aase

Talented Athlete Scholarship Scheme
www.tass.gov.uk

Sport Ireland
www.sportireland.ie

Psychologist

What is Involved?

As a psychologist, you would study the processes and nature of the human mind in order to understand how people behave, how they react to stimuli or circumstances and how they interact in small or large groups. You would use scientific methods to gather information and try to measure what constitutes normal or abnormal behaviour. You would be concerned not just with understanding human behaviour but also with using this understanding to help people and to bring about change.

There are several main specialisms for professional psychologists:

- Clinical psychologists work with people with mental or physical health problems - which might include anxiety and depression, serious and enduring mental illness, adjustment to physical illness, neurological disorders, addictive behaviours, childhood behaviour disorders or personal and family relationships

- Counselling psychologists help people manage difficult life events such as bereavement, past and present relationships and working with mental health issues and disorders;

- Educational psychologists are concerned with children's learning and development, working primarily in schools with teachers and parents

- Forensic psychologists undertake their work in the criminal and civil justice field, working with academic institutions, prison services, the National Health Service, probation services and social services

- Health psychologists are concerned with the application of psychological methods to the study of behaviour relevant to health, illness and health care. For example, why and when people seek professional advice about their health, how patients and health care professionals interact or how patients adapt to illness

- Occupational psychologists are concerned with the performance of people at work and in training, how organisations function and how individuals and small groups behave at work.

Other areas include neuropsychology and sport and exercise psychology

Opportunities for Training

To become a chartered psychologist, you must have a degree in psychology or equivalent qualification accredited by the British Psychological Society. This is often referred to by employers as the GBC or Graduate Basis for Chartered Membership. Your degree would usually offer a broad introduction to the subject but, if you wish to work as a professional psychologist, you would normally undertake postgraduate study in one of the specialist areas.

Requirements for Entry

University admissions requirements for a degree in psychology are usually two or three A level/Advanced Higher, three or four Higher or equivalent qualifications, together with a good spread of GCSE/S Grade passes 9-4/A*-C/1-3, including English and maths. There is no need to take psychology as a pre-university subject, although you should be able to demonstrate that you have an understanding of what is involved. Entry is competitive and you should research the exact requirements of each course that interests you.

Kind of Person

You would have to work with a wide range of people. Depending on what type of psychologist you become, you could find yourself dealing with children or adults with learning difficulties, patients with brain damage or disease, prisoners or people at work. You would need good communication skills and an ability to mix with people. In addition, you should have keen investigative skills and should be sufficiently numerate to understand statistical methods.

Broad Outlook

Around 15 to 20% of psychology graduates end up working as professional psychologists, with a third of these going into public service (such as the health service, education, the civil service or the armed forces), a further third entering industry or commerce, and the remainder going on to a wide variety of different areas. The Health and Care Professions Council (HCPC) is the statutory regulator for practitioner psychologists in the UK. In order to offer services to the public as a psychologist in one of the nine domains regulated by the HCPC, you need to complete an HCPC approved programme of postgraduate training.

Related Occupations

You may be particularly interested in other professions concerned with helping people, such as: careers adviser/guidance counsellor, speech and language therapist, teacher (secondary), human resources manager, probation officer or social worker.

Impact on Lifestyle

This is very dependent on the type of psychology that you choose to pursue as a career. An occupational psychologist working with companies in industry and commerce would usually work normal office hours; an educational psychologist dealing mainly with schoolchildren would be busiest during term time. On the other hand, a forensic psychologist may be called out to collaborate with the police at unsocial hours.

Earnings Potential

Earnings vary considerably between the different branches of psychology and between the different countries of the United Kingdom.

As a psychologist working in the National Health Service, you would start in Band 7 at £31,696 and could eventually earn over £100,000 as head of a large department. As an educational psychologist, you would earn £35,731 to £52,903 on Scale A and £44,797 to £66,276 as a senior or principal educational psychologist on Scale B. As an occupational psychologist, you might generally start at around £20,000 to £30,000 but this could rise to over £100,000 with experience and with fees negotiated for consultancy work.

Further Information

British Psychological Society
www.bps.org.uk

Careers in Psychology
www.careersinpsychology.co.uk

Association of Educational Psychologists
www.aep.org.uk

Health and Care Professions Council
www.hcpc-uk.org

Psychological Society of Ireland
www.psihq.ie

Public Relations Executive

What is Involved?

As a public relations (PR) executive, you would specialise in the business of looking after the reputation of your clients, making a planned and sustained effort to establish goodwill and mutual understanding between them and the public. Your clients might include a business, a profession, a government department, a public service or an organisation concerned with health, culture or education. You would aim to find out the concerns and expectations of a client's customers, employees, suppliers, investors or other audience and feed these back to the management.

A large organisation might have its own in-house PR department, whilst smaller organisations would use an independent PR consultancy. You could find yourself organising receptions, entertaining clients at sporting events or gauging public reaction to a government initiative. At its best, PR helps an organisation to see its own role more clearly and helps it to react effectively to public perception of its performance.

Opportunities for Training

There are a number of routes into PR. You might enter the profession after working in another area, such as journalism, law, advertising or any industry of which you have experience. If you are looking to go into PR as your first job, you would almost certainly need a relevant qualification and work experience.

It is not essential but you could consider a first degree course specifically in public relations, approved by the Chartered Institute of Public Relations (CIPR). Alternatively, you could take a postgraduate course. Once you have a job in PR, you could work towards CIPR, PRCA (Public Relations Consultants Association) or CAM (Communication, Advertising and Marketing Education Foundation) professional qualifications.

The CIPR Chartered Practitioner scheme awards chartered status on an individual basis to members who have completed a rigorous assessment of their professional expertise.

Requirements for Entry

To gain admission to a degree course, you would need two or three A level/Advanced Higher, three or four Higher or equivalent qualifications, together with a good spread of GCSE/S Grade passes at 9-4/A*-C/1-3. The minimum requirement for the CAM exams is five GCSE/S Grade passes at 9-4/A*-C/1-3, including maths and English but the vast majority of new entrants are graduates. Relevant work experience would be essential.

Kind of Person

Exceptionally good 'people' skills are needed here. You would need to be able to communicate and to remember that this is a two-way process. You would need flexibility to cope with a variety of projects at the same time, together with thorough attention to detail. The ability to get on with a variety of people and work with others as part of a team would be essential.

You would have to be assertive and determined, able to cope with pressure and tight deadlines and to make your point in discussions without alienating people. You would also need to be very well organised, with good IT and literacy skills. You would probably be expected to give presentations.

Broad Outlook

After a very tough period in 2008 and 2009, the world's two largest markets for PR - the US and the UK - both saw a return to growth from 2010 to 2015, with further growth predicted for 2017. This is according to the World Report from the International Communications Consultancy Organisation. Digital and social media services are playing an increasingly important role in PR strategies.

The issue of attracting talent, and then retaining it, is one of the biggest concerns for PR consultancies, since growing the business depends upon achieving the right mix of skills and experience and having the ability to form lasting relationships with clients. There is a clear trend at present for people to leave the uncertainty of consultancy work for the relative security of in-house PR. At the same time, there is deep concern about jobs within the public sector.

There is no standard promotion pattern in PR but, on successful completion of an initial training programme, you might expect to spend one to two years as a junior account executive, two or three years as an account executive and two to three years as a senior account executive or account manager before moving to associate or account director.

Related Occupations

You might also consider: journalist, solicitor, advertising account executive, marketing executive, market researcher, social media manager or events manager.

Impact on Lifestyle

You would be mainly office based and work normal office hours. However, when necessary you would be expected to work longer hours to meet deadlines. Depending on the nature of the work, you could find yourself travelling around the country or abroad on promotional tours or attending conferences. You might have to give presentations or organise functions in the evening or at weekends.

Earnings Potential

Starting salaries can be around £19,000 to £27,000, rising with experience to between £30,000 and £60,000. Account directors and heads of corporate affairs can earn £80,000 to £100,000 a year.

The CIPR reports that 34%, 39% and 35% of private sector, consultancy and freelance practitioners earn a salary in excess of £50,000. This contrasts with just 19% in the public sector and 20% in not-for-profit organisations. The average annual earnings figure for 2016 is £48,196.

Further Information

Chartered Institute of Public Relations
www.cipr.co.uk

PR Week
www.prweek.com/uk

CAM Foundation
www.camfoundation.com

Public Relations Consultants Association
www.prca.org.uk

International Communications Consultancy Organisation
www.iccopr.com

Public Relations Institute of Ireland
www.prii.ie

Publisher

What is Involved?

The publishing industry includes books, newspapers, magazines, journals, directories and electronic media, although this article is concerned primarily with the editorial side of publishing books. Of the many thousands of books published each year, a small percentage are mass-market titles, while others include educational textbooks, academic research works or STM (scientific, technical and medical) publications. Your role as a publisher would involve working with colleagues in selecting or commissioning new books, revising existing titles, in design, marketing and sales to ensure that each publication makes maximum impact in its particular market, reaching as many readers as possible and recouping the initial investment made in it.

As a commissioning editor, you would decide whether to accept manuscripts submitted by literary agents or authors or whether to use your specialist knowledge of a particular market to commission specific books and projects. All manuscripts passing through your hands would need to be read and given an initial assessment, often by readers employed for the purpose; a number would then need a second opinion, perhaps from a specialist. You would have to weigh up the opinions of your readers, plus, in many cases, sales and marketing colleagues, before making a commitment to proceed.

You might also become concerned with the contractual side of publishing, including the drawing up of the initial contract between the publisher and the author, and the handling of subsidiary rights, such as translation, book club and serial rights.

As a copy editor, you would concentrate on preparing accepted manuscripts for the printers. You would need an exact eye for details such as repetition, contradiction, spelling mistakes, punctuation and grammar, and would have to discuss and agree all changes with the author. You might also have to discuss details of manufacture and presentation with the production, design and marketing departments.

Opportunities for Training

Some publishing houses run their own in-house training schemes or send new recruits on short courses run by specialist agencies but there are no universally recognised approaches to training and qualification. It is possible at a number of United Kingdom universities and colleges to take a first degree in publishing or a broader arts/humanities degree with a publishing option. There are also a small number of postgraduate courses, which could follow almost any first degree.

Requirements for Entry

New entrants are often graduates but there are no absolute entry requirements and you could be successful without formal qualifications if you can demonstrate sufficient technical ability, commitment, enthusiasm and commercial awareness. Even with a degree, the actual subject is often unimportant, although you would usually be expected to have specialist qualifications on the design side (see our separate article on Graphic Designer) and a business course would be a useful preparation for marketing.

Kind of Person

You would need an interest in people, places and events, knowledge of current affairs and a love of words. That includes understanding grammar, spelling and punctuation, especially for work as a copy editor. In all areas of publishing, computer and web skills are at the very least a definite asset and usually essential. Knowledge of foreign languages can be a particular asset in dealing with translation rights.

Adaptability can often be the key to developing a career in book publishing: it is worth trying - and working hard at - whatever is available in order to gain experience, taking on general duties within a small publishing house in order to learn the business.

Broad Outlook

Self-publishing and ebooks are at the heart of a process that is creating great uncertainty in the world of traditional book publishing. Most opportunities tend to be in London and the south east, with many more openings in non-editorial than editorial specialisms. Indeed, competition for editorial posts is so intense that you would be well advised to develop skills, perhaps through specialist training, individual initiative or work experience, that make you stand out from the crowd. Good personal contacts are important, together with detailed knowledge of the sector in which you choose to develop your career.

Related Occupations

You might also consider: magazine journalist, journalist, broadcasting/media researcher, graphic designer, marketing executive or sales executive.

Impact on Lifestyle

Many people in publishing work a standard Monday to Friday, nine to five week, although additional hours are often required as publication deadlines approach. If your work involves dealing with international clients, you may be expected to travel extensively or to make telephone contacts at the appropriate time for the Far East or the United States.

Earnings Potential

"When you're starting out," says the Society for Young Publishers, "be prepared to work long hours for low pay." Salaries vary widely, with editorial trainees starting on around £18,000 to £20,000 and working their way up through the system to £50,000 or more. Although the negotiation of freelance fees is a matter for the individual and client to resolve, the SfEP suggests minimum hourly rates as a starting point for negotiations. These include £23.35 for proofreading, £27.15 for copy-editing and £31.30 for substantial editing and rewriting.

Further Information

Publishers Association
www.publishers.org.uk

Association of Learned and Professional Society Publishers
www.alpsp.org

Publishing Training Centre
www.publishingtrainingcentre.co.uk

Society for Editors and Proofreaders
www.sfep.org.uk

Society of Young Publishers
www.thesyp.org.uk

Book Careers
www.bookcareers.com

Quantity Surveyor

What is Involved?

As a quantity surveyor, sometimes known as a cost consultant or commercial manager, you would be concerned with the financial and contractual aspects of construction projects. You would be involved at all stages of the project and would usually be appointed by the architect or engineer who has designed the construction. You would be acting as the financial overseer of a particular project, translating the plans into detailed costs. This would involve working out the timings of each process and the materials needed.

You might advise on alterations to the initial designs; you could be involved in obtaining funding for a particular project; you might be asked to draw up a feasibility study of a project and advise on how to reduce the risks involved. During the construction phase you are likely to be responsible for making sure that the contractors keep to the specification and to the quoted price.

Opportunities for Training

You would need to take a degree course approved by the Royal Institution of Chartered Surveyors (RICS), followed by the RICS Assessment of Professional Competence (APC). This involves two years of structured, practical training with an employer, ending with an RICS professional assessment.

There are some four-year sandwich courses available, which include a year spent working in a quantity surveying practice. This year can count towards your required training period, provided that it has been approved in advance by the RICS. There are also some courses accredited by the Chartered Institute of Building.

If you have a foundation degree or HNC/D in surveying, you may be able to start work as a quantity surveying technician before completing further study to qualify as a quantity surveyor.

RICS also provides degree apprenticeships for trainee surveyors, leading to chartered status (MRICS). This new route - the first chartered surveying degree apprenticeships opened to entrants in September 2015 - involves a part-time undergraduate degree together with in-work experience and training over a period of four to five years.

Requirements for Entry

For a degree course, the minimum stated requirements are at least three A level/ Advanced Higher, four Higher or equivalent qualifications, together with five GCSE/S Grade passes at 9-4/A*-C/1-3. These should usually include English and maths.

Kind of Person

To be a successful quantity surveyor you would need to be a practical person with a logical and methodical approach to problem solving. You would need a high standard of numeracy, together with the ability to analyse the content of complicated documents. A good understanding both of construction techniques and technology and of the relevant laws and health and safety requirements would be essential.

You should have good communications skills as you could be required to express your views and opinions both verbally and on paper. You are also likely to be involved in negotiating with a wide variety of people. This means that you would have to listen to the points of view of others as well as expressing your own opinion. In addition, you are likely to be working as a member of a team, which may require you to motivate and lead people on site. Finally, you would have to be familiar with specific computer programmes.

Broad Outlook

The demand for quantity surveyors depends to a great extent on the state of the construction industry and the picture now is starting to look encouraging, as the sector recovers from the severe downturn that started in 2008. Indeed, the UK construction industry has turned around to become one of the fastest-growing sectors in the economy, offering new hope for quantity surveyors in the years to come.

It is estimated that the construction industry lost 375,000 workers between 2008 and 2010. These include architects, quantity surveyors and construction managers, as well as bricklayers, carpenters, plumbers, electricians and other trades. While cuts in public spending may continue to depress demand for construction projects in the public sector, the commercial sector is showing clear signs of a return to sustained growth.

There are three main areas in which you could find employment: private practice; with a large building or civil engineering contractor or with local and central government.

Related Occupations

You might consider another specialism as a surveyor (general practice) or building surveyor, or perhaps another profession allied to the building industry, such as architect, building services engineer, town planner, housing manager or civil engineer.

Impact on Lifestyle

You are likely to spend the majority of your time indoors, working regular office hours. You would also have to spend at least some time on site and you may have to start early or finish late to match the daylight hours usually worked by site contractors.

You could be out in all weathers, sometimes exposed to wet, cold and muddy conditions. Buildings under construction are likely to be dirty and potentially dangerous places. You would need to wear protective clothing at times and be prepared to climb ladders or scaffolding.

Earnings Potential

When you first start working you could expect to earn between £20,000 and £30,000. If you start working for a large contractor, you could earn more as you may get paid for working site hours: £22,000+ is a more typical starting salary in such cases. Your salary could easily rise with experience to £35,000 to £80,000, and you could earn substantially more if you become a principal partner in private practice.

Further Information

Royal Institution of Chartered Surveyors
www.rics.org

Chartered Institute of Building
www.ciob.org

Chartered Surveyors Training Trust
www.cstt.org.uk

Building
www.building.co.uk

Society of Chartered Surveyors, Ireland
www.scsi.ie

Radiographer

What is Involved?

There are two types of radiography: diagnostic and therapeutic. As a diagnostic radiographer, you would produce and interpret high quality images of the body to diagnose injury and disease; as a therapeutic radiographer, you would plan and deliver prescribed treatment using X-radiation and other radioactive sources. Your work as a diagnostic radiographer would normally encompass a wide range of different imaging investigations, such as ultrasound, magnetic resonance imaging and x-rays, although you might later specialise in one particular area.

You would provide a service for most departments within a hospital, including Accident and Emergency, outpatients, operating theatres and wards. Therapeutic radiographers work closely with doctors, nurses, physicists and other members of the oncology team to treat patients with cancer. You would use ionising radiation (mostly high-energy X-rays) to deliver an accurate dose of radiation to the tumour/cancer whilst minimising the dose received by the surrounding tissues. The work would often involve the care of the cancer patient from the initial referral clinic stage, where pre-treatment information is given, through the planning process and treatment to the post-treatment review (follow-up) stages.

Opportunities for Training

You would need to complete a qualifying radiography course at honours degree level. In England and Wales, these courses are three years full-time whereas in Scotland and Northern Ireland they are normally four years full-time. You would usually spend equal amounts of time in your university and in hospital departments. Alternatively, you could qualify as a radiographer at postgraduate level if you have a relevant first degree or another professional healthcare qualification. Qualifying courses in diagnostic radiography are currently offered at 24 higher education institutions in the UK and in therapeutic radiography at 14.

Requirements for Entry

Entry requirements vary between universities but you would usually need two or three A level/Advanced Higher, three or four Higher or equivalent qualifications including a science subject, together with three GCSE/S Grade passes 9-4/A*-C/1-3, including maths and a science subject. A visit to a radiography department or radiotherapy centre is advisable before applying. There are no age limits in either diagnostic or therapeutic radiography, and mature students are especially welcome.

Kind of Person

Both diagnostic and therapeutic radiographers need good interpersonal skills to deal with patients of all types and ages, many of whom require reassurance and counselling as well as an explanation of the radiographic procedure with which they are being examined or treated. You would also need to be able to communicate well with the other professionals in the healthcare team to ensure that the most appropriate treatment is given to each patient. You must be confident about working with complex high-technology equipment and would need to give great attention to detail while remaining flexible enough to treat each patient as an individual case. The continuing development of radiographic techniques and treatments means that you would be constantly learning new skills. You would need to be able to think quickly and to be prepared to make decisions yourself.

Broad Outlook

The NHS employs most radiographers, although there are also opportunities to work within the armed forces and in the private sector. Within the NHS there is a career structure that gives the opportunity to take on management responsibilities or specialist skills. This means that you could develop a wide range of transferable skills that would equip you for management at all levels within the NHS, industry or higher education.

You might develop your career by taking further part-time specialist postgraduate training in subjects such as ultrasound, computed tomography (CT scanning), magnetic resonance imaging, or palliative care and counselling. You could also go on to specialise as a sonographer or ultrasonographer, which involves completing a one-year post-registration course approved by the Consortium for Accreditation of Sonographic Education.

There is currently a worldwide shortage of both diagnostic and therapeutic radiographers and the UK qualification is normally transferable to most overseas countries. State registration is the most important factor for your career development, indicating that you meet the high ethical standards required, have achieved educational and professional excellence, and are committed to duty of care.

Related Occupations

You might also consider: doctor (general practice), doctor (hospital), nurse, medical physicist, biomedical scientist, occupational therapist, physiotherapist or photographer.

Impact on Lifestyle

It is normal to work a 35-hour week but, for diagnostic radiographers, this would include night and weekend shifts for emergency cover. Allowances are given for this flexible working. Therapeutic radiographers work more regular hours, seeing patients by appointment in a radiotherapy or oncology centre, although pressure to reduce waiting lists can involve overtime working. Exposure to x-rays can be dangerous and there is always a need to meet strict health and safety requirements.

Earnings Potential

A newly qualified NHS radiographer would start in Band 5, on a scale ranging from £22,128 to £28,746 This could rise to £41,787 for a specialist at the top of the scale and to over £69,000 for a consultant. Additional allowances are paid for appointments in and around London, ranging from 20% of basic salary for Inner London, to 15% for Outer London and 5% for the London Fringe. Salaries in the private sector are often linked to NHS levels but may be higher.

Further Information

Society of Radiographers
www.sor.org

British Institute of Radiology
www.bir.org.uk

Radiography careers
www.radiographycareers.co.uk

British Medical Ultrasound Society
www.bmus.org

Irish Institute of Radiography and Radiation Therapy
www.iirrt.ie

Research Biologist/Bioscientist

What is Involved?

Biology is the study of living organisms of all types. As a research biologist you might choose to work with plants, animals or micro-organisms. A relatively new and expanding area of biology is biotechnology, which combines biology with technical developments such as genetic engineering. The UK government is currently investing in synthetic biology, a suite of technologies that can effectively produce anything from renewable resources. The bioscience research community is generating the raw materials that will help businesses innovate now and in future.

Working as a research biologist, you would be at the cutting edge of your chosen specialised area, trying to discover new information and identify solutions to specific problems. In addition to working in universities in a pure research role, there are opportunities to work in food research institutions, in medicine-related areas or in such industries as pharmaceuticals or food production and brewing.

Opportunities for Training

To become a research biologist, you would need a good degree in biology. Most universities have relevant three- or four-year courses, offering biology as a single subject or in combination with a range of other subjects. There are also sandwich courses available which allow you to spend some time working in industry whilst you are studying. Some employers and large companies might sponsor you.

You might look, in particular, for Integrated Masters degrees (MSci, MBiol, MBiolSci), which usually involve four years (five in Scotland) of study. These degrees allow you to undertake a more in-depth study of biology or a specialised area of biology and graduate with a Masters level qualification. Integrated Masters normally include a significant research project or work placement and can provide good preparation for a career in research.

Most research biologists would carry out postgraduate study and go on to take a PhD. You should consider working towards Chartered Biologist status.

Requirements for Entry

Degree entry requirements vary between universities. Most would specify biology at A level/Advanced Higher/Higher or equivalent and some would also want chemistry at a similar standard. The minimum requirements are normally stated as two A level/Advanced Higher, three Higher or equivalent qualifications, together with GCSE/S Grade passes 9-4/A*-C/1-3 in five subjects. Sometimes maths and English are specified.

To be accepted for postgraduate study leading to a career in research, you would normally need a degree passed with first or upper second class honours. A doctorate (PhD) is usually required for research associate/senior scientist roles and above.

Kind of Person

As a research biologist you would need to have a deep interest in your subject and to be prepared to continue your academic study for many years. You would be working at the forefront of your specialised area of biology and as such could be moving the subject forward. In order to do this you would need an enquiring mind and an imaginative and creative approach to problem solving. If you do not find practical laboratory work interesting at the moment, this would probably not be the career for you. You would be expected to show accuracy and precision in recording your experimental results.

You are likely to be part of a team of scientists and to be involved with discussing your ideas and findings with other scientists. In addition, you may be expected to explain your research or developments in your field to others who do not have the same scientific background as you. You would almost certainly need to use computer technology both for your research and to communicate with others in the field.

Broad Outlook

People all over the world need healthy food, new medicines, clean water, sustainable agriculture and carbon neutral fuel. Without well-trained research biologists, these needs will not be met.

You could work in the public or private sector, with opportunities in, for example, the pharmaceutical, agricultural or food industries, carrying out research and product development or scientific analysis and investigation. You might specialise in environmental biology or ecology, and could work with international aid agencies, charities, research institutions and organisations such as the Environment Agency.

You could also move into management, teaching or the media.

Related Occupations

You may be interested in other careers based in the field of biology, such as microbiologist or forensic scientist. Alternatively, a career based in another science might appeal to you, including biochemist or pharmacologist.

Impact on Lifestyle

You are likely to be working regular laboratory/office hours for five days a week most of the time. However, there may be occasions when you are under pressure to meet deadlines and would have to work late. You may need to read or write papers or journal articles in your free time. If you choose to work in an environment that is attached to a university, you may find yourself involved in some sort of lecturing role as well as being a researcher. In addition, you would be expected to travel to conferences and to other laboratories to keep up to date with your subject

Earnings Potential

A PhD studentship, which allows you to study for a doctorate while carrying out research work, is usually set at the minimum Research Councils UK rate of £14,296, maybe higher. Your earnings should rise to £25,000 to £35,000 for a postdoctoral research associate and £33,000 to £57,000 for a research fellow. Professors can achieve salaries of £60,000 and beyond. Industry salaries, especially in the biotechnology and pharmaceutical sectors, are generally greater than those paid by the academic and public sectors.

Further Information

Royal Society of Biology
www.rsb.org.uk
Biotechnology and Biological Sciences Research Council
www.bbsrc.ac.uk
National Institute for Health Research
www.nihr.ac.uk
Vitae
www.vitae.ac.uk
Microbiology Society
www.microbiologysociety.org
Environment Agency
www.gov.uk/government/organisations/environment-agency
Institute of Biology of Ireland
www.ibioli.net

Research Chemist

What is Involved?

As a research chemist, you would deal with the nature of atomic and molecular substances, their properties, chemical bonding and interaction. You might work in industry - in pharmaceuticals, foodstuffs, agriculture, oil and chemical manufacture or polymers, for example - or you might choose to stay within a university environment and carry out research that is primarily academic but could have major commercial potential. Increasingly, universities and their staff are patenting and licensing their discoveries - which can significantly increase their available revenues.

Opportunities for Training

The Royal Society of Chemistry (RSC) accredits chemistry courses which are of a high standard in terms of intellectual challenge and content. These are usually integrated Masters degree courses, designated MChem or MSci rather than BSc. These are extended programmes that last four years, whilst BSc courses last three years. The first two years are usually identical to those of the Chemistry BSc course at the same institution. Students then take different routes in year 3 or 4.

Accredited courses satisfy the academic requirements for the award of Chartered Chemist (CChem). Graduates who are awarded an RSC accredited degree and are RSC members are eligible to apply for CChem once they have gained several years of chemistry-related work experience. The award of CChem recognises the experienced practising chemist who has demonstrated an in-depth knowledge of chemistry, significant personal achievements based upon chemistry, professionalism in the workplace and a commitment to maintaining technical expertise through continuing professional development (CPD). You may also apply for Chartered Scientist (CSci) status with the Science Council.

Having a PhD can be a great asset in a research career, so you would need to be prepared for further postgraduate study. This can be expensive but some companies might be prepared to help fund your studies.

Requirements for Entry

A level/Advanced Higher or Higher qualifications in chemistry and ideally in maths or another science are likely to be required for entry to a chemistry degree. However, if you choose to combine chemistry with a very popular subject, such as law, you may need to obtain higher grades than are required for chemistry alone. It is possible for students without these qualifications to take a foundation course before starting their degree, either at a university or a college of further education. The entry requirements for the MChem/MSci courses are generally a little higher than those for the corresponding BSc courses.

Kind of Person

As a chemical researcher you would need to have a very keen interest in your subject and an enquiring mind, constantly asking why reactions occur and examining the effects of chemical changes. You would be expected to keep yourself up to date with overall developments in the field and to show an analytic and logical approach to problem solving.

Accuracy and precision would be very important in making observations and in recording data. At times you would need to persevere in order to solve a particular problem and to be technically imaginative in your thinking. You would also need to work with other people as part of a research team and to be able to explain your ideas, theories and discoveries to others who may not be as expert as you.

Broad Outlook

There are generally good prospects of employment for chemists, especially now that industry is recovering from the economic downturn that started in 2008. As a graduating chemical scientist, you could choose to work in a field vital to the future, such as addressing climate change, providing energy, securing food and water or developing new technologies in healthcare, communication and security.

This is a competitive field and you would always be under pressure to complete work on time and to publish your results in regular departmental reports or in learned papers. You may find that you will need to study further in order to gain recognition and promotion. Many researchers in industry move onto the sales, administration or management areas of their companies.

Related Occupations

You may be interested in other careers in the field of chemistry, such as: pharmacologist, biochemist, biomedical scientist or science technician. Alternatively, you might like to think about another scientific career such as: metallurgist, research biologist/bioscientist or forensic scientist.

Impact on Lifestyle

You are likely to be working regular office hours on weekdays most of the time. You should be prepared to travel for conferences and other meetings. Your work would always involve reading journals and other papers outside your normal work hours to keep up to date in your own field. At times, when you are making especially good progress or are under pressure to find a solution to a problem, you may need to work extra hours to meet deadlines.

If you choose to work in a university, carrying out research, you are likely to be involved in some sort of supervision of laboratory work and even to lecture to undergraduates at times.

Earnings Potential

A PhD studentship, which allows you to study for a doctorate while also carrying out research work, is usually paid at the minimum Research Councils UK rate of £14,296. This should increase to £25,000 to £35,000 when you first start as a research scientist. At a senior level, you might earn £50,000 to £70,000, with larger salaries possible in some large manufacturing companies. Larger companies usually pay research scientists higher salaries than smaller, specialist employers, although the latter may offer you earlier responsibility and opportunities to remain in your preferred scientific area.

Further Information

Royal Society of Chemistry
www.rsc.org

The Science Council
www.sciencecouncil.org

Society of Chemical Industry
www.soci.org

Engineering and Physical Sciences Research Council
www.epsrc.ac.uk

Institute of Chemistry of Ireland
www.chemistryireland.org

Residential Care Home Manager

What is Involved?

As a residential care home manager, you would be responsible for looking after long- or short-stay residents in a particular home or hostel. You are likely to find yourself caring for children, elderly people or adults with physical disabilities, mental health or behavioural problems. Your job would be to help clients come to terms with their problems and, if possible, to become independent.

You could find yourself teaching, giving one-to-one counselling sessions, running group therapy classes and, at times, offering basic support such as help with dressing or feeding. You are likely to be involved with supervising the daily routine of the home and also with providing educational and recreational activities as appropriate. Other duties might include attending meetings and writing reports, dealing with staffing issues and checking the budget. You may not be resident yourself but you would usually be expected to sleep in for a certain number of nights on a rota basis.

Opportunities for Training

You would need relevant qualifications and management experience to become a care home manager, perhaps gaining promotion from a deputy manager's position.

It is recommended that you start the level 5 Diploma in Leadership for Health and Social Care and Children and Young People's Services within three months of taking up your role, with a view to completing it within two to three years.

The Diploma has six pathways to choose from, depending on the service your organisation offers:

- Management of Adult Services
- Management of Adult Residential Services
- Practice in Adult Services
- Management of Children and Young People's Services
- Management of Children and Young People's Residential Services
- Practice in Children and Young People's Services

To manage a home that provides nursing care, you will usually need to be a registered nurse with a qualification in management.

If you're new to social care work, an Apprenticeship could prove a good way to learn about the sector. You'll work alongside experienced staff and develop your skills and knowledge, achieving nationally recognised qualifications while earning a wage. There is also a national graduate management training scheme, open to graduates in any subject if you can demonstrate the right core values.

Requirements for Entry

Entrants to care home management need experience of working in social or medical care. Many managers have worked as care home assistants or deputy managers, and for many jobs there is a specified minimum length of experience.

The national minimum standards for care home managers require you to have the qualifications, competence and experience to run the home and meet its stated purpose, aims and objectives. These standards are issued by the Department of Health and can be found on the Care Quality Commission website.

Kind of Person

You would need to be extremely flexible and adaptable, showing great patience and tact in building relationships with residents. You would be involved with helping them to realise their potential and try to regain control of their lives. This can make your work environment quite tense and stressful, so you would need to be emotionally stable and resilient in order to cope. You are likely to be motivated by a desire to help people to make more of themselves and to be content with sometimes very slow progress towards that goal. You would need to be a good listener who can accept a wide variety of people without judgement. Your job would involve working with a number of other people as part of a team.

Broad Outlook

For many years, the highly labour intensive social care sector has been largely outsourced to independent providers of different types and sizes. This has led to a diverse and open market of provision, offering people choice in the care available. However, the downside of entrusting vital care services to private equity companies has emerged since the economic downturn that started in 2008. Britain's largest care home provider went out of business in 2011, and many other providers are facing similar financial problems. In the wake of extremely negative reports in the news media, the government reviewed its social care policy and introduced the Care Act 2016, designed to ensure that people will have protection and support and will be treated with compassion when in hospital, care homes or their own home.

Related Occupations

You might consider: social worker, nurse, probation officer or youth worker.

Impact on Lifestyle

Spending some nights sleeping in, often in self-contained accommodation attached to the unit, including weekend and holiday period shifts, can severely disrupt your family and social life.

Earnings Potential

Salaries for residential care home managers vary according to the type and size of home and the level of responsibility involved. Starting salaries are usually around £21,000 to £30,000 a year, rising with experience to between £30,000 and £40,000 a year. Some managers may earn over £45,000 a year.

Further Information

Think Care Careers
www.skillsforcare.org.uk/Care-careers/Think-Care-Careers

Care Quality Commission
www.cqc.org.uk

Scottish Social Services Council
www.sssc.uk.com

Social Care Institute for Excellence
www.scie.org.uk

Social Care Wales
www.ccwales.org.uk

Northern Ireland Social Care Council
www.niscc.info

Social Care Ireland
www.socialcareireland.ie

Restaurant Manager

What is Involved?

As a restaurant manager, you could work in locations from small exclusive dining establishments or wine bars to fast food outlets, mass-appeal eating-houses, hotels, clubs and branches of major chain organisations. As well as having a working knowledge of food and wine, you would need to meet the expectations of your customers and ensure that they return in the future.

If you work for a national chain organisation, you would have to fit in with company menu policies; in other areas, your chef or catering manager would be responsible for selecting the items on the menu but you would have an overview. You would have overall responsibility for cleanliness and hygiene, health and safety, air pollution and compliance with by-laws together with recruitment, training and staff motivation.

Budgetary control would normally be an important part of your job, including ordering supplies, publicising the business, paying staff, banking each day's takings and investing for future development.

Opportunities for Training

There are many possible avenues for training. You could start as a chef or food service assistant, for example, and work your way through progressive levels of recognised vocational qualifications. You might at the same time study part-time or by distance learning for the professional qualifications offered by the Hospitality Guild.

You could take a national diploma course at a local college or you could continue into higher education for a degree, foundation degree or higher national diploma (HND) in a subject such as hospitality or catering. At this level, you may secure a place on a management training scheme run by one of the large hotel or restaurant groups.

Another possible training route would be to join an apprenticeship training programme. There is, for example, an advanced apprenticeship in Hospitality and Catering (Supervision and Leadership).

Requirements for Entry

Experience, motivation and commitment would generally count for much more than examination success. Depending on the training route you choose, you could enter the restaurant industry with no examination passes at all, with GCSE/S Grade passes at 9-4/A*-C/1-3, with A level/Advanced Higher, Higher or equivalent qualifications, with a degree or HND. You should research options carefully and talk them through with your careers or personal adviser.

Kind of Person

You would need a bright, extrovert personality and the ability to communicate well with everyone you meet. You should by nature be customer-orientated and service-focused, with a solid base of common sense and a resistance to pressure and stress, together with a sense of humour and tact, business flair and administrative thoroughness. Crises can often occur in the heat of a busy kitchen and you would need to be able to think quickly and act decisively to solve problems, while maintaining an atmosphere of unhurried and unflappable professionalism in the dining area. You should have a reasonable standard of numeracy to cope with the financial side of the business and sufficient IT skills to use specialist software packages for restaurants.

The Hospitality Guild website offers a personality test to consider how well you might match your chosen role.

Broad Outlook

The hospitality workforce is forecast to increase by 3.5% every year until 2020, but this view may be complicated by the UK leaving the EU and such possible consequences as the rising price of imports and changing nationality and residence requirements for employees.

Having successfully managed a single restaurant, you might progress into area management, for which extensive knowledge of a particular chain and a strong background of practical experience are normally required. An area manager may typically manage four to six restaurants, depending on the size of the establishments. It is also possible to move into an operations management or head office role.

Many restaurants in the UK are owner-managed or run by the owner in partnership with a manager. With the right experience and financial backing, you could set up and run your own restaurant.

Related Occupations

You might also consider: hospitality/hotel manager, events manager, catering manager or chef.

Impact on Lifestyle

Demands on your personal time would be substantial, with long hours, split shifts and late working, including evenings, weekends and public holidays. Indeed, the better you are at your job, the longer into the night your clients might want to stay. Your working hours would start long before the first customers arrive and finish after the last ones leave. Clearly your social and family life would be affected to such an extent that everything else would have to revolve around your work.

Earnings Potential

The range of remuneration is wide. As an assistant restaurant manager, you might start at around £18,000 to £23,000, rising with experience to between £30,000 and £40,000. A senior manager in a large restaurant could earn in excess of £50,000, possibly up to £70,000. If you set up your own restaurant, your income would depend entirely on your own ability to establish a profitable business.

Further Information

Hospitality Guild
www.hospitalityguild.co.uk

Institute of Hospitality
www.instituteofhospitality.org

People First
www.people1st.co.uk

Academy of Food and Wine Service
www.afws.co.uk

British Hospitality Association
www.bha.org.uk

Apprenticeships
www.getingofar.gov.uk

Irish Hospitality Institute
www.ihi.ie

Retail Manager

What is Involved?

Your role as a retail manager would depend very much on the type of retailing in which you were involved. You could be selling goods and services online, in a retail park, shopping mall or high street; you might work in a supermarket, a large department store or a specialist boutique. If you were the manager of a large store, you might have a large team of assistant managers dealing with, for example, individual departments, customer services, finance, buying and human resources.

In a smaller organisation, you might take on many of these functions yourself. The basic principles would remain the same: to maximise profits by setting and reaching sales targets, persuading customers to choose your outlet and training and getting the best out of all members of staff. You would expect to spend some of your time on the shop floor, to see how customers are reacting to your latest range of products and to check that customers are being properly handled by staff. You would attend meetings with your staff and deal with administrative matters in your office.

Opportunities for Training

You could work your way to the top through sheer hard work and talent. However, more emphasis is now being placed on qualifications. Many large stores and chains have their own training schemes, for both graduates and non-graduates, and the competition for places on these schemes can be fierce. Diploma courses in retail management are available at different levels for candidates with GCSEs/S grades, A levels/Advanced Highers/Highers or equivalent qualifications. Universities and other institutions of higher education offer relevant degree, foundation degree and higher national diploma courses.

There are also apprenticeships available for this type of work.

Requirements for Entry

While there are no precise educational requirements laid down for entry into retail management, employers are increasingly looking for staff who have reached a certain educational level or have completed a period of training. Graduates are generally offered places on fast-track management schemes.

The actual subject of your degree would not be crucial, since the training would cover all the necessary topics, but subjects allied to retailing, including business studies, would obviously be helpful. For entry into other relevant marketing, retail management, and other degree courses you would need two A level/Advanced Higher, three to four Higher or equivalent qualifications.

Kind of Person

You would need an outgoing personality, together with excellent communication skills, both spoken and written, since you would be dealing with a wide variety of people, including staff, suppliers and customers. Quick thinking and problem-solving ability would also be necessary in a busy environment where many different things are happening at once. Physical and mental stamina would be important, as the hours could be long, and as manager you would be expected to be on hand to deal with anything that cropped up. A smart appearance would be necessary. You should be numerate and have a good eye for business.

Broad Outlook

The UK retail sector has been hit by three main problems since 2008:

- The recession has sapped consumer confidence and reduced borrowing. Consumers are spending less

- Retail balance sheets and the rents retailers pay were historically focused on continued growth and reckless consumer spending. Because consumers have curbed their spending, the economics of current-day retailing no longer work
- The rapid growth of online spending, which now accounts for more than 12% of retail sales, has occurred mainly at the expense of conventional shops, supermarkets and department stores, resulting in even lower spending in physical retail stores

2012 proved to be the worst year for bankruptcies and failures since the start of the recession in 2008, with 54 significant retailers going into administration, affecting 3,951 stores and 48,000 employees. In January 2013, another four retail failures were responsible for 991 stores closing and 10,700 redundancies.

There has been a slow improvement in retail career prospects recently, but the British Retail Consortium predicts that there will be over 8,000 fewer shops by 2020, putting 80,000 jobs at risk.

Related Occupations

You might also like to consider: advertising account executive, buying executive, hospitality/hotel manager, management/business consultant, marketing executive, office manager, operational researcher/management scientist, human resources manager or public relations executive.

Impact on Lifestyle

Retail management can be a demanding occupation and store opening hours are becoming ever longer (even 24 hours). While you would not be expected to be present all the time, you would probably have to work some evenings and certainly some weekends.

Earnings Potential

Pay scales vary enormously, depending on the size and scope of the organisation, and the amount of responsibility undertaken. Trainee managers in multiple stores could start at anything from £20,000 to £26,000, rising with experience to £34,000 to £70,000. There would also be other benefits offered by larger employers, such as bonuses, commission, enhanced pension scheme, staff discount and good social facilities. Small retail organisations tend to pay less.

Further Information

British Retail Consortium
www.brc.org.uk

Institute of Grocery Distribution
www.igd.com

British Independent Retailers Association
www.bira.co.uk

Apprenticeships
www.getingofar.gov.uk

People First
www.people1st.co.uk

Sales Institute of Ireland
www.salesinstitute.ie

Retail Ireland
www.retailireland.ie

Royal Air Force Officer

What is Involved?

As an officer in the RAF, you would be part of the service which guards the airspace of the UK and other areas for which Britain has responsibilities, including its operations under NATO. You would be responsible for leading and managing non-commissioned personnel on bases at home and overseas, either in an active role in flying or in any of the numerous support services on which pilots depend. RAF aircraft are divided into three groups: fast jets, multi-engine and helicopters. If you were a pilot, you would specialise in one of these and would devote most of your time to flying duties.

Apart from pilots, officers in the RAF are employed in a variety of specialised areas, including: navigators who plan routes and guide pilots; fighter controllers who use radar to direct pilots in action; air traffic controllers who provide pilots with flight information and help them take off and land safely; intelligence officers who interpret photographic and other images from reconnaissance aircraft; engineers who keep aircraft in operation; RAF Regiment officers who defend airfields and other installations; administrators, physical training personnel, training officers, police officers, lawyers, chaplains, doctors, dentists and nurses.

Opportunities for Training

Initial Officer Training takes place at the RAF College Cranwell in Lincolnshire, the world's first military air academy. Over three ten-week terms, you would receive an introduction to military life and to the principles of leadership; you would build up your leadership skills and learn, in simulated military operations, how to gain trust and command respect; you would shadow RAF personnel to see leadership skills in practice; and undertake further practical exercises to put your own skills into action. Once commissioned, you would proceed to the specialist training of your choice. For pilots, you would be selected for training on fast jets, multi-engine planes or helicopters on the basis of your performance after a short period of initial training and flying with an instructor.

Requirements for Entry

For basic entry, you must have at least two A level/Advanced Higher, three Higher or equivalent qualifications, together with five GCSE/S Grade passes at 9-4/A*-C/1-3 including English and maths. You must also meet RAF nationality and residence requirements and pass a series of selection tests - including aptitude and initiative tests, interviews and a medical - held at the RAF College at Cranwell. Many posts - but not all - have rigorous eyesight requirements.

If you want to go to university first, you will find that graduates are welcome in all branches of the service, particularly if your degree is in a technological or other relevant discipline. Currently about 40% of applicants are graduates.

You can seek financial support through a sixth form scholarship or sponsorship at university. A Flying Scholarship could provide some free flying training.

Kind of Person

You must be confident and capable as a leader, able to work in a team but also able to stand apart and make decisions, often very quickly. You must be physically fit and prepared to accept responsibility for both personnel and very expensive equipment. Good communication skills are vital.

Each branch of the RAF requires its own mix of personal qualities: thinking and reacting quickly for a pilot or air traffic controller; working logically for an engineer, for example.

Most branches need officers with a keen interest in the operation of advanced technical equipment.

Broad Outlook

In common with other branches of the UK's armed services, the RAF has faced cuts as a result of the 2010 Strategic Defence and Security Review (SDSR). Following the loss of more than a quarter of trainee pilot places in 2011, redundancies in 2012 included 30 group captains, 40 wing commanders and 115 squadron leaders. Further job losses have come from engineers, logistics, personnel and air traffic controllers. The SDSR target is 31,750 by 2020.

The RAF is still recruiting, but it is clearly changing to become a smaller, faster and more flexible fighting force.

Related Occupations

You may also consider: Royal Navy/Royal Marines officer, Army officer, airline pilot, air traffic controller or aircraft maintenance engineer.

Impact on Lifestyle

You would have to be available for duty 24 hours a day, 7 days a week, but for much of the time you would work normal office hours from Monday to Friday, extended occasionally into weekends. During operations and in emergency situations, you would be expected to work whatever hours the circumstances demand. This and overseas commitments could take you away from family and friends, often for extended periods of time.

There is special provision for female officers who become pregnant either to seek early release from their commission or to take maternity leave before resuming their commission.

Earnings Potential

Your officer rank and pay scale would depend on your qualifications and chosen specialist area. As a Pilot Officer, for example, you would start on £25,984, rising to £30,923 to £35,743 as a Flying Officer, £40,025 to £50,123 as a Flight Lieutenant and £50,417 to £64,199 as a Squadron Leader.

There are different pay scales for some specialist officers and professionally qualified entrants. If you join as a qualified dentist, for example, you would earn £53,800 plus benefits after training. Benefits include subsidised accommodation and food, through-life education and training, annual allowances for educational courses, free sports and adventure training and extensive travel opportunities.

Further Information

RAF Careers
www.raf.mod.uk/recruitment

Defence Forces Ireland
www.military.ie

Royal Navy/Royal Marines Officer

What is Involved?

As a young naval officer, you would have a management responsibility for people and for state-of-the-art equipment. Eventually you might find yourself in command of a warship, flying a helicopter, supervising the safe operation of a submarine nuclear propulsion plant or providing emergency medical care. You would be trained as a specialist to perform key operational roles, working together with the Royal Marines to carry out vital work in ships, submarines, aircraft, naval air stations and shore establishments. Officer specialisms include warfare, aviation, diving, Royal Marines, hydrographic surveying, meteorology, engineering, supply and training management. Then there are medical and dental officers, nurses and chaplains. Closely linked to the Royal Navy, the Royal Marines are a specialist amphibious commando force able to operate at very short notice in a variety of terrains, often under considerable threat.

Opportunities for Training

Royal Navy officer training begins with 15 to 30 weeks of initial training at Britannia Royal Naval College (BRNC) in Dartmouth. This Initial Naval Training (INT) for officers is split into three distinct phases: Militarisation, Marinisation and Initial Fleet Time, with the first two phases taking place at BRNC and the third on board a warship.

The ten-week militarisation phase covers the basic skills and knowledge you need to go from being a civilian to a member of the armed forces. These include team-based physical training, map reading and navigation and field craft and survival skills. You spend two weeks at HMS Raleigh, undergoing weapon training, and also go through Chemical, Biological, Radiological, Nuclear and Damage Control (CBRNDC) training.

During the marinisation phase, you learn to apply your military skills to a maritime environment. This includes tuition on topics such as strategic studies and maritime operations, and a lot of time on the River Dart, learning boat handling skills in the college's motor whaler and picket boats.

In the third part of your INT, you spend nine weeks at sea in one of the Royal Navy's major warships, working in every department on board, learning how they operate and how they contribute to the ship as a whole.

Once you have mastered the essential basic military and maritime command skills, you can begin training as a specialist in the officer role you have chosen.

Requirements for Entry

With five GCSEs or equivalent (including Maths and English) and two A levels or equivalent, you could join direct as an officer, starting as a midshipman and rising to sub-lieutenant after two years. If you are studying maths and science subjects, you could apply to read for an engineering degree. Some 75% of officers enter as graduates or obtain degrees during training. You would have to go through a rigorous selection process known as the Admiralty Interview Board (AIB). This gives both you and the Navy a chance to assess whether a career in the Royal Navy is right for you. The main aim of the AIB is to assess your potential. It lasts two days and takes place at HMS Sultan, a naval base near Gosport in Hampshire. There are nationality and residence requirements as well as strict eyesight standards. You must also be male if you want to take part in mine clearance diving, serve in submarines or join the Royal Marines.

Kind of Person

Life on board ship and in submarines requires very particular qualities of officers. You must be able to live and work under the pressures of confined space with large numbers of other people. This requires broadmindedness and high levels of self-discipline. As an officer responsible for the men and women under your command, you need good management, communication and interpersonal skills. You need to be quick thinking and resourceful, able to show initiative in sudden events which may be of a 'life or death nature' in the event of combat. Long spells working away from home require qualities of self-sufficiency and drive to get on with the job. An interest in science and technology is important in many areas of work. The hard physical nature of the commando training of the Royal Marines requires a very special level of fitness, stamina and determination.

Broad Outlook

In common with other branches of the UK's armed services, the Royal Navy faced cuts following the 2010 Strategic Defence and Security Review (SDSR). The SDSR target was that the Navy would be reduced by around 5,000 personnel by 2015. Some 1,600 Navy personnel were laid off in the first tranche of redundancies in September 2011, including 121 officers up to the rank of captain from the warfare, engineering, medical and logistics branches.

Cuts were much smaller in 2012 (17 captains and 19 Royal Marines officers) and this was the last round of actual redundancies, with natural wastage and a recruitment freeze in some areas making up the remaining cuts. The programme for 2015 to 2020 is much more positive.

Related Occupations

You may consider: army officer, merchant navy officer, Royal Air Force officer or air traffic controller.

Impact on Lifestyle

You would be working in an environment where much is expected of you and where you would be on call 24 hours a day. On exercise and operational duty, shifts and hours can be long and demanding, both physically and mentally. Communal living in often cramped conditions away from families for various periods of time requires a calm outlook on life and a high level of tolerance. You must be prepared to serve anywhere in the world.

All officers join on an initial twelve-year commission (Royal Marines eight years), although there are options to leave early in certain cases.

Earnings Potential

As soon as you join Britannia Royal Naval College or Commando Training Centre Royal Marines, you earn £25,727, increasing to £30,923 once you pass out. After a year of service, you would earn £31,741 to £34,180 as a Sub-lieutenant (Royal Marines 2nd Lieutenant), and could go on to £39,629 to £47,127 as a Lieutenant (Royal Marines Captain). Salaries rise significantly on further promotion and officers receive additional allowances for such things as flying, serving in submarines or being at sea. A Captain (Royal Marines Colonel) currently earns from £84,878 to £93,304.

Further Information

Call 0345 607 5555 or visit your local Armed Forces Careers Office
www.royalnavy.mod.uk/careers

Defence Forces Ireland
www.military.ie

Rural Practice Surveyor

What is Involved?

As a rural practice surveyor, sometimes known as an agricultural surveyor, you would be involved in offering advice on a range of aspects of countryside management and development. You might undertake the sale or purchase of rural holdings, value land, property and livestock and organise auctions; you might issue shooting or fishing permits or advise on leisure activities such as golf courses, outward-bound activities or tourist accommodation; you might be involved with managing an estate or large farming enterprise.

You could be employed as a consultant offering advice to farmers or landowners on such things as buildings, livestock, and investment in machinery or other possible uses for farmland. You could become involved with insurance, tax or compensation issues. Another area that is becoming increasingly important is that of conservation and the environment. As these examples show, this can be a very varied job, concerned with a full range of countryside issues.

Opportunities for Training

There are several possible routes to qualification, including distance learning, taking an accredited degree or following a relevant postgraduate course. Whatever academic route you follow, you can work towards chartered membership of the Royal Institution of Chartered Surveyors (RICS) by completing a period of structured practical training with an employer, ending with the RICS Assessment of Professional Competence. There are also some courses accredited by the Central Association of Agricultural Valuers (CAAV).

The CAAV suggests initial training on one of three programmes:

- Rural Enterprise and Land Management at Harper Adams University
- Real Estate at Reading University (Henley Business School)
- Rural Land Management at the Royal Agricultural University, Cirencester

All three institutions offer undergraduate and postgraduate provision, and all carry RICS accreditation.

There are also courses supporting the profession at Cambridge University (Department of Land Economy) and University College of Estate Management (Reading)

Requirements for Entry

For entry to a degree course you are likely to be asked for two or three A level/ Advanced Higher, three or four Higher or equivalent qualifications, together with supporting GCSE/S Grade passes at 9-4/A*-C/1-3, including English and maths. Some courses will accept more practical qualifications in place of the above.

Kind of Person

You would need to have a good basic understanding of the countryside and of rural matters. In addition to your agricultural interests, you should have a sound knowledge of the law and of financial matters. You could be involved with such things as valuations, managing accounting systems and budgeting, so you would need to be numerate. You should enjoy solving problems and applying your knowledge to find practical and logical solutions.

You could find yourself working for or with a wide range of different people and you would need to be able to communicate with them all clearly and with authority. You would need to enjoy being part of a rural community and out in the countryside in all weathers. You are likely to be walking some distance and clambering around buildings, which means that you would need to be reasonably fit and agile.

Broad Outlook

There are a number of different areas of employment for rural practice surveyors. You might work in the public sector for a local authority or a government department, such as the Ministry of Defence or the Department for the Environment, Food and Rural Affairs. You might equally find work with a major rural charity such as the Royal Society for the Protection of Birds or the National Trust. However, the major area of employment is the private sector, where you might be employed directly by an estate or large farm, indirectly by a group of smaller properties or within the rural department of a firm of general practice surveyors. There is increasingly work involving conservation issues and the diversification of use of rural land.

Related Occupations

You might also consider: estate manager/land agent, ecologist, environmental consultant, farm manager, horticultural manager, landscape architect, town and country planner or land/geomatics surveyor, hydrographic surveyor, building surveyor or quantity surveyor.

Impact on Lifestyle

This is certainly not a Monday to Friday, nine to five job. The hours would depend greatly on the season and the consequent demands of the countryside. You would be working outside in all sorts of weather and at times likely to get wet, cold and muddy. You would need to spend a lot of time talking to farmers and other rural clients, listening to their problems and worries. You may be expected to travel quite long distances to get to your work.

Earnings Potential

Traditionally, this is not the best-paid branch of surveying, the compensation being that it offers an attractive lifestyle if you enjoy the country life. If you enter the profession as a graduate, you may start on £20,000 to £25,000. This is likely to rise to around £40,000 to £50,000 when you achieve full professional status and gain experience. The current average salary of rural practice surveyors working in the UK is £41,808 plus a bonus of £7,455. Sometimes you may be offered accommodation as part of the payment package.

Further Information

Royal Institution of Chartered Surveyors
www.rics.org/rural
University College of Estate Management
www.ucem.ac.uk
Chartered Institute of Building
www.ciob.org
Central Association of Agricultural Valuers
www.caav.org.uk
Harper Adams University
www.harper-adams.ac.uk
Royal Agricultural University
www.rau.ac.uk
Reading University (Henley)
www.henley.ac.uk/undergraduate/course/bsc-real-estate-n231
Society of Chartered Surveyors, Ireland
www.scsi.ie

Sales Executive

What is Involved?

As a member of a sales team (you might also be known as a sales representative or sales manager), you would be involved in selling products or services and ensuring that your clients are fully aware of your organisation's presence in the market place. You would usually be responsible for a range of products or services and might travel widely to meet customers and establish good relationships with them. Your work could include dealing with enquiries regarding specifications or prices, helping to solve any problems of supply or quality, seeking advice on technical issues and reporting any information on competitor activities to your sales and marketing colleagues.

You would usually work within a framework laid down by your head office marketing and sales department, who would generate enquiries from potential buyers by means of advertising, sales literature, the Internet and press and television announcements. You would normally have to meet revenue targets and generate new business in addition to maintaining relationships with existing customers.

Opportunities for Training

Many companies operate their own in-house courses for trainee sales staff, usually covering product knowledge, sales techniques and company sales policy. There are also relevant part- and full-time courses available at colleges and training centres and by distance learning, while bodies such as the Institute of Sales and Marketing Management, the Managing and Marketing Sales Association and the Chartered Institute of Marketing offer qualifications linked to grades of membership.

Increasingly, degree courses are available covering sales and related aspects of business management. These could provide a sound foundation for a future career in sales, although graduate opportunities are usually open to students of any discipline. You might need a degree in, say, IT or engineering for some specific technical sales areas.

Requirements for Entry

While there are no specific entry requirements for a career in sales management, employers often recruit graduates and people with experience in relevant fields. You would generally enhance your prospects with a broad platform of GCSE/S Grade passes at 9-4/A*-C/1-3, including maths and English, and would have even greater choice - including degree course entry - with A level/Advanced Higher, Higher or equivalent qualifications.

Kind of Person

You should have a confident, outgoing personality, a readiness to make new contacts, sensitivity to others and the ability to listen carefully to comments or requests. You would need to believe in your own products or services and to know enough about your clients to be able to suggest the right products to meet their needs.

You would have to be persuasive in explaining the special features of your products or services, aware of competition in the marketplace, efficient in handling orders and well organised in keeping appointments and maintaining your records. You would usually be expected to dress smartly. Other qualities needed would include numeracy, the ability to cope with rejection, patience to deal with awkward customers and the energy to keep going all day long.

Broad Outlook

There is usually no shortage of sales executive opportunities anywhere in the UK, although the 2008 recession has had a lasting and severely negative effect on selling activity. Despite recent overall improvement, the outlook is uncertain due to possible negative effects to the economy as the UK leaves the EU.

Promotion would normally depend on your track record to date and could lead to regional or national sales manager posts and eventually to a position as sales or export director. You may find that you need to move fairly regularly to other companies or parts of the country if you want to progress more rapidly, broaden your experience or take on more responsibility.

Related Occupations

You might also consider: buying executive, marketing executive, advertising account executive, retail manager or public relations executive.

Impact on Lifestyle

You would work under a great deal of pressure to meet targets and you might be expected to travel widely. Deadlines could intrude on your family and social life, and your customers would expect you to place them top in your priorities. In some jobs, you could spend days or even weeks away from home and you might have to write up your reports and prepare presentations in the evening or at weekends.

Earnings Potential

There are no set pay scales but you might expect to start on around £18,000 to £35,000 as a graduate trainee. This could rise to £22,000 to £45,000 with around five years' experience and to £40,000 to £100,000 plus for a senior sales manager. It is essential to check the full remuneration package before you join a company, as your earnings might be linked with commission, bonuses, a car or car allowance and travelling and accommodation expenses. Salaries are usually based on success in meeting sales targets, and may be advertised as OTE or 'on target earnings'. Salaries in specialised areas such as pharmaceuticals, chemicals and technological equipment tend to produce higher rewards.

Further Information

Institute of Sales and Marketing Management
www.ismm.co.uk

Chartered Institute of Marketing
www.cim.co.uk

Management and Marketing Sales Association
www.mamsasbp.com

UR the Brand
www.urthebrand.co.uk

Institute of Promotional Marketing
www.theipm.org.uk

Marketing Institute of Ireland
www.mii.ie

Secretary Linguist

What is Involved?

As a secretary linguist (or bilingual/trilingual secretary or bilingual PA), you would be able to offer practical speaking and writing skills in one or more foreign languages in addition to the full range of secretarial skills. The exact nature of your job would vary considerably from one employer to another but could include anything from word processing in your different languages, translating correspondence and making phone calls abroad to receiving and entertaining overseas visitors, making foreign travel arrangements and keeping up to date with the political or commercial climate in relevant countries.

You may receive occasional requests for translating or interpreting but it should be clear that you are not a specialist in either of these fields. (See our separate articles on these occupations.) You would normally be based in an office and should have access to keyboards, software packages and reference materials specific to the languages you would be using.

Opportunities for Training

You may find it helpful to have a recognised qualification in administration before you look for work. Colleges offer a wide range of full- and part-time courses, including certificates and diplomas. The greatest need is usually for western European languages such as French, German, Spanish and Italian, but other languages like Russian, Chinese, Japanese and Arabic are also in demand.

You might then develop your career with part-time training for a qualification such as:

- OCR awards from entry level up to level 4 in French, German, Italian, Japanese, Mandarin Chinese, Russian or Spanish

- ABC award from entry level up to level 3 in Practical Languages (14 languages available)

Requirements for Entry

You would need to be fluent in writing and speaking the languages you offer, and it would be a distinct advantage to have a sound understanding of the cultural, economic and social situation in the countries where your languages are spoken. Depending on the level you are aiming at, you may need A level/Advanced Higher, Higher or equivalent passes in one or more languages and you could find a degree valuable. However, experience of travelling or living overseas and using foreign languages on a regular basis could count for as much as examination success. Whatever your linguistic background, you would need a high-level secretarial qualification.

Kind of Person

You would need excellent communication skills and the confidence to enter into multilingual conversations on the telephone or in face-to-face meetings. You should have a keen interest in keeping your language skills up to date and a willingness to learn specialist vocabulary. Attention to detail, advanced IT skills and good organisational ability would all be important.

You should be able to get on with people easily, especially if your work involves welcoming foreign visitors to your organisation and making them feel at ease. A willingness to travel would quite likely be part of your interest in using languages and could enhance your employment opportunities.

Broad Outlook

With accelerating globalisation and the continuing development of the European Union, demand is healthy for people with genuine bilingual or trilingual ability (as opposed to a superficial smattering of language awareness). Most opportunities relate to the major European languages, especially French, German and Spanish, but there are also openings for specialists in Russian, Arabic, Japanese, Chinese and Eastern European languages.

A career as a secretary linguist presents above-average openings for late start, career break, flexitime, temping and freelance initiatives. There are also many job opportunities abroad, including the option of working as an English language specialist in a country where you can communicate easily in the local language.

Related Occupations

You might also consider: secretary/personal assistant, teacher (secondary), translator, interpreter, or another specialist role such as farm secretary, medical secretary or legal secretary.

Impact on Lifestyle

Many posts would involve a normal business week from Monday to Friday, but you could have to work unsocial hours if you need to be in regular contact with people in other time zones or if you are looking after overseas visitors. You may be expected to travel abroad as part of your job.

Earnings Potential

Levels of pay would vary considerably from one job to another, depending on the location and your ability and experience, but you could expect a salary higher than the normal secretarial rate, perhaps between £22,000 and £28,000, with additional allowances for out-of-hours working and overseas travel. This should rise with experience to £30,000 to £40,000 and could be higher for a senior post in a large international organisation.

Further Information

Institute of Administrative Management
www.instam.org

Skills CFA
www.skillscfa.org

Asset Languages alternative qualifications
www.ocr.org.uk/qualifications/by-type/asset-languages

Chartered Institute of Linguists
www.ciol.org.uk

International Management Assistants
www.ima-network.org

ABC Awards - Languages
www.abcawards.co.uk/languages

SCILT - Scotland's National Centre for Languages
www.scilt.org.uk

Shipbroker

*W*hat is Involved?

As a shipbroker, your role would be to facilitate the business of international bulk shipping by bringing together ship owners with vessels to fill and charterers with cargoes to transport by sea. You would also be involved with the purchase and sale of very large ships such as bulk carriers, container vessels, oil tankers and specialist ships. The main centre of international shipbroking operations is the Baltic Exchange in London, with some 50% of all tanker broking and up to 40% of dry bulk chartering carried out by about 3,000 shipbrokers working in around 600 shipbroking companies (there are 20,000 shipbrokers worldwide).

Other major shipping markets are found in Tokyo, Singapore, Shanghai, Hong Kong and New York as well as in European centres like Hamburg, Copenhagen and Oslo. Your work would include making presentations to potential clients, negotiating the main terms of a contract or sale, providing your clients with market intelligence and advice, entering tonnage into the company's database, checking the technical nature of a cargo and building up your own personal contacts throughout the world of shipping. Good relationships are vital if you wish to succeed.

*O*pportunities for Training

While there are no specific qualifications required, you might wish to apply for membership of the Institute of Chartered Shipbrokers (ICS) and to undertake some of its courses. Learning is available in a variety of ways: the aptly named TutorShip is a distance learning programme, which provides the option of studying at your own pace, but is also offered in 16 learning centres worldwide. Successful completion of ICS examinations is the only route to chartered shipbroker status.

ICS courses cover maritime law, international shipping and trade, economics and bulk transport. The Baltic Exchange also runs regular training courses on many aspects of the shipbroking business.

Many new recruits are graduates entering shipbroking after completing a degree in maritime business, although any academic subject would be acceptable.

*R*equirements for Entry

There is no required shipbroking qualification but you would gain much relevant background information from a business degree with a shipping specialism.

*K*ind of Person

You should be prepared to take a high level of responsibility, to mix well socially, to express views clearly and logically in both written and oral format, to have well-honed negotiating skills with a flair for maintaining contacts. Your intellectual credentials would be tested in the tenacity required to push through deals. Physical demands can also be high, with long hours, a global timescale, frequent exhausting travel, 24-hour availability in times of urgency and an extremely competitive global arena.

The highest levels of reliability, accuracy and integrity are essential. The motto of the Baltic Exchange - 'Our Word Our Bond' - symbolises the importance of ethics in trading. Members need to rely on each other and, in turn, on their principles for many contracts verbally expressed and only subsequently confirmed in writing. You would need good IT skills to cope with the sophisticated online information system at the Exchange.

Broad Outlook

Shipping markets have faced difficult times since the global economic downturn that started in 2008. However, free trade between nations - and shipbrokers are at the heart of this - is a cornerstone of the still sluggish world economic recovery. Despite stiff competition from other shipping centres around the world, the London market looks likely to remain very significant for many years to come. A very positive sign for the future is that the ICS has recently experienced record levels of examination registrations.

The Baltic Exchange is becoming increasingly computerised and brokers acting for ship owners can place shipping information, including the technical details of ships, directly online. However, negotiation is still handled completely by the brokers personally, since this is too complex to be automated by computer. Every ship, port and cargo is different.

Related Occupations

You might also consider: logistics/supply chain manager, freight forwarder, stockbroker, insurance underwriter or marketing executive.

Impact on Lifestyle

The global market ensures that shipbroking services spread over 24 hours a day, seven days a week. Periods of frenzied activity occur regularly when there is a need to find employment for a fleet and, as a broker, you would wish to prove the value for money of your services to the ship owners and charterers. Typically, your day could start early in the morning, in time to catch the important Far Eastern Markets, or could go on late into the night for the USA. You would be working by telephone and email for much of the time and might need to make frequent trips abroad.

Earnings Potential

Medium to high levels of pay can be expected, with a starting salary of around £26,000 to £28,000, rising to £70,000 to £100,000 for an experienced shipbroker. In good years, bonuses can easily double these figures.

Further Information

Institute of Chartered Shipbrokers
www.ics.org.uk

Baltic Exchange
www.balticexchange.com

International Chamber of Shipping
www.ics-shipping.org

British International Freight Association
www.bifa.org

Chartered Institute of Logistics and Transport
www.ciltuk.org.uk

Institute of Chartered Shipbrokers Ireland
www.icsireland.ie

Site Engineer/Construction Estimator

What is Involved?

As a site engineer or construction estimator, sometimes known as a building technician, you are likely to find yourself specialising in one or more of the areas of work involved in managing a construction site. For example, you could be working from an architect's or engineer's drawings to estimate the costs of a project or plan the stages of construction. Taking account of the materials and manpower needed, you would calculate the time and costs involved. You might be involved with buying the materials needed and working out how to store the equipment and materials on site. Alternatively, your work could take you on to the site itself, where you would check the progress and standard of the work being carried out and possibly take responsibility for site security, health and safety and the organisation and supervision of material and human resources.

Opportunities for Training

There are several possible training routes. You could, for example, take a degree in construction studies or a part- or full-time higher national certificate/diploma (HNC/D) at a college or training centre; you could take a lower level construction course at a local college or you could train in a craft skill - such as bricklaying or plastering - before taking a vocational qualification at technician level. Another way of training would be to take a construction apprenticeship or higher apprenticeship, in which you could study part-time while in paid employment. This would probably take three or four years to complete.

You may improve your career prospects by taking the level 4 Certificate and Diploma in Site Management qualifications offered by the Chartered Institute of Building. You would take units that most closely matched your job role and would then be able to work towards the level 6 Diploma in construction site management.

Requirements for Entry

Practical experience of working on a building site or in a construction environment is usually the most important requirement. For the HNC/D route, you would normally need at least one A level/Advanced Higher, two Higher or equivalent qualifications, together with four GCSE/S Grade passes at 9-4/A*-C/1-3, including English, maths and a science. Similar GCSE/S Grade requirements would apply to most apprenticeships and college courses for this type of work. You would often be able to enter a craft level course by passing a selection test.

Kind of Person

You would need to be a practical person with a logical and sensible approach to problem solving. In order to be successful you would need to learn a considerable amount of technical information about the building industry and also gain some knowledge of law and health and safety issues. Your job is likely to involve computers, so you would need to be computer literate. Your job would involve dealing with a large variety of people and you would need to have good communication skills. You might, for example, be negotiating with other professionals or supervising workers on a building site.

In either case you would need to make yourself clearly understood. You are also likely to be involved with interpreting plans and with making calculations based on the information you are given. You may need to organise your own work and that of others and should be able to work on your own initiative.

Broad Outlook

There are opportunities to work for local and central government, for large building contractors and for large organisations that have property portfolios such as hotel chains or major retailers. The demand for site engineers/construction estimators depends to a great extent on the state of the construction industry and the picture has recently begun to look encouraging, as the sector recovers from the severe downturn that started in 2008. You may choose to change employers and job roles over time in order to gain the experience necessary to develop your career and perhaps set up your own business.

Related Occupations

You might consider other construction-related careers, such as: building control officer/surveyor, architectural technician/technologist, town planner, construction manager, surveyor (general practice), estate manager/land agent, estate agent, rural practice surveyor or auctioneer/valuer.

Impact on Lifestyle

If you are working in an office-based job, the hours of work are likely to be around 40 a week. However, you would also be expected to work overtime in the evenings and at weekends, particularly if you have a contract deadline to meet. The hours of work on building sites can be long, especially in the summer to make maximum use of daylight hours. You could also get dirty, wet and cold at times on a building site and would need to wear protective clothing such as a hard hat, boots and a reflective coat.

Earnings Potential

Salaries for site engineers/construction estimators vary between companies and different parts of the country. A trainee could expect to earn around £18,000 to £26,000, rising on qualification to £25,000. Some site engineers earn more than £40,000 as they become more experienced. There are also allowances for working on site and sometimes travel expenses are reimbursed.

Further Information

Careers in Construction
www.citb.co.uk/careers-in-construction

Construction Industry Council
http://cic.org.uk

Apprenticeships
www.getingofar.gov.uk

Chartered Association of Building Engineers
www.cbuilde.com

Chartered Institute of Building
www.ciob.org

National House Building Council
www.nhbc.co.uk

Construction Industry Federation, Ireland
www.cif.ie

Social Worker

What is Involved?

As a social worker, you would provide advice and support to vulnerable individuals, families, and those living on the margins of society. You would also be responsible for helping them to get access to the services they need to improve their situation and well-being. Much of your work would focus on assessing the needs of your clients and planning individual packages of care and support to meet those needs.

You would normally specialise in either adult or children's services, perhaps helping to protect vulnerable people from harm or abuse or supporting people to live independently. You might provide assistance and advice to keep families together, manage adoption and foster care processes, provide support to younger people leaving care, at risk or in trouble with the law, or help children facing difficulties brought on by illness in the family.

You would often work in multi-disciplinary teams alongside other agencies and professionals, including health workers, youth workers, teachers, the police and probation services.

Opportunities for Training

Becoming a social worker in England involves taking an honours degree in social work and registering with the Health and Care Professions Council. The main route is a three-year undergraduate degree course although two-year postgraduate programmes are also available. Some universities offer part-time courses. All students on all courses must successfully complete at least 200 days of assessed practice before being awarded the social work degree.

Similar routes to qualification exist in the other countries of the United Kingdom but you must research options very carefully and consider studying/training in the country where you intend to work.

A new fast-track social work training scheme is in operation in the North East, North West, West Midlands, South East and Greater Manchester. Known as *Frontline*, it aims to train graduates to become social workers specialising in working with vulnerable children and their families. The scheme is an intensive work-based programme spread over two years. Another scheme, *Step Up to Social Work*, is designed to enable high-achieving graduates or career changers who have experience of working with children and young people to become qualified social workers. *Think Ahead* is a two-year diploma or master's programme aimed at training graduates to become mental health social workers.

Requirements for Entry

Entry to the degree course is open to people of all ages. You may be able to gain admission over the age of 21 without formal examination passes, although as a school or college leaver you would normally need at least two A level/Advanced Higher, three Higher or equivalent passes, together with five GCSE/S Grade passes at 9-4/A*-C/1-3. All programmes require you to have some relevant paid or voluntary social work experience.

Kind of Person

You would need to be open minded and prepared to examine and even change your attitudes and possible prejudices. You may need to deal with racism and other forms of discrimination. You would certainly require personal qualities such as patience, determination and the ability to help people face painful and distressing problems. Social work can be both physically and emotionally stressful and not everyone can stand back from situations and assess them in an objective but caring way. Good practice would rely on the intellectual skills of analysis, reflection and adopting a critical perspective.

Broad Outlook

Recent years have proved to be a fraught time for social workers working in children's services as a result of all the adverse publicity surrounding cases such as 'Baby Peter' in London and 'Baby A' in Doncaster. These prompted a serious review of child protection in England and highlighted problems with the 'unmanageable workloads' of social workers.

There are serious pressures in many parts of the country in what is very demanding and difficult work, made harder by the economic downturn increasing workloads further, while media attention is sharply focused on the profession. Ongoing debate about the level of resources directed towards social work offers challenging prospects for future generations of social workers. Perhaps unsurprisingly, some 10% of social worker posts remain unfilled, and both recruitment and retention are causing problems for employers.

Related Occupations

You might also consider: probation officer, residential care home manager, teacher (secondary), nurse, occupational therapist, psychologist, police officer, prison governor or youth worker.

Impact on Lifestyle

Most social workers are involved in a system providing cover 24 hours a day, seven days a week. This means that your hours are likely to be long and irregular. You may well be required to work a rota system or to be on call at times after your official hours of work, for which you may get extra pay. You may find yourself facing difficult situations, which can be unpleasant and at times dangerous. For example, you may need to call on someone with a history of violence or visit clients living in a squat.

Earnings Potential

There are no fixed grades for social workers, as each employing organisation negotiates within certain guidance. A social worker in the National Health Service would normally be on a starting salary of £26,565 to £35,577 (more in London), with opportunities for progression to more senior posts.

Further Information

Step up to Social Work
www.gov.uk/guidance/step-up-to-social-work-information-for-applicants
Frontline
www.thefrontline.org.uk
Think Ahead
http://thinkahead.org
Scottish Social Services Council
www.sssc.uk.com
Social Care Wales
https://socialcare.wales
British Association of Social Workers
www.basw.co.uk/social-work-careers
Community Care
www.communitycare.co.uk
Irish Association of Social Workers
www.iasw.ie

What is Involved?

As a solicitor, your job would be to provide clients with skilled legal advice and representation, including representing them in court. You might, like most solicitors, work in a 'private practice' partnership or you might work as an employed solicitor for central or local government, the Crown Prosecution/Procurator Fiscal Service, the magistrates/district courts or a commercial or industrial organisation. Your work could be general in nature - wills, divorce settlements, property sales, criminal cases and compensation for injury - or you could become expert in, for example, company, criminal, taxation, European, international or environmental law. You could concentrate on work with legally aided clients (although these cases have halved in number since 2013), who could not normally afford a solicitor's fees, or you could specialise in advising multi-national corporate clients on urgent, multi-million pound deals.

Opportunities for Training

The quickest route to qualification in England and Wales is by means of a qualifying law degree. If you take a degree in a subject other than law, you would have to complete a one-year full-time (or two-year part-time) course leading to the Common Professional Examination (CPE) or the Graduate Diploma in Law (GDL). After successful completion of the academic stage, you would have to undertake a Legal Practice Course (LPC), before entering a training contract with a firm of solicitors or other approved organisation (such as a local authority or the Crown Prosecution Service), gaining practical experience in a variety of areas of law. This vocational stage can be full- or part-time. An alternative route would be to train as a legal executive and use this as a stepping-stone to qualification as a solicitor. See our separate article on 'Legal Executive'. Look out also for the new Legal Apprenticeship scheme, which could lead to qualification as a solicitor over a five- to six-year programme.

In Scotland, you would need a degree in Scots Law or a three-year pre-Diploma training contract, together with the 26-week Diploma in Legal Practice. You would follow this with a two-year training contract with a practising solicitor in Scotland, towards the end of which you would have to sit a Test of Professional Competence to determine whether you are a 'fit and proper person' to enter the profession. Separate training routes apply in Northern Ireland and the Republic of Ireland.

Requirements for Entry

Competition for places to read law is exceptionally strong and university admissions tutors expect high grades at A level/Advanced Higher, Higher or equivalent. No particular subjects are specified. You will have to take the National Admissions Test for Law (LNAT) to secure a place on a Law degree at nine of the most prestigious UK universities.

Kind of Person

You would need excellent written, verbal and interpersonal skills, together with the ability to read widely and take in considerable amounts of information. You would spend a lot of time interviewing clients in order to establish the facts of a case and form an opinion. Much of what you are told by clients would be confidential and they would need to be sure that it should remain so. You may be involved with complex financial issues, including company accounts and taxation, so a good standard of numeracy would be important.

Broad Outlook

Like the rest of the world, the legal profession faced a difficult time in the downturn that started in 2008. This has had a knock-on effect for junior lawyers, especially trainees and students, who have found themselves facing a tougher employment market than usual. In the short term, training contract places and newly-qualified positions are proving very difficult to find. The Legal Education and Training Review suggests that competition to enter the profession is likely to continue to be strong for the remainder of the period to 2020, although there was a 9% rise in the number of trainee registrations in 2015.

Related Occupations

You might also consider: advocate/barrister, court legal adviser/justice's clerk/court clerk, legal executive, licensed conveyancer, paralegal, patent attorney, civil service fast streamer or civil service executive officer.

Impact on Lifestyle

The training can be very expensive, especially if you choose not to take a law degree, leaving you with even larger loans to repay when you start training than most other students. Most solicitors work normal office hours, although you may have to put in many additional hours to complete work on time. Sometimes you may be on call, in the evenings or at weekends, to deal with clients who have been taken to a police station. Legal aid work can be poorly paid and demanding but would give you valuable experience in dealing with a wide range of cases.

Earnings Potential

The Law Society recommends that, as a matter of good practice, trainee solicitors should receive a minimum salary of £20,913 in London and £18,547 elsewhere. Commercial firms in the City of London usually offer considerably more, currently around £39,000 to £40,000. The average annual salary for a lawyer is around £51,500. A partner in a large firm would expect to earn £100,000 plus.

The Law Society of Scotland recommends that trainee solicitors be paid £17,545 in the first year of their traineeship and £21,012 in the second, although some of the larger commercial law firms are known to pay trainees significantly higher salaries. As a newly qualified solicitor, you might expect to be paid about £25,000 if you work for a small firm and about £30,000 or over if you work for one of the larger commercial firms in Edinburgh or Glasgow.

Further Information

Law Careers
www.lawcareers.net
Law Society Junior Lawyers
http://communities.lawsociety.org.uk/junior-lawyers
Solicitors Regulation Authority
www.sra.org.uk
Law Central Applications Board
www.lawcabs.ac.uk
Law Society of Scotland
www.lawscot.org.uk
Law Society of Northern Ireland
www.lawsoc-ni.org
National Admissions Test for Law
www.lnat.ac.uk
Law Society of Ireland
www.lawsociety.ie

Speech and Language Therapist

What is Involved?

As a speech and language therapist (SLT), you would be a specialist in communication disorders. The ability to communicate is central to all that we do: who we are, how we learn and how we relate to each other at home, at school and at work. Your aim would be to help the thousands of people who fail to access education, social, economic and career opportunities due to communication difficulties.

In your work, you would assess and diagnose the people under your care or who have been referred to you, developing a programme of care to maximise their communication potential. You would also work to support people with swallowing, eating and drinking difficulties. You would work directly with a person with communication difficulties but would also be involved in breaking down communication barriers by influencing and supporting other people in their communication environment.

You might work with: people who stammer or have hearing impairments; babies with cleft palates or cerebral palsy; children who need help in learning to understand language or putting words together; adults or children involved in road traffic accidents; and adults who have had strokes or other neurological disorders.

Opportunities for Training

All speech and language therapists must complete a recognised three- or four-year degree programme and register with the Health and Care Professions Council before being able to practise.

Programmes combine academic study and practice/clinical placements. Many programmes welcome applications from suitably qualified mature students, although universities may require evidence of recent study. If you already have an honours or equivalent degree, you may be eligible to enter a two-year postgraduate qualifying programme. Subjects in related fields (for example, psychology, social sciences and linguistics) are often preferred.

You would study the normal development of language and production of speech sounds, as well as communication disorders. You would also cover aspects of psychology, particularly normal development, phonetics and linguistics, neurology, physiology and anatomy, together with acoustics and audiology (hearing), as problems in these areas can affect speech and language. The practical side of your training would involve at least 150 hours of clinical placement with a range of client groups (e.g. children with special needs or adults with acquired neurological disorders), in which you would work under the supervision of qualified colleagues.

Requirements for Entry

Most recognised degree programmes require three A level passes or five Scottish Highers as minimum entry qualifications. Some require specific GCSE and A levels, such as English and biology, so check the entry requirements with each university.

Competition for places is keen and requirements are generally higher than the minimum. All courses interview candidates and usually ask about clinical observations. Before interview, therefore, you should seek to arrange a visit to your local speech and language therapy service.

Kind of Person

Good interpersonal skills are essential. It is important that you can communicate clearly and are able to listen and so gain the trust of your patients. You would need skills in observation, analysis and problem solving as you work with patients and clients. You would need a flexible and creative approach because what works with one patient would not necessarily work with another. You should also have an interest in both science and language. It is important to keep records for each patient and monitor their progress. This demands organisational skill and the ability to work independently, as well as to be part of a team.

Broad Outlook

With austerity measures hitting all areas of public services, the Royal College of Speech and Language Therapists fears that the services essential to people who need support with communicating and swallowing could be under threat and that the profession could be heading for a difficult period. As a result, it has set in motion the ongoing 'Giving Voice' campaign to highlight the cost-saving, life-transforming work of SLTs.

Related Occupations

You may be interested in other therapy-based professions in the medical field, such as occupational therapist, radiographer, physiotherapist or podiatrist/chiropodist. Alternatively, you might be interested in becoming a teacher (secondary), teacher (primary) or an educational psychologist or clinical psychologist.

Impact on Lifestyle

NHS SLTs work a 36-hour week, usually Monday to Friday, but you should be prepared to work extra hours occasionally. In private practice, the hours may be longer and can involve some unsocial hours, but the earnings are likely to be higher. You may be required to travel to different locations during your working day.

Earnings Potential

A newly qualified NHS SLT would start in Band 5, on a scale ranging from £22,128 to £28,746. This could rise to £41,787 for an advanced SLT at the top of the scale and to over £69,000 for a consultant. Additional allowances are paid for appointments in and around London, ranging from 20% of basic salary for Inner London, to 15% for Outer London and 5% for the London Fringe. Salaries in the private sector are often linked to NHS levels but may be higher.

Further Information

Royal College of Speech and Language Therapists
www.rcslt.org

Health and Care Professions Council
www.hcpc-uk.org

Health Careers
www.healthcareers.nhs.uk

Association of Speech and Language Therapists in Independent Practice
www.helpwithtalking.com

Afasic - Voice for Life
www.afasic.org.uk

Irish Association of Speech and Language Therapists
www.iaslt.ie

Sports Coach

What is Involved?

As a sports coach, you would help people participating in sports to work towards achieving their full potential. You might support professional sportspeople, community teams or school groups, working with them closely to improve performance. You might also have a role in encouraging under-represented groups or young people to participate in sporting activities.

Your work would involve bringing out ability by identifying needs and planning and implementing suitable training programmes. You would aim to develop participants' physical and psychological fitness and provide the best possible practical conditions in order to maximise their performance.

Beyond the glamour of a handful of top professional opportunities, many coaches combine coaching with another job. Their work is often part-time and unpaid, offering coaching services on a purely voluntary basis.

Opportunities for Training

The national governing bodies (NGB) often provide part- or full-time courses in their own sports areas. For example, bodies such as the LTA (Lawn Tennis Association), the PGA (Professional Golfers Association) and the RYA (Royal Yachting Association) offer courses for coaches and provide official recognition and registration. There is some higher education provision with higher national diploma (HND) courses and foundation degrees in leisure studies, and more especially degree courses in PE, movement studies, sports science or coaching.

The UK Coaching Certificate (UKCC) endorses many NGB qualifications, giving coaches a nationally recognised qualification and also a progressive development pathway. The qualifications begin at Level 1 and go up to Level 4, to help you coach safely and effectively at different stages of your coaching career. There are currently more than 30 sports with UKCC endorsement. Each sport's programme varies, depending on the nature of the sport.

Requirements for Entry

For entry to a sports-related degree or to teacher training, you would normally need two or three A level/Advanced Higher, three or four Higher or equivalent qualifications, together with a good spread of GCSE/S Grade passes 9-4/A*-C/1-3, including English, maths and a science for teacher training courses. HNDs would require one A level/Advanced Higher, two Higher or equivalent qualifications. You would need to be very fit and many courses would look for evidence of sporting achievement.

Kind of Person

In addition to physical fitness, you would need good verbal communication skills, sensitivity to others, the capacity to mix praise and criticism in acceptable doses, powers of analysis, persistence, organisation and stamina. As a professional representative of your sport, you would usually be expected to set an example to others in terms of your behaviour, appearance and adherence to the code of conduct laid down by your governing body.

Broad Outlook

Opportunities for coaching vary depending on the sport. Full-time jobs are mainly in professional sports such as football, cricket, tennis, golf and athletics. Competition for jobs at this level is very fierce. Most other jobs are part-time or voluntary.

With experience and advanced qualifications, you could become a coach development officer or senior coach with a regional or national team, or with an NGB.

Coaches in professional sport are often ex-professional sportspeople who have taken coaching qualifications after retiring.

Related Occupations

You might also consider: PE/PT teacher/instructor, professional sportsperson, youth worker, leisure services/fitness centre manager, teacher (secondary), teacher (primary), physiotherapist, chiropractor or osteopath.

Impact on Lifestyle

This can be only slightly less consuming than for the full-time sportsperson, but possibly without the same level of personal intensity. Nevertheless, it can involve working throughout the day, at weekends and, for indoor sports, during the evenings. This could be seen as one of the most sociable of career fields with the most unsocial of time schedules to meet the likely demands of clients.

Earnings Potential

The number of full-time, paid coaching positions is limited, with little standardisation in rates of pay. Salaries vary depending on the employer, whether the position is full or part-time and at what level coaching is required. In professional sport, you would be likely to receive a basic salary with bonuses, depending on how much prize money is earned or how well an individual or team performs. As a full-time coach, you might expect to start on around £17,000 to £28,000. The hourly rate can depend on how many people are being coached and at what level, but usually ranges from £10 to £25. Experienced coaches working full-time may have the potential to earn up to £100,000, although those in professional football or tennis would anticipate considerably higher financial rewards.

Further Information

Sports Coach UK
www.sportscoachuk.org

Sport and Recreation Alliance
www.sportandrecreation.org.uk

Association for Physical Education
www.afpe.org.uk

SkillsActive, Sector Skills Council for Active Leisure and Learning
www.skillsactive.com

Sports Leaders UK
www.sportsleaders.org

Sport Ireland
www.sportireland.ie

Stage Manager

What is Involved?

As a stage manager, you would liaise with all the members of a theatrical production, including the producer, director, actors, theatre manager and sound, lighting, set and costume designers. You would be the practical co-ordinator, from the planning stage before the rehearsals to the taking down of the set. On tour, you would be in charge of organising travel and accommodation for the cast, and of booking rehearsal space and time. Whatever the production, you would work very closely with the director, helping to implement his or her ideas and stage directions, collecting props and arranging sound effects, relaying the director's ideas to the set designers and making sure that actors were in the right place at the right time for rehearsals. You would also make sure that safety procedures were being followed at all times. During the actual performances, you would be present at the side of the stage, overseeing the smooth running of the production. You would normally head a team including a deputy stage manager, one or more assistants and a number of stagehands, although you might combine all of these roles in a small touring company.

Opportunities for Training

Whilst it may be possible to join a repertory company without formal training, only a very small number of people now enter the profession in this way. The more usual route would be to take a degree or diploma course at a recognised drama school, a BTEC HND in Performing Arts (Production) or a foundation degree or degree in theatre practice, theatre arts or stage management.

You may be able to take a creative apprenticeship in technical theatre and/or work towards recognised vocational qualifications in stage management.

Requirements for Entry

For a degree course entry, you would need two or three A level/Advanced Higher, three or four Higher or equivalent qualifications, together with five GCSE/S Grade passes 9-4/A*-C/1-3. For entry to an HND course you would need a minimum of one A level/Advanced Higher, two Higher or equivalent passes, together with four GCSE/S Grade passes 9-4/A*-C/1-3. There are no set entry requirements for foundation degrees, so you must check with individual providers. In many cases, relevant work experience or involvement in school or other amateur productions would prove as important as academic qualifications when applying for a place.

Kind of Person

As the essential link between all the different people in a theatre company, you would need excellent communication skills and the ability to remain calm when others around you talk of crisis. Tact and diplomacy would be valuable, together with good organisation, an eye for detail, and accuracy in keeping records. The job often calls for a blend of leadership and the willingness to work as part of a team, which would enable you to liaise with confidence between a wide variety of people, often in stressful situations. Practical ability would be useful, and you would need to be interested in both the artistic and technical sides of productions. Physical, emotional and mental stamina would be of prime importance, allied to a strong sense of determination.

Broad Outlook

Employment prospects for graduates of technical courses at drama schools are extremely good, with surveys of recent graduates across the sector showing that virtually 100% achieve employment in the industry. Some people who train and work as stage managers choose to stay in stage management all their working lives, while others might move into administration or producing. Many cross from theatre to television, to trade shows or to the music industry. The skills needed are similar, whatever the area of work. Indeed, film and television producers often look for stage management experience when recruiting for new productions. However, even experienced stage managers have periods out of work.

Related Occupations

You might also consider: actor, floor manager (TV/film)), events manager or public relations executive.

Impact on Lifestyle

You would inevitably be working long and unsocial hours, perhaps rehearsing a new production during the day and managing the current performance each evening. There could also be a good deal of travelling involved, either on tour or moving around from one contract to another. The lifestyle of a stage manager would not necessarily fit well with family or social commitments.

Earnings Potential

A typical starting salary for an assistant stage manager would be around £18,000 to £26,000, rising to around £28,000 to £40,000 for a stage manager. Your salary level would depend on the company and the type of contract under which you are employed. Subsistence and touring allowances may also be paid. Freelance stage managers tend to earn more, particularly in the West End theatres. Minimum rates for stage managers are set by Equity, the performers' and entertainment workers' trade union. The 2014 minimum for a large West End theatre was £735.40 per week.

Further Information

Association of British Theatre Technicians
www.abtt.org.uk

Stage Management Association
www.stagemanagementassociation.co.uk

Equity
www.equity.org.uk

Creative Skillset
http://creativeskillset.org/who_we_help/young_creative_talent

Creative and Cultural Skills
https://ccskills.org.uk/careers/advice/article/stage-manager

Apprenticeships
www.getingofar.gov.uk

National Association for Youth Drama in Ireland
http://nayd.ie

Stockbroker

What is Involved?

Your role as a stockbroker would be to buy and sell securities on behalf of clients. You may be known as an investment manager or wealth manager if your clients are primarily private individuals. Securities are bonds, stocks and shares, which are used by the government and companies when they wish to raise additional capital. Government bonds carry fixed rates of interest but company shares can fluctuate in value in accordance with the fortunes of the company and the shareholder can make a profit or loss on them.

It would be very important, therefore, for you to be aware of the details of a company's performance and state of health, together with the economic trends of the whole stocks and shares market, so that you can advise your clients satisfactorily about whether to invest their money, to hold or to sell those shares they already have. Your clients may be individuals, companies (for example insurance companies) or institutions, such as those acting on behalf of pension funds. Trading is carried out by telephone and computer.

Opportunities for Training

All firms employing stockbrokers must be members of the Stock Exchange and you would have to be registered as an appropriately qualified person with the Financial Conduct Authority (FCA). To achieve this, you must pass the examinations administered by the Chartered Institute for Securities and Investment (CISI) or the CFA Society of the UK. These include the CISI level 4 Diploma in Investment Advice or the level 7 Chartered Wealth Manager, or the CFA Investment Management Certificate. You could also be eligible if you are a Fellow or Associate of the Faculty or Institute of Actuaries, or if you have completed the Financial Services, Planning and Management degree at Manchester Metropolitan University.

You would normally be expected to study for the CISI or CFA examinations at home, in your own time, but your employer would organise an in-house training programme, allowing you to gain experience over a period of time in different departments and perhaps develop a special interest.

Requirements for Entry

While there are no formal educational requirements laid down for entry into stockbroking, it has become virtually an all-graduate profession. Any degree subject could be acceptable but subjects such as economics, business studies, maths, statistics and law would be particularly relevant.

For entry to a degree course, you would need two or three A level/Advanced Higher, three or four Higher or equivalent qualifications, together with a minimum of five GCSE/S Grade passes at 9-4/A*-C/1-3. You might consider a sandwich course, which would include a business placement. You may wish to continue your studies with a postgraduate Master of Business Administration (MBA) course before you apply for a post.

Kind of Person

You should be able to cope with pressure and stress, sufficiently confident to back your own judgement and willing to take risks once you have analysed all the relevant data. You would need a high standard of computer literacy, as all your dealings would work through the Stock Exchange computerised settlement system. Good communication skills would be very important, in order to present detailed information to clients, and honesty and integrity are vital, as you could be dealing with large amounts of other people's money.

Advanced numeracy skills and an understanding of what can affect share prices are also of great importance. Dealing rooms can be fraught and busy places, with an atmosphere of tension and excitement as the brokers try to do their best for their clients by buying and selling at the most advantageous prices.

Broad Outlook

The global economic crisis that started in 2008 was blamed by most commentators on reckless investment in high-risk sectors by professionals who should have known better. In this climate, stockbroking - normally one of the most sought-after careers by the most ambitious graduates - temporarily lost some of its allure. Economic recovery during the last couple of years means that stockbrokers are especially active and career opportunities have regained their former cachet. Many companies use internships as a way of screening potential candidates.

Related Occupations

You might also consider: accountant (professional), actuary, commodity broker, market maker, banking executive, corporate investment banker, economist, financial adviser, insurance broker, investment fund manager or investment analyst.

Impact on Lifestyle

Probably the most obvious effect this career would have on your life would be the high pressure and long hours that it would involve. Global markets may require unsocial hours of work and this would have to be taken into consideration, although it may be a matter of starting early and finishing late rather than working through the night.

It is also quite likely that you would have to take work home with you over the weekend. You would have to be prepared to dress smartly.

Earnings Potential

You might earn £30,000 to £40,000 at the beginning of your career, and progress over the next few years to £50,000 to £80,000, depending on your performance and promotion. Higher earners can make around £150,000 a year, and some stockbrokers earn well in excess of these figures. Performance bonuses can make you exceptionally well paid if you are successful.

Further Information

Chartered Institute for Securities and Investment
www.cisi.org

London Stock Exchange
www.londonstockexchange.com

Financial Conduct Authority
www.fca.org.uk

The Personal Investment Management & Financial Advice Association (PIMFA)
www.pimfa.co.uk

CFA Society of the UK
https://secure.cfauk.org

Trading
https://trading.co.uk

Irish Stock Exchange
www.ise.ie

Structural Engineer

What is Involved?

Working as a structural engineer, you would be involved in a specialist discipline within civil engineering, closely related to architecture. If the architect's job in a building has to do with the human aspects - how it looks, how it functions, how it can be maintained - the structural engineer's job is to ensure that it doesn't fall down in the process by designing it to be structurally sound. You would work on building projects alongside architects, civil engineers and other construction professionals, taking particular responsibility for such things as the design, analysis, building and maintenance of load-bearing or resisting structures. These might include dams, tall buildings and bridges. According to the load-bearing mechanism, your structures could be plates, shells, arches, columns, beams or catenaries.

In addition to the technical requirements of a particular project, you would be expected to consider the impact the structures you are creating could have on the surrounding countryside. This might influence: your choice of materials such as concrete or timber; your ability to recycle or re-use materials or components whilst building the structure and at the end of its life; your emphasis on ensuring minimum waste and maximum efficiency; your measures to reduce energy consumption; and your consideration of the potential to re-use the structure in the future.

Opportunities for Training

There are relatively few universities offering specific degree courses in structural engineering. Sometimes the subject is combined with architectural studies or with civil engineering. There are also civil engineering courses on which you could choose to specialise in structural analysis and design after a year or two. In all cases, it would be important to make sure that you choose a course accredited by the Institution of Structural Engineers within the Joint Board of Moderators. Sandwich courses are available, giving you the opportunity to spend some time working in industry whilst studying.

In order to become a chartered engineer, responsible for research, design and development, you would need to spend at least four years in undergraduate study, followed by postgraduate study and supervised experience. The initial requirement can be achieved by taking a four-year degree course that leads directly to an MEng. Alternatively, you could take a three-year degree course leading to a BEng and follow this with a year of more specialised postgraduate study. To become an incorporated engineer, responsible more for the efficient day-to-day management of projects, you could take the BEng route and follow this with further study and on-the-job training.

Requirements for Entry

In order to be accepted for an MEng in structural engineering, you are likely to need three A level/Advanced Higher, four Higher or equivalent qualifications, including maths and physics, together with at least five GCSE/S Grade passes at 9-4/A*-C/1-3. Entry requirements for the BEng are usually slightly lower but would still normally include maths and physics or engineering at A level/Advanced Higher or Higher.

Kind of Person

Your job would be to solve structural problems in a sensible and practical way. For this you would need to enjoy using your technical knowledge, combined with sound common sense, to reach logical conclusions about the structures you are designing and constructing. You would need a rigorous approach to each project. Much of your work would involve using sophisticated computer technology to model structures and test different design solutions before going ahead with construction.

You would work in a team and would have to be reliable and efficient, able to coordinate the work of others and to give presentations to clients. You would need to explain your ideas and plans clearly to others who often may not share your specialist knowledge.

Broad Outlook

The shift to environmental protection is creating opportunities for innovative projects in such areas as creating zero carbon, zero waste, car-free communities. Engineering UK, for example, predicts that the emerging LCEGS (low carbon and environmental goods and services) sector, also referred to as the 'green economy', will soon grow in value to £4 trillion worldwide, with its worth split across the environmental, renewable energies and low carbon sectors. LCEGS already embraces some 1.4 million companies employing around 28 million people.

There are usually good opportunities for structural engineers in the UK and abroad, as UK qualifications are recognised in many overseas countries. The industry is to a large extent dependent on the state of the economy, which determines how many new projects are likely to be started. Indeed, structural engineering projects were severely affected by the economic downturn that started in 2008. Despite a recent encouraging improvement in performance, the outlook for the sector is uncertain due to possible negative effects to the economy as the UK leaves the EU.

Related Occupations

You might be interested in another branch of engineering, such as: civil engineer, mechanical engineer or marine engineer. Alternatively, you might consider: architect, town planner, naval architect, marine engineer, surveyor (general practice) or construction manager.

Impact on Lifestyle

You are likely to spend quite a lot of time working out of the office and on site, often out of doors in all kinds of weather. You might occasionally get dirty, wet and cold. When you are working on site you may be expected to work site hours, which can be longer than normal office hours, especially during the summer months. In addition, you may be expected to travel quite long distances within the UK and overseas, which could disrupt your social and family life.

Earnings Potential

Salaries for new graduate trainees are in the region of £23,000 to £32,000. After 10 to15 years in the job, with experience and seniority, you should see your earnings rise to £40,000 to £70,000.

Further Information

Institution of Structural Engineers
www.istructe.org
Joint Board of Moderators
www.jbm.org.uk
Engineering UK
www.engineeringuk.com
Engineering Council UK
www.engc.org.uk
Association for Consultancy and Engineering
www.acenet.co.uk
Engineers Ireland
www.engineersireland.ie

Surveyor (General Practice)

What is Involved?

As a general practice surveyor you would be involved in understanding both the built and the natural environments, seeking to gauge the right balance between them, physically measuring them but also measuring their impact on people and business.

A qualification in general practice surveying can prepare you for many different jobs, among them negotiating deals connected with buying, selling and renting property; acting as an agent, buying and selling property and land on behalf of clients; assessing the environmental impact and economic viability of development; valuing land and property; compiling reports for such purposes as mortgage valuations, rent reviews and investment potential; advising on property values, land purchase, tenure issues and related legislation.

You might decide to specialise in an area such as development - working with town planners, architects, and civil and structural engineers to consider new developments and their financial implications; property management - collecting rent on behalf of a landlord, dealing with maintenance and repair and making sure tenancy agreements are followed; investment - advising clients on buying and selling individual investments or managing large property portfolios; Valuation Office Agency work - valuing property on behalf of the government, local authorities and public bodies for business rates, capital taxation, purchase and sale.

You could work in the private or public sector, based in an office for report-writing but more likely spending a lot of your time out of the office visiting sites, buildings, land and farms.

Opportunities for Training

The principal professional body is the Royal Institution of Chartered Surveyors (RICS), which offers many different routes to qualified status. You would most likely meet the academic requirement through a full- or part-time degree or diploma course in a relevant subject, although there are many other options, including postgraduate courses if your first degree is not approved, or starting as a technician and taking further qualifications on a part-time basis. Some employers may offer the opportunity to train on a degree apprenticeship programme. This route allows you to work while you study part-time for a degree in surveying.

On achieving the academic standard, you must complete at least two years structured on-the-job training in a surveyor's office (one year if you have already spent a year with a surveyor as part of a sandwich course) before attempting the Assessment of Professional Competence (APC). Whatever route you follow for the academic stage, it is successful completion of the APC which ultimately confers chartered status.

You can also qualify as a surveyor through the Faculty of Architecture and Surveying of the Chartered Institute of Building.

Requirements for Entry

You would normally need three A level/Advanced Higher, four Higher or equivalent qualifications for admission to an approved degree course. Many students opt for a more vocational route after GCSE/S Grade, following a relevant national award, for example, before progressing to higher education. Course titles include construction, land management or the built environment.

Kind of Person

The RICS stresses that good communication skills, both written and oral, are necessary for negotiating agreements, making presentations and submitting reports to clients.

It also indicates that an aptitude for maths and science can be helpful for the more technical sides of the job and that a logical, practical mind is important.

You would need to be a practical person with good observation skills and you would almost certainly require the ability to drive.

Broad Outlook

The outlook for general practice surveyors can vary depending on the state of the commercial and residential property market, which has been very weak since the recession of 2008, with a massive drop in sales, widespread redundancies, falling house prices and potential buyers finding great difficulty in securing mortgage finance. For a number of years before that, however, the market had been extremely buoyant and all the indicators suggest that it is now staging a remarkable recovery. If you pursue a career in this sector, you must accept that this is a field that fluctuates and that your prospects and your pay could rise or fall in relation to market confidence.

Surveying is an international profession and there may be opportunities to work abroad.

Related Occupations

You might also consider: estate agent, civil engineer, architect, town planner, building surveyor, hydrographic surveyor, land/geomatics surveyor, quantity surveyor and rural practice surveyor.

Impact on Lifestyle

Surveyors tend to work normal office hours, although a considerable amount of that time can be spent out of the office. Depending on your specialisation, you may have to travel considerable distances. If you are involved in estate agency, you may have to work at weekends and in the evenings in order to carry out surveys. It may prove necessary to move several times to build the right experience for your career development.

Earnings Potential

Graduate starting salaries are generally around £20,000 to £25,000, slightly higher in the London area. Salaries for qualified chartered surveyors range from around £32,000 to £45,000, while a principal might earn around £70,000. The current average is around £52,000, although top-end salaries can be over £100,000. Most surveyors receive additional benefits as part of their salary package. These may include a performance-related bonus and a company car.

Further Information

Royal Institution of Chartered Surveyors
www.rics.org

Chartered Institute of Building, Faculty of Architecture and Surveying
www.ciob.org/insight/specialinterest/architecturesurveying

University College of Estate Management
www.ucem.ac.uk

Valuation Office Agency
www.gov.uk/government/organisations/valuation-office-agency

Chartered Surveyors Training Trust
www.cstt.org.uk

Society of Chartered Surveyors, Ireland
www.scsi.ie

Teacher (Primary)

What is Involved?

As a primary school teacher, you would work with children aged between five and eleven in state and independent schools, taking responsibility for their educational, social and emotional development while in your care. In England, you would teach subjects covered by the primary national curriculum at Key Stage 1 (ages 5 to 7) and Key Stage 2 (7 to 11), including English, science, music and art. In some classes, you may have a teaching assistant to help you.

You would usually be responsible for a single class of children, although there might also be scope for teaching a particular subject - such as mathematics or foreign languages - to different classes within the school. You would also have links with parents or carers, in particular at meetings held in the evening, and with other professionals such as educational psychologists and social workers.

As a primary teacher, you would also be able to work with children under the age of five (Early Years Foundation Stage) in such settings as a children's centre or a reception class in a school.

Opportunities for Training

Recognised training is essential for teaching posts in maintained schools. You would need to undertake Initial Teacher Education or Training (ITET) and obtain Qualified Teacher Status (QTS) in England and Wales. Routes are similar in Scotland but are not described in terms of ITT/QTS and courses are geared to the specific needs of the Scottish education system.

There are several different ITET routes and you should undertake some careful research to determine which one would be the best for you. You can, for example, follow a university-led route, training to be a teacher while completing a degree or postgraduate course. This might be a BA or BSc with QTS or, in some cases, a BEd (Bachelor of Education). An alternative would be to take a first degree, usually in a National Curriculum subject, followed by a postgraduate certificate in education (PGCE). The other major route is school-led and employment-based, known either as School Direct or school-centred initial teacher training (SCITT). All ITET routes combine theoretical training with a minimum of 18 weeks' practical experience.

You may be eligible for Teach First, a two-year teacher training and leadership programme for graduates with a good degree (2:1 or higher). Training is based within schools in areas facing social and economic challenges.

Requirements for Entry

The minimum requirements for primary ITET in England/Wales are two A levels or equivalent and three GCSE Grades 9-4/A*-C or equivalent, including English, maths and a science. You will also have to pass professional skills tests in literacy and numeracy before you can be recommended for QTS.

In Scotland, you would need at least two Advanced Higher or three Higher, including English or equivalent, together with S Grades 1-3 in two other subjects, including maths at grade 1/2 or equivalent.

Kind of Person

You would need to enjoy working with children and young people and to be patient with those who find it difficult to learn. You also need to enjoy the subject or subjects that you are going to teach. Training may help you to handle difficult situations in the classroom but the enthusiasm for learning and helping others to learn must come from you. You would need to have very good communication skills, to be well organised, a good member of a team but confident enough to work on your own, and consistent and fair in your treatment of your pupils.

Broad Outlook

There will always be a need for good teachers and there are sometimes shortages, although the situation varies from subject to subject and from area to area. At present, for example, those who want to teach primary maths are in great demand in England and may be eligible for a training bursary. There are also bursaries available for certain other primary training routes. Visit the Get into Teaching website for full details.

Teachers can be promoted to posts of responsibility in academic, administrative and pastoral roles - as heads of department or year group, personal tutors, heads and deputy heads. Allowances can also be offered for additional teaching and learning responsibilities.

Related Occupations

You might also consider: teacher (secondary), educational psychologist, lecturer (further education), lecturer (higher education), nursery/early years teacher, social worker, TEFL/TESOL teacher or youth worker.

Impact on Lifestyle

Teachers are held in great esteem by some and blamed by others for many of the ills of society. Your life would probably be affected by the need to take work home with you, although good organisation and use of time in the holidays should help to cut this down. The holidays (particularly in the summer) are a great asset, though they should not be regarded as completely free - much organisation and forward planning goes on, both in and out of school.

Earnings Potential

A Newly Qualified Teacher (NQT) in England and Wales can expect to start on a scale ranging from £22,467 to £33,160 or £28,098 to £38,241 in Inner London. Headteachers can earn anything from £44,102 to £108,283 a year (£51,476 to £115,582 in Inner London), depending on the size of the school.

Further Information

Get into Teaching (England)
https://getintoteaching.education.gov.uk

Professional Skills Tests
http://sta.education.gov.uk

Teach First
www.teachfirst.org.uk

National Curriculum
www.gov.uk/national-curriculum/overview

Education Workforce Council, Wales
www.ewc.wales

General Teaching Council for Scotland
www.gtcs.org.uk

Department of Education Northern Ireland
www.education-ni.gov.uk

Department of Education and Skills, Ireland
www.education.ie

Teacher (Secondary)

What is Involved?

As a secondary school teacher, you would enable pupils to develop their abilities and aptitudes and fulfil their own individual potential. Much of a typical school day would be concerned with teaching specific subjects but you would also have a pastoral role to play - helping your pupils with personal problems and supporting them when they are faced with difficult decisions. You would also have links with parents or carers, in particular at meetings which are usually held in the evening. Preparation of lessons and marking would take up a good deal of your time. You would usually specialise in one or two national curriculum subjects, which you would teach throughout the school to different age groups from 11 to 16 or up to 19 if your school has a sixth form. Much of the work involves preparing pupils for external examinations, and you may find that you are judged by how well your pupils perform.

Opportunities for Training

Recognised training is essential for teaching posts in maintained schools. You would need to undertake Initial Teacher Education or Training (ITET) and obtain Qualified Teacher Status (QTS) in England and Wales. Routes are similar in Scotland but are not described in terms of ITET/QTS and courses are geared to the specific needs of the Scottish education system.

There are several different ITET routes and you should undertake some careful research to determine which one would be the best for you. You can, for example, follow a university-led route, training to be a teacher while completing a degree or postgraduate course. This might be a BA or BSc with QTS or, in some cases, a BEd (Bachelor of Education). An alternative would be to take a first degree, usually in a National Curriculum subject, followed by a postgraduate certificate in education (PGCE). The other major route is school-led and employment-based, known either as School Direct or school-centred initial teacher training (SCITT). You may also consider Teach First, a two-year teacher training and leadership programme for graduates with a good degree (2:1 or higher). Training is based within schools located in areas facing social and economic challenges.

All ITET routes combine theoretical training with a minimum of 18 weeks' practical experience.

Requirements for Entry

The minimum requirements for secondary ITET in England/Wales are two A levels or equivalent and three GCSE Grades 9-4/A*-C or equivalent, including English and maths. You will also have to pass professional skills tests in literacy and numeracy before you can be recommended for QTS.

In Scotland, you would need at least two Advanced Higher or three Higher, including English or equivalent, together with S Grades 1-3 in two other subjects, including maths at grade 1/2 or equivalent.

Kind of Person

You would need to enjoy working with children and young people and to be patient with those who find it difficult to learn. You also need to enjoy the subject or subjects that you are going to teach. Training may help you to handle difficult situations in the classroom but the enthusiasm for learning and helping others to learn must come from you. You would need to have very good communication skills, to be well organised, a good member of a team but confident enough to work on your own, and consistent and fair in your treatment of your pupils.

Broad Outlook

There will always be a need for good teachers and there are sometimes shortages, although the situation varies from subject to subject and from area to area. At present, for example, those who want to teach secondary physics, maths, chemistry, computing, modern foreign languages, history, English, geography, biology, design and technology, religious education or music are in great demand in England and may be eligible for a scholarship or training bursary.

Teachers can be promoted to posts of responsibility in academic, administrative and pastoral roles - as heads of department or year group, personal tutors, heads and deputy heads. Allowances can also be offered for additional teaching and learning responsibilities.

Related Occupations

You might also consider: teacher (primary), educational psychologist, lecturer (further education), lecturer (higher education), nursery/early years teacher, social worker, TEFL/TESOL teacher or youth worker.

Impact on Lifestyle

Teachers are held in great esteem by some and blamed by others for many of the ills of society. Your life would probably be affected by the need to take work home with you, although good organisation and use of time in the holidays should help to cut this down. The holidays (particularly in the summer) are a great asset, though they should not be regarded as completely free - much organisation and forward planning goes on, both in and out of school.

Earnings Potential

A Newly Qualified Teacher (NQT) in England and Wales can expect to start on a scale ranging from £22,467 to £33,160 or £28,098 to £38,241 in Inner London. Headteachers can earn anything from £44,102 to £108,283 a year (£51,476 to £115,582 in Inner London), depending on the size of the school.

Further Information

Get into Teaching (England)
https://getintoteaching.education.gov.uk

Professional Skills Tests
http://sta.education.gov.uk

Teach First
www.teachfirst.org.uk

National Curriculum
www.gov.uk/national-curriculum/overview

Education Workforce Council, Wales
www.ewc.wales

General Teaching Council for Scotland
www.gtcs.org.uk

Department of Education Northern Ireland
www.education-ni.gov.uk

Department of Education and Skills, Ireland
www.education.ie

Textile Designer

What is Involved?

As a textile designer, you would be concerned with the design of a range of fabrics or textiles that would be used mainly for producing clothes, curtains, furnishing fabrics, carpets or wallpaper. You might work initially on paper but you are more likely to use a computer with a specialist software package allowing patterns and colours to be changed rapidly and the designs to be printed out in colour for consideration and approval by clients. You would then produce samples by weaving, knitting or screen printing, taking great care to ensure the right fabrics are used in each case.

Your work would be very much influenced by changing fashion and lifestyle trends. Clients need new ideas and colour schemes and furnishing fabrics change every year, so you must constantly think ahead and anticipate the current and future moods of manufacturers and buyers. You must also take account of the manufacturing processes involved, ensuring that your designs could actually be put into production without being prohibitively expensive and that you are not specifying unrealistic colours or yarns.

Opportunities for Training

You would need to have a formal training in textile design, usually via one of the specialist courses available at degree or higher national diploma (HND) level in universities and art schools throughout the UK. Some courses focus purely on design and artistic creativity, while others are more orientated towards the technology of manufacturing or the business of marketing. You must check prospectuses carefully when researching possible courses. You might decide to continue your studies to postgraduate level before you enter the labour market.

You may also be able to enter the textile industry through an apprenticeship scheme. The range of apprenticeships in your area will depend on the local jobs market and the types of skills employers need from their workers.

Requirements for Entry

The main entry requirement for study or employment is usually a portfolio of work. This might include samples of knitting, sewing, dyeing or weaving in addition to examples of your drawing skills. Talent and creativity are usually more highly regarded than examination success, although it is always helpful and sometimes essential to have a platform of GCSE/S Grade passes 9-4/A*-C/1-3 and A level/Advanced Higher, Higher or equivalent studies, including an art-related subject.

In England and Wales, you would normally complete a one- or two-year foundation course before progressing to a three-year art and design degree. In Scotland, the foundation course is the first year of a four-year degree. The HND route is normally a year shorter and may be more closely linked to manufacturing processes.

Kind of Person

To be a successful textile designer you would need to combine artistic creativity, drawing skills and an acute awareness of colour and texture with a good understanding of the technical side of the business. You should have a keen interest in fashion and may spend some time visiting exhibitions and fashion shows to spot trends and see what other designers are doing.

You must be able to communicate your ideas visually and verbally to clients or colleagues and may need to persuade buyers to accept your work. You would also have to be prepared to see some of your ideas rejected. You would need good IT skills, especially in using computer design packages, and an understanding of how developments in technology could enhance your design concepts. Poor colour vision could present serious problems.

Broad Outlook

Textile design is a very competitive field. Even well established designers can go out of fashion and find that buyers lose interest in their work. However, the textile business is one of the largest in the world and there will always be a demand for creative and talented people. You could work for a large manufacturer or a smaller independent design house. You could set up your own business and might use an agent to market your collections to prospective buyers. British design training is valued abroad and you might choose to work overseas.

Women currently account for some 75% to 80% of the workforce.

Related Occupations

You might also consider: fashion designer, furniture designer, graphic designer, interior designer, jewellery designer or photographer.

Impact on Lifestyle

This is a global industry which means that, as well as career opportunities abroad, you could find yourself having to travel fairly extensively in order to keep up to date with trends and to visit overseas fabric manufacturers. If you are employed by a large group, you would normally work office hours from nine to five, but could also work at trade shows, which could involve weekend and evening work. As a self-employed designer, you would often need to work very long hours, late into the evening and over weekends, to establish your business and meet the last-minute deadlines of clients.

Earnings Potential

Your pay would depend upon the nature of your employment, whether for a large or small company or self-employed. Junior designers working for a textile manufacturing company usually start at about £20,000 to £25,000, which could increase to £30,000 to £40,000 as you become more experienced. Your earnings as a freelance designer would vary greatly, depending on your reputation. Paying commission to an agent would reduce your fee income but could help you establish a broad client base.

Further Information

Textile Institute
www.textileinstitute.org

Creative and Cultural Skills
http://ccskills.org.uk/careers/advice/article/textile-designer

Creative Skillset
http://creativeskillset.org/creative_industries/fashion_and_textiles

Textile Centre of Excellence
www.textilehouse.co.uk

Chartered Society of Designers
www.csd.org.uk

UK Fashion and Textile Association
www.ukft.org

Style Bible
www.stylebible.com

National College of Art and Design, Dublin
www.ncad.ie/undergraduate/school-of-design/textile-and-surface-design

Tour Operator

What is Involved?

As a tour operator, you would organise the package holidays, leisure activities, tours, expeditions, cruises and coach trips on sale at travel agents or on the internet. Details are publicised on websites, in sales brochures and advertisements, written about in newspapers and magazines and featured on radio and TV travel programmes. Working as a product manager for a tour operator, you might arrange expeditions by elephant or bicycle, journeys by Pullman train or cruise liner, or flights by hot air balloon.

You might organise accommodation in anything from a chalet to a chateau. As a contract manager, you would negotiate availability and prices with the airlines, hotels, local transport companies, attraction owners and others involved in the package. In addition, it would be vital to check the quality of food, sanitation, beaches and entertainment, usually in liaison with your local representatives.

Opportunities for Training

Many tour operators start out on an Apprenticeship, provided by numerous organisations across the country. An alternative route is to complete a relevant degree, foundation degree or diploma course, such as travel and tourism, hospitality/ hotel management, leisure and recreation, business studies, IT, marketing or modern languages. You should ideally look for a course having close links with the travel industry.

The Institute of Travel and Tourism and the Tourism Management Institute both recognise on their websites a range of undergraduate and postgraduate programmes in Tourism Management.

Requirements for Entry

There are no specific requirements needed to become a tour operator, although good GCSE or A level grades or equivalent are likely to be viewed positively. Work experience in the industry is considered highly important.

You would need at least two A level/Advanced Higher, three Higher or equivalent qualifications for degree course entry, slightly less for the HND or foundation degree. Foreign language skills would be a great asset.

Kind of Person

You would need to combine very strong organisational and entrepreneurial qualities with the vision to put together holiday packages that appeal to the public, are competitively priced and demonstrate a concern for the overall comfort and enjoyment of customers. You should enjoy travelling, visiting resorts, making new contacts and establishing friendly and long-term relationships.

Your work would call for considerable attention to detail in such matters as the accuracy of descriptions in your promotional materials or exchange rate considerations and local taxes in determining precise costs. You would also need to write contracts to establish agreements and take out appropriate insurance cover. Marketing, business administration and finance and accountancy skills would all be important, especially an understanding of how to manage cash flow in what can be a highly seasonal business.

Broad Outlook

There is no clearly defined career pathway, and opportunities for career progression will vary from employer to employer. Tour operators range from large international companies to small, specialist tour organisers who organise holidays/travel arrangements for special interest groups, such as sports teams, families, business travellers, those attending language courses and those visiting friends and relatives.

A trend in recent years has been for organisations in travel and tourism to 'integrate vertically', meaning that they become tour operators, airlines and travel agents under the same ownership. This offers the chance to change direction within the organisation, and to move up to middle or senior management. There is also scope to become self-employed, by setting up your own company once you have gained considerable knowledge of the industry.

Sustainable tourism is currently a hot topic, as tour operators try to help us plot a pathway around the planet without leaving too large a carbon footprint.

Related Occupations

You might also consider: travel agent/consultant, events manager or marketing executive.

Impact on Lifestyle

While you might work fairly standard hours in a head office post, you would usually have experienced the complete absence of set hours for a resort representative. You would often have to sort out problems at any time of the day or night in such a post, and would be expected to work for as long as it takes to resolve the issues. Frequent travel and extended absence from home would normally be a significant feature of the work and could disrupt your family and social life.

Earnings Potential

Typical starting salaries are around £15,000 to £22,000 per annum, rising with experience to £25,000 to £45,000. Some roles involving sales offer a basic salary and commission. Salaries can vary widely between employers, depending on such things as the range of duties carried out by the individual and the size of the organisation.

Further Information

Institute of Travel and Tourism
www.itt.co.uk

Association of Independent Tour Operators
www.aito.com

Tourism Management Institute
www.tmi.org.uk

Hospitality Guild
www.hospitalityguild.co.uk

Tourism Concern
www.tourismconcern.org.uk

Apprenticeships
www.getingofar.gov.uk

Incoming Tour Operators Association, Ireland
www.itoa-ireland.com

Town Planner

What is Involved?

Working as a town or spatial planner, your job would be to balance the demand for new development and buildings with the diminishing amount of land available. You would be responsible for maintaining an attractive environment that can also sustain the demands of the population who live there. You would be involved with listening to the views of a number of interested parties, including conservationists, builders, farmers and residents, before advising on planning decisions. You would need to consider future developments and demands on amenities as well as the current situation, taking into account such factors as design features, waste and environmental management, transport, urban renewal and employment or recreation demands.

You would sometimes be implementing national planning policy at a local level, such as, for example, a political preference for building on brownfield sites. You would use various sources of information, including surveys, public opinion and existing legislation, and could be involved with large-scale projects or with decisions on home extensions. You would almost certainly be required to use a wide range of skills in order to produce your reports. Much of the work is based in an office and involves the use of a computer but you would also be expected to make site visits.

Opportunities for Training

In order to work as a town planner, a Royal Town Planning Institute (RTPI) accredited qualification is essential. To become a chartered town planner, the accredited academic qualifications must be supported by two years' work experience.

If you wish to study town planning as your first degree, there are specialist town and country planning or urban studies degrees, accredited by the RTPI. These courses provide the full planning education in four years (five if on a sandwich course), which includes a three-year undergraduate BA degree and a one-year postgraduate diploma. The courses are also available part-time and by distance learning. Graduates who are not from RTPI-accredited planning courses will need a recognised postgraduate qualification. Subjects such as economics, engineering, environmental studies, geography, law, politics or social studies could all help prepare for a career in planning. You then have the option of taking an RTPI-accredited conversion Masters.

There is also an apprenticeship in town planning technical support; this could qualify you to work as a planning technician or enforcement officer.

Requirements for Entry

For a first degree in town planning, you would need two or three subjects at A level/ Advanced Higher, three or four Higher or equivalent qualifications, together with at least three GCSE/S Grade passes at 9-4/A*-C/1-3. A few universities specify particular subjects but most are looking for a combination of arts and science subjects. Geography can be a useful subject to offer. The content of the courses can vary considerably, so it is important to study the prospectus carefully to make sure that the course on offer covers areas of interest to you. Work experience is a good idea because it gives you a chance to find out about the range of options available.

Kind of Person

You should be committed to achieving the best possible quality of life in your area without causing undue damage to the environment. You would need to communicate effectively with a wide range of people and to listen to their views. Your job would involve writing clear reports in language that can be easily understood and you would at times be required to work under pressure to meet tight deadlines. You would have to speak at public meetings and would need to be persuasive or assertive if your audience is hostile. You would probably be responsible for managing other staff.

Broad Outlook

Like the construction industry generally, planning has highs and lows reflecting the state of the national economy. In the downturn that started in 2008, the building sector shrank considerably and with it opportunities for town planners. However, the UK construction industry has turned around over the past couple of years to become one of the fastest-growing sectors in the economy, offering new hope for planners in the years to come if leaving the EU does not reverse the UK economy's fortunes.

The government's new Housing and Planning Act and the National Planning Policy Framework, intended to make the planning system less complex and more accessible, have prompted fierce debate between traditionalists and reformers. Insiders fear that the new proposals could lead to both job cuts in the industry and shortcuts in working practice.

The environmental field is a growing area of work, offering increasing opportunities for professionals to become involved in the planning process for environmentally sensitive development schemes.

Related Occupations

You might also consider: civil engineer, construction manager, building control officer/ surveyor, architect, landscape architect, surveyor (general practice) or cartographer.

Impact on Lifestyle

You may have to travel quite large distances to get to planning sites, or find that you have to move around the country in order to find the job you want or to gain promotion. Most planners who work for local authorities work a 37-hour week although you might be expected to attend planning meetings in the evenings.

Earnings Potential

In the public sector, starting annual salaries range from £18,000 to £28,000, rising with experience to £30,000 to £45,000. Chief planning officers, heads of departments and directors can earn between £55,000 and £80,000, with an average salary of about £64,000. The higher salaries in these ranges are paid by local authorities where there is a scarcity of planners, for example London boroughs or local authorities in the South East.

Pay in the private sector is generally comparable with that in the public sector. There are no set scales and individual salaries are usually a matter for negotiation with the employer.

Further Information

Royal Town Planning Institute
www.rtpi.org.uk

Planning Officers Society
www.planningofficers.org.uk

National Planning Policy Framework
www.gov.uk/guidance/national-planning-policy-framework

RTPI Ireland
www.rtpi.org.uk/the-rtpi-near-you/rtpi-ireland

Trading Standards Officer

What is Involved?

As a trading standards officer (TSO), you would usually work within local government, enforcing the law and regulations that govern goods and services which we buy, hire and sell. You would be championing the rights of the consumer by making sure that they were not being cheated, which could involve anything from checking the scales of a local trader to testing the claims made about a product by its manufacturer or importer.

You might take samples of pre-packed food to ensure that the correct weight is shown; you might check weighing machines, beer and spirit measures and labelling. Another important aspect would be identifying potential hazards or unsafe products.

Sometimes a case may involve action in the criminal court, requiring you to investigate possible criminal offences and attend as a witness or present cases in the Magistrates Court. Although you would have to write up reports in an office, you would also be out in the local community.

The exact nature of the work would vary according to your location. In a rural area, you might spend much time on animal health ensuring, for example, proper transport of livestock to market. As a city-based officer, you could be more concerned with street traders and problems of counterfeit goods. In a port, you might work with customs to vet imported goods.

Opportunities for Training

The most direct entry route is via a consumer-related degree accredited by the Chartered Trading Standards Institute (CTSI) and then a trainee trading standards officer post. Five universities offer approved degrees: Manchester Metropolitan, Nottingham Trent, Teesside, Cardiff Metropolitan, and Glasgow Caledonian. Local authorities sometimes sponsor students on these courses. Trainee TSO vacancies with local authorities are also open to graduates of any subject via a postgraduate diploma course, although a degree in law, retail management or food science may improve your chances.

The Trading Standards Qualifications Framework (TSQF) delivered by CTSI provides three levels of qualification:

- Core Skills in Consumer Affairs and Trading Standards
- Diploma in Consumer Affairs and Trading Standards (DCATS)
- Higher Diploma in Consumer Affairs and Trading Standards

This allows TSQF to be used both as qualification and as continuous professional development. The framework is modular, with each module consisting of both examinations and assessment of a portfolio of evidence. A recognised degree provides exemption from most examinations.

Requirements for Entry

Entry to an approved specialist degree would require two or three A level/Advanced Higher, three Higher or equivalent qualifications, together with five GCSE/S Grade passes 9-4/A*-C/1-3. Relevant experience would be an absolute requirement before you could take the DCATS examinations.

As an alternative to starting with a consumer protection degree, you might apply for a post as a consumer adviser or trainee enforcement officer with a local authority. You would then study towards professional qualifications on the job as you work your way up to TSO. Previous experience of legal, retail or advice work would be useful.

Kind of Person

You would need to be firm but tactful, not easily intimidated. You would need a good memory for all the relevant legislation and the ability for assessing the key facts in each situation. It would be vital to have a very keenly observant eye for possible deviations from the law. You would need the confidence and integrity to stand up for your views and make some unpopular decisions. This could involve explaining your cases with precision and clarity in courts of law, so some public speaking experience could help. You would also need to be able to write clear reports.

Broad Outlook

Trading standards officers are employed throughout the UK and there is a clear promotion structure, i.e. senior officer to section head, divisional officer and then to deputy or chief trading standards officer. Departments are usually small, however, so promotion often calls for mobility.

There are increasing controls and regulations and consumers are complaining more, so there is plenty of work to be done. Local authority budgets have, however, been reduced and finding a training place can be very difficult. You may choose to develop your career by moving into the private sector, where you might advise on quality control or consumer law in the manufacturing, food or retail sectors.

Related Occupations

You might also consider: environmental health practitioner, health and safety adviser, health and safety inspector, police officer or quality assurance manager.

Impact on Lifestyle

You would normally expect to work regular office hours but the process of deregulation means that shops and public houses now have longer opening hours and can trade seven days a week. You may have to follow up certain complaints or queries during these 'non-traditional' times.

Earnings Potential

As a trainee local government trading standards officer, you might expect to earn around £19,000 to £23,000, rising on qualification to £27,000 to £37,000. Senior managers may earn considerably more, usually around £50,000 to £70,000. For further information about salaries for particular positions, contact your local council directly.

Private sector opportunities are usually paid at senior manager level and above.

Further Information

Chartered Trading Standards Institute
www.tradingstandards.uk

Local Government Association
www.local.gov.uk

Department for the Economy, Northern Ireland
www.economy-ni.gov.uk

Regulatory Delivery
www.gov.uk/government/organisations/regulatory-delivery

Contact your local authority and ask to speak to the manager of the trading standards department.

Translator

What is Involved?

As a translator, you would be a highly skilled linguist specialising in the written word. You would normally translate into your mother tongue and would be required to produce authentic, idiomatic and accurate versions, which mirror the tone and levels of meaning of the originals. In literary areas, style and idiom would predominate, but most translation work is in commercial, legal, scientific or technical material, where accuracy and understanding are much more important. Your work may span a very broad spectrum, from medicine, tourism or engineering to law, politics or finance, and could include legal contracts, scientific articles, technical manuals, promotional brochures or business letters.

Opportunities for Training

You would normally be expected to study one or more foreign languages to degree level. It could be helpful if the course includes modules in translation or if you combine language studies with a subject such as business, law, computing or engineering. Almost all courses of this kind would give you the opportunity, which you should take, to spend at least a year abroad. You may be expected to work towards the level 7 diploma in translating and you would usually need to join and pass the examinations of professional organisations such as the Chartered Institute of Linguists (IOL), the Institute of Translation and Interpreting (ITI), and/or the Translators Association of the Society of Authors (for literary work).

Requirements for Entry

For entry to a degree course, you would usually need two or three A levels/ Advanced Highers, three or four Highers or equivalent, including a good pass in at least one foreign language. You would need a good first degree for progression to a postgraduate course. Vocational qualifications do not always require any formal academic record and could prove attractive if you have advanced linguistic skills, cultural awareness or technical knowledge but do not want to go to university. You may, for example, have come to translating through a bilingual upbringing, residence abroad or regular contact with speakers of your second language. You would have to provide evidence of your ability by maintaining a detailed record of texts translated and building a portfolio of your best work.

Kind of Person

You must be able to write impeccably in your mother tongue, preferably in a variety of styles. An enquiring mind would be essential, with a particular interest in researching and understanding commercial or technical issues. In addition to your mastery of at least one foreign language, you must have a thorough knowledge of the institutions, culture, attitudes and practices in the countries where that language is spoken, normally acquired through residence there.

You would need to be capable of working alone in front of a computer screen, armed with specialist dictionaries and reference books, working at speed to find the right words and phrases. Editing and IT skills would come together in the growing use of computerised translating programs, which produce fast but rough drafts for revision to an acceptable final standard.

Broad Outlook

While some international organisations, government departments, multinational companies and aid agencies employ their own translating teams, the majority of translators are self-employed. Languages in demand in business include Japanese, Chinese and European Union languages, especially those of the newer member states.

Competition for contracts is intense and you would need to be very skilled, professional and businesslike to succeed. A lot of work is passed on by the recommendation of colleagues, so it would be an advantage to make yourself known to others in the profession.

Related Occupations

You might also consider: teacher (secondary), secretary linguist, interpreter, tour operator or diplomatic service officer.

Impact on Lifestyle

You can choose your own hours if you are working from home, sending and receiving material by email. However, the work can be unpredictable and you may need to supplement your income with other activities, especially teaching. As a staff translator, you would be more likely to work normal office hours from Monday to Friday, with occasional overtime if a translation is needed urgently.

Earnings Potential

How much you earn could depend on your language combinations, your subject areas and your speed and reputation. You would normally quote a freelance rate based on every 1,000 words translated, ranging from around £75 to £100 per 1,000 words for French or German to £180 for every 1,000 Chinese characters. Translators often agree fees per project, based on a word count of around 2,000 to 3,000 words per day. Salaries for full-time employment vary considerably, starting at around £19,000 to £21,000 for a young graduate. Generalist translators earn between £25,000 and £30,000, and specialist translators between £30,000 and £35,000. Senior translators earn £60,000 plus. The European Commission and United Nations are the best paying employers of senior translators.

Further Information

Institute of Translation and Interpreting
www.iti.org.uk

Chartered Institute of Linguists
www.ciol.org.uk

Careers with the European Union
http://europa.eu/epso/index_en.htm

Association of Translation Companies
www.atc.org.uk

Society of Authors Translators Association
www.societyofauthors.org/Groups/Translators

Irish Translators' and Interpreters' Association
www.translatorsassociation.ie

Travel Agent/Consultant

What is Involved?

As a travel agent or travel consultant, you would sell holidays on behalf of tour operators, together with air, ferry, train and coach tickets, hotel reservations, car hire services, tours and expeditions, theatre seats and insurance. You might work with the general travelling public or specialise in services for business customers and you would sometimes be asked to arrange complete itineraries.

Some travel agencies are independently owned, while others are part of chains that market their own tours and package holidays as well as those of other tour operators. Traditionally, most travel agencies in the UK had high street, shop-front premises, where you would inform and negotiate with clients and check availability before completing a sale. However, online agencies now account for over half of the industry's revenue.

Opportunities for Training

Many young people enter through Apprenticeships provided by national and local training providers. They work towards vocational qualifications at levels 2 and 3 in travel and tourism, together with other appropriate travel-related qualifications. Some gain qualifications in customer service.

It can be helpful to have qualifications in travel and tourism, gained through a college course and/or previous employment, but this is not essential. Useful qualifications include:

- Level 1 Certificate/Diploma Introduction to the Travel and Tourism Industry
- Level 1/2 Certificate in Travel and Tourism (Air Fares and Ticketing)
- Level 2 Award in Principles of Customer Service in Hospitality, Leisure, Travel and Tourism
- Level 2 Certificate/Diploma in Travel and Tourism

Some colleges also offer the Guild of Travel Management Companies (GTMC) Certificate in Business Travel, available at three levels for those who want to specialise in this area.

Alternatively, you might consider a degree, foundation degree or higher national diploma (HND) in travel and tourism or a related subject.

Requirements for Entry

Experience is generally regarded as far more important than academic success. There are no specific entry requirements, although individual employers might look for GCSE/S Grade passes 9-4/A*-C/1-3, including English, maths, geography and modern languages. You would need at least two A level/Advanced Higher, three Higher or equivalent qualifications for degree course entry, slightly less for the HND.

Kind of Person

To be a successful travel agent, you would need to be a good communicator and come across as friendly and helpful. You would be selling holidays and travel-related products and would therefore need to be enthusiastic and a good salesperson. A retentive memory and a thorough knowledge of hotels, resorts and travel possibilities would be very helpful in building trust and retaining your clients, together with a good working knowledge of geography for discussing possible destinations.

You would have to be very efficient and organised, as you would often be dealing with more than one client at a time and it would be essential not to make mistakes with reservations and tickets. You would be dealing with prices and overall costs of holidays, so you would need to be numerate. You should also have good IT skills, as computers are always used for making bookings and finding up-to-date information. You should have a smart appearance and you should have the ability both to listen carefully and to make suitable travel suggestions.

Broad Outlook

The travel industry has been very volatile in recent years, with many well-known brands disappearing and a small number of large organisations dominating the market. If Brexit does not halt the UK economy's recent improvement, the future will hold better prospects than travel agents have seen since the recession started in 2008.

Opportunities exist with organisations ranging from small, independent travel agencies to large travel chains with many branches, together with business travel management companies. You may choose to specialise in a niche market, catering specifically for customers looking for a certain type of holiday - e.g. safari holidays, or sports holidays. As more people use the internet to make their travel arrangements, there is also work available in online contact centres, selling holidays to customers.

Sustainable tourism is currently a hot topic, as travel specialists try to help us plot a pathway around the planet without leaving too large a carbon footprint.

Related Occupations

You might also consider: tour operator, leisure services/fitness centre manager, customer service manager or resort representative.

Impact on Lifestyle

You would normally work shop hours from Monday to Saturday, although you may have to work some evenings and Sundays as well in a busy shopping centre. You may find that you are required to go to resorts abroad for research purposes but this would usually be seen as an occasional perk of the job.

Earnings Potential

Salaries vary greatly between agencies, with larger chains generally paying higher rates. As a recent graduate, you might start on around £15,000 to £25,000. Typical salaries at senior level range from £25,000 to £45,000.

Further Information

Careers That Move
http://careersthatmove.co.uk
Hospitality Guild
www.hospitalityguild.co.uk
Institute of Travel and Tourism
www.itt.co.uk
ABTA - The Travel Association
http://abta.com
Guild of Travel Management Companies
www.gtmc.org
Apprenticeships
www.getingofar.gov.uk
TTG Media
www.ttgmedia.com
Irish Travel Agents Association
www.itaa.ie

TV/Film Camera Operator

What is Involved?

As a camera operator in the TV/film industry, you would use different types of camera to record action on film, videotape or digital media. You might work on large- or small-scale productions in a studio; you might be part of an outside broadcast team covering sports fixtures or public ceremonies; or you might use special lightweight equipment in a small newsgathering team.

You would mostly be expected to follow instructions from a director, although you would usually be invited to contribute ideas for camera positions and shots during rehearsals. Depending on the budget and resources of the project on which you are working, you may be part of a team or you may have to operate sound and other equipment in addition to your main work with the camera.

Most camera operators begin their careers as trainees or runners, progressing to 2nd assistant camera (clapper loader) and, as they gain more experience, to 1st assistant camera (focus puller). Once they achieve a high level of competence when operating a variety of cameras, they may become a director of photography or a camera operator.

Traditionally, you would have had to specialise in either film or television work, as there were differences in equipment and techniques. However, digital cameras and HD technology now make it easier for camera professionals to work across all sectors.

Opportunities for Training

No specific qualifications are required for this type of work, although film schools and training courses offer a good basic grounding in the skills and knowledge required. In practice, many camera operators study for higher level qualifications before starting work. The most useful courses offer practical experience and may also include work experience placements. Relevant courses include City and Guilds courses, BTEC HNC/HNDs, foundation degrees, first degrees and postgraduate qualifications in media, film and TV production or cinematography. Basic stills photography, which develops visual and composition skills, also provides a useful starting point.

You may be able to train through an advanced apprenticeship in Creative and Digital Media. Visit the Creative Skillset website for more information. There may also be limited training opportunities with Creative Scotland. It is important to get practical experience in any way you can, even if it means initially working for nothing. The Trainee Finder programme could help you find a work placement, develop skills and cultivate strong networks in the film industry.

Requirements for Entry

You should have a portfolio of photographs or film - ideally a showreel DVD of productions that you have worked on - and you should be able to demonstrate a keen interest in film and television. It would help if you had A level/Advanced Higher, Higher or equivalent qualifications and enough understanding of maths and physics to appreciate the technical aspects of film-making and broadcasting. You would need to be physically fit to be able to move equipment that is often heavy.

Kind of Person

In order to succeed in this kind of work you would need to be passionately interested in film photography and prepared to put up with short-term contracts, uncertainty of employment, lots of pressure and long working hours. You must be a team player, with a good eye for colour and composition. The work can be creative but also requires a high standard of technical awareness. Good eyesight and normal colour vision are essential, together with good hand/eye co-ordination. Some camera positions call for a head for heights!

Broad Outlook

You would almost certainly work on a freelance basis, building up a network of personal contacts and establishing a reputation for certain types of work. Small independent production companies spring up on a regular basis, in addition to the established film and television organisations, usually offering new work opportunities but most often on short-term contracts. You will increase your chances of a successful career if you are prepared to go anywhere in the UK or overseas to work. It is common to get work by contacting companies yourself, networking and word of mouth, and using a crew directory or diary service to market yourself. Competition for work is fierce.

Related Occupations

You might wish to consider: photographer, production assistant/runner, videographer, or - with sufficient experience - film/TV director.

Impact on Lifestyle

Initially, you can expect long hours, low wages and endless pressure. The early jobs are not likely to be very glamorous although later on they may well be. In the world of film and television, the hours always tend to be irregular, starting early, finishing late and often involving waiting around for hours on standby. If you work as a news camera operator, you may find yourself abroad, sometimes in potentially dangerous situations.

Earnings Potential

You could find yourself sometimes working for next to nothing, gaining experience and hoping that you will receive a retrospective payout if the film turns out to be a commercial success. At other times, you might be on a daily or weekly rate, depending on the project. Working in TV drama may earn you around £1,500 for a full week's work. On a low-budget feature film, you may earn around £1,900 a week, rising to around £2,350 a week on a major feature film. On commercials, you may earn around £460 for 10 hours a day. You would need your own camera kit (which can cost thousands of pounds) or to hire equipment. You would also need to keep equipment up to date. BECTU offers advice on its website about freelance rates.

Further Information

Creative Skillset
www.creativeskillset.org
BBC Academy
www.bbc.co.uk/academy
Trainee Finder
https://app.hiive.co.uk/traineefinder
Creative Scotland
www.creativescotland.com
Guild of Television Cameramen
www.gtc.org.uk
BECTU (Broadcasting Entertainment Cinematograph and Theatre Union)
www.bectu.org.uk
Guild of British Camera Technicians
www.gbct.org
Irish Film and Television Network
www.iftn.ie

Veterinary Nurse

What is Involved?

As a veterinary nurse, you would be involved in caring for animals before, during and after treatment by a veterinary surgeon. You could be required to carry out treatments such as administering drugs, taking x-rays and preparing animals for surgery. You may also offer advice to owners, for example on post-operative care.

You would be working mainly with domestic pets but could be required to cope with horses, farm animals or even zoo animals.

Your job would also include clerical and administrative work in a veterinary practice, such as keeping records, filing reports, answering the telephone and dealing with reception.

Opportunities for Training

There is a non-statutory register of veterinary nurses, for which you would need a qualification recognised by the Royal College for Veterinary Surgeons (RCVS). For many people, the level 3 diploma in veterinary nursing is the recognised training route. It normally takes two to three years to complete. This qualification comprises a core and two option pathways, one in small animal nursing and one in equine nursing. You must complete the core units and an optional pathway in order to gain the Diploma. Your work-based clinical skills will be recorded using an electronic Nursing Progress Log (NPL), which will provide a record of all the clinical skills you have learned, practised and reached competence in. You may be able to train via an advanced apprenticeship in Veterinary Nursing. To enrol, you will need to find work as a trainee with an approved veterinary training practice before you can start.

Alternatively, you can undertake a Veterinary Nursing foundation or BSc honours degree. Training takes between three and four years, depending on the type of course you choose.

Requirements for Entry

You would need a minimum of five GCSE/S Grade passes 9-4/A*-C/1-3, including English, maths and a biological or physical science. Alternatively, an Animal Nursing Assistant (ANA) or Veterinary Care Assistant(VCA) qualification (with Functional Skills Level 2 in Application of Number and Communication) would be acceptable for enrolment.

Entry to a degree course is usually with five GCSE/S grade passes 9-4/A*-C/1-3 and two A levels/three H grades. One A level/two H grades may be required for a foundation degree or HND course.

Volunteering or work experience opportunities may be available in your local area, allowing you to demonstrate your commitment to a prospective employer.

Kind of Person

You would need a genuine concern for animals and a wish to care for them. At the same time, you would need to take an unsentimental approach as, inevitably, you would be involved with putting animals down or with unsuccessful surgical procedures. The work is likely to be messy and unpleasant at times as it frequently involves clearing up after animals. In addition to handling a variety of animals, you would need to be able to communicate clearly and sympathetically with their owners. You would have to work as part of the team within the practice and you would need some office skills for keeping records and booking appointments.

Broad Outlook

It can be difficult securing a position in a training practice, and you may find the lack of student places available and the fierce competition for them fairly frustrating. Many veterinary practices choose existing staff members for student placements, meaning that you may be advised to accept a ward assistant or receptionist role to enable you to build up some experience before you are successful in finding a training position.

Most veterinary nurses work for vets in a private practice but there are opportunities to work for animal welfare organisations or in zoos. There are also jobs within veterinary hospitals, universities, breeding establishments, laboratories and research centres, and there may be opportunities to work overseas. In large veterinary practices or animal hospitals, there may be chances for promotion to supervisor, senior practice nurse or manager. Some veterinary nurses move into training, lecturing or working in animal pharmaceutical companies.

Related Occupations

You may be interested in other occupations working with animals, such as RSPCA/ SSPCA inspector or zoo keeper.

Impact on Lifestyle

You may be involved in working long and unsocial hours, including evenings and weekends, perhaps on a shift basis. The work can be physically demanding and emotionally draining, not to mention smelly and unpleasant at times. You would wear a uniform and would add protective clothing when necessary. There may be opportunities for part-time work.

Earnings Potential

There are no set salary scales for veterinary nurses. However, a salary survey conducted in 2014 by the British Veterinary Nursing Association and the Society of Practising Veterinary Surgeons shows median student earnings of £14,061, rising to £20,229 for all qualified nurses and to £22,565 for those with an Advanced Diploma. There are considerable regional variations. Some veterinary nurses are offered a share in the profits of the practice or other perks to compensate for a lower salary.

Further Information

British Veterinary Nursing Association
www.bvna.org.uk

Royal College of Veterinary Surgeons
www.rcvs.org.uk

College of Animal Welfare
www.caw.ac.uk

Society of Practising Veterinary Surgeons
www.spvs.org.uk

British Equine Veterinary Association
www.beva.org.uk

Irish Veterinary Nursing Association
www.ivna.ie

Veterinary Surgeon

What is Involved?

As a veterinary surgeon, you would be concerned with the health and welfare of animals, including household pets, zoo animals, farm animals and horses. This may involve diagnosing and treating them when they are unwell or injured or advising on their living conditions and on steps that can be taken to ensure they stay in good health.

Vets also offer advice on such topics as breeding stock, any government or EU regulations regarding animals and vaccination programmes. Some vets are concerned with research and others work for government agencies ensuring that standards are maintained, particularly in animals destined to join the food chain.

Opportunities for Training

You would have to be registered with the Royal College of Veterinary Surgeons (RCVS) before you could practise veterinary surgery in the UK. This means that you must complete an approved degree in Veterinary Science. The degree usually takes five years, with some students opting to take an additional science subject for a year. At Cambridge it is a six-year course for everyone. The degree courses combine theory and practical work.

There are currently eight universities in the UK offering a degree in Veterinary Science, although you are restricted to a maximum of four applications. Competition for places is very intense and the grades required are high. There is also a course at University College Dublin.

For the first year or so after graduation, you must complete the RCVS Professional Development Phase, during which you record online your experience across a range of clinical skills and procedures in small animal, equine and/or farm animal practice.

Requirements for Entry

Generally, universities are looking for 3 A levels or equivalent at grades ranging from AAB to A*AA. All veterinary schools require biology at A level/Advanced Higher/ Higher, some specify chemistry as well, while others want one or two subjects from maths, physics or chemistry. Some universities will accept a third A level/Advanced Higher/Higher in a non-science subject if it is considered to be an academic subject. Cambridge also requires you to take the Biomedical Admissions Test. It is important to check with individual veterinary schools to be sure of their requirements.

Veterinary schools usually insist that you show evidence of your interest and commitment by having gained experience of working in a veterinary practice and working with and handling animals including livestock. However, practical experience is not a substitute for academic qualifications.

Kind of Person

You would need a lot of determination to get onto the course in the first place: only about a third of applicants are successful. You then have to be dedicated and prepared to work hard throughout your training and when you start your career. As well as having top academic credentials and a good scientific understanding, you must have a real interest in animals. You also need to be unsentimental about them and prepared to face some hard decisions. Dealing with the owners is also very important: you must appear confident, in control and able to explain clearly both the problems and the treatments. You would need to be compassionate when dealing with a sick but much-loved family pet; at other times, when you find evidence of neglect for example, you would need to be firm and insist on correct standards of care. Handling large animals requires a reasonable level of physical fitness.

Most vets need to spend at least some time travelling to see their clients so you should be able to drive. You would be likely to work as part of a team whilst at the same time having to take decisions for yourself. You may also need to have good business skills to handle the business side of the practice.

Broad Outlook

There is currently a decline in the need for large animal vets because of challenges within the farming industry; however, there is an increased demand for horse vets and small animal vets who look after people's pets. Buying a share in an established practice can be an expensive commitment for a young vet.

Related Occupations

In the medical field, you might consider training as a doctor (general practice), doctor (hospital), homoeopath, radiographer or physiotherapist. Other options might include agricultural adviser/consultant or agricultural research scientist, farm manager or RSPCA/SSPCA inspector.

Impact on Lifestyle

Every veterinary surgeon has an obligation to deal with emergencies in any species at any time. It is a 24-hour service, 365 days a year. Being a vet is not a job where it is possible to work regular hours as animals require attention at all times of the day and night. Conditions of work can be unpleasant, smelly, dirty and very physically demanding and can involve a great deal of travelling.

Earnings Potential

Once qualified, most vets start working in a general practice as a veterinary assistant. Starting salaries vary greatly. According to data from the Society of Practising Veterinary Surgeons, a typical remuneration package - which includes a car, fuel allowance, accommodation and training - is £31,150 for a newly qualified vet and £69,021 for a practitioner with more than 20 years' experience. Should you become a partner, your earnings would depend on the size and location of the practice but could be substantial.

Further Information

Royal College of Veterinary Surgeons
www.rcvs.org.uk

Society of Practising Veterinary Surgeons
www.spvs.org.uk

British Veterinary Association
www.bva.co.uk

Biomedical Admissions Test
www.admissionstestingservice.org/for-test-takers/bmat/about-bmat

Veterinary Council of Ireland
www.vci.ie

Youth Worker

What is Involved?

As a youth worker, you would work with young people aged between 11 and 25, particularly those aged between 13 and 19, to promote their personal and social development and enable them to have a voice, influence and place in their communities and society as a whole. Youth work is carried out in different situations and locations, using a range of approaches. You might, for example, operate from a youth club or centre, offering some activities for all young people in the area and some targeted at specific groups. You might be a detached or outreach youth worker, making contact with young people who do not use youth centres. You could work in a school or college, contributing in particular to PSHE (personal, social and health education), citizenship and study support programmes. You might be involved with young people who have been excluded from school, who persistently misuse drugs or alcohol, or who have been involved in crime.

You would often work with other services - such as social services, housing, leisure, and health - to develop and improve provision for young people.

Opportunities for Training

To become a professional youth worker in England, you will need to gain at least a BA Honours degree in youth work, recognised by the National Youth Agency (NYA). Depending on your previous qualifications, you could take either:

- BA honours degree (three years full-time, or part-time equivalent); or
- postgraduate certificate, diploma or MA (one year full-time, or part-time equivalent, if you already have a degree in any subject)

The NYA website has a full list of recognised courses. You may be able to start via an apprenticeship, which will give you the chance to earn a salary while you learn on the job, and then take work-based qualifications to meet the degree entry requirements.

Because youth workers operate in a wide range of settings, higher education qualifications reflect different occupational needs and have a range of titles, including youth and community, community and youth studies, childhood and youth studies, and informal and community education.

Different training arrangements apply in Scotland, Wales and Northern Ireland.

Requirements for Entry

Degree course entry requirements can vary, so you should check with each university or college. You may be accepted without formal qualifications if you have relevant work experience and the potential to succeed on the course. It is important that you obtain experience (paid or unpaid) of working with young people. You will often need at least a year's experience to apply for professional youth work courses and jobs. Indeed, most people enter youth work as either a volunteer or paid worker/apprentice and are typically called youth support workers. They undertake training via a level 2 certificate or level 3 certificate or diploma in youth work practice.

Kind of Person

You would need to build relationships with young people based on trust and respect, offering them new experiences and challenges and encouraging them to think critically about their lives and values. You would encourage young people to take on greater responsibility for themselves and others and to work effectively as a team, judging when to stand back and when to intervene. This may mean letting them make mistakes but ensuring that they learn from them. You would use a range of interpersonal skills such as counselling, advocacy and group work. You could not be expected to be an expert on everything affecting young people but you should be aware of other local agencies and what they offer, and to recognise when you need to involve people with specialist skills and knowledge, while continuing to support the young person concerned.

Broad Outlook

Local authorities have made significant reductions in funding to non-statutory services, including youth support, due to spending cuts imposed by central government. In most local authorities this has seen a severe reduction in youth worker positions. Indeed, according to the Community, Youth and Play Workers in Unite union, we now face the biggest assault on youth and community work jobs in history, in both voluntary organisations and local authorities. They accuse employers of 'dismantling their open access youth provision and along with it their commitment to a highly skilled professional workforce'.

It is clear that opportunities for youth workers may be restricted for some time by public sector spending cuts.

Related Occupations

You might consider: social worker, probation officer, teacher (secondary), careers adviser/guidance counsellor or education social worker/welfare officer.

Impact on Lifestyle

As a full-time worker, you would be contracted to work a set number of hours, usually 35 to 37 a week. Your contract would almost certainly specify evening and weekend sessions.

Earnings Potential

Starting salaries depend on your qualifications and your employing organisation. The current professional range pay scale starts at £23,213 and rises to £39,173. A small number of senior manager posts can rise to around £60,000. There are additional allowances for posts based in and around London.

Further Information

National Youth Agency
www.nya.org.uk

British Youth Council
www.byc.org.uk

Youth Council for Northern Ireland
https://youthcouncilni.org

Choose Youth
www.chooseyouth.org

Youth Link Scotland
www.youthlinkscotland.org

Community, Youth and Play Workers in Unite
www.cywu.org.uk

National Youth Council of Ireland
www.youth.ie

Additional Career Outlines

Lack of space prevents us from giving a complete WORKBRIEF analysis of every possible career idea but we do list in this section a range of further occupational titles.

Our top priority here is to include the majority of careers mentioned under 'Related Occupations' in the main section but not described in their own detailed chapters.

Acupuncturist

Practises the ancient Chinese holistic therapy of acupuncture. This is based on the theory that the body depends on life energy being balanced to maintain good health. An acupuncturist treats imbalances in energy by inserting fine needles into key pressure points in the body. Some practitioners are qualified healthcare professionals, such as a doctor or a nurse, who add skills in acupuncture to their overall practice; others take a degree-level training course accredited by one of the professional organisations for acupuncture.

British Acupuncture Council
www.acupuncture.org.uk

Acupuncture Society
www.acupuncturesociety.org.uk

British Medical Acupuncture Society
www.medical-acupuncture.co.uk

Agricultural Adviser/Consultant

Works within the land-based sector, providing technical or business consultancy and research advice to farmers, the horticultural industry, government and levy bodies, food processors, food retailers and the agricultural supply industry. A relevant degree is usually an essential minimum requirement. This could be in agriculture, crop and plant science, horticulture, soil science, agricultural engineering, environmental science or a biological science. Wide-ranging experience is also needed before progressing to an advisory or consultancy post.

Agricultural Development and Advisory Service
www.adas.uk

Agricultural Biologist

Specialises in the application of modern biological techniques to the study of ways to improve the production of plants or animals, their reproduction, genetic make-up, nutrition, health and diseases. Specialist career opportunities might include agronomist, animal geneticist, animal physiologist, botanist, entomologist, horticulturist or toxicologist. Given that much of the work is in applied research, a good degree in a biological science is often a minimum starting point.

Royal Society of Biology
www.rsb.org.uk

Agricultural Chemist

Conducts wide-ranging research and assists in the development of agricultural products, such as molecules or compounds for pest or weed control. Also tests compounds in order to determine the impact of included chemicals on the environment and in food, and seeks ways to control the causes and effects of biochemical reactions related to plant and animal growth. Would normally have a first degree in chemistry or a chemistry-related subject, together with postgraduate qualifications.

Royal Society of Chemistry
www.rsc.org

Agricultural Inspector

Ensures that official standards are met and maintained in the land-based (agriculture, horticulture, forestry) sector, especially in such areas as health and safety in the workplace, animal health and welfare - including identification, transportation and disease control - and food assurance. In the UK, may work for the Department of Environment, Food and Rural Affairs (Defra) or the Health and Safety Executive.

Department of Environment, Food and Rural Affairs (Defra)
www.gov.uk/government/organisations/department-for-environment-food-rural-affairs

Health and Safety Executive
www.hse.gov.uk

Agricultural Research Scientist

Specialises in the application of scientific research techniques to the study of areas such as animal/plant diseases, pest control methods, the use of chemicals in farming, crop production methods, or breeding and rearing livestock. Research may be undertaken at universities, in research institutions or within businesses, such as with manufacturers of agricultural chemicals. The aim may be to find ways of improving crop yields to study, fungal, insect and weed control, or to breed new disease-resistant strains of grains, fruit or vegetables.

Agroscience Services
www.eurofins.com/agroscienceservices.aspx

Air Cabin Crew

The main point of contact for passengers during a flight, air cabin crew work to ensure that passengers enjoy a safe, pleasant and comfortable journey. They oversee boarding and disembarkation, ensure that hand luggage is safely stored and that passengers are wearing seat belts, inform passengers of aircraft safety procedures, serve and sell meals, drinks, gifts and duty-free products during the flight, and deal with any problems or other issues. Personal qualities, appearance and good health and fitness are normally more important than academic qualifications, although nursing, travel, tourism, leisure industry or language qualifications or experience may be helpful.

Cabin Crew
www.cabincrew.com/career-advice

Aircraft Maintenance Engineer

Inspects, maintains and repairs civil and military aircraft. May be a mechanical engineer, specialising in scheduled maintenance, restoration and re-fit of airframes, power plants, fuel systems and associated pneumatic, hydraulic and air-conditioning systems, or an avionics engineer, concerned with scheduled maintenance, restoration and modification of communication, navigation and radar equipment, and guidance and control systems including auto-pilot/auto-land and cabin entertainment. Must meet very strict training and licensing regulations.

Association of Licensed Aircraft Engineers
www.alae.org

Royal Aeronautical Society
www.aerosociety.com

Royal Air Force
www.raf.mod.uk/careers

Alexander Technique Teacher

Shows people how to improve their postural and positional habits, with particular emphasis on the relationship between the head, neck and spine. Also encourages people to change their mental approach, helping them become more alert, poised and self-confident. The Technique aims to help people with a range of conditions, including back, neck and shoulder problems, breathing and voice disorders, chronic fatigue syndrome and problems with movement or co-ordination. May also work with people who want to improve their performance in sport or the performing arts.

Alexander Technique
www.alexandertechnique.com/ats

Analytical Chemist

Assesses the chemical structure and nature of substances for a variety of purposes - including drug development, forensic analysis and toxicology - using a range of modern analytical techniques, including ion/electro-chromatography, gas/high performance liquid chromatography, and spectroscopy. May specialise in an area such as toxicology, pharmaceuticals, quality control or forensics, after achieving a good honours degree in a relevant subject such as chemistry, applied/analytical chemistry or biochemistry.

Royal Society of Chemistry
www.rsc.org

Biochemical Society
www.biochemistry.org

Animal Nutritionist

Specialises in the effect of diet on the health, well-being and productivity of animals. Works mainly in agriculture but may also be involved with food-related issues concerning zoo animals or domestic pets. Will usually have a science-based degree - perhaps in agriculture, animal science, bioscience, dietetics, veterinary science or zoology - together with postgraduate qualifications.

Association for Nutrition
www.associationfornutrition.org

Animator

Produces multiple frames of images, which can be rapidly sequenced together to create the illusion of movement known as animation. The frames can be made up of digital or hand-drawn images, models or puppets. Must have skills in drawing, modelling or using computer animation packages; can be entirely self-taught, although an animation or art-related course may be a useful starting point. Computer-generated animation features prominently in film and television special effects, as well as in internet websites and the computer games industry.

Creative Skillset
http://creativeskillset.org/creative_industries/animation

I Could – real stories to inspire your career
http://icould.com

Antiquarian Bookseller

Runs a specialist bookshop dealing in valuable books, often buying or selling through auction houses, or by direct contact with collectors or other dealers. Needs to develop a detailed knowledge of sales prices and of the levels of supply and demand, to avoid overbidding at auctions and to be able to answer the questions of the public. May enter the trade by first finding work with an established dealer, library or auctioneer.

Antiquarian Booksellers Association
www.aba.org.uk

Antiques Dealer

Buys and sells antique furniture and other collectable artefacts and works of art, often specialising in an area such as ceramics, glass, paintings, sculpture, clocks or books. May also offer valuations for insurance purposes. Central to the work are auctions and fairs, where dealers may sell or buy in stock, observe levels of buyer interest and develop their expertise. They often buy for collectors and export to other countries. No particular qualifications are required, apart from a passionate interest in the particular objects in which the dealer specialises.

British Antique Dealers' Association
www.bada.org

Arboriculturist

Also known as a tree surgeon or arborist, is involved with all aspects of work with trees, including pruning and removal, planting, hazard assessment and pest control. Must be physically fit, with a good head for heights. Training is often in such specific skills as chainsaw operation, working from a rope and harness, use of elevated work platforms, working at heights and manual handling.

The International Society of Arboriculture provides an arborist certification programme, and the Royal Forestry Society (RFS) endorses ABC Awards qualifications in Arboriculture at Levels 2 through to 6 (Professional Diploma in Arboriculture).

Arboricultural Association
www.trees.org.uk

International Society of Arboriculture
www.isa-arbor.com

Royal Forestry Society
www.rfs.org.uk

Archaeological Illustrator

Prepares detailed drawings to help people understand archaeological information and to record archaeological sites and finds. Illustrations are a key part of academic papers, textbooks, reference books, instruction manuals and archaeological websites. Practitioners need to be able to draw and to use a computer, and they must have sufficient archaeological knowledge to understand the significance of what they are illustrating.

Graphics Archaeology Group
www.gag-cifa.org

Archaeological Surveyor

Undertakes field surveys of land and structures for future archaeological investigations and excavations, using a range of surveying techniques, instruments and software packages. May also assess the risks that development projects might pose to archaeological heritage. In a non-intrusive survey, nothing is touched, just recorded. An accurate survey of the earthworks and other features can enable them to be interpreted without the need for excavation. An intrusive survey may involve removing all artefacts of archaeological value, or drilling small bore holes to determine the depths at which one might find cultural artefacts worthy of excavation.

Graphics Archaeology Group
www.gag-cifa.org

Archivist

Manages and preserves historical records and documents, working with collections of all types, from books, photographs and maps to audio, film and electronic files. The work involves carefully identifying, dating, cataloguing and indexing archive materials. Qualification normally involves a degree - in any subject, although history, library studies, computing or foreign languages might prove useful - followed by a postgraduate course.

Archives and Records Association
www.archives.org.uk

Aromatherapist

Works as a holistic therapist, using aromatic oils from herbs, flowers, trees, spices or fruit to help improve a patient's sense of wellbeing and to relieve symptoms of ill health. The oils are applied by full or partial body massage. No qualifications are needed to do this job, although career prospects may be enhanced by working towards membership of a professional body and registering with the Complementary and Natural Healthcare Council.

International Federation of Aromatherapists
www.ifaroma.org

Art Gallery Curator

Acquires, identifies, interprets, cares for and exhibits a collection of artefacts or works of art in order to inform, educate and entertain the public. Would usually need a degree in a subject such as art or art history. Many curators also have a postgraduate qualification. One of the best ways to get started, to gain experience and to help build a network of useful contacts, is through pre-entry work experience. This can be achieved via an internship or through voluntary work.

Creative and Cultural Skills
http://ccskills.org.uk/careers/advice/article/what-is-a-curator

Art Gallery/Museum Assistant

Supports an art gallery curator or museum keeper with all aspects of the display, storage and administration of collections. May have specific responsibility for customer care and security, talking to visitors and answering their questions. No particular qualifications are required, although competition for jobs means that those who have suitable background knowledge and enthusiasm can considerably improve their prospects.

Museums Association
www.museumsassociation.org

Creative and Cultural Skills
http://ccskills.org.uk

Art Restorer/Conservator

Repairs, cleans and renovates damaged works of art, using a scientific knowledge of materials used in the past, deterioration processes and modern materials compatible with the originals. Usually needs a degree in a subject such as fine art, ceramics and glass, textiles or archaeology, followed by a postgraduate qualification in conservation.

British Association of Paintings Conservator-Restorers
www.bapcr.org.uk

Art Therapist

Uses a variety of artistic skills and media - such as clay, paper and paint - to encourage individuals and groups experiencing a range of medical and emotional conditions to express their feelings and communicate ideas. Would need to achieve a postgraduate qualification in art therapy, usually after completing a degree level course in art, although qualified teachers, social workers, psychologists and other professionals are also considered. Might work with paints of all kinds, canvasses, papers, pastels, clay, fabrics, collages, carving, sculpture or weaving materials, to allow clients to express and share their innermost thoughts and feelings.

British Association of Art Therapists
www.baat.org

Art Valuer

Assesses how much individual artworks or collections - including paintings, sculpture, jewellery, porcelain, books and furniture - might be worth. Usually specialises in a particular period or type of artwork, such as 18th century paintings or 20th century sculpture. May work for a specialised auction house or an art dealership. Clients might include individuals or organisations seeking to sell, buy or insure.

Sotheby's Institute of Art
www.sothebysinstitute.com

Christie's Education
www.christies.edu

Arts Administrator

Plans and organises a wide range of cultural events and activities in association with theatres, galleries, museums, arts festivals, arts centres, dance companies, community arts organisations and local authorities. The work might involve programme planning, booking venues and artists, negotiating sponsorship, front of house management, public relations, marketing and education. There are no set qualifications for becoming an arts administrator, although a degree can be a good starting point. Volunteering or temporary work is also an established way of developing a network of contacts within the industry.

Arts Council England
www.artscouncil.org.uk

Arts Council of Northern Ireland
www.artscouncil-ni.org

Creative Scotland
www.creativescotland.com

Arts Council of Wales
www.arts.wales

Arts Marketing Association
www.a-m-a.co.uk

UK Theatre
www.uktheatre.org

Astronomer/Astrophysicist

Collects and analyses data from satellites and spacecraft using optical and radio telescopes to study the structure and nature of the universe and to discover the scientific principles upon which it is based. Advanced physics, mathematics, computing and other technologies are used to coordinate and analyse data. Astronomy is more an area of academic research than a career title, and opportunities to work as a professional astronomer would normally involve a first degree followed by a postgraduate research qualification

Royal Astronomical Society
www.ras.org.uk

UK Space Agency
www.gov.uk/government/organisations/uk-space-agency

British Astronomical Association
www.britastro.org

Astronomy Ireland
www.astronomy.ie

Author/Creative Writer

Creates original pieces of written work, such as novels, poems, plays or biographies, in fictional and non-fictional genres. Academic qualifications are not essential, although many authors find it useful to pursue a degree or postgraduate course in creative writing. These are often taught by published authors with hands-on experience of writing for publication, and help develop thought processes through textual and practical exploration. The goal for most authors is to identify and develop a unique voice and channel this through writing.

Writers' Guild of Great Britain
www.writersguild.org.uk

Society of Authors
www.societyofauthors.org

BBC Writersroom
www.bbc.co.uk/writersroom

Avionics Engineer

Specialises in electronic equipment used in the air, from the engine computers to the fly-by-wire flight control system. It will include, in a military aircraft, weapon aiming and release and, in a civil airliner, the cabin entertainment system. The very latest aircraft can have hundreds of on-board computers, not to mention over 500 kilometres of wiring. Systems engineers work on new aircraft at the conceptual stage, studying and defining what technologies can be applied; they generate detailed equipment specifications at the design stage, and conduct and support flight trials and manufacture.

Careers in Aerospace
www.careersinaerospace.com/careers-areas/engineering2/avionics.html

Biophysicist

Considers the physical, electrical and mechanical properties of living tissues and cells, their protein structures and nerve impulse transmissions, thereby playing an important part in biological and medical research. Noteworthy examples of the application of biophysics to new techniques for analysing organisms include: EM (Electron Microscopy), CAT (Computer-Aided Tomography), MRI (Magnetic Resonance Imaging), PET (Positron Emission Tomography) and X-ray crystallography. Biophysicists may also apply biological knowledge to problems in physics. For example, the DNA of salmon has been found to improve the performance of light-emitting diodes.

Institute of Physics
www.iop.org

Royal Society of Biology
www.rsb.org.uk

Bodyguard/Close Protection Officer

Protects individuals or groups from the risk of personal attack, harassment or kidnapping, in any situation which could be considered potentially harmful. May have a background in the armed forces or the police, although this is not essential. Needs to be physically fit, with good eyesight and hearing. May sometimes need to stand out in a crowd but at other times to blend into the background.

Security Industry Authority
www.sia.homeoffice.gov.uk/Pages/home.aspx

British Security Industry Association
www.bsia.co.uk

Bookseller

Interacts with customers in a bookshop to help them locate particular books and to offer information and advice about the range of appropriate titles; may also be involved with ordering and displaying stock and working with publishing company representatives; may specialise in a particular kind of bookselling, such as antiquarian or foreign language books. Needs to be enthusiastic about books, with a broad range of reading interests.

Antiquarian Booksellers Association
www.aba.org.uk

Booksellers Association of the United Kingdom and Ireland
www.booksellers.org.uk

European and International Booksellers Federation
www.europeanbooksellers.eu

Border Force Officer

Protects national borders by enforcing immigration and customs regulations. The Border Force has responsibility for securing borders 24 hours a day, 365 days a year, at all ports and airports, together with postal depots and the rail network. The work may involve questioning passengers at entry points, detaining suspicious individuals, and boarding and searching aircraft, boats and vehicles for illegal immigrants, drugs or other goods and activities that could cause harm.

Border Force
www.gov.uk/government/organisations/border-force

Botanist

Identifies, records and monitors plant species, from trees and flowers to algae, fungi, lichen, ferns, grasses and mosses, to protect, manage and enhance plant life. Must have at least a first degree in a subject such as botany, plant biology, environmental science or ecology. Postgraduate study to doctorate level is usually essential for research posts. Would-be botanists are encouraged to demonstrate their enthusiasm by undertaking voluntary fieldwork and conservation activities.

Botanical Society of Britain and Ireland
www.bsbi.org.uk

Broadcast Engineer

Operates, updates and repairs equipment used in radio, television, webcasts and other media, ensuring that programmes are broadcast on time and to the highest quality standards. At professional level, a degree in electrical, electronic or broadcast engineering is needed. For testing or servicing, academic qualifications are less important, although employers still require a keen interest in technology and an aptitude for the work.

International Moving Image Society
www.societyinmotion.com

Young Creative Talent
http://creativeskillset.org/who_we_help/young_creative_talent

Building/Construction Contractor

Usually the manager or owner of a building company, undertakes construction contracts either directly with private clients, development companies or local authorities, or under the guidance of an architect, surveyor or engineer. It would help to have a foundation degree, higher national certificate or diploma or a degree in a subject such as building studies and building engineering, surveying and civil engineering, construction engineering or construction management. Whatever the course, skills in management, project management, economics, IT and accounts are essential, together with considerable experience of the construction industry.

Chartered Institute of Building
www.ciob.org

Careers in Construction
www.citb.co.uk/careers-in-construction

Construction Industry Federation, Ireland
www.cif.ie

Building Control Officer/Surveyor

Carries out regular inspections to ensure that regulations are followed when houses, offices and other buildings are under construction. The regulations include public health, fire safety, energy conservation and building accessibility. While a degree is not essential for entering this area of work, it is important in the process of working towards professional recognition. Useful subjects include architecture, building control, building surveying, civil or structural engineering, construction, or town planning.

Royal Institution of Chartered Surveyors
www.rics.org

Chartered Association of Building Engineers
www.cbuilde.com

Construction Industry Council
www.cic.org.uk

Building Society Executive/Manager

Runs one or more retail ('high street') branches of a building society, with responsibility for managing staff, meeting sales targets for financial products and services, maintaining customer relationships and attracting new customers. Would normally need a degree qualification to join a management trainee scheme, although it is possible to gain experience in branch operations and work up to managerial level.

Building Societies Association
www.bsa.org.uk

Cabinet Maker

Makes fine furniture, such as chairs, tables, chests of drawers, desks and display cabinets, using modern as well as traditional production methods; may also restore antiques or repair damaged furniture. Entry is usually via an apprenticeship scheme or by completing a full-time college course in furniture making. No particular entry qualifications are required, although they would be necessary for, say, a degree or foundation degree in furniture design.

Guild of Master Craftsmen
www.guildmc.com

Cell Biologist

Researches how cells work in both healthy and diseased states, working across animal, plant and medical science. Can develop new vaccines, more effective medicines, plants with improved qualities and a better understanding of how all living things live. A doctoral qualification is typically preferred for cell biologist jobs in academic and research institutions. Private companies and laboratories may employ cell biologists with a bachelor or master degree in life sciences, chemistry or biology.

British Society for Cell Biology
http://bscb.org

Ceramics Designer

Designs and often creates a range of pottery objects made by shaping and firing clay, including domestic and commercial kitchenware and tableware, ceramic sculpture, garden ornaments, gifts, jewellery, and wall and floor tiles. May work as a self-employed ceramicist or produce commercial designs for mass production in a large company. There are no essential academic requirements, although many practitioners will have studied ceramics or three-dimensional design to degree level.

Studio Pottery
www.studiopottery.co.uk

Crafts Council
www.craftscouncil.org.uk

Charity Fundraiser

Works to boost the income of a charity by encouraging individuals, communities, businesses and other organisations to make donations. Organises events, seeks legacies and major gifts, raises awareness of the charity's goals, while constantly exploring new fundraising opportunities. There are no essential entry requirements, although a degree can be useful - especially if linked with experience in management, marketing, media, public relations, events organisation, advertising, sales or finance.

Institute of Fundraising
www.institute-of-fundraising.org.uk

Charity Officer

Employed by a charity, voluntary or non-profit-making organisation, works to undertake a variety of tasks. Specific responsibilities tend to vary according to the size of the charity but common duties can include: recruiting, training and managing employees and volunteers; administering accounts; organising meetings; liaising with relevant organisations; undertaking mail shots and similar publicity tasks; implementing IT/administrative systems. Commitment to the voluntary sector is often seen as more important than academic qualifications, although a business studies, management or social administration degree may be helpful.

Knowhow Non-profit
http://knowhownonprofit.org

Chef

Prepares, cooks and presents food to an accepted standard in the kitchen of a restaurant, hotel or other eating establishment; may specialise in a certain area of the kitchen, such as vegetables or pastries, or in a particular cuisine, such as French, Italian, Thai or Indian. May not need any academic qualifications to start work as a kitchen assistant or trainee/commis chef, progressing with experience to section chef, sous chef and finally head chef. Work at head chef level can include responsibility for creating and updating menus, and for meeting financial targets.

Institute of Hospitality
www.instituteofhospitality.org

Hospitality Guild
www.hospitalityguild.co.uk

Choreographer

Creates dance routines and works with dancers to achieve the desired level of performance for the stage, TV, film/video or other event. Would normally specialise in a particular style of dance, such as classical ballet, modern dance, musical theatre or ballroom. Most choreographers start as professional dancers and may begin choreographing whilst still working as a dancer.

Dance UK - Choreographers
www.danceuk.org/choreographers

Classical Musician

May play one or more instruments and/or sing. Could be a performer or composer, a teacher working from home or in a school, college or university, an administrator, publisher, record company executive, instrument manufacturer, librarian, broadcaster or journalist. Many musicians combine some of these activities, especially those who both perform and teach. An orchestral player may spend many years with one orchestra or work freelance, taking session work for concerts, recordings and other activities. Specialist music colleges and conservatoires offer three- or four-year degree courses with the emphasis on performance, while university courses tend to have more academic content.

Incorporated Society of Musicians
www.ism.org

Clinical Psychologist

Works with clients of all ages, treating mental or physical health problems such as anxiety, depression and schizophrenia, addictive behaviour, eating disorders, personal and family relationship problems, adjustment to physical illness, learning disability, and neurological disorders. Would normally follow an accredited degree in psychology with a further three years of study for a doctorate in clinical psychology.

British Psychological Society
http://careers.bps.org.uk/area/clinical

Clinical Scientist

Also known as a healthcare scientist, works in one of three major areas - life sciences, physiological sciences or medical physics and clinical engineering - researching new methods of diagnosis, interpreting test results and suggesting methods of treatment. The normal career route is to take a degree in a relevant subject and follow this with a master-level course as part of the three-year healthcare scientist training programme.

Association of Clinical Scientists
www.assclinsci.org

Clothing/Textile Technologist

Carries out technical, investigative and quality control work on clothing and textiles, ensuring that products perform to specifications. The work includes the development of products, improvement of production efficiency and quality, and liaison with people involved in the production process.

British Textile Technology Group
www.bttg.co.uk

Textile Institute
www.textileinstitute.org

Coastguard

Part of the UK Maritime and Coastguard Agency, co-ordinates a 24-hour search and rescue service around the coast and in the international search and rescue region, and investigates illegal shipping activities and pollution incidents. Must have good hearing and eyesight, together with a good standard of literacy and numeracy. Considerable seagoing experience is also essential.

Maritime and Coastguard Agency
www.gov.uk/government/organisations/maritime-and-coastguard-agency/about

Columnist

Regularly expresses opinions or gives a commentary for newspapers, magazines, online blogs, radio or television. The topics can range from advice to editorial comment, gossip or food and the tone can vary from serious to light-hearted or satirical. No specific qualifications are required, although a background in journalism or broadcasting may be useful.

Media.info
http://media.info/uk

Journalism UK
www.journalism.co.uk

National Society of Newspaper Columnists (US)
www.columnists.com

Commissioning Editor

In book publishing, identifies authors and titles that will sell well and enhance the publisher's list; in magazine publishing, commissions writers to produce specific features. May start as editorial assistant and work up to commissioning role. Many commissioning editors are graduates, although there are no specific entry requirements. For some areas, such as scientific or medical publishing, employers may prefer a relevant degree.

Society for Editors and Proofreaders
www.sfep.org.uk

Professional Publishers Association
www.ppa.co.uk

Commodity Broker/Trader/Dealer

Buys and sells, on behalf of clients, physical commodities ranging from coffee, grain and sugar to crude oil, gas and non-ferrous metals; also deals in derivatives (futures and options), based on physical commodities; usually specialises in a particular group of commodities. Most opportunities arise in London and other major cities. Any degree discipline is acceptable for entry, although employers may prefer qualifications in management, business, financial or numerate subjects.

Financial Conduct Authority
www.fcacareers.org.uk

London Metal Exchange
www.lme.com

Intercontinental Exchange
www.theice.com

Communications Engineer

Works with many of the information technologies upon which society depends. Depending on training and specialism, may be an expert in telecommunications, computer systems or related types of communications. To work at a professional level, a degree in engineering or a physical science would be needed. Useful subjects include electronic engineering, telecommunications, computer science or information technology. An apprenticeship may offer a starting point for work at technician level.

Institute of Telecommunications Professionals
www.theitp.org

Institution of Engineering and Technology
www.theiet.org

Community Arts Worker

Helps local communities to plan and participate in arts activities such as creative writing, dance, drama, painting, photography, and film and video production. Must normally be qualified and experienced in at least one specialist area of the creative arts. There are no absolute entry requirements, although a degree or foundation degree in a subject such as drama, theatre, dance or performing arts, music, art and design, media, film or photography, event management or teaching would be useful.

Voluntary Arts Network
www.voluntaryarts.org

Community Development Worker

Organises action with people - individuals, families or larger groups - in communities usually perceived to be disadvantaged, perhaps because of problems related to age, race, ability, drugs, poverty or geography; aims to empower communities to regain control over the conditions and decisions affecting their lives and to improve the quality of life for all who live in them. While commitment and relevant experience are generally more important than academic qualifications, a degree in social sciences may improve career prospects.

Community Development Foundation
www.cdf.org.uk

Federation for Community Development Learning
www.fcdl.org.uk

Scottish Community Development Centre
www.scdc.org.uk

Community Education Officer

Ensures that appropriate educational, developmental and recreational provision is available to meet the needs of all members of the local community, and encourages people to take part in the courses on offer. Academic qualifications are not an essential requirement, although many people in this area of activity are graduates with experience of teaching, adult education or youth and community work.

Workers' Educational Association
www.wea.org.uk

Compliance Professional

Ensures that banks or financial institutions operate in line with regulations imposed on them. The role can carry huge accountability and requires constantly updated knowledge of financial products and the regulatory environment. Many UK compliance roles are centred on the financial hubs of the City of London and Canary Wharf.

Compliance Professionals
www.complianceprofessionals.co.uk

Conservator

Cares for cultural artefacts, such as books, paintings, textiles, ceramics and furniture, by applying scientific methods to preserve and restore them. Much of the work involves monitoring and controlling the environment in which objects are stored or displayed to prevent deterioration. A degree in conservation followed by work-based development is a typical entry route into a museum/gallery conservator role. Alternatively, a relevant postgraduate qualification is essential if the first degree is not in conservation.

Institute of Conservation
www.icon.org.uk

Constituency/Political Party Agent

Works either at constituency level or at party headquarters, undertaking promotional, administrative and fundraising activities, analysing electoral rolls, recruiting for party membership and organising election campaigns. Employment is often dependent on having a good degree. Preferred subjects include politics, government, public/social administration, social policy, law, history, business studies and economics. A postgraduate qualification may be beneficial, particularly for graduates without a relevant first degree. It is also normally essential to hold substantial relevant experience, which can be gained via paid or voluntary employment with the appropriate party.

UK Parliament
www.parliament.uk

Association of Professional Political Consultants
www.appc.org.uk

Consumer Psychologist/Scientist

Helps organisations adapt and improve their marketing by studying the behaviour of consumers, how they select one product rather than another, how they react to advertising, in order to develop a psychology of consumer choice. Using the 'psychologist' title requires a degree in psychology; otherwise a degree in marketing, statistics or consumer studies would be useful.

The National Skills Academy – Food and Drink
http://nsafd.co.uk/nations

Food Standards Agency
www.food.gov.uk

Control and Instrumentation Engineer

Designs, develops, installs and maintains equipment used to monitor and control engineering systems, machinery and processes; may work in the manufacture and supply of equipment or for organisations that use it. May have a specific control and instrumentation engineering degree, although entry is also possible with a degree qualification in electronic, computer, mechanical or systems engineering.

Institute of Measurement and Control
www.instmc.org

Copy Editor

In publishing, ensures that material is clear and consistent, complete and credible, and that text is well written and grammatically correct. May work on a range of publications, including books, journals, newspapers, websites and other electronic resources. Many copy editors are graduates. Most degree subjects are accepted, although publishing, media or a related subject may be useful. For some specialist areas, a related degree may be necessary. For example, an engineering degree for specialist engineering publications or an architecture degree for architectural journals.

Society for Editors and Proofreaders
www.sfep.org.uk

Publishers Association
www.publishers.org.uk

Copywriter

Within marketing, advertising and public relations, writes the text or verbal content of advertisements, promotional literature, press releases and suchlike. May specialise in, say, radio and television scripts, website design, social networking or other marketing media. Must have creative instinct, be organised and able to work well under pressure. Anyone interested in creative writing, with or without experience, can become a copywriter, although a degree in journalism or communications can be a useful starting point.

Creative Skillset
http://creativeskillset.org

Corporate Investment Banker

Provides a range of financial services to companies, institutions and governments, advising on such issues as acquisitions, bond and share issues, management buyouts, mergers, privatisation, raising capital and securing deals. Almost all new recruits are graduates, although the actual degree subject is less important than a high level of numeracy, commercial awareness and a knowledge of financial markets.

British Bankers Association
www.bba.org.uk

Corporate Lawyer

Primarily a transactional specialist, advises companies on the purchase or sale of other businesses, and helps them raise funds. Globalisation means that there is often an international element to the work. The regulatory environment in which companies operate is constantly evolving and the range of corporate actions undertaken varies according to the market cycle. The term 'lawyer' can apply to solicitors, barristers or legal executives, although a corporate lawyer is usually a qualified solicitor.

Law Careers
http://allaboutlaw.co.uk

Costume Designer

Researches and designs clothes and costumes used in theatre, film and television productions. Creative skills can be more important than qualifications, but many costume designers have a degree in costume design or fashion. Another route is to start as a wardrobe assistant or costume maker and work up from there.

Costume Society
www.costumesociety.org.uk

Angels Costumiers
www.angels.uk.com

Counselling Psychologist

Helps people deal with problems associated with life events such as bereavement, sexual abuse, relationship issues or domestic violence, and mental health issues such as anxiety, depression, eating disorders, post-traumatic stress disorder or psychosis. Must have an accredited degree-level qualification in psychology, together with a postgraduate doctorate or similar qualification in counselling psychology.

British Psychological Society
http://careers.bps.org.uk/area/counselling

Counsellor

Works with individual clients in a confidential setting to explore difficulties they are facing. Does not make judgements, give advice or direct clients to a specific solution, but rather listens and encourages clients to think clearly about their situation in order to find a way forward. There are several different approaches to counselling, each with its own theoretical basis. Personal qualities are at least as important as academic achievement for this area of work.

British Association for Counselling and Psychotherapy
www.bacp.co.uk

British Psychological Society
www.bps.org.uk

Counselling and Psychotherapy in Scotland
www.cosca.org.uk

Court Legal Adviser/Justice's Clerk/Court Clerk

A qualified solicitor or barrister, advises magistrates (who do not necessarily possess legal qualifications) and district judges in accordance with the Courts Act and other legislation. Manages court schedules, reads charges to the court and may advise on sentencing. Must have completed at least the academic stage of training to be a solicitor or barrister.

Skills for Justice
www.sfjuk.com

HM Courts and Tribunals Service
www.gov.uk/government/organisations/hm-courts-and-tribunals-service

Critic

Writes articles or makes comments in various branches of the media, expressing opinions and assessment on a wide range of topics. These could be books, plays, films, exhibitions, musical events, restaurants or programmes on television or radio. Tends to specialise in specific areas. There are no fixed qualifications for becoming a critic, although many are graduates. Some of the most famous critics studied completely unrelated subjects at university. Experience in journalism is often a good starting point.

Media.info
http://media.info/uk

Journalism UK
www.journalism.co.uk

International Association of Theatre Critics
www.aict-iatc.org

Customer Services Manager

Usually the first point of contact in client communication, offers expertise regarding products or services offered by an organisation; may handle complex customer questions, complaints and special orders. Previous experience of working with customers, such as in a shop, hotel, restaurant, call centre or office, is usually required before entering this area of work.

Institute of Customer Service
www.instituteofcustomerservice.com

Cybernetics/Systems Specialist

Deals with systems and their control; these may be technological systems as in robots, biological as in the control of human body temperatures, or environmental as in studies of global warming; spans several academic disciplines, including such subjects as robotic systems, biomedical engineering, environmental science and computer technology.

Cybernetics Society
www.cybsoc.org

UK Systems Society
www.systemsforum.org

Dancer

Communicates ideas visually, physically and musically in ballet, contemporary dance and in entertainment generally, working in films, television, pantomime, cabaret and sometimes in education. Hours can be long and irregular, with rehearsals and classes during the day and performances in the evening. The work is physically very demanding, and dancers must practise and keep fit even when not performing.

Council for Dance Education and Training
www.cdet.org.uk

Debt Counsellor

Offers free, impartial and confidential advice on money management to people whose debts have become too large or complex to handle; may cover aspects of personal finance such as credit cards, mortgages, credit reporting agencies, bankruptcy, budgeting, interest rates, fees, consolidation loans, and financial education. The usual starting point for this sort of work is to volunteer in an advice centre. Experience in consumer advice, welfare rights work or debt recovery is usually seen as more important than academic qualifications.

Wiser Adviser
www.wiseradviser.org

Institute of Money Advisers
www.i-m-a.org.uk

Dental Hygienist/Therapist

Works closely with dentists, carrying out procedures such as scaling and polishing teeth, and applying topical fluoride and fissure sealants. May also be known as an oral health practitioner, and may carry out dental health promotion work in the community. To work in the UK, must be registered with the General Dental Council and possess an approved diploma in dental therapy, or a degree in oral health sciences, or dental therapy and dental hygiene.

British Society of Dental Hygiene and Therapy
www.bsdht.org.uk

Dental Nurse

Supports a dentist in all aspects of patient care; this includes preparing instruments, mixing materials and ensuring patient comfort. Also takes notes from dentist's dictation for patient records and, after the patient has left, tidies the surgery and sterilises all instruments. There are usually no academic qualifications needed to work as a trainee dental nurse, but must study for an approved course in dental nursing and must be registered with the General Dental Council.

British Association of Dental Nurses
www.badn.org.uk

National Examining Board for Dental Nurses
www.nebdn.org

DJ

Plays recorded music on the radio or to entertain the audience at a live venue. Must be interested in music trends and able to operate a range of technical equipment. Needs to be confident and outgoing, usually chatting or telling jokes between tracks. There is no clear entry point to a career as a DJ and no particular route to qualification. Many people start with a passion for a particular style of music and build a collection of music and equipment, developing at the same time their own style of presentation and gaining practical experience of using decks, mixers and sampling equipment.

Creative and Cultural Skills
http://ccskills.org.uk/careers/advice/any/music

Domestic Bursar/Accommodation Officer

Responsible, as a domestic bursar, for non-academic day-to-day operations of an independent school or university college; more likely known as accommodation manager in a conference centre, hotel, hospital, care home or youth hostel. Usually ensures that the establishment is run efficiently, problems are quickly rectified, standards of cleanliness and maintenance are upheld (in rooms, bathrooms and public areas), budgets are controlled and teams of staff are well trained and managed.

Independent Schools' Bursars Association
www.theisba.org.uk

Drilling Engineer

Plans and supervises all operations necessary for drilling oil and gas wells. Might work for a multinational corporation engaged in the exploration, extraction and production of oil or gas, an engineering consultancy or an onshore, offshore or mobile drilling contractor. Usually has at least a first degree in minerals, mining or petroleum engineering or geology, earth or natural sciences.

My Oil and Gas Career
www.myoilandgascareer.com/careers

Ecologist

Studies the relationship between animals, people and plants and their environment, usually choosing a specialist area, such as fauna, flora, freshwater, marine or terrestrial, and then carrying out a wide range of scientific tasks related to the specialism. Normally needs at least a first degree in a biological science or environmental subject, such as ecology, environmental or conservation biology, botany/plant science, marine biology or zoology. Some employers also look for postgraduate qualifications.

Chartered Institute of Ecology and Environmental Management
www.cieem.net

British Ecological Society
www.britishecologicalsociety.org

Editor

May work for a newspaper, magazine, academic journal, news agency, website, book publisher or broadcaster, carrying responsibility for the quality and content of everything that is printed or broadcast, and ensuring a consistent standard and style of presentation. Must have a thorough knowledge of a particular subject area. A background in journalism or broadcasting is often seen as essential, together with strong communication skills.

National Council for the Training of Journalists
www.nctj.com/want-to-be-a-journalist/careers

Education Administrator

Organises and manages the administrative and support systems required to facilitate the effective management of educational provision; may be based in a local authority, in further or higher education, or in an individual state or private school. Sometimes has a generic role but could specialise in an area such as data management, examinations, finance, human resources or quality assurance. Many of the specialist roles require both a degree and a relevant professional qualification.

Association of University Administrators
www.aua.ac.uk

Education Officer - Armed Services

A commissioned officer in one of the armed services with particular responsibility for education and training support; may organise anything from initial training for new recruits to specialist instruction in military engineering or tutoring officers for promotion. Must normally have a degree and for certain posts this should be in, say, engineering, mathematics or physics. The ability to lead and motivate as an officer is the most significant entry requirement.

Royal Navy
www.royalnavy.mod.uk

British Army
www.army.mod.uk

Royal Air Force
www.raf.mod.uk

Royal Marines
www.royalnavy.mod.uk/careers/role-finder/roles/royalmarinesofficer

Education Social Worker/Welfare Officer

Works with schools, pupils and families to support regular school attendance. May investigate problems of children whose education is being threatened by a wide range of social, behavioural, financial, transport, dietary or health factors. Visits schools to identify the causes of problems, talks to the children and their families and devises solutions to overcome difficulties. While entry requirements vary, local authorities often look for a degree or other qualification in social or human sciences, together with experience of working with children and families.

National Association of Social Workers in Education
www.naswe.org.uk

Educational Psychologist

Works to enhance the learning of children experiencing problems in education, including social or emotional problems or learning difficulties. Uses observation, interviews and test materials to assess each child, before offering a range of appropriate interventions, such as learning programmes and collaborative work with teachers or parents. Must have an accredited degree or equivalent in psychology, together with an approved postgraduate qualification in educational psychology.

British Psychological Society
http://careers.bps.org.uk/area/educational

Association of Educational Psychologists
www.aep.org.uk/careers

Electronic Music Performer

Uses computer-based performance technologies, including sequencing, synthesis, sound design, audio-editing, mixing and mastering, to create contemporary electronic music. Needs a combination of technological understanding and creative musical talent. May specialise in recording, radio, television or advertising, or - more likely - work freelance across several industries. Learning is mainly through hands-on experience, although there are music technology courses available at several different levels.

Music Match
www.media-match.com/uk/music

Emergency Planning Officer

Works as part of a team set up to anticipate and respond to threats to public safety, such as epidemics, major industrial accidents, natural disasters or terrorist acts. The work involves liaising with the police, fire, ambulance and other services to co-ordinate and prepare emergency plans, procedures and activities to meet the challenge of any major emergency. Experience of working in one of the emergency services could be useful for entry, although some employers may prefer a postgraduate qualification in, say, disaster management.

Emergency Planning Society
www.the-eps.org

Energy Engineer

Researches ways to generate energy, improve energy efficiency, reduce emissions from fossil fuels, and minimise environmental damage by developing renewable or sustainable sources, including biofuels, hydro, wind and solar power. To become a chartered energy engineer with the Energy Institute, would need an accredited engineering degree together with a relevant postgraduate qualification.

Energy Careers
http://careers.energyinst.org/courses

Engineering Geologist

Assesses the integrity of soil, rock, groundwater and other natural conditions prior to major construction schemes, such as tunnelling, laying of pipelines, planning of buildings, docks and harbours; may also advise on the suitability of appropriate construction materials. Would normally have an accredited geoscience degree in a subject such as geology, geophysics, geotechnology, engineering geology or mineral/mining engineering.

Association of Geotechnical and Geoenvironmental Specialists
www.ags.org.uk

Geological Society
www.geolsoc.org.uk

Institute of Materials, Minerals and Mining
www.iom3.org

Engineering Physicist

Specialises in the engineering applications of physics in areas such as microelectronics, optics and electromagnetism; takes a creative approach to solving issues related to materials science, electronics and computer modelling. May work in industry or in academic research. Other specialisation areas could include aerodynamics, acoustics, electrochemistry and photovoltaics.

Institute of Physics
www.iop.org

Entertainment/Talent Agent

Represents actors, musicians, singers, television and radio presenters, writers and other performers, seeking to secure the best possible work for them, at the best possible rates. May also run all aspects of the business affairs of clients, from new acts to major stars. Experience, enthusiasm and extensive personal contacts are usually much more important in this work than academic qualifications.

The Agents' Association
www.agents-uk.com

Environmental Consultant

Addresses a variety of environmental issues on behalf of commercial or government clients, including air, land or water contamination, environmental impact assessment, environmental audit, waste management or the development of environmental management systems. Would normally have at least a first degree in a science, environmental, engineering, agricultural/horticultural or land studies subject, with a postgraduate qualification preferred.

Institute of Environmental Management and Assessment
www.iema.net

Equality and Diversity Officer

Promotes best practice in the community or in the workplace in terms of ensuring equality of opportunity and of combating discrimination in such areas as gender, race, disability, age, religion and sexual orientation. Proof of commitment to this area of work, particularly if linked to experience in local government or the voluntary, faith or community sectors can be more important than academic qualifications.

Diversity Link
www.diversitylink.co.uk

Ergonomist

Sometimes known as a human factors specialist, ensures that equipment, facilities and systems are designed and organised to the highest standards of comfort, efficiency, health and safety for the people using them. The work involves the scientific study of the relationship between people, environments and equipment and using findings to improve human interaction with processes and systems. Areas of work include product/equipment design, production systems, information and advanced technology, and transport design.

Chartered Institute of Ergonomics and Human Factors
www.ergonomics.org.uk

Estate Manager/Land Agent

Manages an estate, farm, amenity horticulture site or forestry operation. May at times be responsible for developing leisure and recreational facilities, such as fishing, shooting, golf and hill walking, or establishing and marketing holiday accommodation for tourists. Usually has a qualification in farming/agriculture/estate management or in rural practice surveying.

Royal Institution of Chartered Surveyors
www.rics.org

University College of Estate Management
www.ucem.ac.uk

European Union Official *

Works for one of the European Union (EU) institutions, including the European Commission (the civil service of the EU), the Court of Justice and the European Parliament. Must be a citizen of an EU member state, interested in current affairs and able to speak more than one EU language. Administrator grade posts require a university degree, sometimes but not always in a specific subject such as law, economics, statistics or a science. Specialist jobs at higher grades require at least three years' professional experience and a degree in a specific subject.

European Commission Job Opportunities
http://ec.europa.eu/civil_service/job/index_en.htm

* UK citizens will no longer be eligible for this area of work once the process of UK withdrawal from the European Union is complete

Exhibition/Display Designer

Creates attractive displays for major events, trade shows, conferences, art galleries and museums, using graphics, props, lighting and sound to make the most of the exhibition space. Must balance aesthetics and innovation with the limitations of space and budget. Designs start from an interpretation of the client's ideas and requirements, with the addition of flair and originality to enhance both the product concept and its customer appeal. There are no absolute entry requirements, although many exhibition designers have a foundation degree or degree in a relevant subject.

British Display Society
www.britishdisplaysociety.co.uk

Association of Event Organisers
www.aeo.org.uk

Creative and Cultural Skills
http://ccskills.org.uk/careers

D and AD
www.dandad.org

Exploration Geologist

Uses drilling, seismic, acoustic, aerial photography and other methods to collect and interpret geological data, thereby locating mineral deposits, such as oil, petroleum, gas, platinum, gold, copper and nickel. Employs field-mapping techniques and makes calculations to estimate the size and locations of the reserves.

Association of Geotechnical and Geoenvironmental Specialists
www.ags.org.uk

Geological Society
www.geolsoc.org.uk

Institute of Materials, Minerals and Mining
www.iom3.org

Farm Secretary

Works closely with farmers and farm and estate managers to ensure the smooth running of the business side of a farm or estate; deals with management and livestock records, handles financial accounts, plans budgets, calculates pay, and works with buyers and suppliers. May work for one employer, be freelance or be sent out by an agency to a number of farms. Some knowledge of farming is useful, together with qualifications in, say, bookkeeping, accounting, secretarial work or business administration.

Institute of Agricultural Secretaries and Administrators
www.iagsa.co.uk

Fashion Buyer

Specialises in buying attractive garments for sale within fashion and dress shops or large retail store groups, attending exhibitions where fashion houses show their latest collections to UK, European and International buyers. There is no guaranteed entry or single training route to this sort of work. See Buying Executive.

Chartered Institute of Procurement and Supply
www.cips.org

Retail Apprenticeships
www.people1st.co.uk/retail-apprenticeships

Fashion Retail Academy
www.fashionretailacademy.ac.uk

Fashion Editor

Commissions and edits feature articles for a specialist fashion magazine. Alternatively, might write or edit a fashion section in a newspaper. Reports on all the latest trends, attends fashion shows, and keeps up to date with and comments on fashion available in retail stores. See also: Fashion Designer, Fashion Journalist, Fashion Photographer, Journalist, Magazine Journalist.

The Fashion Spot
www.thefashionspot.com

Fashion School Review (US)
www.fashionschoolreview.com

Fashion Journalist

A specialist journalist fully in touch with trends in fashion - a subject which attracts considerable interest from a clothes conscious market - must be able to make value judgements in this very creative field and to write with professional authority, flair and insight. A degree in fashion design could provide a strong foundation but there is no guaranteed route into this relatively small career field. See Journalist.

National Council for the Training of Journalists
www.nctj.com

Fashion Photographer

Takes photographs of models displaying the latest clothes, accessories, hairstyles and make-up. This involves working with the editors of fashion magazines, with fashion houses for their publicity literature, choosing locations and arranging lighting. Fashion photography is seen as one of the most glamorous areas of photography and it is certainly one of the most competitive. The lure of exotic locations, foreign travel, and joining the celebrity circuit must be weighed against working long hours and having to meet tight deadlines. See also: Photographer.

Alec
www.alec.co.uk/free-career-assessment/career-in-fashion-photography.htm

Fashion Sales Executive

Works in all aspects of fashion retail, including promoting the products of fashion houses/labels, store management, customer service, visual merchandising, buying, design, computer technology and marketing. See also: Fashion Designer, Fashion Buyer, Sales Executive.

Fashion Retail Academy
www.fashionretailacademy.ac.uk

Fashion and Retail Personnel
www.fashionpersonnel.co.uk/candidates/retail-job-sectors/sales-executive-manager

London Fashion Week
www.londonfashionweek.co.uk

Film/TV Director

Carries overall responsibility for defining the style and structure of a film or television programme, visualising it and bringing it to life, using creativity, organisational skills and technical knowledge to manage the entire production process. Duties include casting, script editing, shot composition, shot selection and editing. There are no formal entry requirements, although relevant degree courses exist. An alternative is to obtain work experience as a 'runner' on a film set or in a production office before working up through various positions over many years. The key is to observe successful directors at work, whilst becoming totally immersed in the practical process of filmmaking.

Directors Guild of Great Britain
www.dggb.org

British Film Institute
www.bfi.org.uk

Financial Risk Analyst

Sometimes known as a risk manager or risk surveyor, identifies and analyses areas of potential risk threatening the assets, earning capacity or success of organisations in the industrial, commercial or public sector. A degree in risk management, finance, mathematics or statistics would be a useful starting point, although not essential.

Institute of Risk Management
www.theirm.org

Association of Insurance and Risk Managers
www.airmic.com

Fine Art Dealer

Displays original paintings, sculptures and other works of art for purchase by the public or by members of the art trade; usually specialises in a particular type, field or period of painting, sculpture or ceramics. Attends art auctions or buys direct from the public and needs to become expert in such areas as valuation, restoration and authentication.

Society of London Art Dealers
www.slad.org.uk

Fish Farmer

Breeds and rears shellfish and fish such as salmon, trout and halibut; mainly for sale as food, although sometimes to stock lakes and rivers for angling purposes, and sometimes to stock ornamental ponds. Monitors water conditions and fish health, follows feeding routines and harvests stock for sale. There are no formal entry requirements, although it could be useful to take a college course in fish husbandry or fisheries management.

Institute of Fisheries Management
www.ifm.org.uk

Fisheries Officer

Conserves and protects freshwater or marine fisheries, carrying out surveys of aquatic life and water quality. As a sea fisheries officer, works to sustain the marine environment. This includes inspecting fishing vessels at sea and enforcing technical conservation measures. Would normally have a degree in a subject such as aquaculture, biology, environmental science, fisheries management, marine science or oceanography.

Institute of Fisheries Management
www.ifm.org.uk

Fitness Instructor

Leads group and individual exercise programmes to help people improve their health and fitness. May work across a range of activities or specialise in a particular one, such as aquagym, keep fit, Pilates, weight training or yoga. Could also work with specialist groups, such as senior citizens, children, people with disabilities or people referred by a doctor. Would normally have a recognised qualification in health, fitness and exercise instruction.

Register of Exercise Professionals
www.exerciseregister.org

Floor Manager (TV/Film)

The link between the director and the many people involved in a production, ensures that events go according to plan and that people taking part know their particular roles; also checks that sets and technical equipment are safe, ready to use and in the right position prior to filming. There are no specific entry requirements and many floor managers gradually work their way up from a more junior role.

BBC Careers
www.bbc.co.uk/careers/home

Creative Skillset
http://creativeskillset.org/creative_industries/film

Floral Designer/Florist

Uses creative skill and knowledge of plants and flowers to design and assemble flower arrangements. Flowers play a key role in everything from births, deaths and marriages to corporate events or budding romance. The UK fresh-cut flower and indoor-plant market is worth £2.2bn at retail level.

British Florist Association
www.britishfloristassociation.org

Footwear Designer

Creates practical designs for boots, shoes and other footwear. May specialise in one particular area, such as High Street fashion shoes, boots and sandals, catwalk and high-end couture footwear, or sportswear such as football boots and training shoes. In high-end couture, designers usually work on their own fashion labels, producing one-off shoes or exclusive ranges. Most footwear designers start their career after gaining a degree in fashion or product design.

Creative Skillset
http://creativeskillset.org/job_roles_and_stories/job_roles/667_footwear_designer

SATRA Footwear Training
www.satra.co.uk

Foreign Correspondent

A journalist with considerable experience and a proven track record, seeks out news for television, radio, newspapers, magazines and news agencies. May be based in one country or may travel around the world whenever a major news event occurs.

National Council for the Training of Journalists
www.nctj.com

Broadcast Journalism Training Council
www.bjtc.org.uk

Forensic Psychologist

Works mainly in prisons, conducting individual assessments and developing offender treatment and rehabilitation programmes. May occasionally be involved with criminal profiling to help police investigations, although this is a minor role. Must normally have an accredited degree in psychology together with a postgraduate qualification at master or doctoral level.

British Psychological Society
http://careers.bps.org.uk/area/forensic

Forensic Scientist (Biology)

Searches for and examines traces of material which might establish or exclude an association between a suspect, a victim and a crime scene. Evidence is acquired by exploring areas of biology including molecular biology, chemistry and analytical sciences. Evidence might include blood and other body fluids, hairs, textile fibres, glass fragments and tyre marks. Would normally have a first degree in biology, biochemistry, biomedical science or forensic science, together with a recognised postgraduate qualification.

Chartered Society of Forensic Sciences
www.csofs.org

Forensic Scientist (Chemistry)

Uses principles of chemistry, together with a range of specialist techniques, to analyse evidence - such as blood and other body fluids, hairs, textile fibres, glass fragments and tyre marks - that might link a suspect with a crime scene. Would normally have a first degree in chemistry, biochemistry, pharmacology, physiology, or materials, biomedical or forensic science, together with a recognised postgraduate qualification.

Chartered Society of Forensic Sciences
www.csofs.org

Fragrance Evaluator

Acts as the link between the client, typically a large corporation, and the perfumer. The evaluator is in charge of translating the often intangible descriptions that clients submit as a brief for a new product. Works closely with the perfumer to interpret this brief and to bring the client's imagination to life in a fragrance. Training is usually by in-house apprenticeships with many evaluators starting out as laboratory technicians, helping perfumers with the preparation of their compositions.

British Society of Perfumers
www.bsp.org.uk

Fragrance Foundation
www.fragrancefoundation.org.uk

Furniture Designer

Uses a range of skills to design furniture and related products for industrial, commercial and domestic clients. The work may involve anything from bespoke design to batch runs or mass production. Must balance innovative design, functional requirements and aesthetic appeal. Would often have a degree in furniture design or a related subject, although it is possible to start via an apprenticeship.

Chartered Society of Designers
www.csd.org.uk

Crafts Council
www.craftscouncil.org.uk

Creative and Cultural Skills
http://ccskills.org.uk/careers/advice/article/furniture-designer

Genealogist

Helps people trace their family roots and history by researching and studying archived information, especially records of births, deaths and marriages. May concentrate on a specific geographical area or track travelling ancestors anywhere in the world. There are no specific entry requirements, although knowledge of history, library/archive work and Latin could all be useful. Most genealogists have some other source of income.

Explore Genealogy
www.exploregenealogy.co.uk/becoming-professional-genealogist.html

Geneticist

Studies genes - the working parts of DNA or deoxyribonucleic acid - and the chromosomes that house them, perhaps to diagnose and treat disease, to improve crops, to develop new drugs and therapies, to conserve endangered species or to preserve the environment. Genes tell the body, for example, how to make all the proteins it needs to survive and grow, and healthcare scientists working in genetics examine samples of patients' DNA to identify genetic abnormalities that may be responsible for inherited diseases or conditions, such as cystic fibrosis or cancer.

Genetics Society
www.genetics.org.uk

British Society for Genetic Medicine
www.bsgm.org.uk

Geochemist

Specialises in studying the distribution of chemical elements in rocks and minerals, and observing the potential movement of these elements into soil and water systems. May work in oil exploration, water quality management or toxic waste site clearance. Usually has a degree in geochemistry, geology, chemistry, chemical engineering or marine science, and may find that a postgraduate qualification can be an advantage.

British Geological Survey
www.bgs.ac.uk

Geological Society
www.geolsoc.org.uk

Petroleum Exploration Society of Great Britain
www.pesgb.org.uk

Geographer

Explores the relationship between people and the physical world, particularly in terms of human values and how these guide our interaction with other creatures, the environment and the sustainability of the planet. Would usually start with a geography-related degree and then progress to a more specifically vocational postgraduate qualification.

Royal Geographical Society
www.rgs.org

Geophysicist

Studies physical aspects of the earth, using complex equipment to collect data on earthquakes and seismic waves, may analyse and interpret data in order to create maps of the build up of hydrocarbons. A degree in physics, geology/geoscience or geophysics is usually required, together with a postgraduate qualification.

British Geophysical Association
http://britgeophysics.org

British Geological Survey
www.bgs.ac.uk

Petroleum Exploration Society of Great Britain
www.pesgb.org.uk

Society of Exploration Geophysicists
www.seg.org

Goldsmith/Silversmith

Designs, produces and sometimes repairs a range of rings, brooches, pendants, bracelets and other items such as gold commemorative plates and medallions or silver cutlery, drinking cups and candlesticks, using fine precision tools to cut, saw, file and polish. Training can range from an apprenticeship to a full-time college or university course, but highly skilled smiths always train at the bench, as practical experience is vital. Students who go to college or university may have more design and theoretical knowledge but usually need to build up their hand skills.

The Goldsmiths' Company
www.thegoldsmiths.co.uk/craft-industry

National Association of Jewellers
www.naj.co.uk

Golf Course Designer

Commissioned to develop a new project or to make alterations to an existing course, usually works in the following areas: conceptual design, covering the ideas and development of the concept of a project; detailed design, focusing on the engineering detail and associated documentation of the architecture to greens, tees, bunkers, drainage, irrigation and so on; design management, involving inspections and supervisory visits during the construction and irrigation phases; establishment management, making final visits and inspections.

European Institute of Golf Course Architects
www.eigca.org

British Association of Golf Course Constructors
www.bagcc.org.uk

British Association of Landscape Industries
www.bali.org.uk

Grants Officer

Assesses applications for grants and funding from individuals, charities, community groups or university research departments. May award funding directly, or may refer applications to a senior grants officer, programme director or committee for a final decision. While there are no specific entry requirements, organisations tend to look for experience in the type of projects that they fund, such as the arts, community work, conservation or scientific research.

Association of Charitable Foundations
www.acf.org.uk

Health and Safety Adviser

Uses knowledge and skills to prevent or reduce injuries, accidents and health problems in the workplace; creates health and safety policies, covering such areas as fire safety, occupational health, noise, safe use of machinery and control of hazardous substances. While it is not essential, a degree level qualification can be a useful starting point, particularly if linked with previous experience of risk assessment, or a background in construction, manufacturing, engineering or scientific work.

Institution of Occupational Safety and Health
www.iosh.co.uk

Health Psychologist

Applies psychological methods to research behaviour relevant to health, illness and healthcare; may, for example, study when and why people seek professional advice about their health, why healthcare professionals do or do not recommend preventative measures, how patients and healthcare professionals interact, or how patients adapt to illness. Also seeks ways to encourage people to improve their health, such as helping them to lose weight or stop smoking. Must normally have an accredited degree in psychology, together with a postgraduate qualification in health psychology.

British Psychological Society
http://careers.bps.org.uk/area/health

Health Visitor

A qualified and registered midwife or nurse, works in the community to promote good health and prevent illness, mainly visiting new parents in their homes to assess the support they need to help give the child the best possible start in life. Must follow nurse or midwifery training with an approved programme in specialist community public health nursing/health visiting.

Health Careers
www.healthcareers.nhs.uk

Community Practitioners' and Health Visitors' Association
www.unitetheunion.org/cphva

Helicopter Pilot

Flies single- and multi-engined helicopters within the armed services or for business, leisure or emergency response purposes. Duties may range from active warfare to ferrying oil workers to offshore rigs or transporting private clients as part of a charter service. May either sign up for pilot training with one of the armed services or follow a rigorous and usually expensive programme of training to obtain a commercial licence.

British Helicopter Association
www.britishhelicopterassociation.org

Flying Start
www.flying-start.org

Herbalist

Treats a range of illnesses, allergies and chronic physical conditions by using plant medicines to maximise the human body's healing capacities. Herbal medicine is a holistic health system that explores the underlying causes as well as the symptoms of illness. Must have an accredited degree and complete an initial professional development programme before being able to practise as a medical herbalist.

National Institute of Medical Herbalists
www.nimh.org.uk

European Herbal and Traditional Medicine Practitioners Association
www.ehtpa.eu

Heritage Manager

Usually has responsibilities that involve the preservation of the fabric and character of a building of historical importance or a significant site in terms of cultural or industrial heritage, while at the same time seeking to generate an income by attracting visitors. There are no specific entry requirements, although many heritage managers are graduates. A degree in history, history of art, archaeology or museum studies could be useful.

Creative and Cultural Skills
http://ccskills.org.uk/careers/advice/article/heritage-manager

Higher Education Careers Adviser

Provides information, advice and guidance, through individual interviews and group work, to help undergraduates, graduates and postgraduates assess their values, interests, abilities and skills and relate these to opportunities for employment, further study and training. There are no specific entry requirements, although many advisers have a degree, work experience and a postgraduate guidance qualification.

Association of Graduate Careers Advisory Services
www.agcas.org.uk

Historic Buildings Inspector

Reports and advises on buildings, structures and areas of special historic, architectural or artistic interest. The role includes helping to protect and enhance all forms of building, from castles and dungeons to churches, lighthouses, windmills and residential property. A degree relevant to the built environment - in, say, architecture, civil engineering, planning or surveying - is a useful but not essential starting point; some practitioners offer qualifications in subjects such as history, architectural history or heritage management.

Institute of Historic Building Conservation
www.ihbc.org.uk

Historical Researcher

Applies key historical approaches, sources and methods to a particular subject area; the role often requires wide-ranging research, with importance placed on the use of architecture, field trips, material culture, archaeology and literature to aid historical understanding. This small field of work often overlaps with other career areas such as university lecturer or museum curator, but can also include specialised research. A postgraduate qualification is likely to be required, following a first degree in a history-based subject.

Institute of Historical Research
www.history.ac.uk

Horse Riding Instructor

Teaches people of all ages, levels of ability and experience to ride, either as a leisure activity or to prepare for competitions such as show jumping, eventing or dressage. May work in a commercial riding establishment or private yard or as a freelance coach. There are no academic entry requirements, but must have a high standard of horsemanship and good communication skills. To work in the UK, would usually have qualifications from the British Horse Society or the Association of British Riding Schools.

British Horse Society
www.bhs.org.uk

Association of British Riding Schools
www.abrs-info.org

Association of Irish Riding Establishments
www.aire.ie

Housing Manager

Works for a local authority, housing association or other accommodation provider, maintaining regular contact with tenants, collecting rental income, and dealing with repairs, redecoration and community living issues. Personal qualities and experience tend to be more important than academic qualifications, although a higher national diploma or degree in a subject such as estate or property management, planning, urban studies or sociology could be useful.

Chartered Institute of Housing
www.cih.org

Hydrogeologist

Specialises in the theory and practice of groundwater science and engineering; may work for a scientific, engineering or environmental consultancy organisation, for a water company or for a government scientific or regulatory service, or in academic research. Would normally follow a degree in a subject such as geoscience, engineering, physics, mathematics, chemistry, bioscience or environmental science with a specific postgraduate course.

UK Groundwater Forum
www.groundwateruk.org

Geological Society
www.geolsoc.org.uk

Immigration Officer

Applies national immigration rules and policy by checking the right of entry to the UK of all individuals arriving at seaports, airports and via the Channel Tunnel; examines passports and conducts personal interviews with travellers when necessary. May also gather intelligence and use legal powers to detain or remove illegal entrants. There are no set qualification requirements, but many applicants are graduates. Degree subject is not important, although ability in modern languages can be useful.

UK Visas and Immigration
www.gov.uk/government/organisations/uk-visas-and-immigration

Immunologist
Investigates the functions of the body's immune system and uses this knowledge to work towards treating and controlling a range of diseases and disorders. The work includes understanding the processes and effects of inappropriate stimulation, which are associated with the development of autoimmune diseases, allergies and transplant rejection. Immunologists work within clinical and academic settings, as well as in industrial research.

British Society for Immunology
www.immunology.org

Medical Research Council
www.mrc.ac.uk

Indexer
Compiles lists of searchable terms relating to the content of documents such as books, periodicals, technical manuals or reports, websites or large collections to help users find the information they need. Although there are no fixed entry requirements, many indexers have a degree-level qualification.

Society of Indexers
www.indexers.org.uk

Industrial Production Manager
Plans and supervises manufacturing processes, ensuring that goods are produced efficiently and meet targets. May work anywhere in the manufacturing sector, including motor vehicles, brewing, food, textiles, pharmaceuticals and building materials. Could start as a production worker and progress with experience to management level; alternatively, could complete a degree in manufacturing before joining a graduate management training programme.

Chartered Management Institute
www.managers.org.uk

International Aid Worker
May focus on working with developing countries to implement sustainable solutions to problems in fields such as agriculture, education, health and sanitation; may alternatively be involved with short-term humanitarian/disaster relief assignments. Work opportunities can cover just about anything from education, healthcare or irrigation to economics, human rights or flood relief. Many aid workers are graduates, sometimes with a specific qualification in, say, healthcare or engineering, sometimes with a more broadly-based degree in social sciences, development studies, languages or economics.

United Nations Junior Professional Officer Service Centre
www.jposc.undp.org

International Banking Executive

Supports commercial customers across an international network, offering such services as debt financing, risk management and financial transactions; also provides balance sheet advisory and structuring services to help firms get the most out of their financial resources. International work may be offered to the highest-flying graduate trainees. A useful starting point is to offer a good degree (minimum 2:1) in a finance-related subject.

British Bankers Association
www.bba.org.uk

Chartered Banker Institute
www.charteredbanker.com

International Marketing Executive

Manages the process of improving an organisation's market share and profitability by identifying, anticipating and satisfying customer requirements in other countries. May specialise in market research, brand management or marketing communications. A degree or postgraduate qualification in marketing is a considerable asset, although employers value skills such as good communication, numeracy and the ability to work under pressure.

Chartered Institute of Marketing
www.cim.co.uk/insight/tools-and-templates/getin2marketing

International Trade Adviser

Works with UK based businesses to ensure their success in international markets through exports; may also encourage and support overseas companies to look at the UK as the best place to set up or expand their business. Would normally be of graduate calibre, with wide-ranging, senior level experience in international trade.

Institute of Export
www.export.org.uk/professional-qualifications/certified-international-trade-advisor

Investment Fund Manager

Provides financial advice and services to private and corporate clients about a range of investment matters including buying and selling unit/investment trusts and shares/ bonds. Works closely with investment analysts, using their recommendations to take decisions. Almost all entrants are graduates, often with a professional qualification in a related field and with experience of a specialist market sector.

Association for Financial Markets in Europe
www.afme.eu

Chartered Institute for Securities and Investment
www.cisi.org

CFA Society of the UK
https://secure.cfauk.org

Jazz Musician

Creates and/or performs jazz music as an instrumentalist, singer or composer. The work often includes both live performance and studio recording, either as a soloist or as part of a group of musicians. May also work in other genres, such as classical, rock or folk music. There is no standard training programme and no fixed career path, although there are degree courses available. Any performing career would demand very high standards, simply because the competition is so intense.

Jazz School UK
www.jazzschool.co.uk/advice.html

Jewellery Designer

Creates a variety of hand-made or mass-produced jewellery, silverware and similar items, including pieces using precious metals and gems, costume jewellery using synthetic stones and less precious metals, and fashion accessories made from other materials. There are no set requirements for becoming a jewellery designer, although some training would be useful. Provision ranges from short craft level courses to honours degree standard.

The National Association of Jewellers
www.naj.co.uk

Contemporary British Silversmiths
www.contemporarybritishsilversmiths.org

Jockey

Licensed to ride horses at race meetings, either on a flat racetrack or across jumps in what is known as National Hunt racing. Often gains initial experience by working as a stable hand before applying for a 12- to 18-month racing apprenticeship. There are no academic entry requirements but age, eyesight, physical fitness and weight are usually important considerations.

Careers in Racing
www.careersinracing.com

Landscape Scientist

Works closely with landscape architects/designers, carrying out ecological and habitat surveys of a site, advising on planting, creating new habitats and drawing up wildlife management plans. Usually specialises in, say, botany, conservation, ecology, geology or soil science. Must have a relevant degree, followed by a period of study at work in order to qualify fully as a chartered landscape scientist.

Landscape Institute
www.landscapeinstitute.org

Lecturer (Further Education)

Teaches one or more subjects to mainly post-16 students in a college, community centre or similar environment; courses may be academic, vocational (covering anything from catering to hairdressing or motor vehicle repair) or focused on hobbies and leisure activities. Must have an accredited qualification in the subject being taught, together with a recognised teaching certificate or diploma.

FE Advice
www.feadvice.org.uk

University and College Union
www.ucu.org.uk

Lecturer (Higher Education)

Teaches and carries out research in a university or similar institution, delivering undergraduate and postgraduate lectures, seminars and practical demonstrations, in an academic or vocational subject area, to students over the age of 18. Would usually need a relevant first degree, a postgraduate qualification and the desire to carry out original research and have work published. In some vocational areas, a professional qualification and several years' relevant work experience would be necessary.

Higher Education Academy
www.international.heacademy.ac.uk

University and College Union
www.ucu.org.uk

Lexicographer

Compiles, edits and updates dictionaries, monitoring and recording uses of language and using databases to check a wide range of evidence. Considers both the meaning and usage of words and phrases before compiling authoritative definitions. If working as a bilingual lexicographer, translates words and expressions rather than defining them. Would normally have a degree in English, linguistics, modern languages or classics, although other subjects could also be acceptable.

Chambers
www.chambers.co.uk

HarperCollins
www.harpercollins.co.uk

Oxford University Press
http://global.oup.com

Society for Editors and Proofreaders
www.sfep.org.uk

Lifeguard

Patrols a beach, swimming pool, lake or inland waterway, working to keep swimmers safe. Observes and supervises swimming areas to prevent accidents and make swimmers aware of dangerous situations; uses life-saving techniques in the event of an emergency. Must be physically fit and a strong swimmer, in possession of specific qualifications relating to either pool or beach work.

Surf Lifesaving Great Britain
www.slsgb.org.uk

Swimming Teachers' Association
www.sta.co.uk

Literary Agent

Acts as a link between writers and the publishing and media industries; uses contacts and experience to negotiate rates on behalf of writers and to sell novels, books and screenplays to publishing houses and media production companies. There are no academic entry requirements for starting out, usually by joining an agency as a reader, and it is almost impossible to progress without a considerable collection of personal contacts.

Creative and Cultural Skills
http://ccskills.org.uk/careers/advice/article/being-a-literary-agent

Loss Adjuster

An independent specialist, investigates large or complex claims on behalf of insurance companies. May specialise in domestic or commercial claims, assessing the scale and causes of loss or damage, and making sure that claims are valid. These could cover anything from fire or flood damage to loss through theft or fraud. There are several routes to qualification, including starting as a claims technician and working towards insurance industry qualifications, or joining a graduate training scheme.

Chartered Institute of Loss Adjusters
www.cila.co.uk

Magazine Journalist

Researches and writes feature articles and news items for one or more periodicals, including consumer titles, business journals and trade publications. Magazines tend to have a defined readership and focus on a specialist area or interest. While there are no absolute entry requirements, many magazine journalists have a degree or equivalent qualification.

National Council for the Training of Journalists
www.nctj.com

Magazine Publisher

Manages one or more printed or online periodicals, taking responsibility for making them an editorial and commercial success. Establishes overall editorial direction, sets budgets and controls business operations to balance high quality content with revenue and profit. Must have good knowledge of the marketplace, outstanding business acumen and strong editorial experience.

Professional Publishers Association
www.ppa.co.uk

Make-up Artist

Applies cosmetics and styles hair for performers, presenters, models or others before they appear in front of a camera or a live audience. May work in film, television, theatre, music, photographic sessions or fashion shows. While there are no specific entry requirements, many practitioners start with a course in fashion, theatre and media make-up and gain practical experience in such areas as amateur dramatics, student film and photography projects, or charity fashion shows.

National Association of Screen Make-up Artists and Hairdressers
www.nasmah.co.uk

Market Maker

Uses specialist knowledge to facilitate trade in global markets by buying (when the price is low) and selling (when the price is high) commodities such as foreign exchange, equities, crude oil, metals, gold, vegetable oils, and grains. Most entrants have a degree, usually in a subject such as business, economics, finance, accountancy or mathematics.

Chartered Institute for Securities and Investment
www.cisi.org

Mathematician/Mathematical Researcher

May work in an academic, commercial or public service environment, applying mathematical principles to identify trends in data sets or developing mathematical models to explain, quantify or predict almost any situation or event. Would normally have at least a good first degree in mathematics or a related subject and would often be expected to have a postgraduate qualification.

Institute of Mathematics and its Applications
www.ima.org.uk

Maths Careers
www.mathscareers.org.uk

Medical Illustrator/Clinical Photographer

Supports other healthcare professionals within a hospital environment; specialises in clinical photography, graphic design, medical art or videography, producing resource materials for use in patient care, education and research. Qualification as a clinical photographer requires a specific degree or an accredited degree in another photographic discipline followed by a postgraduate certificate. Medical illustrators and graphic designers are expected to have a degree in design or other relevant media discipline and to complete a postgraduate distance-learning course.

Institute of Medical Illustrators
www.imi.org.uk/section/education-and-careers

Medical Secretary

Trained in the use of medical terminology, keeps the medical records of patients and handles medical correspondence and filing. May work in a hospital or in private practice, for individual doctors/consultants or in a health centre.

Association of Medical Secretaries, Practice Managers, Administrators and Receptionists
www.amspar.com

Member of European Parliament (MEP) *

Elected once every five years by voters of the European Union (EU), on behalf of its 500 million citizens, represents a particular city or region in one of the 28 member states (the UK, for example, has 73 of the 751 MEPs); scrutinises proposals for new EU laws and questions and lobbies the European Commission and the Council of Ministers. The European Parliament and its MEPs are mostly based in Brussels, but they also meet in Strasbourg to amend and vote on draft legislation and policy. MEPs do not generally sit in national delegations in the Parliament but in multinational political groups.

European Parliament
www.europarl.europa.eu

* The UK will no longer be represented in the European Parliament once the process of UK withdrawal from the European Union is complete

Member of Parliament (MP)

Represents a local constituency in the UK House of Commons in London; attends sessions in parliament, debates issues, raises questions and votes on new laws and policies. Also holds surgeries in constituency and takes up constituents' issues and concerns. Usually a member of a political party, although some MPs stand for election independently. May eventually hold a position of national responsibility, such as being a government minister or party spokesperson on a particular issue. There are no academic entry requirements.

UK Parliament
www.parliament.uk

Electoral Commission
www.electoralcommission.org.uk

Member of Scottish Parliament (MSP)

Represents a constituency in the Scottish Parliament in Edinburgh, the law-making body in Scotland for devolved matters. These include health, education, justice, police and fire services, housing, local government, the environment, social work and agriculture. MSP work might include lodging a motion to get support for an issue, attending committee meetings, speaking in debates, introducing bills to change the law, and proposing amendments to a bill.

Scottish Parliament
www.scottish.parliament.uk

Minerals Surveyor

Explores and maps mineral deposits in potential mining and quarrying sites in order to consider their commercial exploitation. Uses specialised equipment and techniques to construct a precise three-dimensional model of the site. Normally needs a degree or accredited professional qualification. Relevant degree subjects include mining engineering, geology, surveying, civil engineering or geomatics.

Institute of Materials, Minerals and Mining
www.iom3.org

Model Maker

Designs and makes three dimensional scale models, such as prototype models of new products prior to sale, architectural models of construction developments or visual special effects for exhibitions, museums, film, TV and theatre. May use techniques including wood machining, metal working and sculpting with clay, finishing processes such as hand colouring and spray painting, together with a range of hand, power and machine tools and computer-assisted equipment. Most model makers are self-employed and work on a project-by-project basis. Clients include engineers, designers, architects, advertising companies, museums, and film and TV companies.

Creative and Cultural Skills
http://ccskills.org.uk/careers/advice/article/model-maker

Institution of Engineering Designers
www.ied.org.uk

Molecular Biologist

Studies how organisms transmit genetic information to successive generations. Also analyses viruses and bacteria to assist with the diagnosis and treatment of infections found in humans, plants and animals. Needs at least a first degree in molecular biology or a closely related field such as biology or biochemistry, with a master or doctoral level qualification required for work in research or university teaching.

Royal Society of Biology
www.rsb.org.uk

Music Publisher

Secures contracts with composers and songwriters to have the publishing rights of current and/or future compositions; actively seeks to exploit these rights by licensing material for recording, airplay, inclusion in films and television, and many other commercial uses. A degree in management, marketing or law could prove useful but is not as essential as knowledge of the recording industry, awareness of music trends and performers, familiarity with business contracts and understanding of copyright law.

Music Publishers Association
www.mpaonline.org.uk/careers

Music Teacher

Gives music lessons - for playing an instrument, singing, understanding theory or performance - to people of all ages and abilities, individually, in small groups or in larger classes; may offer private tuition or work in a school, college, conservatoire or university. May be able to become a private teacher without qualifications, although a recognised qualification is advisable. Must have full qualified teacher status to work in the state school sector.

Get into Teaching
https://getintoteaching.education.gov.uk

Incorporated Society of Musicians
www.ism.org

Music Therapist

Usually a trained musician with a postgraduate qualification in music therapy, works with people of all ages, using music as a form of self-expression for clients with a variety of mental health problems, communication disorders and serious physical illness. A high level of musicianship is essential, together with strong personal skills. Entrants usually have a music degree or equivalent, although graduates from courses such as medicine, nursing, psychology or education may be considered if they possess the key musical skills. Postgraduate training can be full- or part-time.

British Association for Music Therapy
www.bamt.org

Musical Instrument Maker/Repairer

Uses highly specialised practical skills to create new musical instruments or repair ones that have been damaged; usually works with a particular family of instruments, such as keyboards, strings, percussion or brass, using wood, metal, plastic and other materials. There are no set qualifications for this area of work, although there are many short courses available. Outstanding woodwork or metalwork skills are often a starting point, together with fine appreciation of pitch and quality of sound.

Institute of Musical Instrument Technology
www.imit.org.uk

National Association of Musical Instrument Repairers
www.namir.org.uk

Nanny

Cares for babies and young children, working in a private home. Duties might include feeding, bathing, dressing and changing nappies; teaching basic social skills and hygiene; helping children to learn through play; organising play opportunities to help children mix with others; preparing meals and snacks; and tidying up and cleaning rooms used by the children.

Professional Association for Childcare and Early Years
www.pacey.org.uk

Council for Awards in Care, Health and Education
www.cache.org.uk

Naturopath

Practises the branch of complementary medicine based on the belief that the human body is self-regulatory and capable of self-repair if given the right conditions. Treatment may consist of special diets or fasting, coupled with hydrotherapy and osteopathic techniques. Qualification is not essential but it is advisable to complete a three-year diploma and register with one of the professional organisations for complementary therapists.

General Council and Register of Naturopaths
http://gcrn.org.uk

General Naturopathic Council
www.gncouncil.co.uk

Neuropsychologist

A chartered psychologist within the field of clinical or educational psychology, works with patients of all ages who have had traumatic brain injury, strokes, toxic and metabolic disorders, tumours and neurodegenerative diseases. Requires not only general clinical skills and knowledge of the broad range of mental health problems, but also a substantial degree of specialist knowledge in the neurosciences.

British Psychological Association
http://careers.bps.org.uk/area/neuro

Newspaper Publisher

Manages one or more printed or online newspapers, taking responsibility for making them an editorial and commercial success. Establishes overall editorial direction, sets budgets and controls business operations to balance high quality content with revenue and profit. Must have good knowledge of the marketplace, outstanding business acumen and strong editorial experience.

News Media Association
www.newsmediauk.org

Media.info
http://media.info/uk/newspapers

Notary

Verifies, authenticates and records deeds, documents and facts for cross-border transactions, performing a vital function in international trade and business. Most notaries are also solicitors and do their general legal work in that capacity; others, including the Scrivener notaries in London, practise only as notaries, undertaking commercial and property work (including conveyancing) and family and private client work (including wills, probate and the administration of estates).

The Notaries Society
www.thenotariessociety.org.uk

Nuclear Engineer

Works on the production and use of nuclear fuels to generate electric power, and the design, construction, control and safety of nuclear reactors. May also be involved in reactor decommissioning, developing nuclear-powered submarines or medical research. Would normally have a degree in nuclear engineering or in a related subject, such as chemical, electrical or mechanical engineering.

Nuclear Industry Association
www.niauk.org

World Nuclear Association
www.world-nuclear.org

Nursery/Early Years Teacher

Works with children aged from three to five years in day nurseries, nursery schools and reception classes. Specialises in early childhood development, planning, organising and running a range of learning and play activities in a safe and supportive environment. Must have either Early Years or Qualified Teacher Status, for which there are several pathways available, each requiring a degree or equivalent qualification and a professional skills test in literacy and numeracy.

Get into Teaching
https://getintoteaching.education.gov.uk

Professional Association for Childcare and Early Years
www.pacey.org.uk

Pre-School Learning Alliance
www.pre-school.org.uk

Nutritional Therapist

Advises clients on how to improve their overall health and wellbeing by careful assessment of what their bodies need in terms of food, vitamins and minerals. Nutritional therapy is considered a complementary therapy and is often used alongside orthodox medicine.

British Association for Applied Nutrition and Nutritional Therapy
www.bant.org.uk

Nutritional Therapy Education Commission
www.nteducationcommission.org.uk

Occupational Hygienist

Assesses potential risks to workforce safety in environments including factories, offices and building sites; responsible for recognising, evaluating and controlling environmental hazards resulting from physical, chemical or biological factors in the workplace. Often working within a team with other professionals, such as doctors, nurses and engineers, enables organisations to respond effectively to the requirements of legislation on issues such as asbestos, noise and manual handling.

Chartered Society for Worker Health Protection
www.bohs.org

Institution of Occupational Safety and Health
www.iosh.co.uk

Occupational Psychologist

Applies psychological theory and practice to workplace issues, especially those relating to recruitment, training and retention; may use psychometric tests or assessment centres to gauge particular personality traits and ability levels; may advise on the work environment. Must have an accredited degree or equivalent in psychology, together with a doctorate-level qualification in occupational psychology.

British Psychological Society
http://careers.bps.org.uk/area/occupational

Office Manager

Ensures that every aspect of an organisation's administration is carried out efficiently, dealing with outgoing and incoming information and communication and its accurate storage and retrieval. May have a team of clerical and administrative assistants to deal with day-to-day office duties, such as answering queries, typing letters, taking and passing on messages, providing help at meetings and filing information.

Institute of Customer Service
www.instituteofcustomerservice.com

Association of Medical Secretaries, Practice Managers, Administrators and Receptionists
www.amspar.com

Institute of Legal Secretaries and PAs
www.institutelegalsecretaries.com

Institute of Agricultural Secretaries and Administrators
www.iagsa.co.uk

Council for Administration
www.skillscfa.org

Institute of Administrative Management
www.instam.org

Ophthalmologist
Undertakes surgery of the eye, usually with the aid of an operating microscope and lasers, and cares for patients with minor and major eye injuries, and those with long-term diseases of the eye such as diabetic retinopathy and age-related macular degeneration. Must be a fully qualified doctor, following a degree in medicine with two foundation years as a junior doctor and seven years of specialist training.

Royal College of Ophthalmologists
www.rcophth.ac.uk

Health Careers
www.healthcareers.nhs.uk

Organic Farmer
Produces food for human consumption whilst avoiding chemicals such as pesticides, herbicides and artificial fertilisers; relies on traditional principles of crop rotation, composting and weed and pest control to protect both wildlife and ecosystems that benefit the soil. Many practitioners start from a sense of personal conviction but there are several courses, at a variety of levels, teaching the principles and techniques of organic farming and food production.

Garden Organic
www.gardenorganic.org.uk

Orthotist/Prosthetist
Supplies and fits either orthoses - splints, braces and special footwear to aid movement, correct deformity and relieve discomfort - or prostheses - artificial replacement limbs for patients who have lost or were born without a limb. Must successfully complete an approved three- or four-year degree in prosthetics and othotics.

British Association of Prosthetists and Orthotists
www.bapo.com

Outdoor Activities Instructor
Teaches skills in a variety of pursuits, ranging from canoeing, climbing and orienteering to skiing and snowboarding; must be able to plan activities to suit the needs, abilities and experience of different client groups, and ensure adherence to strict safety regulations. There are no particular entry standards, although recognised coaching or instructor qualifications in at least one major outdoor activity would normally be the minimum required.

Institute for Outdoor Learning
www.outdoor-learning.org

Chartered Institute for the Management of Sport and Physical Activity
www.cimspa.co.uk

Outward Bound Trust
www.outwardbound.org.uk

Paralegal

Performs substantive legal work that requires knowledge of the law but is not a qualified solicitor or barrister. May work for, or be retained by, solicitors within the legal profession or may work within a legal environment in commerce, industry or the public sector. There are no specific rules about qualifications and training but many graduates and postgraduates, who have completed a law degree or professional training course, take jobs as paralegals while still looking for a training contract as a solicitor or a pupillage as a barrister.

All about Law
www.allaboutlaw.co.uk

Skills for Justice Career Pathways
www.skillsforjustice-cp.com

Paraplanner

Processes personal information provided by clients when meeting a financial adviser or planner, researching solutions to meet each client's financial needs. Does not give advice but can produce letters, reports and supporting evidence for consideration by the client. There are no specific entry requirements for this still emerging career area, although most practitioners gain experience through working in a support or administrative function within a paraplanning or financial advice organisation.

Financial Planning
www.financialplanning.org.uk/sites/financialplanning.org.uk/files/user/role_of_ the_paraplanner_2010_0_0.pdf

Passenger Transport Manager

Plans, coordinates and supervises passenger transport operations, including air, bus, coach, ferry, ship, train and tram services. The actual role can vary considerably, depending on the nature of the transport system involved, but often includes performance and safety targets. While it is possible to start as a driver or administrative assistant and work up to managerial level, many people enter with a degree in, say, logistics, supply chain management or transport management.

Careers that Move
www.careersthatmove.co.uk

Pathologist

A fully qualified doctor, uses a variety of investigative techniques to detect disease. The work can be vital in accurate and early diagnosis, improving the prospects for treatment. Also works to identify sources of disease and reduce the possible risks of further spread. Must first obtain a medical degree, which takes approximately five years, followed by a two-year foundation programme. Doctors wishing to train in pathology then apply for specialty training in one of five branches: chemical pathology/clinical biochemistry, haematology, histopathology, medical microbiology and virology, or immunology.

Association of Clinical Pathologists
www.pathologists.org.uk

Perfumer

An expert in creating perfume compositions, often regarded as an artist in conveying a mood or a feeling through scent. Must have an incredibly keen sense of smell and extensive knowledge of a large variety of ingredients, their smells and chemical compositions. Training is usually by an in-house apprenticeship with a fragrance house such as International Flavours and Fragrances (IFF) or Givaudan.

British Society of Perfumers
www.bsp.org.uk

Givaudan
www.givaudan.com/Careers

Physician Associate

Works under the supervision of a doctor, performing such tasks as carrying out a complete physical examination, making an initial diagnosis, ordering and interpreting investigations and developing an initial treatment plan for patients with a variety of illnesses. Usually follows a science degree or a qualification in, say, nursing, physiotherapy or working as a paramedic with a two-year postgraduate course.

Faculty of Physician Associates
www.fparcp.co.uk

Picture Researcher

Uses visual knowledge and experience to find the 'right' pictures for any given project, whether for a book, newspaper, magazine, advertisement, television programme, film, exhibition, brochure, CD, DVD, or website. There are no formal academic requirements, although visual arts qualifications - such as fine art, photography, publishing, illustration or graphic design - may be helpful.

Picture Research Association
www.picture-research.org.uk

Pilates Teacher

Helps people correct their posture and improve their body strength with special stretching and conditioning exercises, including relaxation, coordination, stamina and breathing. Must be able to design exercise routines specific to certain people, such as those with particular injury problems. Might run group classes or one-to-one sessions. Usually needs experience in exercise, movement or another physical therapy, followed by training with one of the organisations in the Pilates industry.

Pilates Foundation
www.pilatesfoundation.com

Planning and Development Surveyor

Works closely with town planners, architects and construction professionals, advising on the effective use of land and property resources. Considers such issues as site planning, development, conservation and transport options, all in relation to current market conditions. Usually needs an accredited degree or professional qualification in a subject such as planning and development, building surveying, property development or estate management.

Royal Institution of Chartered Surveyors
www.rics.org

Political Researcher

Assists with the formulation of a political party's policies and campaigns, advising politicians on policy decisions and researching issues to generate new policies. May draft speeches and articles for politicians to describe party policy, or to respond effectively in media interviews. Also provides politicians with the necessary information to attack opponents' policies and performance. Must have a keen interest in politics and current affairs, and often has a degree in a subject such as politics, government, law, economics, history or international relations.

Working for an MP
www.w4mp.org

European Parliament
www.europarl.europa.eu

Politician's Assistant

Provides administrative support to an elected politician, usually helping with secretarial tasks, research and publicity. The role may include responding to enquiries, managing the politician's diary, making travel arrangements and taking minutes. Although there are no specific entry requirements, many new entrants are graduates with a keen interest in politics and current affairs.

Working for an MP
www.w4mp.org

European Parliament
www.europarl.europa.eu

Pop/Rock Musician

Performs live in front of an audience or makes recordings for broadcast, CD or download. May sing or play alone as a soloist, or work with a group of musicians, using knowledge of voice production, melody, harmony and rhythm to interpret music. Might also undertake session work for backing tracks, advertisements and films. Talent, dedication, a passion for music and a strong desire to perform are the essential entry requirements.

Careers in Music
www.careersinmusic.co.uk

Presenter (Radio/TV)

Links together the different parts of programmes broadcast on television, radio and the internet, introducing guests, playing music, delivering reports, reviewing books, recordings or films, conducting interviews and interacting with the audience. Genuine flair, charisma and a captivating personality are more important than academic qualifications, although news presenters, for example, need skills in journalism and current affairs, weather presenters need meteorological training, and political/financial presenters need detailed understanding of parliamentary and City developments.

Creative Skillset
www.creativeskillset.org

Broadcast Journalism Training Council
www.bjtc.org.uk

Press/Information Officer

Acts as the official contact for a public or private organisation - from a charity or government agency to a multinational corporation - handling all media interest. Prepares, writes and distributes press releases, responds to media queries and liaises with journalists. Also tracks media coverage relating to the organisation and organises press conferences. Most new entrants are graduates, often with previous experience of journalism, broadcasting or public relations.

Chartered Institute of Public Relations
www.cipr.co.uk

National Council for the Training of Journalists
www.nctj.com

Printing Technologist/Manager

Organises and controls the flow of work in a printing company, monitoring quality, ensuring deadlines are met, complying with health and safety standards, managing production staff and liaising with customers. There are many routes into this work, ranging from progression to management after gaining experience on the shop floor to direct entry with a degree in, say, print media management, graphic communications or business studies.

Institute of Paper, Printing and Publishing
www.ip3.org.uk

Prison Governor

Carries responsibility for the management and security of prisons, remand centres and young offenders' institutions. Must be able to enforce discipline while at the same time taking a close interest in the welfare and future prospects of prisoners. It is possible to progress to governor level after gaining experience as a prison officer or to complete a degree in any subject and seek direct entry to the National Offender Management Service graduate programme.

Prison Governors Association
http://prison-governors-association.org.uk

HM Prison Service
www.gov.uk/government/organisations/hm-prison-service

Scottish Prison Service
www.sps.gov.uk

Northern Ireland Prison Service
www.justice-ni.gov.uk/topics/prisons

Prison Officer

Supervises inmates in prisons, remand centres and young offenders' institutions, with duties including security, training and rehabilitation. In addition to custodial duties, must be able to establish and maintain positive working relationships with prisoners. Entry is by selection test, with no specific academic requirements. Experience of working in the police or armed forces, as a security officer or probation officer, or with an organisation that supports ex-offenders can be useful.

HM Prison Service
www.gov.uk/government/organisations/hm-prison-service

Scottish Prison Service
www.sps.gov.uk

Northern Ireland Prison Service
www.justice-ni.gov.uk/topics/prisons

Private Investigator

Carries out confidential enquiries for clients - who may be private individuals, businesses, solicitors, insurance companies or government departments - to investigate such issues as missing persons, infidelity in personal relationships, suspected fraud or industrial espionage. Must have excellent observational skills, personal integrity and knowledge of the law. People often enter this work after gaining experience in the police or armed services.

World Association of Professional Investigators
www.wapi.com

Institute of Professional Investigators
www.ipi.org.uk

Association of British Investigators
www.theabi.org.uk

Producer (Film/Television/Video)

Oversees a film, television or video project from conception to completion, setting a budget, arranging finance and working closely with a director and other production staff; may also be involved in marketing and distributing the completed production. There are no specific academic entry requirements, although many producers are graduates. The overwhelming need is to have a significant track record in the industry, perhaps gaining experience as an assistant producer or in research, marketing or scriptwriting.

Broadcast
www.broadcastnow.co.uk

Creative and Cultural Skills
http://ccskills.org.uk/careers

BBC Academy
www.bbc.co.uk/academy/production/job-hunting/getting-in

Product Designer

Combines creative design skills with an understanding of technology, materials and manufacturing methods to develop products that might cover anything from a toaster to a television set, from a washing machine to a car. Usually needs a degree or equivalent in a subject such as product, spatial, three-dimensional or industrial design.

Creative and Cultural Skills
http://ccskills.org.uk/careers/advice/any/design

Chartered Society of Designers
www.csd.org.uk

Production Assistant/Runner

Provides administrative, organisational and secretarial support during a film, television or video production. The role usually includes assisting actors and crew, issuing scripts, dealing with travel and accommodation and sorting out associated paperwork. While there are no specific academic entry requirements, it is critically important to have significant experience, enthusiasm and contacts. May start as a runner, the most junior role in the production department.

Broadcast
www.broadcastnow.co.uk

Creative and Cultural Skills
http://ccskills.org.uk/careers

BBC Academy
www.bbc.co.uk/academy/production/job-hunting/getting-in

Project Manager

Plans and manages all the elements necessary to make a project a success, from planning and execution to monitoring and closing. A project can be any set of activities with a defined start and end, with specific objectives to be completed within a certain time and cost. May use project management methods such as PRINCE2 (Projects in Controlled Environments) or PMBOK (Project Management Body of Knowledge) to break down each project into stages and monitor its progress. Many project managers are qualified to degree or postgraduate level, either in project management or a subject relevant to their particular industry; others come into the work on the strength of their experience.

Association for Project Management
www.apm.org.uk

Project Management Institute
www.pmi.org

Proofreader

Carefully checks written text after it has been edited but before it is printed or published, providing a final quality check to ensure that there are no spelling or grammatical mistakes, that pages are correctly numbered and that nothing has been omitted. There are no set entry qualifications, although many proofreaders are graduates. Some experience in publishing, journalism or a related area can be useful.

Society for Editors and Proofreaders
www.sfep.org.uk

Property Developer

Engages in a range of property related activities - from finding the best locations, sourcing funds and obtaining planning permission to building from scratch, organising renovations or repairs or leasing property - with the goal of making a profit on each particular project. There are no particular entry requirements and there is no clear template for success, although some knowledge of building, interior design or finance could be useful.

Be Constructive
www.citb.co.uk/bconstructive

Prosecutor (Crown Prosecution Service)

Reviews and, where appropriate, pursues criminal cases following investigation by the police in England and Wales; also advises the police on matters relating to criminal cases. Must be a solicitor admitted in England and Wales with a full current practising certificate, or a barrister called to the English Bar who has completed pupillage, with a thorough knowledge of criminal offences ranging from motoring to murder.

Crown Prosecution Service
www.cps.gov.uk/careers

Psychotherapist

Works on an individual, group, marital or family basis to help people overcome stress, emotional difficulties, relationship problems or troublesome habits. Encourages clients to analyse past behaviour, assess their way of thinking and develop strategies for coping. While there are currently no minimum entry requirements, applicants for postgraduate psychotherapy training usually have a degree in a relevant subject and/ or qualifications and experience as a healthcare practitioner, such as a psychiatrist, psychologist, mental health nurse or social worker.

British Psychotherapy Foundation
www.britishpsychotherapyfoundation.org.uk

British Psychoanalytic Council
www.bpc.org.uk

Public Affairs Consultant

Also known as a lobbyist, uses knowledge of political developments to advise clients, who may be private sector companies, trade associations, charities, not-for-profit organisations or overseas governments, on how best to promote and protect their interests. While there are no specific entry requirements, most practitioners are graduates in a subject such as politics, public relations, social policy or journalism and have a keen interest in politics and decision making.

Public Affairs Networking
www.publicaffairsnetworking.com

Purchasing Manager

Obtains the products and services needed by an organisation to support its key activities. This could include purchasing raw materials for manufacturing, sourcing spare parts for machinery maintenance, ordering merchandise for a retail outlet or updating IT facilities. While there are no specific entry requirements, most employers look for a degree or equivalent qualification. This could be in any subject, although supply chain management, business studies, management science, computing or logistics could be useful. In the engineering/manufacturing industries, a technological qualification would be an advantage, as would chemistry in the chemical industry or computing in IT.

Chartered Institute of Procurement and Supply
www.cips.org

Quality Assurance Manager

Coordinates the activities required to ensure that the product or service provided by an organisation is consistent, fit for purpose and in line with both internal and external requirements, including legal compliance and customer expectations. Some areas of work, such as the manufacturing and processing industries, require a technical background, but others are open to graduates with a degree in any subject or to non-graduates with substantial relevant experience.

Chartered Quality Institute
www.quality.org

Recording/Sound Engineer

Makes high quality recordings of music, speech and sound effects, using complex electronic equipment to capture sound for uses such as commercial music recordings, radio, TV, film and advertisements, websites, computer games and other types of interactive media. There are no specific entry requirements, although it is useful to have a good knowledge of music, physics and electronics. Many entrants start with a music technology course at college or university.

Joint Audio Media Education Support
www.jamesonline.org.uk

Plasa Entertainment Technology
www.plasa.org

Recruitment Consultant

Works on behalf of client organisations, attracting candidates - by advertising, headhunting or networking - and matching them to temporary or permanent positions. Usually screens candidates, conducts interviews and carries out background checks. May specialise in, for example, engineering, IT, nursing/medical or office vacancies. There are no specific entry requirements, although relevant training and experience could be useful in a specialised consultancy role.

Recruitment and Employment Confederation
www.rec.uk.com

Recycling Officer

Plans and manages environmental conservation, waste reduction and recycling policies in a local community. Ensures that appropriate recycling facilities are available and promotes recycling in local schools, community groups and the media. There are many routes into this work, ranging from experience in recycling and conservation to an apprenticeship in sustainable resource management or an accredited degree in waste management.

Waste and Resources Action Programme
www.wrap.org.uk

Chartered Institution of Wastes Management
www.ciwm.co.uk

Reflexologist

Applies pressure to certain areas of the body, known as reflexes, to stimulate energy pathways in the therapeutic treatment of such issues as stress, sleep disorders, sports injuries and back pain. Works mainly on the feet, but also on other parts of the body, such as the lower leg, hands, face and ears. In order to practise, must have appropriate insurance and be a member of a professional body. This requires a minimum level of qualification, such as a diploma in reflexology or complementary therapies. There are also foundation degrees and degrees in complementary or holistic medicine.

Association of Reflexologists
www.aor.org.uk

Resort Representative

Looks after groups of holiday-makers at a holiday destination, working to ensure that everything runs smoothly. Meets groups when they arrive, organises excursions and deals with emergencies like illness, lost passports or money or difficulties with accommodation. There are no specific entry requirements but representatives usually need to be able to speak one or more foreign languages, and may need special skills - such as ability to ski - for certain types of holiday.

Careers that Move
www.careersthatmove.co.uk

Take Off in Travel
www.takeoffintravel.com

Retail Merchandiser

Ensures that products are available in the right store or on the right website, at the appropriate time, attractively displayed and in sufficient quantity. Must work closely with a buying team to forecast trends accurately, plan stock levels and monitor sales performance, and with a visual merchandiser to create special promotional displays. A new entrant often begins as an allocator, distributor or merchandise administrative assistant, allocating stock to stores and liaising with suppliers over delivery times.

British Display Society
www.britishdisplaysociety.co.uk

Robotics Engineer

Combines knowledge of mechanical engineering, electronic engineering and computing to develop intelligent systems for tele-operated, semi-autonomous and autonomous robots to carry out complex and precise tasks in manufacturing, aerospace and the nuclear industry. Entry is usually via a degree in robotics or mechatronics or a postgraduate course following a first degree in mechanical or electrical engineering.

British Automation and Robot Association
www.bara.org.uk

RSPCA/SSPCA Inspector

Looks after injured animals, investigates complaints of neglect and cruelty, bringing perpetrators to court, carries out animal rescues and inspects animal establishments. Must be able to handle animals confidently and to deal with unpleasant and distressing situations. Needs to demonstrate a genuine commitment to animal welfare, with proven experience of working with animals. Must be physically fit and in possession of a full driving licence.

RSPCA
www.rspca.org.uk

Scottish SPCA
www.scottishspca.org

Science Technician

Might work in industry, perhaps involved with quality control during the production process; alternatively, might work with scientists in a research and development department, investigating new products or manufacturing processes. This work could be in industries such as food and drinks, agriculture, pharmaceuticals or oil and chemical manufacture. There are also opportunities to work within the civil service as an assistant scientific officer, in the health service and in schools and universities. The work would tend to focus on the more routine tasks essential to support research and development

Supporting Practical Science and Technology in Schools and Colleges
http://science.cleapss.org.uk

Sector Skills Council for Science, Engineering and Manufacturing Technologies
http://semta.org.uk/careers

Scriptwriter/Screenwriter

Creates original ideas or adapts existing material, such as a true story, novel, play or comic book, to bring stories to life by writing scripts for feature films, TV drama, comedies and other programmes and computer games. Writing talent, creative flair and considerable self-belief are more important than formal qualifications, although many screenwriters develop their skills through a degree or postgraduate course in, say, creative writing, journalism or English.

BBC Writers' Room
www.bbc.co.uk/writersroom

Industrial Scripts
http://screenplayscripts.com

Writers' Guild of Great Britain
https://writersguild.org.uk

Sculptor

Creates original pieces of three-dimensional art to express an emotion or record an event. May carve images in solid materials, such as stone or wood, or use newer products and technologies to produce art forms that are diverse and sometimes controversial. While it is possible to succeed in this area with no formal qualifications, many sculptors seek to develop their skills through a degree in fine art with a sculpture specialism.

Royal British Society of Sculptors
http://rbs.org.uk

Secretary - Personal Assistant

As a secretary, deals with correspondence and other communications, organises meetings, liaises with other departments, companies or customers, and sometimes acts on behalf of the manager. As a personal assistant (PA), goes beyond basic secretarial duties, acting as close support to a manager or executive, handling the day-to-day running of an office to allow them to make the most efficient use of their time.

Institute of Administrative Management
www.instam.org

Skills CFA
www.skillscfa.org

Institute of Agricultural Secretaries and Administrators
www.iagsa.co.uk

Association of Medical Secretaries, Practice Administrators and Receptionists
www.amspar.com

PA Assist
www.pa-assist.com

Security Officer

Works to protect buildings, people or valuables from theft, attack or damage. Duties might range from patrolling premises at night to supervising entry during working hours, guarding cash or other valuables, searching aircraft or guarding airport boundaries. There are no specific entry requirements, although experience of working in the police or armed services could be useful. May need a front line licence from a body such as the Security Industry Authority.

International Professional Security Association
www.ipsa.org.uk

Skills for Security
www.skillsforsecurity.org.uk

Security Industry Authority
www.sia.homeoffice.gov.uk

Set Designer

Sometimes known as a production or stage designer, creates the overall look and feel of a film, television or theatre production. Must work within a budget, relating the design to the script and researching historical, contemporary or futuristic details for the production. Needs a high level of design skill, which can be developed through relevant work experience or through a specific degree course at university, art college or drama school.

Society of British Theatre Designers
www.theatredesign.org.uk

Creative and Cultural Skills
http://ccskills.org.uk/careers/advice/any/theatre

British Film Institute
www.bfi.org.uk

Creative Skillset
http://creativeskillset.org/creative_industries/film

Film London
http://filmlondon.org.uk

Shorthand Writer/Court Reporter

Sometimes known as a stenographer or verbatim reporter, works in Crown Courts, the House of Commons and the House of Lords, recording proceedings in shorthand or by using stenography equipment (civil courts use audio recording equipment). In Scotland, works in the High Court, Court of Session and the Sheriff Court. Must be able to work quickly and accurately, with a good standard of English grammar and an interest in law.

Skills for Justice
www.sfjuk.com

Sorene Verbatim Reporter Training Services
www.sorene.co.uk

Verbatim Reporters
www.verbatim-reporters.com

British Institute of Verbatim Reporters
http://bivr.org.uk

Singer

May specialise in one of many fields, such as folk, opera, classical or rock, performing live in front of an audience or making recordings for broadcast, CD or download. Interprets music by using knowledge of voice production, melody, harmony, and rhythm. Might do session work for backing tracks, advertisements and films; may sing alone as a soloist, work with a group of musicians or sing with others in a choir. Training requirements depend on the field of music. Many rock and folk singers, for example, rely upon on-the-job training, while classical and opera singers might spend several years in voice training. A good voice and a strong musical sense are always the most important entry requirements.

Careers in Music
www.careersinmusic.co.uk

Singing Careers
www.vocalist.org.uk/singing_careers.html

Social Researcher

Uses a variety of methods - including interviews, questionnaires and focus groups - to investigate the views of population samples on such issues as unemployment, gender equality, crime, transport, social services, healthcare, education or the environment. Usually needs a degree or postgraduate qualification in a discipline that includes social research methods and statistics.

Social Research Association
http://the-sra.org.uk/sra_resources/careers

National Centre for Social Research
www.natcen.ac.uk

Soil Scientist

Interprets and evaluates the biological, chemical and physical properties of soil, with the aim of understanding how soil resources contribute to agricultural production, biodiversity, environmental quality and human health issues. Usually has a degree in a subject such as biology, chemistry or environmental science, together with a postgraduate qualification in soil science.

Agricultural Development and Advisory Service
www.adas.uk

Land Information System Soil Portal
www.landis.org.uk

Songwriter

May work in some or all of: writing, arranging, orchestrating, conducting and performing musical compositions. The music may be in any style, from classical, rock, pop or jazz to folk, country, soul, rap or easy listening. There is no single entry route, although composers of many styles of music do have some formal musical training. It is important to be able to play at least one instrument and read and write music.

Careers in Music
www.careersinmusic.co.uk

Sonographer

Uses ultrasound imaging to produce images of structures of the human body, which can then be observed on a monitor screen or printed as photographs. This is a specialist area within radiography.

Society of Radiographers
www.sor.org

British Medical Ultrasound Society
www.bmus.org

Special Educational Needs Teacher

Works with children and young adults who need extra support to complete their learning successfully. May help individuals who are physically or mentally disabled, sensory impaired or emotionally vulnerable, or have speech and language or behavioural difficulties. Must have recognised teacher status, which most often requires degree level study and a postgraduate qualification.

Get into Teaching
https://getintoteaching.education.gov.uk

General Teaching Council for Scotland
www.gtcs.org.uk

Northern Ireland Department of Education
www.education-ni.gov.uk

Sport and Exercise Psychologist

Works with athletes, teams and officials involved in sport, at any level, helping them deal with the pressures of the sport and improve their personal performance. May also work with the general public, encouraging them to exercise as part of a healthy lifestyle. Must normally have an accredited degree in psychology and a postgraduate award in sports and exercise psychology.

British Psychological Society
http://careers.bps.org.uk/area/sport-exercise

Sport and Exercise Scientist

Applies scientific principles to sport and exercise performance, looking particularly at physiology - the way the body responds to training, biomechanics - the interaction of the body with apparatus, and psychology - human behaviour in sport and exercise settings. Would normally have a degree in sport science or a degree in a related subject, such as physical education, physiology or psychology, followed by a postgraduate qualification.

British Association of Sport and Exercise Sciences
www.bases.org.uk

Sports Administrator

Ensures the smooth running of a sports organisation, which might be a small local club, a major Premier League brand, a funding or governing body or a local authority development office. May focus on organising events, promoting sport and running sports facilities. Must have a strong interest in sport and an awareness of issues affecting the sports sector, although actual sporting ability is less important than commercial awareness and skills in, say, marketing, media, human resources or events management.

Sport and Recreation Alliance
www.sportandrecreation.org.uk

Skills Active
www.skillsactive.com

Statistician

Collects, analyses, interprets and presents quantitative data, using mathematical techniques and software to produce information on which decisions can be made. May work in such sectors as education, finance, government, health, insurance, market research or transport. There are no absolute academic requirements but most new entrants have a degree in a subject containing formal statistical training, such as mathematics, economics or operational research.

Royal Statistical Society StatsLife
www.statslife.org.uk/careers

Stunt Performer

Stands in for an actor when the script calls for spectacularly dangerous, violent or specialised action on a film or TV set. This might include boxing, martial arts, swordfights, crashing cars and motorcycles, swimming, diving or falling out of aeroplanes. Must be physically fit and have high standard qualifications and skills in at least six different sporting areas.

Joint Industry Stunt Committee
http://jigs.org.uk/stunts

Swimming Coach/Teacher

As a swimming teacher, helps people of all ages and abilities to develop swimming skills and techniques, and to exercise in water; as a swimming coach, trains and develops competitive swimmers. May specialise in swimming, synchronised swimming, diving or water polo. To train, must choose one of these four disciplines and work through three levels of qualification.

Careers in Aquatics
www.swimming.org/careers

Tax Adviser

Uses knowledge of tax legislation to ensure that clients pay the correct amount of tax at the right time and benefit from any tax advantages and exemptions. Must keep up to date with changing tax laws and explain complicated legislation and its implications to clients. There are many routes to qualification, ranging from starting as a taxation technician and working through the competency structure to joining the profession as a qualified accountant, solicitor, company secretary or tax inspector. Must be a chartered tax adviser to practise in the UK.

Chartered Institute of Taxation
www.tax.org.uk

Association of Taxation Technicians
www.att.org.uk

Tax Professional

Calculates the tax liability of businesses and individuals, checking tax returns, examining financial accounts and related documents, and detecting and investigating cases of suspected fraud or tax evasion. May also advise on taxation matters. It may be possible to progress internally by demonstrating the right level of ability, but new entrants must normally have a good honours degree in any subject.

HM Revenue and Customs, Graduate Recruitment
www.gov.uk/government/organisations/hm-revenue-customs/about/recruitment

Technical Author

Communicates technical information in a user-friendly way, writing instruction manuals, training guides and reference documentation for a variety of products and services. May also produce material in the form of software demonstrations and interactive tutorials. While there are no specific entry requirements, many technical authors are graduates. A science or technology degree can be useful for certain areas of work.

Association of British Science Writers
www.absw.org.uk

Institute of Scientific and Technical Communicators
www.istc.org.uk

Technical Brewer

Manages the process of brewing and packaging beer, taking responsibility for the quality and consistency of the finished product. The role includes sourcing raw materials and exploring new recipes in response to changing consumer tastes. Must normally have a degree in a subject such as applied chemistry, process engineering, biological science or food science/technology, although it is sometimes possible to work up from production assistant level.

Institute of Brewing and Distilling
www.ibd.org.uk

TEFL/TESOL Teacher

Works with adults and children whose native language is not English, helping them develop written and spoken communication skills. May work in a commercial language school, a state or independent school, in industry or in a further or higher education establishment. Must have a very high standard of English, with a degree required by some employers. This need not be in any particular subject, although English, linguistics, modern foreign languages or education studies might be useful. With or without a degree, a certificate from either Trinity or Cambridge is a qualification recognised around the world.

International Association of Teachers of English as a Foreign Language
www.iatefl.org

National Association for Teaching English and Community Languages to Adults
www.natecla.org.uk

Telecommunications Engineer

Operates in such sectors as internet, mobile and wireless communications, data networks, and programming and security for telecommunications. Current issues include cloud computing, software defined networking and network function virtualisation. Strong problem solving abilities and excellent communication skills are essential, together with a degree in a subject such as electronic and communication engineering, telecommunications, computer science, physics, mathematics or information technology.

Institute of Telecommunications Professionals
www.theitp.org

Institution of Engineering and Technology
www.theiet.org

Theme Park Manager

Ensures the smooth running of a very large entertainment complex, usually covering many acres of land, where visitors can enjoy thrill rides, landscaped gardens, themed buildings and displays, other leisure-based attractions and on-site catering. There are no specific entry requirements, although employers often ask for experience and qualifications in such areas as hospitality, leisure, travel or tourism management, marketing, or facilities or human resources management.

British Association of Leisure Parks, Piers and Attractions
www.balppa.org

Tourism Officer

Develops and promotes the merits of a specific region or site in order to attract tourists, create employment opportunities and generate revenue. May focus on areas such as marketing, visitor management or developing new attractions. Personal qualities, skills and experience of working in a customer-focused or tourism role are often more important than academic qualifications, although a relevant degree or diploma would be useful.

Institute of Travel and Tourism
www.itt.co.uk

Tourism Management Institute
www.tmi.org.uk

Tourism Society
www.tourismsociety.org

World Travel and Tourism Council
www.wttc.org

Toxicologist

Studies the adverse health and environmental effects caused by exposure to chemical, drug, biological, radiation or physical hazards, carrying out laboratory experiments and field studies to identify, isolate and quantify toxic substances. Usually has a first degree in a subject such as chemistry, biochemistry, pharmacology, pharmacy, medicine, medical science, veterinary medicine or environmental sciences, followed by a postgraduate qualification in toxicology.

Association for Clinical Biochemistry and Laboratory Medicine
www.acb.org.uk

British Toxicology Society
www.thebts.org

Trade Mark Attorney

Provides advice on the suitability of a word or logo, for example, as a trade mark, undertaking searches to see if others are already using the same sign and helping determine the range of goods and services to be protected by the trade mark. Although a degree is not essential, many trade mark attorneys are graduates. A law degree can be especially useful, as it gives exemption from some professional examinations.

The Chartered Institute of Trade Mark Attorneys
www.citma.org.uk

Transport Planner

Assesses the impact of transport issues on the public and works on policies and projects to improve existing transport systems or develop new ones. This includes air travel, rail networks, roads and the use of cars, lorries and buses, bicycle lanes and pedestrian paths. Normally needs a degree in a subject such as geography, civil engineering or environmental science, followed by a postgraduate qualification in transport planning.

Transport Planning Society
www.tps.org.uk/main/careers

United Nations Official

Works as part of the 44,000-strong, multi-cultural United Nations workforce, with people from the 193 member states, seeking solutions to complex global problems - from ending conflict and alleviating poverty to combating climate change and defending human rights. Might, for example, monitor elections, disarm child soldiers, coordinate relief in humanitarian crises or provide administrative and logistical support to carry out a particular mandate. Must be willing to travel and work anywhere at a moment's notice, and able to thrive in an environment that is truly international.

United Nations Careers Portal
https://careers.un.org

Videographer

Records moving images and sound, usually using a digital hard-drive, flash card or tape-drive video camera. May engage in electronic news gathering (ENG) of news stories for television, or operate a camera in a studio, usually as part of a larger television crew; may work alone, specialising in corporate and event videography, such as commercials, documentaries, live events, short films, training videos and weddings.

Mandy
www.mandy.com

Broadcasting, Entertainment, Cinematograph and Theatre Union
www.bectu.org.uk

Volunteer Organiser

Recruits, trains and manages volunteers in a variety of organisations, including hospitals, social services, and charitable or other voluntary groups. May interview prospective volunteers, match individuals to vacancies, arrange training and provide ongoing support. While there are no set academic requirements, many new entrants have a degree or equivalent qualification, together with extensive experience of working in the voluntary sector.

Association of Volunteer Managers
http://volunteermanagers.org.uk

Warehouse Manager

A key part of the supply chain process in a distribution depot, retail superstore or manufacturing plant, oversees the efficient receipt, storage and dispatch of goods such as food, clothing, healthcare products, manufacturing parts and household items. May move into management after gaining experience in warehouse or distribution work, or may join a graduate training scheme after completing a degree in, say, transport, distribution, logistics or supply chain management.

Waste Management Officer

Carries responsibility for the development, management, supervision and control of waste disposal and recycling facilities. Some posts combine waste management and recycling functions, whilst others split the functions into separate jobs. The UK produces over 400 million tonnes of waste a year. It is the responsibility of the waste management industry, working with local authorities, to dispose of waste safely, with due consideration for the environment.

Chartered Institution of Wastes Management
www.ciwm.co.uk

Waste Management Industry Training and Advisory Board
www.wamitab.org.uk

Water Engineer

Specialises in water-based projects, including the provision of clean water, disposal of waste water and sewage, and prevention of flood damage. May be involved in designing and maintaining reservoirs, pumping stations or sea defence walls. Usually has a degree in civil engineering, although entry is also possible with a degree in an environmental or physical science followed by an approved postgraduate qualification in engineering.

Water UK
www.water.org.uk

Chartered Institution of Water and Environmental Management
www.ciwem.org

Water Quality Analyst

Safeguards all aspects of water quality through, for example, carrying out laboratory testing of samples, checking potential sources of pollution or contamination, investigating pollution reports and arranging emergency action in response to incidents. Usually has a degree in a subject such as chemistry, environmental science, biology, biochemistry, microbiology or geoscience.

Water UK
www.water.org.uk

Chartered Institution of Water and Environmental Management
www.ciwem.org

Wine Merchant

Buys wine from growers and shippers to sell on to hotels, restaurants, retail outlets and other clients. May travel to find new wines, visit vineyards, negotiate prices, check production standards and maintain relationships with producers. Must have a good sense of taste and smell, together with strong communication and negotiation skills. There are no academic entry requirements, although fluency in the languages of major wine-producing countries can be extremely useful.

Wine and Spirit Education Trust
www.wsetglobal.com

Institute of Masters of Wine
www.mastersofwine.org

Zoo Keeper

Cares for animals in zoological parks or aquariums, maintaining captive exotic animals for conservation, research, public education and recreation. May care for a diverse collection of animals - from mammals and birds to reptiles, amphibians, fish and invertebrates - or may specialise in an area such as an animal hospital, exotic birds, great apes, elephants or reptiles. Important basic duties include daily cleaning and maintenance of animal enclosures and proper feeding of the animals. Must also be an excellent observer, learning about habits and behaviour, and able to detect subtle changes in an animal's physical or psychological condition. These responsibilities are essential in maintaining a healthy and reproductively successful animal collection.

Association of British and Irish Wild Animal Keepers
http://abwak.org

British and Irish Association of Zoos and Aquariums
www.biaza.org.uk

Zoologist

Studies animals and their behaviour, either in their natural environment or in captivity, usually specialising in a particular area, such as insects, reptiles, parasites, reproductive systems, genetics or the effects of pollutants on animal life. Normally needs at least a first degree in a subject such as zoology, animal ecology, animal behaviour or conservation. Academic research usually requires postgraduate qualifications at master's or doctoral level.

Institute of Zoology
www.zsl.org/science

Royal Society of Biology
www.rsb.org.uk

Religious Careers

If you have strong religious beliefs, you might wish to consider a career as a vicar, priest, rabbi, elder, imam or whatever is appropriate for your particular faith. Many different religions are practised in the United Kingdom and we cannot possibly do justice to them in a book of this kind. You are probably already an active member of a religious group and we suggest that you start by discussing your career aspirations with a local representative of your religion.

Each religion has its own training methods but most involve a period of college-based study in the United Kingdom or overseas. You can obtain further information by visiting relevant websites from the list below.

Baptists Together – **www.baptist.org.uk**

Buddhist Society – **www.thebuddhistsociety.org**

Church of England – **www.cofe-ministry.org.uk**

Church of Ireland – **www.ireland.anglican.org**

Church of Scotland – **www.churchofscotland.org.uk**

Hindu Council UK – **www.hinducounciluk.org**

Islam – **www.islamic.org.uk**

Judaism – **www.jewfaq.org/judaism.htm**

Methodist Church in Britain – **www.methodist.org.uk**

Methodist Church in Ireland – **www.irishmethodist.org**

Catholic Church in England & Wales – **www.catholic-ew.org.uk**

Catholic Church in Ireland – **www.catholicireland.net**

Catholic Church in Scotland - **www.bcos.org.uk**

Sikhism – **www.sikhs.org** & **www.sikhnet.com**

You might also explore the following:

Information Network on Religious Movements – **www.inform.ac**

Inter Faith Network for the UK – **www.interfaith.org.uk**

UK Priest – **www.ukpriest.org**

Index